ARCHAEOLOGY
OF THE BIBLE

The Greatest Discoveries
From Genesis to the Roman Era

BEST-SELLING AUTHOR OF *In the Footsteps of Jesus*

JEAN-PIERRE ISBOUTS

NATIONAL GEOGRAPHIC

WASHINGTON, D.C.

CONTENTS

Page 1: A rare fourth-century C.E. gold medallion from Syria depicts the Annunciation to Mary. Pages 2-3: The Dead Sea fortress of Masada, where rebels faced off against the Roman Tenth Legion during the final phase of the Jewish War (66-73 C.E.). Page 4: Archers, possibly members of the Persian Guard of the Immortals, march on this wall of molded enameled brick from Darius's palace at Susa, dated circa 510 B.C.E.

*The purpose of biblical archaeology is not to
"prove" the Bible ... [but] to shed light on the history
that is important to biblical studies.*

ROBERT I. BRADSHAW, *ARCHAEOLOGY AND THE PATRIARCHS*

INTRODUCTION
The Enduring Fascination With Archaeological Discovery

WHY DO ARCHAEOLOGICAL DISCOVERIES IN THE HOLY LAND ROUTINELY MAKE headlines around the world? The reason, no doubt, is the enduring role of the Judeo-Christian Bible in our times. While for some it is the bedrock of faith, for others it serves as a moral compass for interpreting the complexities of human existence and the ethical issues raised by an ever changing modern society.

At the same time, we live in a world that is radically different from biblical times. In our society, every event, every idea, indeed every word can be instantly captured and communicated around the world. That is why the dark and distant past of the biblical era is so tantalizing to us. We yearn to imagine this strange and ancient world where, despite the fact that no mass media existed at all, words were spoken that still resonate thousands of year later.

Of course, the stories of the Bible did not originate in a vacuum. They were shaped by the most powerful civilizations of their time: Mesopotamia, Egypt, Assyria, Babylonia, Persia, Greece, and the world of Imperial Rome. By traveling through the world of the Bible, we truly follow the full arc of ancient civilization.

Furthermore, the past decade or so has witnessed a number of dramatic discoveries, partly by chance and partly by virtue of new technologies such as drone photography and seismic imaging. These finds include:

• The 2007 excavation of the Davidic palace of Khirbet Qeiyafa near the Israeli city of Beit Shemesh, where a sherd with what some say is the oldest Hebrew text was found—possibly corroborating the reign of King David

• The discovery in 2000 of fully functional boats in Abydos, Egypt, predating the Old Kingdom, which may shed light on the description of Noah's ark in Genesis

• The excavation in 2007 of a synagogue in the ancient city of Magdala, the birthplace of Mary Magdalene, which may date to the period of Jesus' ministry

• The sensational excavation in 2008 of King Herod's tomb on the Herodium, which corroborates the account in the works of the Jewish first-century historian Josephus

• Possible evidence of a meteoric burst or perhaps a meteor impact near the Dead Sea, first published in 2013, which was of such intense heat that it melted pottery and even

Opposite: *The triumphal gate of the Hellenistic city of Gerasa (modern Jerash, Jordan) once led to the main forum, the city's religious and commercial center.* **Right:** *A clay tablet from the eighth-century B.C.E. Neo-Babylonian period contains a Sumerian-Akkadian vocabulary.*

This sesterce with the legend "Judaea Capta" ("Judea captured") was struck after the defeat of the Jewish Rebellion in 70 C.E.

fused sand into glass, and could be correlated to the story of the destruction of Sodom and Gomorrah

- In 2015, confirmation that Herod's Jerusalem palace was located underneath today's Tower of David Museum. For Christians, this is particularly exciting, for as we will see, Herod's palace is one of two possible places where Jesus was imprisoned awaiting his trial.
  - And finally—and perhaps most spectacular—the excavation, also in 2015, of a first-century courtyard house in Nazareth, very close to the current Annunciation Church, which may be the childhood home of Jesus.

These and many other fascinating finds have inspired the development of this book. It aims to provide, for both casual readers and serious students of Israel's history, a comprehensive overview of the most important archaeological discoveries related to stories in the Bible. Based on several years of research at Near Eastern sites, as well as museums in Israel, Turkey, Russia, Italy, Germany, Britain, France, and the United States, this book offers a sweeping overview of forensic testimony that may illustrate the events of Hebrew Scripture and the New Testament.

Does the Bible need such evidence? Of course not. The Bible requires no proof, for it is above all a document of faith rather than history. Nevertheless, every story in the Bible emerged in a specific time and place, and within a distinct social, cultural, and literary milieu. It is this intersection of story and science that forms the subject of this book.

THE ORGANIZATION OF THIS BOOK: *Archaeology of the Bible* is organized in six chapters, inspired by the division of the Tanakh or Hebrew Scripture ("the Old Testament" in Christian parlance) as well as the New Testament, each consonant with a major period of the Ancient Near East:

CHAPTER 1: THE ARCHAEOLOGY OF THE PATRIARCHS
This chapter links the stories of Genesis to discoveries in ancient Mesopotamia (today's Iraq and Syria), Canaan (today's Israel and Jordan), and the Old Kingdom of Egypt.

A lion of glazed brick from the early sixth century B.C.E. once guarded the Processional Way of Babylon, leading to the Temple of Marduk.

CHAPTER 2: THE ARCHAEOLOGY OF THE EXODUS
This chapter seeks a historical connection between the remainder of the Pentateuch—from Exodus to Deuteronomy—and Egypt's Second Intermediate Period.

CHAPTER 3: THE ARCHAEOLOGY OF THE KINGDOMS OF ISRAEL
This chapter identifies discoveries that may attest the history of the ancient kingdoms of Israel as described in the Book of Joshua through the Kings.

CHAPTER 4: THE ARCHAEOLOGY OF THE SECOND TEMPLE PERIOD
This chapter seeks archaeological data for the period after the Babylonian exile up to the Roman conquest of Judea, based on Chronicles and I and II Maccabees.

CHAPTER 5: THE ARCHAEOLOGY OF THE LIFE OF JESUS

This chapter shows archaeological finds related to the life and times of Jesus in Galilee, Samaria, and Judea, as described in the Gospels of Matthew, Mark, Luke, and John.

CHAPTER 6: THE ARCHAEOLOGY OF EARLY CHRISTIANITY

This chapter is focused on the decades after Jesus' Passion and the growth of early Christianity and Rabbinic Judaism in Syria, Asia Minor, Greece, Rome, and beyond.

THE BIBLE BOOKS BY CHAPTER

The first two chapters of this book are focused on the first division of Hebrew Scripture, known as the Pentateuch or "Five Books of Moses," and the Torah or "Law" in Jewish parlance. Chapter 1 describes the historical roots of the stories of Genesis, up to the saga of Joseph. Chapter 2 is devoted to the historical and archaeological context of the Exodus, as described in the books of Exodus through Deuteronomy.

The books of Joshua, Judges, Samuel, and Kings form the basis for Chapter 3. A parallel history known as the Chronicle History, as well as the books of Ezra and Nehemiah, which take us into the exile and postexilic era, are covered in Chapter 4. We also look at the archaeological framework of certain other religious works, called "apocrypha" or "deuterocanonical" works, which were written between 300 B.C.E.

Excavators are at work uncovering the remains from Roman, Arab, and medieval periods underneath the Cathedral of La Seu in Lisbon, Portugal.

A gold bracelet with terminals in the form of griffins, made in Asia Minor circa 250 B.C.E., was a popular motif in Hellenistic art.

and the late first century C.E. and are accepted by some Christian traditions as an integral part of the Bible.

The New Testament forms the basis for Chapters 5 and 6. Chapter 5 highlights the most important archaeological finds related to the story of Jesus as described in the Gospels, and Chapter 6 follows the growth of early Christianity in Asia Minor, Greece, and Rome, based on the remaining books of the New Testament, ending with Revelation.

A NONDENOMINATIONAL PERSPECTIVE

This book is deliberately written from a nondenominational perspective, using a style that is accessible to lay readers. It does not conform to any particular theological orientation, but rather treats the biblical texts as historical documents so as to appeal to the broadest possible readership.

This is also true for the question whether the figures of the Bible were, without exception, historical characters, or whether some stories are rooted in myth or biblical legend. No scholar will ever question the Bible's moral and religious significance, but many authors have challenged the Bible as a reliable source of historical information. This

An aerial of Khirbet Qeiyafa offers an overview of the citadel that some archaeologists believe dates from the putative period of King David, circa tenth century B.C.E.

book takes no position in the debate. It treats every biblical story as a valued conveyor of meaning, regardless of its putative historicity. On that basis, throughout this book, we will look for parallels between the biblical stories and historical sources, including evidence of ancient cities and monuments, as well as tablets, letters, and works of art.

Hebrew Scripture has come down to us in Hebrew (with certain segments in Aramaic) or, in the case of the Septuagint, in a translation in Greek. The New Testament is also written in Greek, in a dialect known as *koinè*. The English translations in this book are taken from the 1989 New Revised Standard Version translation (NRSV) of the Old and New Testament.

As is now common practice, *Archaeology of the Bible* uses the nondenominational temporal indicators of B.C.E. (before the Common Era) instead of the traditional B.C. (before Christ), and likewise C.E. (Common Era) rather than A.D. (anno Domini or in the year of the Lord) to identify dates in history.

THE ILLUSTRATIONS

In true National Geographic tradition, this book is illustrated with over 350 color photographs of archaeological sites and artifacts from across the Near East. To place these finds in their proper geographical context, this book also includes no fewer than 38 highly detailed maps, exclusively developed by National Geographic's cartographic staff.

To further sustain the chronological thread of the narrative, a time line runs throughout the book. The markers in this time line refer to the emergence of civilizations, the span of royal dynasties, or the construction of cities or key monuments throughout the world of Antiquity as attested by archaeology and historical research.

This raises the thorny question of how to date biblical episodes, another topic of ongoing scholarly debate. For example, it is very difficult to identify actual dates for biblical events prior to the reign of Kings David and Solomon. Even then, much of the subsequent biblical chronology up to the Greco-Roman era is subject to debate. For consistency, however, we follow the principal time line markers as used in my previous National Geographic books.

A newly discovered piece of pottery at a dig in Ashkelon, Israel, is carefully dusted off by an archaeological assistant.

For example, in *The Biblical World* (2007) we looked at the biblical *stories* in their literary, geographical, and cultural context. With *Who's Who in the Bible* (2013), we focused our attention on the *people* of Judeo-Christian scripture. This book complements this triptych by looking at the *archaeological* record; we see to what extent these discoveries can illustrate Scripture and help us to re-create the world of the Bible.

So join me now as we plunge into the ancient lands of the Fertile Crescent—the crescent-shaped territory that once curved from ancient Egypt and Israel to Mesopotamia and beyond. ∎

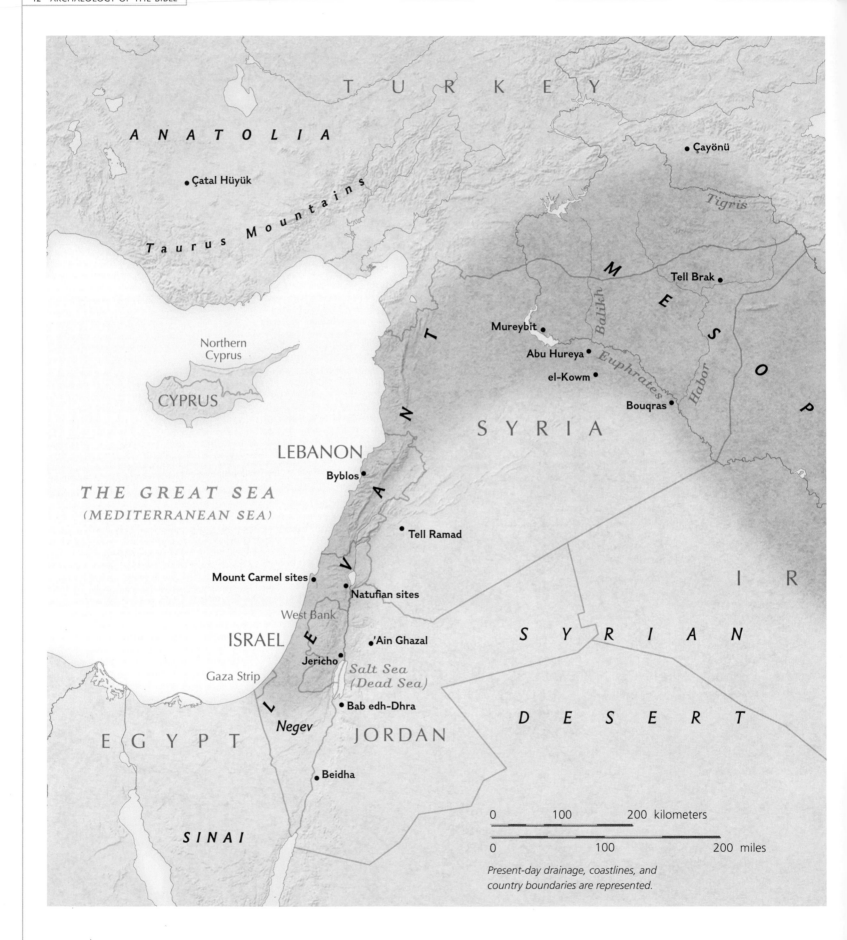

TURKEY

ANATOLIA

• Çayönü

• Çatal Hüyük

Taurus Mountains

Tigris

MESOP

Tell Brak •

Balikh

Mureybit •

Abu Hureya •

Euphrates

el-Kowm •

Habor

Bouqras •

Northern
Cyprus

CYPRUS

SYRIA

THE GREAT SEA
(MEDITERRANEAN SEA)

LEBANON

Byblos •

Tell Ramad •

Mount Carmel sites •

Natufian sites •

West Bank

ISRAEL

'Ain Ghazal •

Jericho •

Salt Sea
(Dead Sea)

Gaza Strip

Bab edh-Dhra •

EGYPT

Negev

JORDAN

SYRIAN

IR

DESERT

Beidha •

SINAI

| 0 | 100 | 200 kilometers |

| 0 | 100 | 200 miles |

*Present-day drainage, coastlines, and
country boundaries are represented.*

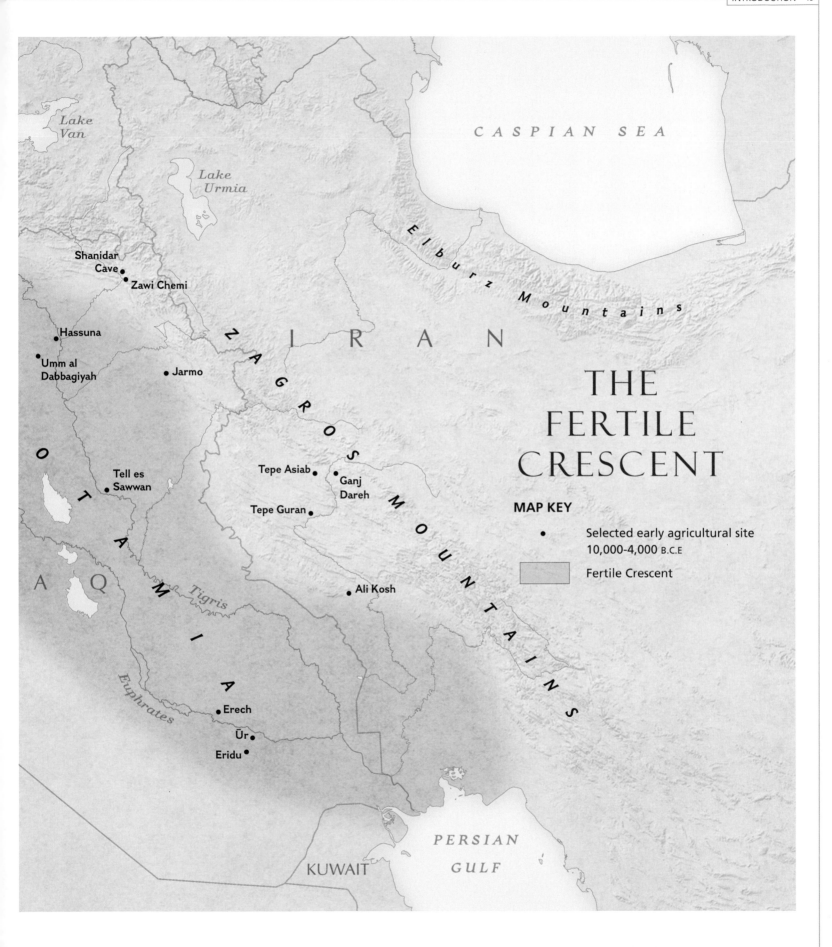

THE
FERTILE
CRESCENT

Lake Van

Lake Urmia

CASPIAN SEA

Elburz Mountains

IRAN

ZAGROS MOUNTAINS

Shanidar Cave

Zawi Chemi

Hassuna

Umm al Dabbagiyah

Jarmo

Tell es Sawwan

Tepe Asiab

Ganj Dareh

Tepe Guran

Ali Kosh

Tigris

Euphrates

Erech

Ūr

Eridu

A Q

O T A M I A

KUWAIT

PERSIAN GULF

MAP KEY

• Selected early agricultural site 10,000-4,000 B.C.E

Fertile Crescent

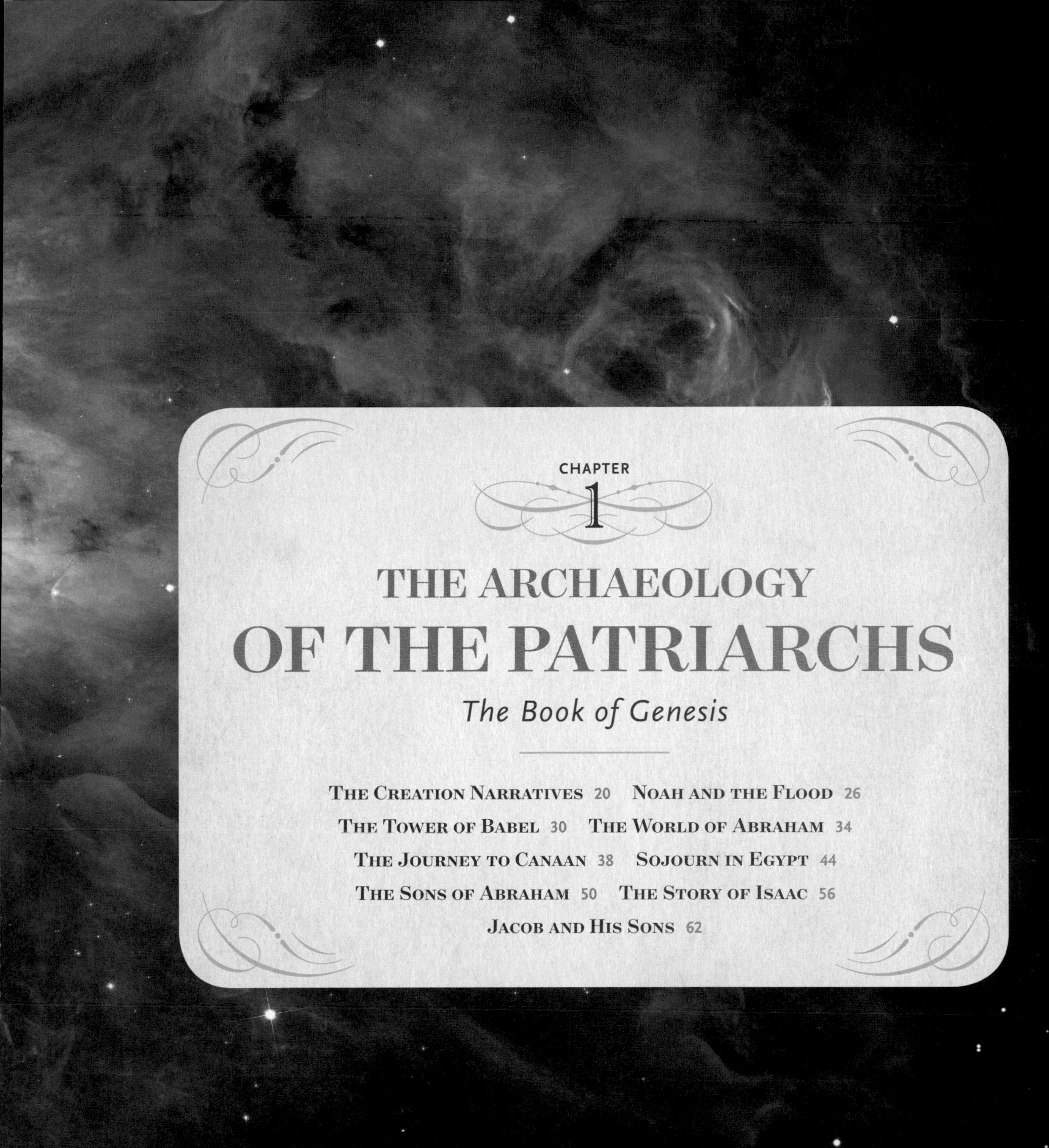

CHAPTER

1

THE ARCHAEOLOGY
OF THE PATRIARCHS

The Book of Genesis

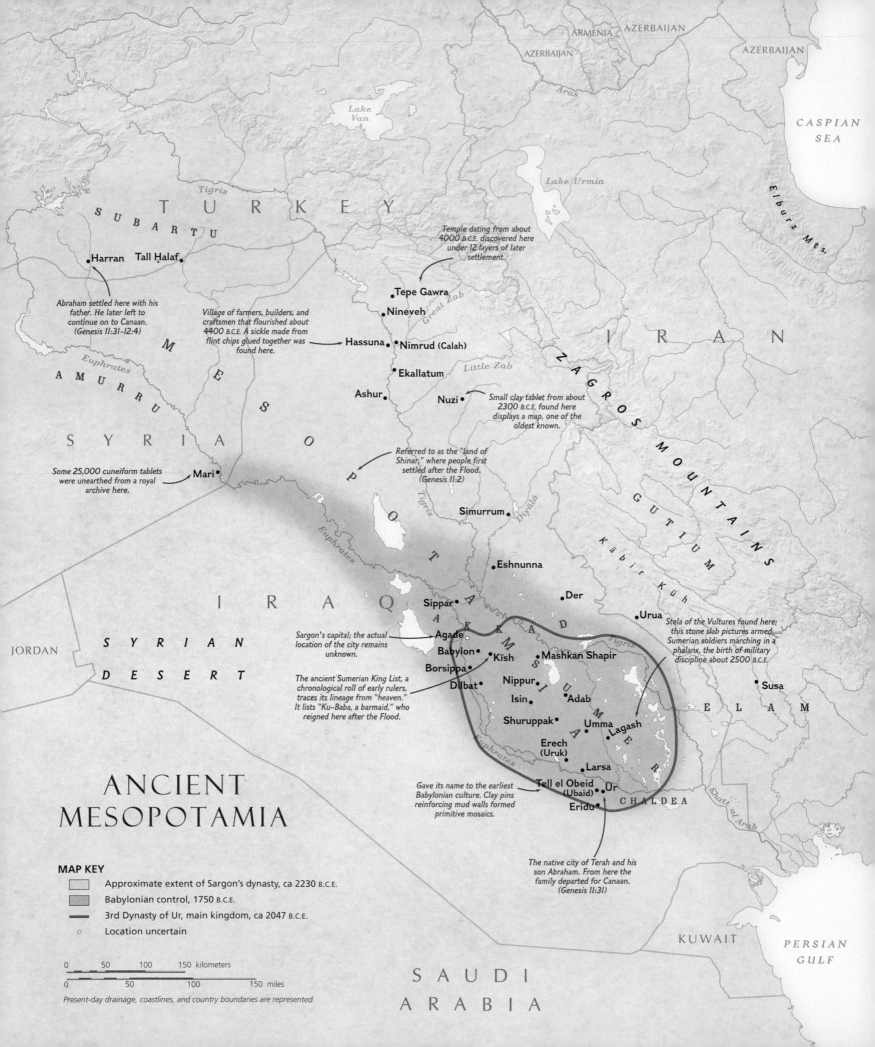

CASPIAN
SEA

ARMENIA
AZERBAIJAN
AZERBAIJAN
AZERBAIJAN

Lake Van

Lake Urmia

Aras

Elburz Mts.

TURKEY

Tigris

S U B A R T U

●Harran Tall Ḥalaf●

Abraham settled here with his father. He later left to continue on to Canaan. (Genesis 11:31–12:4)

Village of farmers, builders, and craftsmen that flourished about 4400 B.C.E. A sickle made from flint chips glued together was found here.

Tepe Gawra
●

Temple dating from about 4000 B.C.E. discovered here under 12 layers of later settlement.

●**Nineveh**

Great Zab

I R A N

Hassuna● ●**Nimrud (Calah)**

Z A G R O S

●**Ekallatum**

Little Zab

A M U R R U

Ashur● **Nuzi**●

Small clay tablet from about 2300 B.C.E. found here displays a map, one of the oldest known.

M E S O P O T A M I A

S Y R I A

Euphrates

Some 25,000 cuneiform tablets were unearthed from a royal archive here.

●**Mari**

Referred to as the "land of Shinar," where people first settled after the Flood. (Genesis 11:2)

Tigris

M O U N T A I N S

Diyālā

Simurrum●

G U T I U M

Kabir Kūh

●**Eshnunna**

●**Der**

I R A Q

Sippar●

Euphrates

●**Urua**

Stela of the Vultures found here; this stone slab pictures armed Sumerian soldiers marching in a phalanx, the birth of military discipline about 2500 B.C.E.

JORDAN

S Y R I A N

Agade○

Sargon's capital; the actual location of the city remains unknown.

Babylon● **Kīsh**●

Mashkan Shapir●

Tigris

D E S E R T

Borsippa●

The ancient Sumerian King List, a chronological roll of early rulers, traces its lineage from "heaven." It lists "Ku-Baba, a barmaid," who reigned here after the Flood.

Dilbat●

Nippur●

Isin●

Adab●

Susa●

E L A M

Shuruppak●

Umma●

Lagash●

Erech (Uruk)●

Larsa●

Tell el Obeid (Ubaid)● ●**Ur**

Euphrates

Gave its name to the earliest Babylonian culture. Clay pins reinforcing mud walls formed primitive mosaics.

Eridu●

C H A L D E A

Shatt al Arab

ANCIENT MESOPOTAMIA

The native city of Terah and his son Abraham. From here the family departed for Canaan. (Genesis 11:31)

MAP KEY

▨	Approximate extent of Sargon's dynasty, ca 2230 B.C.E.
▨	Babylonian control, 1750 B.C.E.
▬	3rd Dynasty of Ur, main kingdom, ca 2047 B.C.E.
○	Location uncertain

KUWAIT

PERSIAN GULF

0   50   100   150 kilometers

0   50   100   150 miles

Present-day drainage, coastlines, and country boundaries are represented.

S A U D I

A R A B I A

*In the beginning when God created
the heavens and the earth, the earth was a formless
void and darkness covered the face of the deep.*

GENESIS 1:1-2

THE WORLD IN 3000 B.C.E.

The Dawn of Civilization, Circa 3000 B.C.E. to 1650 B.C.E.

WHEN DID INTELLIGENT LIFE BEGIN? THE QUESTION IS QUITE RELEVANT FOR OUR story, since the Bible has one view on the matter that—on the surface, at least—seems to contradict what scientific discovery has revealed to us to date. For example, paleoanthropology tells us that the origin of humankind probably began with a long evolutionary process, many millions of years ago, which involved several groups of ancestors known as hominids. These were primates with an average height of three or four feet who distinguished themselves by walking upright and using primitive tools such as flints to hunt and gather their food. The earliest evidence—a group of fossilized animal bones bearing marks from stone tools—was found in 2010 in the Lower Awash Valley in Ethiopia and is now believed to be 3.4 million years old.

In the next phase, some of these hominids began to develop larger brains. This gave them the ability to communicate verbally with one another, coordinate their attack on prey, and form a community so as to share the security and well-being of their offspring. One of the earliest groups of these humans, the *Homo erectus* type, first appeared in Africa some 500,000 years ago.

Preceding pages: A dramatic infrared image, captured by the Hubble Space Telescope, shows the birth of stars in a haze of gases and dust. Right: *This figure from Syria, made from solid copper and dated around the third millennium B.C.E., may depict a Canaanite deity.*

This human skull of a 40-year-old man is believed to be around 100,000 years old, dating from the Middle Paleolithic Period.

An Early Cypriot jug, dated around 2300 B.C.E., depicts a man and a deer.

Their prey ranged from deer, gazelle, and wild boar to migratory birds, which they felled with bows and arrows or sharpened stone blades. They also scoured the fields for wild cereals and fruits, including almonds, acorns, and pistachios, for which they would sometimes be forced to cover large distances.

Finally, around 100,000 B.C.E., *Homo sapiens* began to emerge almost simultaneously in Europe, Africa, and Asia. These were early modern hunter-gatherers who developed a more complex lifestyle, such as burying their dead according to set rituals; one typical example was found in the Wadi el-Mughara Caves on Mount Carmel, Israel.

THE ROLE OF CLIMATE CHANGE

The next key factor was climate change, which challenged the intellect of these early humans to develop a number of survival strategies. Several glacial periods sharply reduced the Earth's temperature and lowered the level of the oceans. The cooler temperatures forced these humans to husband fire as a source of warmth, and possibly as a means to cook their food, prompting major changes in their diet, and perhaps explaining their increased brain size. One theory suggests that cooler temperatures could have prompted several tribes to walk over a land connection between Siberia and North America.

After the last glacial period, which ended some 12,000 years ago, other changes took place that once again compelled human protocultures to adapt. The gradual warming of the Earth caused several animal species to become extinct, not only because of the hotter temperature but also because of changes in vegetation, water sources, and overhunting. These changes would have deprived many communities of their food supply were it not that the warmer climate also allowed new and different edible crops and plants to prosper in the wild like never before.

As a result, the transition from the last Ice Age to the Neolithic or New Stone Age (circa 7000 to 2500 B.C.E.) saw a major psychological shift in the way humans sustained themselves. People moved from a destructive to a productive lifestyle, from the hunting of animals to the raising of livestock, and from the gathering of wild plants to the sowing of seeds. They learned to take some form of control over their destiny by figuring out how to cultivate crops, such as emmer wheat, einkorn wheat, and barley. Of course, this was a gradual process, and many early farmers continued to hunt to supply their grown foods, especially during the winter. But the shift to cultivating crops and domesticating animals was perhaps the most critical transformation in the evolution of humankind. It encouraged the creation of permanent settlements in which villagers could pool their resources, increase harvest yields beyond subsistence levels, and thus allow certain individuals to specialize in other tasks, such as the production of tools, clothing, and pottery. Therein lay the seeds for the rise of human civilization.

The dawn of these early cultures can be glimpsed in places like Jericho in Israel and Ain Ghazal in Jordan, when skillful hands learned to spin sheep wool into textiles, weave reeds into baskets, and bake mud into brick. From the sixth millennium B.C.E. onward, certain communities learned to fire their own pottery from clay, thereby developing distinctive patterns of production and decoration. The recovery of these potsherds in a prehistoric stratum, or excavated layer, is extremely valuable to archaeologists, for these shards are the primary means by which the date of a layer can be established.

The growth of communities also fostered a sense of continuity with both the past and the future. This led to a funerary cult that recognized one's ancestors and the familial bonds of a clan. In some of these early cults, skulls were removed from the skeleton after decomposition, and plastered and painted, perhaps in an attempt to restore the person's original appearance.

THE EARLY BRONZE AGE

The advent of the Early Bronze Age around 3500 B.C.E. witnessed another set of important innovations. The development of the plow greatly increased agricultural yields. Copper ores were mined and alloyed with tin or other metals to produce bronze tools. Trees were planted in dedicated "orchards" for the production of large quantities of olives and olive oil. To move these goods, the donkey emerged as the principal beast of burden.

Especially in a dry climate like the Near East, cultivation depends on a steady supply of water. This problem was tackled with the development of irrigation systems, which may rank as the greatest invention of the Early Bronze Age. The earliest canalization appears around 3000 B.C.E. in Mesopotamia, in the territory of Sumer (today's Iraq) where it was used to channel water from the Euphrates and Tigris Rivers to arable lands far inland.

Such large-scale projects require planning, organization, and the cooperative use of capital and labor. Not surprisingly, it is in Mesopotamia (literally "the land of two rivers") that we see the rise of the first major cities. One of the earliest and most powerful of these city-states was Uruk (the biblical Erech, and possibly the root of the word "Iraq"). Another was Eridu, which the Sumerian King List—a stone prism tentatively dated to 2100 B.C.E. documenting Sumer's rulers—identifies as the first city-state on Earth. All of these cities boasted large agricultural markets where farmers could sell the region's surplus and where the worship of various regional deities slowly coalesced into a national cult. Inevitably this concentration of wealth also led to a commensurate concentration of power and the emergence of royal dynasties, including the line of the legendary King Gilgamesh.

A similar development took place in another region blessed with a perpetual source of water: ancient Egypt. Here, only a modicum of irrigation was necessary, because each year the Nile River rose like clockwork to deposit mineral-rich alluvial sediment all over the adjoining fields, producing what the Egyptians referred to as fertile *kemet,* or "black land." The result was a process of cultural growth very similar to what was happening many hundreds of miles to the east, in Mesopotamia. Thus, when around 2500 B.C.E. the climate changed once more and warmer temperatures robbed many regions in the Near East of their access to water, Egypt and Mesopotamia emerged as the two leading civilizations of the Early Bronze Age. ■

A lonely traveler sets out into the desert at sunset with his beast of burden.

THE CREATION NARRATIVES

God Creates the First Man and Woman

*B*ere'shit (be-rey-SHEET), or "In the beginning." These are the opening words of Hebrew Scripture and the Book of Genesis, describing the creation of the Earth and the origins of humankind. Based on strands from several traditions, Genesis is one of the most complex books in the Bible. Its main purpose is to do two things: to describe the origins of the world as the work of God and tell the story of Israel's prehistory through the lives of its founding fathers, the Patriarchs. Thus, Israel's origins are traced in terms of direct divine involvement from the very beginning of time.

Genesis' dominant theme is that of an omnipotent and devoted god who appoints humankind as stewards of nature, only to see his creation corrupted by man's disobedience, selfishness, and evil. Stymied in his attempts to achieve perfect harmony, God turns to one specific individual, Abraham, and designates him and his descendants as guardians of a covenant that will ultimately become the world's salvation.

To make its case, Genesis does not hesitate to borrow literary motifs from traditions that its Iron Age audience would have been familiar with. The purpose of these allusions is to present the idea of a single, all-powerful god using the symbolic vocabulary of ancient myths and traditions.

For example, Genesis presents God creating the heavens and the Earth as a magnificent cycle of six days. First, God shaped "the heavens and the earth," followed by the creation of Day and Night, the Sky and the Sea, and dry land that he named Earth. Then God brought forth vegetation, plants, and trees that bore fruit. He placed lights in the dome of the sky: the greater light, the sun, to rule the day, and a lesser light, the moon, to rule the night. Then God said, "Let the waters bring forth swarms of living creatures, and let birds fly above the earth across the dome of the sky" (Genesis 1:1-20). This was followed by the creation of animals on dry land. Finally, God created humankind, "in our image, according to our likeness" (Genesis 1:26).

Right: *Lava flows from a massive eruption of the Nyamuragira volcano in the Democratic Republic of the Congo.* **Insets:** *Male and female figurines from Syria, dated around 3200 B.C.E., are among the earliest surviving sculptures in bronze alloy from the Near East.*

ca 6500
Legendary date of
the founding of Ur

ca 5500
Early communities in Near East
learn to fire clay pottery

ca 5000
Legendary foundation
of Eridu in Sumer

ca 4500
The Chalcolithic Age
witnesses communities with
mud-brick dwellings

Opposite: A sunny oasis in the desert evokes the setting of stories in the Book of Genesis, including the depiction of the Garden of Eden. Right: Genesis posits that fish were one of the earliest forms of life. Modern science agrees that the first living species were marine vertebrates, which first appeared around 500 million years ago.

A similar narrative can be found in the Babylonian creation epic, recorded on Akkadian tablets from the first millennium B.C.E., although their origins probably stretch back into the days of ancient Sumer. According to this epic, the Earth was formed by the god Marduk in six days after he vanquished the evil ocean goddess Tiamat. Marduk first created the Earth and the firmament. Next, the epic tells us, "he constructed stations for the great gods, fixing their astral likeness as constellations." He then "caused the moon to shine," and appointed him "a creature of the night to signify the days." On the seventh day, Marduk created "a savage—'man' shall be his name. He shall be charged with the service of the gods."

Both epics share a pattern. First, the firmament and the Earth are created as separate entities. Next, time is instituted as the measure of life, anchored in a seven-day week. Then the sun and the moon are placed in the heavens, followed by living creatures, the last of which is man. Most striking, both Genesis and the Babylonian creation epic argue that heaven and Earth were created out of a shapeless void by divine command.

Since the 19th century, scholars have recognized that the Genesis stories are composed of several different strands. The creation of mankind, for example, is told in two ways: first as the culmination of the six-day creation process (Genesis 1:26) and then in a separate episode where God formed man "from the dust of the ground" (Genesis 2:7). This is reflected in the man's name, Adam; the root, *adama* in Hebrew, means "earth." When God saw that the man was lonely, he caused him to fall into a deep sleep and took one of his ribs, which he made into a woman (Genesis 2:22). Later in the story she is named Eve, or *Hawwah*, the "mother of all things" or "source of life."

It was long believed that Genesis and the other four books of the Pentateuch—Exodus, Leviticus, Numbers, and Deuteronomy—were composed from four different traditions, generally designated as the Y (or J), E, D, and P source. More recent research, however, suggests that the so-called Y, or Yahwist tradition, which refers to God as "YHWH" or *Yahweh*, is the dominant source and that other strands, such as the E or Elohist source (which refers to God as *El* or *Elohim*) and the P or Priestly source, are essentially additions and revisions of a later era. The dominant theory in biblical scholarship today is that the Book of Genesis reached its final form during the exile and postexilic era of the sixth century B.C.E. For example, Deuteronomy is essentially a retelling of much of the legal codes found in Exodus.

THE GARDEN OF EDEN

Genesis tells us that Adam and Eve dwelled in a beautiful Shangri-la, a garden called Eden. Its meaning is uncertain, although a Babylonian cuneiform tablet uses "Eden" as a term for "uncultivated plain." Some authors suggest that Eden may be linked to the Sumerian legend of a utopian land called Dilmun, sometimes identified with present-day Bahrain. Many centuries later, when the Genesis tradition came under Persian influence during the exile, the Garden of Eden acquired a new name: "paradise," rooted in the Old Persian word *pardis*.

The Garden of Eden had many trees, and Adam and Eve were encouraged to eat from every branch with the exception of the so-called tree of knowledge of good and evil (Genesis 2:17). The tree as a symbol of life has a very long pedigree in the cultures of Sumer

So God created humankind in his image,
in the image of God he created them;
male and female he created them.

GENESIS 1:27

The First City of Enoch

After God cast him out, Cain settled in a land east of Eden named Nod, which literally means "the Land of Naught," a place of aimless wandering. There he married a woman who would bear him a son named Enoch. Cain, says Genesis, then "built a city, and named it Enoch after his son Enoch" (Genesis 4:17). This is the first reference in the Bible to "a city," which suggests that at this time, farmer settlements had sufficiently grown to become walled communities. Genesis also tells us that among Cain's descendants was a man named Jabal, "the ancestor of those who live in tents and have livestock," a clear reference to nomadic tribes. Jabal's brother was named Jubal; "he was the ancestor of all those who play the lyre and pipe" (Genesis 4:20-21). Archaeologist Sir Leonard Woolley found a lyre and flute in a tomb near Tell al-Muqayyar, in today's Iraq.

and Babylonia, and even appears in Assyrian reliefs. But in Genesis, the tree is the setting for a parable, a morality tale. Despite God's injunction, Adam and Eve decide to eat from the tree of knowledge, thus breaching God's trust. For this, they are evicted from paradise and condemned to sustain themselves by tilling the land.

From a literal perspective, then, the biblical view of the origins of humankind is quite different from the evolutionary process described in the Introduction. But such comparisons miss the point. Genesis does not aim to provide a historical or scientific depiction of Earth's origins, for the simple reason that this was not its primary purpose. If the author(s) of Genesis had wanted to do so, they could have availed themselves of some very advanced theoretical models. Babylonian scholars, for example, had already developed the sexagesimal numeral system (the basis for our 60-minute, 24-hour daily cycle), a highly developed planetary model that could accurately predict solar eclipses, and a superb grasp of mathematics and early physics.

But that is not what Genesis is about. The book's principal objective is to show that in contrast to the polytheistic cultures of its time, a *single* deity, the God of Abraham, was responsible for the creation of Earth and all who dwell upon it.

CAIN AND ABEL

Devoid of their childlike innocence, Adam and Eve became aware of their nakedness—and sexual attraction. They became man and wife. In due course, Eve gave birth to her first son, and she named

him Cain. Here is an example of the many wordplays or double entendres of which Genesis is so fond, for *qayin* means "that which has been acquired or produced." When Eve gave birth, she said, "I have produced a man with the help of the Lord" (Genesis 4:1).

As soon as Cain became of age, he followed in the footsteps of his father, Adam, and became a farmer. Eve then gave birth to another son, named Abel, who eventually decided to become a shepherd. Here, the story of Genesis intersects with what we saw in the previous chapter: humankind's transition from hunting and gathering to a process of domestication. The Cain and Abel story also highlights the growing tension between the two principal forms of domestication: the sedentary lifestyle of the settled farmer versus the peripatetic movement of the pastoralist, the nomadic shepherd in search of fresh pastures. Throughout the Genesis story,

"The Garden of Eden With the Fall of Man" was painted by Flemish Renaissance artist Jan Brueghel the Elder (1568-1625).

This large clay vessel from Asia Minor, one of the earliest of its kind, is tentatively dated to the fifth millennium B.C.E.

both constituencies—farmers and shepherds—clash repeatedly over control of precious resources, such as wells. Indeed, the name "Abel" means "emptiness," evoking the image of a shepherd roaming aimlessly through great stretches of empty land in search of fields of green.

In due course, both brothers presented their offerings to God. Abel offered the "firstlings of his flock, their fat portions," while Cain sacrificed "the fruit of the ground" (Genesis 4:3-4). This is the first reference in the Bible to animal sacrifice, which would later be developed into an elaborate sacrificial cult centered in the tabernacle or Temple in Jerusalem. It is possible that this part of the story reflects some of the earliest traditions of sacrifice, common in Mesopotamia, to appease the gods so as to ensure a fertile harvest and a healthy flock.

God accepted Abel's animal offering, but surprisingly, Cain's fruit of the Earth was not to his satisfaction (Genesis 4:3-5). The Bible does not offer an explanation for this choice; it may simply reflect the rivalry between farmers and nomads. Incensed, Cain lured his brother, Abel, to a field, and killed him—the first instance of homicide in the Bible. For this, God decided to cast Cain from the land. He became a fugitive, stripped of his tribal protection. Cain was shocked and exclaimed, "Anyone who meets me may kill me!" (Genesis 4:14). This verse suggests that the Earth was already populated by other people, which is interesting. The Bible doesn't say, for example, whether Adam and Eve had children before Cain and Abel. Perhaps, then, this episode took place many generations after the time of Adam and Eve. Here, too, we may see different traditions at work. ■

NOAH AND THE FLOOD

A Massive Flood in the Land of the Two Rivers

After Abel's death and Cain's flight to a land called Nod, "when Adam had lived one hundred and thirty years," Eve gave birth to another son, named Seth (Genesis 5:3). Seth became the father of Enosh and a long line of descendants; many of these names are similar to the genealogy that Genesis ascribes to Cain's son, who is called Enoch. One of these descendants was a man named Noah, son of Lamech.

Around this time, says Genesis, "people began to multiply, and daughters were born to them." This development was keenly observed by a mysterious group of beings that Genesis refers to as "sons of God." These "sons" saw that the daughters "were fair, and they took wives for themselves" (Genesis 6:2). Who are these sons of God? In Mesopotamian myths as well as in later Greek mythology, demigods often became romantically involved with mortal women. But scholars are divided over the meaning of this verse. Some believe "sons" refers to fallen angels. Others reject this notion, since many ancient texts argue that angels are ephemeral beings incapable of sexual relations with human beings. Another interpretation, proposed by theologian and Bible scholar Meredith Kline, suggests that "sons of God" are the kings of the earliest city-states that emerged in antediluvian Sumer around 3000 B.C.E. To cement their power and dynastic authority, these kings invariably claimed divine sanction for their exalted status. If that is true, then this verse could reflect one of the oldest strands in the Genesis saga.

In the next passage, Genesis refers to another enigmatic group, known as Nephilim. The term also returns in the Book of Numbers to describe giants living in Canaan (Numbers 13:33). Genesis calls them "heroes that were of old, warriors of renown." One of the Dead Sea Scrolls (4Q 417) refers to the Nephilim as children of Seth, whom God had condemned. In this case, the association with "fallen angels" may be more plausible, since the name also appears in the Book of

Job, where it refers to "heavenly beings" or angels (Job 1:6; 2:1).

It is in this turbulent period of demigods, heroes, and mortals, says Genesis, that the Earth's population became corrupt. "The wickedness of humankind was great in the earth," says the Bible (Genesis 6:5). God now regretted that he had placed human beings in charge of his creation and decided to destroy them. Only one man and his family would be saved. His name was Noah.

NOAH'S ARK

The name Noah is believed to be rooted in the word *niham*, which literally means "rest." The instrument of Noah's survival was a boat, a very large ship made of gopher wood and covered in pitch. God even gave Noah detailed specifications of how this ark should be built: "the length of the ark three hundred cubits, its width fifty cubits, and its height thirty cubits. Make a roof for the ark, and finish it to a cubit above … And of every living thing, of all flesh, you shall bring two of every kind" (Genesis 6:15, 19).

Did the technology to build such a large ship exist? The sensational discovery of a group of boats in Abydos in 2000 suggests that as early as 3000 B.C.E., the ancient Egyptians had mastered the art of assembling a wooden hull using curved wooden planks, fused together with mortise and tenon joints and sealed with reeds. But these flimsy ships were essentially river barges for coastal traffic, even though some scholars claim that they could have sailed along the Mediterranean coast as far as Syria and the gateway to northern Mesopotamia. It is also interesting to note that the ark's specifications in Genesis do not provide for either a rudder or a sail, which may suggest that it was not meant to be navigated at all, merely carried on the waters by the protective hands of God.

Once Noah, his family, and all the animals were safely stowed aboard, God sent

This clay figurine of a woman from Ur, dated around 700 B.C.E., probably served to protect women during childbirth.

ca 4000
Early farming settlements in Egypt

ca 3500
Early Bronze Age begins

ca 3400
First city-states emerge in Mesopotamia

ca 3300
Nomes, or regions, of Egypt are organized in two separate kingdoms

*At the end of forty days Noah opened the window
of the ark that he had made and sent out the raven;
and it went to and fro until the waters
were dried up from the earth.*

GENESIS 8:6

*This modern reconstruction of Noah's ark is
based on the detailed specifications provided
by the Book of Genesis. Inset: A seventh-
century B.C.E. Assyrian tablet from Nineveh
relates part of the famous Epic of Gilgamesh,
including the story of a great flood.*

ca 3200
First examples of pictographic
writing in Sumer

ca 3100
Egyptians develop mummification
to preserve the dead

ca 3000
First canalization
appears in Sumer

ca 3000
Uruk becomes dominant
city-state in Sumer

Populating the Earth

According to Genesis, the sons of Noah—Shem, Ham, and Japheth—became the new progenitors of the people on Earth, as described in a lengthy Genesis genealogy known as the Table of Nations (Genesis 10:1-7). The children of Japheth, for example, are seen as inhabiting Greece and Asia Minor, whereas the descendants of Ham would populate North Africa, Canaan, and Mesopotamia. Shem became "the father of all the children of Eber," which some authors have linked to the Akkadian/Egyptian name *apiru* or *habiru*, meaning "sandweller" or "migrant," and possibly the root of the word "Hebrew" (Genesis 10:21). Another prominent name in the Noah genealogy is that of Nimrod, son of Cush and great-grandson of Noah, and "a mighty hunter before the Lord" (Genesis 10:8-9). Some authors have tried to see a parallel between Nimrod and Marduk in Mesopotamian mythology. Nimrod then founded a kingdom in the land of Shinar; the prophet Micah would later associate this with the empire of Assyria (Micah 5:6).

down rain for forty days and nights, "and all the fountains of the great deep burst forth, and the windows of the heavens were opened" (Genesis 7:11-12). Some historians interpret this passage as the exact reversal of the original Creation sequence, in which the waters were separated. Eventually the waters subsided, and the ark came to rest "on the mountains of Ararat" (Genesis 8:4). *Harê Ararat*, the plural of "mountains of Ararat," has often been mistaken for the singular "Mount Ararat," the name of the tallest mountain on the border of Turkey and Armenia.

THE GREAT MESOPOTAMIAN FLOOD

There are countless references to a "great flood," orchestrated by divine power, in the literature of ancient Mesopotamia. No doubt this was inspired by the unpredictability of the Tigris and Euphrates Rivers, which could rise at any moment to destroy the painstakingly built network of irrigation. In the Atrahasis Epic, for example, the gods decide to destroy humankind with an immense inundation. But the water god Enki takes pity on a man named Atrahasis and urges him to build a boat. This vessel, the god instructs him, should be filled with all of his possessions, including animals and birds. The Sumerian King List is even organized in two separate periods: one before the Flood and one after the Flood.

Some passages in the famous Epic of Gilgamesh offer an even closer parallel to the story of Noah in Genesis. In this story, it is Gilgamesh's ancestor Utnapishtim who is told to build a large ship. "These are the measurements of the barque as you shall build her," the god Ea tells him. "Let her beam equal her length, let her deck be roofed like the vault that covers the abyss; then take up into the boat the seed of all living creatures."

But did such a catastrophic flood actually take place? The Sumerian King List indicates that it must have happened before 2600 B.C.E. In 1922, while excavating the royal tombs of Ur near Tell al-Muqayyar in today's Iraq, British archaeologist Sir Leonard Woolley discovered a deep layer of "perfectly clean clay, uniform throughout, the texture of which showed that it had been laid there by water." The layer was eight feet deep and then completely disappeared. His discovery prompted headlines around the world: Here, at last, was proof of the biblical Flood!

But in the years since, archaeologists have found evidence of many other greater and lesser floods in the area. It shows that the ancient "land between the two rivers" was simply prone to frequent and sometimes catastrophic flooding. But modern research has found traces of an exceptionally large flood that must have occurred around 2900 B.C.E. Scientists base this theory on the radiocarbon dating of river sediments near Shuruppak (today's Tell Fara in Iraq). This vast deluge would undoubtedly have destroyed many of Sumer's incipient city-states. This in turn may have prompted a power shift from the city of Uruk to a fast-rising center on the Sumerian plain: the city of Ur, the putative birthplace of Abraham. ∎

The so-called Royal Standard of Ur from around 2600 B.C.E. depicts scenes of war and peace. It features the wheel-borne wagon, a Sumerian invention.

A modern reconstruction depicts the White Temple of Uruk where An, the Sumerian god of heaven and ruler of the constellations, was venerated.

This finely detailed model of a boat with rowers and a single steering oar dates from the Middle Kingdom reign of Amenemhat I (circa 1981-1975 B.C.E.).

And God said to Noah ... "Make yourself an ark of cypress wood; make rooms in the ark, and cover it inside and out with pitch."

GENESIS 6:14

THE TOWER OF BABEL

Early Humans Attempt to Reach to the Heavens

Numerous clay figurines found in today's Iraq and Syria show that, from the very beginning, the civilizations of ancient Mesopotamia were grounded in the collective worship of a pantheon of gods. Given that agriculture was the principal economic activity of ancient Sumer and the threat of flooding or drought was always present, it is not surprising that these earliest deities were closely intertwined with agricultural needs. Each god was believed to be responsible for a key element of crop growth—such as water *(Enki)*, sun *(Utu)*, earth *(Ninhursag)*, air *(Enlil)*, and fertility *(Inanna)*. By appeasing these deities with worship and sacrifice, it was believed, human beings could assert some control over prevailing climate conditions so as to secure a good harvest.

The earliest idols from Sumer are rather shapeless depictions of men and women with enlarged genitals, which suggests some form of fertility ritual. Over time,

A clay relief of a Babylonian goddess popularly known as "Queen of the Night" is dated between 1792 and 1750 B.C.E. during the reign of King Hammurabi.

however, the Sumerian artists developed considerable artistry in shaping the images of their gods, as well as their earthly rulers.

Eventually a form of national worship emerged, though some deities remained closely associated with a particular region or city-state. This worship inevitably fostered the emergence of a dedicated priesthood, whose task it was to develop and maintain an elaborate liturgy of cultic practice. This cadre grew into an powerful constituency; records from the 3rd Dynasty of Ur refer to a community of 62 priests, both male *(Ensí)* and female *(Nin)*, whose rituals were accompanied by a dedicated choir and orchestra some 180 strong.

Gods were worshipped in a dedicated structure known as a temple. In Uruk, for example, the dominant deity was Inanna, goddess of fertility, sexual love, and war; she was venerated in the Pillar Temple at the heart of the city. Another important figure, An, the god of heaven and ruler of the constellations, was venerated in a structure with multiple elevated levels known as the White Temple. Thus, the worship of these gods stimulated a new form of artistic endeavor known as architecture.

THE PYRAMID

The concept of planned architecture originated at roughly the same time in both Mesopotamia and Egypt, but for different purposes. In Saqqara, Egypt, a man called Imhotep, the first named architect in history, designed a large complex of buildings as the principal mortuary precinct of his patron, King Djoser. Completed around 2650 B.C.E., it included elaborate temple facilities and a 180-foot-high stepped pyramid. To adorn this vast complex, Imhotep created certain architectural features that would remain valid in Egyptian and European architecture for the next 5,000 years: fluted pilasters and columns, capitals adorned with lotus or papyrus leaves, and ornamental friezes decorated with reliefs. Many of these buildings were built in limestone, rather than baked brick, and remain in astonishingly good condition to this day.

Why Djoser chose a pyramid to mark his tomb continues to be a subject of scholarly debate. One prevailing theory is that the shape naturally emerged from the use of a *mastaba*, or "stepped mound," to mark the grave of a nobleman. These mounds may have symbolized the primeval mound from which the Earth was originally created and to which the deceased were destined to return. Others have argued that Imhotep's pyramidal shape represented the hierarchical arrangement of a unified Egyptian society under the benevolent rule of King Djoser. Still others again have put forth the theory that pyramids were used for astronomical observations or for manipulation of the projection of sunlight, given that Ra, the ancient sun god, was a leading deity in the Egyptian pantheon.

The partially reconstructed mud-brick ziggurat of Ur, Mesopotamia, was built by King Ur-Nammu during the 3rd Dynasty of Ur (circa 2113-2006 B.C.E.).

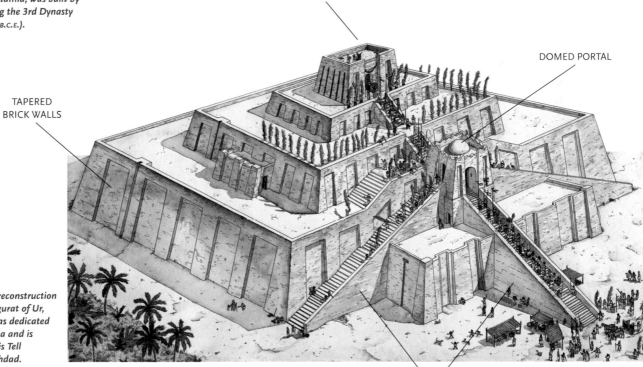

TEMPLE OF NANNA

DOMED PORTAL

TAPERED BRICK WALLS

This diagram shows a reconstruction of the 80-foot-high ziggurat of Ur, shown above, which was dedicated to the moon god Nanna and is located in what today is Tell al-Muqayyar near Baghdad.

MAIN ACCESS RAMPS

ca 2900	ca 2770	ca 2770	ca 2650
Massive flood destroys most of the cities in Sumer	2nd Dynasty of Egypt begins	Hieroglyphic writing emerges in Egypt	King Djoser of the 3rd Dynasty assumes throne in Egypt

The stepped pyramid of King Djoser in Saqqara, Egypt (circa 2650-2575), is the oldest surviving structure built entirely of stone.

Below: This gypsum figure of a woman in prayer, known as an orant, *dates from around 2400 B.C.E.*

Uruk is a key example. As evidenced by the Epic of Gilgamesh, it was one of the first planned cities in human history with spacious streets, market squares, temples, and gardens, surrounded by a protective wall and linked to the nearby harbor via a canal. Zoned districts carefully distinguished between residential and commercial areas, civic centers, and religious precincts, all arranged with the temple at its core— not unlike the way medieval cities would slowly coalesce around their principal cathedral.

THE RISE OF THE ZIGGURAT

Through the late fourth and the early third millennium, these religious shrines grew from simple single-hall structures to sophisticated designs that, as in the case of ancient Egypt, aspired to the heavens. Their main purpose was to create a mediating space between the gods and humankind, between Earth and the firmament. Because the Earth's laws of gravity are universal, this naturally led to a pyramidal form, though the Mesopotamian solution differed from the design of Egyptian pyramids. In the Egyptian Old Kingdom, architects sought to create a perfect pyramidal shape with smooth triangular shapes on all four sides, rising from a square base to a single point on top. In Mesopotamia, by contrast, pyramids were shaped as a series of receding platforms with tapered walls, rising from a square, oval, or rectangular mound of rammed earth. And unlike the Egyptian pyramids, the summit was shaped as a flat platform, accessible through a series of external ramps and stairways.

Archaeologists have uncovered the remains of 32 of these ziggurats, including very large specimens near Baghada and Nasiriyah in Iraq and Khuzestan Province in Iran. The ziggurats' exposed facades were usually covered with glazed or colored brick that either extolled the deity to whom the ziggurat was dedicated or the king responsible for its construction. Some have astrological references, which suggests that ziggurats were

The Saqqara stepped pyramid set the trend for pharaohs to come; some 135 pyramids have been identified in Egypt. Eventually the stepped design was clad with a veneer of limestone so as to create a smooth surface. A small interior access way, designed with several false turns to confuse tomb robbers, led to the chamber in which the pharaoh's sarcophagus was placed. Smaller pyramids and tombs were built nearby to house the royal family and the pharaoh's closest advisers. The greatest examples of these Egyptian pyramids are still standing in Giza, near Cairo, including the pyramids of Khufu (or Cheops) and Khafre (or Chephren).

In Mesopotamia, the beginning of the third millennium B.C.E. also saw the rise of planned monumental architecture, but for a different reason: to honor the gods rather than deceased kings. Nor did the Sumerians as yet recognize the need for a professional architect, since most of the designing was left to skilled scribes. Nonetheless, monumental architecture was held in great esteem in the Sumerian city-states and considered one of the greatest gifts that the gods had bestowed onto humankind.

Therefore it was called Babel, because there the Lord confused the language of all the earth.

EXODUS 11:9

also used for celestial observation. One of the most impressive examples is Ur's 80-foot-high ziggurat, dedicated to the moon god Nanna. This ziggurat, partly restored, can still be admired near the excavations of Tell al-Muqayyar near Baghdad, though it suffered from bombing during the 2003 Iraq War.

Another unique aspect of these structures and their surrounding shrines is that they contained images not only of the deity but also of the faithful. Archaeologists have discovered scores of figurines with outstretched or clasped hands, usually made of clay or gypsum, that appear to be worshippers *(orants)*. Perhaps their primary function was to assure these gods that they were attended with around-the-clock worship. Excavations throughout Mesopotamia have yielded a veritable hoard of these votive statues. Most depict either a male or female worshipper dressed in fringed skirt or gown, hands tightly clasped in front of him or her, which may signify a Sumerian gesture of worship and piety. The eyes are large and exaggerated, often still marked with a thin trace of paint. The men invariably have long and carefully stylized beards.

Sumer's building prowess was not limited to the construction of temples alone. The Royal Tombs, excavated by Leonard Woolley in 1922, feature fully developed arches some 3,000 years before their reappearance in Roman architecture.

THE TOWER OF BABEL

It is possible that the Mesopotamian ziggurat is the inspiration, if not the setting, for the story of the Tower of Babel. At a time, says Genesis, when "the whole earth had one language and the same words," the people of the city of Babel invented the technology of making bricks from baked clay (Genesis 11:1). This too may refer to Mesopotamian precedent, for ziggurats were usually built from mud brick and mortar made of bitumen. "Come," the people of Babel said, "let us build ourselves a city, and a tower whose top may reach unto heaven; and let us make a name for ourselves" (Genesis 11:4). This initiative did not remain hidden from God for long. "The Lord came down to see the city," says Genesis, "and the tower which the children of men had built." Rather than destroying this monumental project, God decided to "confuse their language there, so that they will not understand each other's speech" (Genesis 11:5,7). Unable to communicate with one another, the builders left the city and were scattered abroad.

The name "Babel" is one more example of Genesis' penchant for double entendres. The Akkadian word *bab-ili* means "the gate of the gods," which is possibly the root of the word "Babylon," the city that was founded in the 1860s B.C.E. by the Amorites, a group of people who originally hailed from Syria-Canaan. But *balal* in Hebrew also means something "sowing confusion," not unlike the English verb "to babble," suggesting that Babylon, Israel's future enemy, came about amid great turmoil. ■

The Unification of Egypt

While the civilization of Mesopotamia was spread over multiple autonomous city-states, the disparate regions, or *nomes*, of Egypt were organized in two separate kingdoms as early as 3300 B.C.E. Lower Egypt, located in the north, ran from the Mediterranean to today's Cairo and included the fecund region of the Nile Delta, permeated with tributaries of the Nile that over the centuries had deposited layers of rich alluvial sediment. The other kingdom, Upper Egypt, ran along a narrow ribbon of fertile land bordering the Nile, past its cataracts into Nubia and present-day Khartoum. In this desert landscape, the Egyptian pharaohs would build some of their greatest monuments, including Abydos, Thebes, and Abu Simbel. Around 2920 B.C.E., both kingdoms were unified by a king named Narmer, who founded the 1st Dynasty (2920-2770 B.C.E.)—the first of 31 dynasties that would govern Egypt over a span of 3,000 years.

The famous Great Sphinx of Giza is believed to be a portrait of Pharaoh Khafra (circa 2558-2532 B.C.E.).

THE WORLD OF ABRAHAM

A Family Leaves Their Native City of Ur

After the brief interlude of the Tower of Babel, Genesis resumes the thread of the descendants of Adam and Noah. Nine generations after the Great Flood, the Bible says, there lived a man named Terah who became the father of three sons. He named them Abram (later renamed Abraham), Nahor, and Haran (Genesis 11:26). Abraham and Haran took wives, but sadly, Abraham's wife, Sarah (or Sarai as she was known at this point), turned out to be barren. Then an even greater tragedy struck the family: Abraham's brother Haran died, leaving his son, Lot, and daughters Milcah and Iscah without a father.

Genesis says that at this point, Terah's family still lived in the city of their birth: *'Ur Kaśdim*, usually translated as "Ur of the Chaldeans" (Genesis 11:28). The identification of this city is hotly debated, but many historians are prepared to accept that the Bible is referring to the Sumerian city-state of Ur. The Bible often refers to Babylon as "the land of the Chaldeans" (Jeremiah 50:45). Chaldea was a small nation of Semitic people who were gradually absorbed in Neo-Babylonia after the seventh century B.C.E., when Ur still retained some prominence. As late as the sixth century B.C.E., when many scholars believe the Torah reached its final form, Assyrian king Nabonidus, who hailed from Babylon, spared no effort in reconstructing the magnificent ziggurat of Nanna in the Ur's city center.

The choice of Ur as Abraham's city of origin may therefore have been deliberate, since even in ancient times it was recognized as one of the oldest centers of human civilization. The city is believed to have been founded by farmers from northern Mesopotamia as early as 6500 B.C.E. As we saw, these early settlements were entirely wiped out by a large flood that swept the region around 2900 B.C.E. But Ur eventually recovered, notably under the rule of the so-called 1st Dynasty, established by King Mesh-Ane-padaa, as the Sumerian King List tells us. This dynasty succeeded in gradually taking control of all of southern Mesopotamia, making Ur one of the most prosperous centers of the Early Bronze Age.

Life for Arabs living in the marshes of the Tigris and Euphrates Rivers has changed little over the millennia.

Inset: A statue of superintendent Ebih-Il was found in the Temple of Ishtar at Mari and is dated around 2400 B.C.E.

ca 2650	ca 2575	ca 2550	ca 2530
Imhotep builds the mortuary complex of Djoser in Saqqara	Old Kingdom Period of Egypt begins	King Mesh-Ane-padaa establishes the 1st Dynasty of Ur	King Khufu (Cheops) builds Great Pyramid in Giza

ca 2500
Hotter climate causes
changes in Canaan's urbanization

ca 2500
Cotton and potatoes
are cultivated in today's Peru

ca 2500
Overland trade routes develop
from the Balkans to Spain

ca 2500
Acupuncture is
invented in China

A modern reconstruction of the city of Ur during the 3rd Dynasty (circa 2113-2006 B.C.E.) shows the sacred precinct with the Temple of Nanna at its center.

Several women found in the Royal Tombs of Ur were buried with diadems, earrings, and necklaces made of gold leaves, lapis lazuli, and carnelian.

EARLY PICTOGRAPHIC WRITING

The great wealth of this period is dramatically attested by a series of royal tombs that were excavated by Sir Leonard Woolley near Tell al-Muqayyar in 1922. The tombs contained the remains of 74 people, 68 of whom were female, whose bodies were arranged as if they were lined up in a funerary procession. This led Woolley to suggest a rather macabre scenario: On the death of the king, everyone in his entourage—including wives, officials, and servants—was put to death as well so as to serve the deceased ruler in the afterlife. This royal retinue was equipped with every imaginable luxury, including jewels,

headdresses, statues, musical instruments, mosaics, games, and superbly crafted cups and vessels. The so-called Standard of Ur, a wooden box decorated with scenes of a peaceful banquet as well as a military campaign, shows another important invention: a wheel-borne wagon.

Perhaps the greatest contribution of Sumerian civilization was its development of an early form of pictographic writing around 3200 B.C.E., when the trade in surplus crops grew into a major intrastate economic activity. These merchants began to carve small symbols in soft clay representing the type and quantities of goods they traded, such as sheaves of wheat or barrels of beer. Through daily use, these pictograms became more stylized and simplified into a script of wedge-shaped marks known as cuneiform.

The importance of this development can hardly be overstated. Unlike parchment or paper, clay tablets are more durable and often survive fire. That is why entire libraries of ancient cuneiform tablets have survived to this day, while thousands of parchment scrolls of much later eras have been lost to fire, destruction, or simple decay.

THE RISE OF THE 3RD DYNASTY

The great 1st Dynasty of Sumer, roughly contemporaneous with the 3rd and 4th Dynasties of Egypt, came to an end near the 24th century B.C.E. A prolonged drought led to excessive evaporation in the region's irrigation network, thus causing increased saline levels and a dramatic drop in crop yields. But the greatest disruptive force was the invasion from a warlike people known as the Akkadians, led by legendary King Sargon I. The Akkadians are the first population group known as Semites, since their language would form the basis for the development of Hebrew as well as Aramaic, Assyrian, and Syriac. By 2280 B.C.E., the new Akkadian Empire would stretch from the Taurus Mountains in today's southern Turkey to Lebanon in the west and the Persian Gulf in the east.

Only in the 21st century B.C.E., when the Akkadian realm began to disintegrate, did Ur regain some of its former power under King Ur-Nammu, the founder of Ur's 3rd Dynasty. A vast new public works program was begun, including a large-scale reconstruction of the city's irrigation networks, as well as the construction of the ziggurat dedicated to Nanna. King Ur-Nammu also developed one of the first legal codes in history, which would greatly influence the more famous Code of Hammurabi some 300 years later.

But the revival of Ur's 3rd Dynasty was short-lived. During the reign of King Ibbi-Sin, who ascended the throne in 1963 B.C.E., Mesopotamia was visited by a new wave of invasions, this time by Elamites who hailed from what today is the Iranian plateau. This conflict led to a profound destabilization of the region, when much of the population was forced to flee.

THE JOURNEY TO HARRAN

It is possible that the Elamite invasion forms the framework for Terah's decision to pack up his family and move northward, to the city of Harran, in today's southern Turkey. Harran (*harranu* in Akkadian), which means "crossroads," was one of the farthest outposts of the Sumerian trade network near the end of the third millennium B.C.E. All of the main caravan routes heading north along the course of the Euphrates terminated in this city before branching out westward to Anatolia, or Canaan and Egypt to the south. A rough-and-tumble frontier town, Harran couldn't possibly match the high living standard of Ur, Mesopotamia's most sophisticated city. This may indicate that the move to the north was not a voluntary one. Was Terah a merchant himself perhaps?

The discovery of ancient texts in Mari and Ugarit, both in present-day Syria, may shed some light on the question. Excavated by French archaeologists from the 1930s onward, both sites yielded a vast cache of cuneiform tablets. These texts show that the boundaries between sedentary and pastoral clans were more fluid than we would otherwise expect. Indeed, while Abraham was a nomad, his son Isaac would "sow seed in that land, and reap a hundredfold" (Genesis 26:12).

At some point after the family arrived in Harran, Terah failed to rise from his bed. The mantle of leadership was now transferred to his oldest son, Abraham. As Genesis tells us, this is when he first heard the voice of God, telling him that Harran was not his final destiny. ■

After 3500 B.C.E., Sumerian merchants began to record their trade with a pictographic script carved in soft clay. This eventually led to cuneiform writing.

Terah took his son Abram and his grandson Lot son of Haran,
and his daughter-in-law Sarai, his son Abram's wife,
and they went out together from Ur of the Chaldeans.

GENESIS 11:31

THE JOURNEY TO CANAAN

Abraham Travels From Harran to Shechem

Who was Abraham? Is he a historical character, or a composite of different traditions from Israel's prehistory? Up to this point, Genesis has not given us much information about the key protagonists of its story, but that changes with the figure of Abraham. No fewer than 15 chapters are devoted to this fascinating nomadic figure as he slowly rises to the astonishing opportunity that God has offered him: One day, he will be the ancestor of a great nation. The character who emerges from these pages is a strong and loyal individual, but also a morally flawed one who doesn't hesitate to pass off his wife as his sister (and available bedmate) as long as it suits him.

The historicity of Abraham has long been the subject of debate, but for Genesis' immediate audience, such questioning was probably beside the point. In Antiquity, listeners didn't care if the protagonist was a historical personality or a literary composite; what mattered was the meaning, the essential message of the story. And for Genesis, the meaning is very clear: that after a series of bruising conflicts with humankind—the expulsion from the Garden, the Great Flood, the Tower of Babel—God now turns to a single man to reset the course of human beings. That reset is a covenant, a promise whereby God will guide and protect his people as long as they, in turn, remain true in their faith and obedience to God.

Until this point, the geographic setting of the Genesis stories has been rather indistinct, but the story now shifts to a specific location. "Go from your country and your kindred and your father's house," God tells Abraham while he is still in Harran, "to the land that I will show you" (Genesis 12:1).

Abraham obeys without question. That's rather surprising, since nothing in the story suggests that Abraham has had any prior contact with God. As a son of Ur, he most likely grew up in a household that

Harran, or Harranu in Akkadian, is located in modern-day Turkey and is known for its beehive-shaped houses made of stone and brick.

Inset: This head of a Mesopotamian matriarch is tentatively dated to around 2000 B.C.E.

ca 2280
The Akkadian Empire stretches
from today's Turkey
to the Persian Gulf

ca 2150
Akkadian Period
comes to an end

ca 2134
Political upheaval marks Egypt's
1st Intermediate Period

ca 2100
The Sumerian King List documents
all kings of Sumer to date

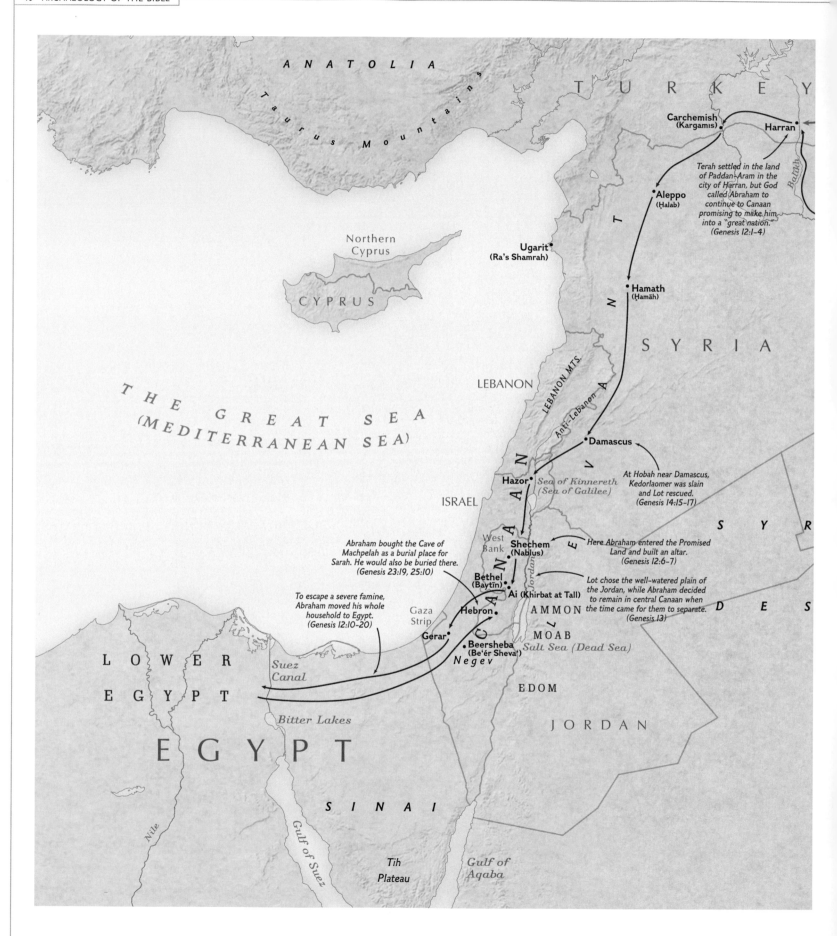

ANATOLIA

Taurus Mountains

TURKEY

Carchemish
(Kargamış)

Harran

Terah settled in the land
of Paddan-Aram in the
city of Harran, but God
called Abraham to
continue to Canaan
promising to make him
into a "great nation."
(Genesis 12:1-4)

Balikh

Aleppo
(Ḥalab)

Northern
Cyprus

Ugarit
(Ra's Shamrah)

CYPRUS

Hamath
(Ḥamāh)

SYRIA

LEBANON

LEBANON MTS.

Anti-Lebanon

A
N
T
I

THE GREAT SEA
(MEDITERRANEAN SEA)

Damascus

Hazor

Sea of Kinnereth
(Sea of Galilee)

At Hobah near Damascus,
Kedorlaomer was slain
and Lot rescued.
(Genesis 14:15-17)

S
Y
R

ISRAEL

West
Bank

Shechem
(Nablus)

E

Here Abraham entered the Promised
Land and built an altar.
(Genesis 12:6-7)

Abraham bought the Cave of
Machpelah as a burial place for
Sarah. He would also be buried there.
(Genesis 23:19, 25:10)

Bethel
(Baytīn)

Ai (Khirbat at Tall)

Jordan

Lot chose the well-watered plain of
the Jordan, while Abraham decided
to remain in central Canaan when
the time came for them to separate.
(Genesis 13)

D
E
S

To escape a severe famine,
Abraham moved his whole
household to Egypt.
(Genesis 12:10-20)

Gaza
Strip

Hebron

AMMON

C
A
N
A
A
N

MOAB

Gerar

Beersheba
(Be'ér Sheva')

Salt Sea (Dead Sea)

Negev

LOWER

Suez
Canal

EDOM

EGYPT

JORDAN

Bitter Lakes

EGYPT

SINAI

Nile

Gulf of
Suez

Tih
Plateau

Gulf of
Aqaba

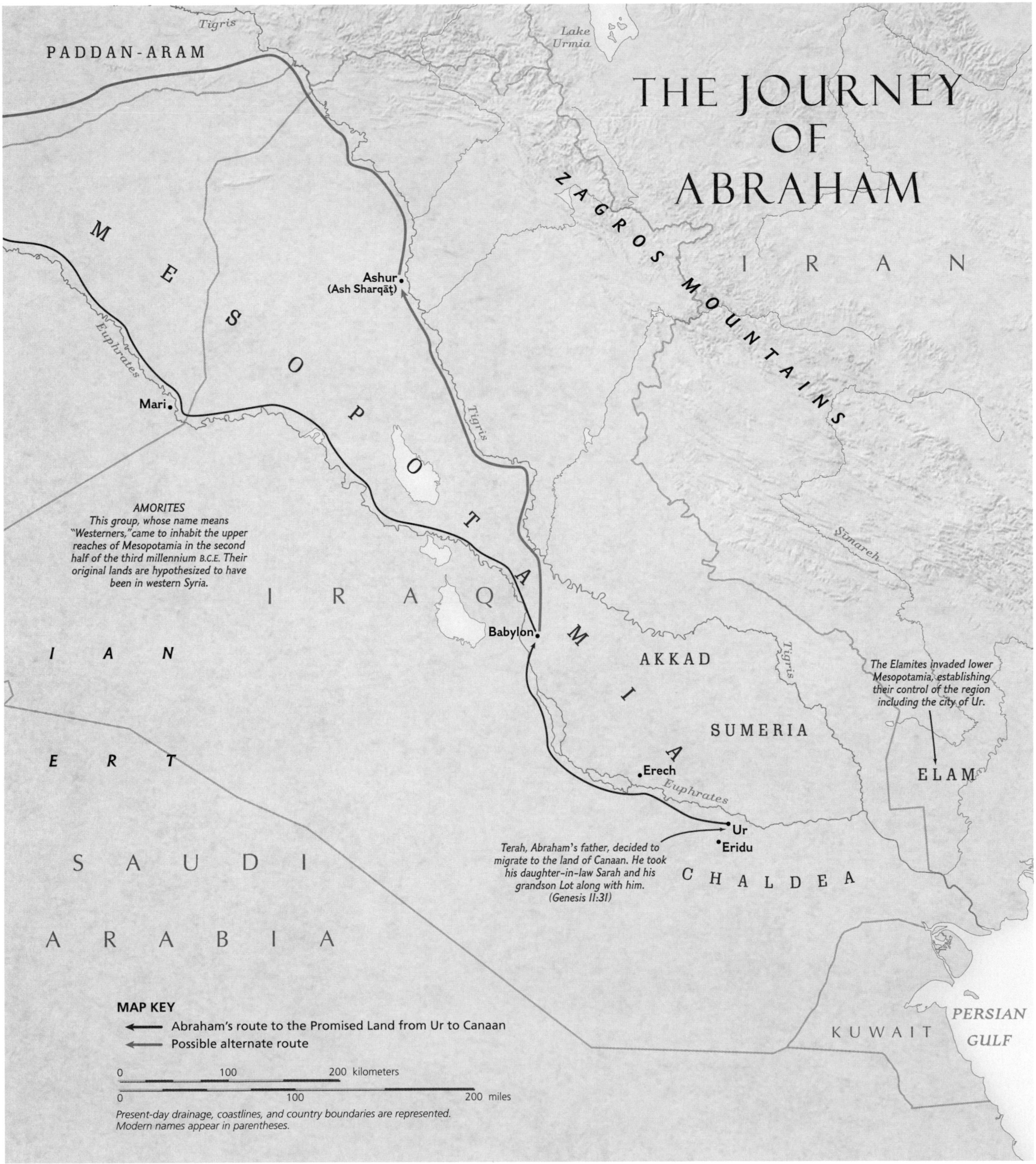

Tigris

PADDAN-ARAM

*Lake
Urmia*

THE JOURNEY
OF
ABRAHAM

ZAGROS MOUNTAINS

I R A N

M
E
S
O
P
O
T
A
M
I
A

Euphrates

Mari

Ashur
(Ash Sharqāt)

Tigris

AMORITES
*This group, whose name means
"Westerners," came to inhabit the upper
reaches of Mesopotamia in the second
half of the third millennium B.C.E. Their
original lands are hypothesized to have
been in western Syria.*

I R A Q

Babylon

AKKAD

Tigris

The Elamites invaded lower
Mesopotamia, establishing
their control of the region
including the city of Ur.

Sīmareh

I A N

E R T

SUMERIA

ELAM

Erech

Euphrates

S A U D I

Ur

Eridu

*Terah, Abraham's father, decided to
migrate to the land of Canaan. He took
his daughter-in-law Sarah and his
grandson Lot along with him.
(Genesis 11:31)*

C H A L D E A

A R A B I A

PERSIAN
GULF

KUWAIT

MAP KEY

⟵ Abraham's route to the Promised Land from Ur to Canaan

⟵ Possible alternate route

0	100	200 kilometers
0	100	200 miles

*Present-day drainage, coastlines, and country boundaries are represented.
Modern names appear in parentheses.*

worshipped the idols of the region, such as Marduk, Anu, or Nanna, Ur's patron deity. But therein lies the fundamental point that Genesis tries to make: Abraham obeys this unseen God without hesitation, even though he has not yet been told his ultimate destination, thus setting the benchmark of unquestioned obedience for the future nation of Israel.

God also said that Abraham should "go from his kindred." And indeed, the surviving family of Terah must now be separated, for Nahor and his wife, Milcah, cannot go with him. Perhaps they have made a life for themselves in Harran and see no need to uproot their family once more. Only Abraham's faithful wife, Sarah (known then as Sarai), agrees to come along, as well as his nephew Lot, whom Abraham has adopted as a son. Together with their servants and livestock, they set out on the long journey south.

THE ENTRY INTO CANAAN

The encounter with Canaan must have come as a shock. Unlike the endless stretches of the Mesopotamian plain, Canaan was a rugged and untamed land of sharp contrasts, a narrow strip of craggy rocks and wild shrub, of fertile fields and dry desert, squeezed between the Arabian Desert and the Mediterranean Sea. Fed by three small streams—the Banyas, the Dan, and the Hazbani—the Jordan River was a far cry from the mighty Euphrates, but even so, the fecundity of this land was quite astonishing. Here was the most fertile valley in all of the Near East, the Jezreel, which in Hebrew means "God sows." Also known as the plain of Esdraelon in the Bible, the valley produced crops as varied as wheat, corn, chickpeas, and melons in abundance.

But, says Genesis, "the Canaanites were in the land," and these natives were not about to let their fields be overrun by nomads and interlopers from the north. That may have been the reason that Abraham moved farther south, to the hills of Samaria, where the soil was much drier but where patches of olive trees and terebinth could offer shade to a weary traveler. Here, in a place called Shechem, Abraham decided to build an altar to mark his arrival. God affirms this by saying, "To your offspring I will give this land" (Genesis 12:7). With these words, the Bible articulates a territorial claim that will determine much of Israel's history—well into our own conflicted times.

THE CITY OF SHECHEM

Shechem, located in a mountain pass between Mount Ebal and Mount Gerizim, is one of the oldest attested cities in Canaan. It appears as early as the 25th century B.C.E. in the Ebla tablets recovered at Tell Mardikh, and on a stela from the reign of King Senusret III of Egypt around 1850 B.C.E. Five hundred years later, it is mentioned as *Šakmu* in the Amarna Letters, the correspondence between Egyptian administrators and the kings of the 18th Dynasty, when Canaan was ruled as an Egyptian vassal state. No doubt the reason was Shechem's strategic location at the nexus of various trade routes crossing the Samarian mountains on their way to Syria or Egypt. The place also served as a central market for crops, including wheat, grapes, and olives, from all the surrounding lands. Shechem would later play an important part in Israel's early history and well into the Christian era, when it was recognized as a leading Samaritan city. It is here, at Jacob's Well, that the Gospel of John sets the encounter between Jesus and a Samaritan woman (John 4:5-10).

Ancient Shechem has been excavated at Tell Balata, an archaeological site adjacent to the Balata refugee camp in the West Bank.

I will make you exceedingly fruitful;
and I will make nations of you, and kings shall come from you.

GENESIS 17:6

Shechem is now identified as Tell Balata, an archaeological site adjacent to the Balata refugee camp on the West Bank. Excavated by several American schools starting in 1956, when the region still formed part of Jordan, the site contains a number of buildings, including a temple, a ceremonial courtyard, and a monumental gate, surrounded by a cyclopean wall and dated to the Middle Bronze Period (IIB) (1750-1650 B.C.E.).

Abraham's next destination was "the hill country to the east of Bethel," where he "pitched his tent with Bethel on the west and Ai on the east" (Genesis 12:8). Beth-el means "house of the Lord." The place has been identified with the Palestinian village of Beitin, also on the West Bank. Local excavations have yielded pottery and tool samples that may be as old as 3200 B.C.E., though the nearby remains of Canaanite tombs and homes are roughly dated to 1750 B.C.E. Bethel would also figure prominently in Genesis, particularly as the place where Jacob dreamed of a ladder to heaven.

But Abraham's journey was far from over. Moving farther south, he led his entourage past the city of Rushalimum, residence of the Egyptian governor, which in the centuries to come would be known as *Yerushalayim*, or "Jerusalem." He then "journeyed on by stages toward the Negeb," establishing the cycle of migration between the highlands and the Negev that would return throughout the remainder of the Abraham story. It is possible that this reflects the seasonal migration of nomadic clans as they looked for pastures at high elevation in summer and grazing lands in the desert after the arrival of the winter rains. ■

The highlands between Mount Ebal and Mount Gerizim where Abraham dwelled are today located in the West Bank.

Inset: *This bronze figure holding a golden ring probably denotes an unknown Canaanite deity.*

SOJOURN IN EGYPT

Abraham and Sarah at the Court of Pharaoh

Although the primary form of sustenance in Canaan was cultivation, this was a tenuous practice, and good harvests were not always guaranteed. While the valleys of Lower Galilee and the Jezreel drew their primary water supply from large underground aquifers, that was not the case for the rest of the land. In the Mediterranean coastal regions, as well as the Samarian and Judean highlands and the desert regions farther south, the primary source of water was rain. But rain was subject to climate trends, which to this day tend to be erratic. In the middle of the third millennium B.C.E., for example, a period of extended drought so ravaged the region's fields that it prompted a gradual abandonment of many of the Early Bronze Age cities and forced much of the population back into a nomadic lifestyle.

Thus it does not come as a surprise when Genesis informs us that soon after Abraham's arrival in the Negev, "there was a famine in the land" (Genesis 12:10). In times such as these, many Canaanites would flee to the one area where harvests were assured regardless of climate changes: the fertile Nile Delta of Egypt. Abraham and his family had no choice but to follow the migration to Egypt's fields of wheat, as his descendants, the sons of Jacob, would do many centuries later. The frescoes in the tomb of Khnumhotep, who served Amenemhat II as provincial governor, depict exactly such a train of refugees from Retenu, as the Egyptians called Canaan. In striking contrast to the elegantly dressed and dark-skinned Egyptian officials, the migrants are wearing ill-fitting woolen coats. The women's hair is unkempt and worn loose around the shoulder, while the men grow strange, Asiatic-looking beards. The leader of this foreign tribe, tasked with negotiating with the Egyptian border guards, is identified as a certain Abishai. There is no record of this name in Genesis, though there is a tantalizing reference to "Abishai, the son of Zeruiah" in the first Book of Samuel, many hundreds of years later.

A dish found in a tomb from the New Kingdom (1529-1075 B.C.E.) contains emmer wheat and earth almonds.

ca 2100	ca 2100	ca 2050	ca 2040
Epic of Gilgamesh is recorded	Middle Bronze Age begins (2100-1550 B.C.E.)	Ur-Nammu establishes 3rd Dynasty of Ur	Beginning of the Middle Kingdom in Egypt

In times of drought and famine, which occurred frequently in the Near East, the people of Syria-Canaan often sought refuge in Egypt, the breadbasket of the region.

A statue of Rehuankh, mayor of Abydos and senior priest of the cult of Osiris, dates from the 12th Dynasty of the Middle Kingdom (1860-1830 B.C.E.).

ca 2000
First use of the
plow in Canaan

ca 2000
Minoan civilization is
dominant in Aegean Sea

ca 2000
Amorites conquer Ur and establish
Babylon as the capital

ca 2000
Aryan-speaking Indo-Europeans
spread into Asia Minor

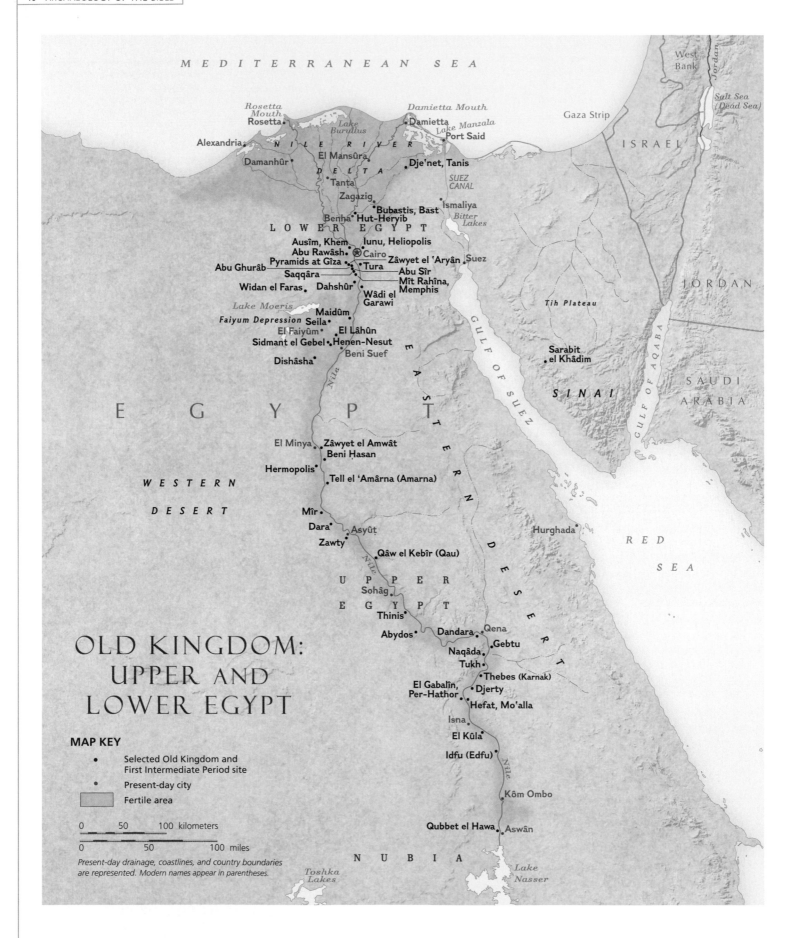

MEDITERRANEAN SEA

Rosetta Mouth
Rosetta
Lake Burullus
Damietta Mouth
Damietta
Lake Manzala
Gaza Strip
West Bank
Salt Sea (Dead Sea)
Alexandria
NILE RIVER
Port Said
El Mansûra
Dje'net, Tanis
ISRAEL
Damanhûr
SUEZ CANAL
Tanta
DELTA
Zagazig
Ismaliya
Bubastis, Bast
Bitter Lakes
Benha Hut-Heryib
LOWER EGYPT
Ausîm, Khem
Iunu, Heliopolis
Abu Rawâsh
Cairo
Zâwyet el 'Aryân
Suez
Pyramids at Gîza
Tura
Abu Ghurâb
Abu Sîr
Saqqâra
Mît Rahîna, Memphis
Widan el Faras
Dahshûr
JORDAN
Wâdi el Garawi
Tih Plateau
Lake Moeris
Maidûm
Faiyum Depression Seila
El Lâhûn
El Faiyûm
Sidmant el Gebel
Henen-Nesut
Sarabit el Khâdim
Beni Suef
SINAI
Dishâsha

GULF OF SUEZ

E G Y P T

GULF OF AQABA

SAUDI ARABIA

WESTERN
El Minya
Zâwyet el Amwât
Beni Hasan
DESERT
Hermopolis
Tell el 'Amârna (Amarna)
EASTERN
Hurghada
RED
SEA
Mîr
DESERT
Dara
Asyût
Zawty
Qâw el Kebîr (Qau)
U P P E R
Sohâg
E G Y P T
Thinis
Dandara
Qena
Abydos
Gebtu
Naqâda
Tukh
Thebes (Karnak)
El Gabalîn, Per-Hathor
Djerty
Hefat, Mo'alla
Isna
El Kûla
Idfu (Edfu)

Kôm Ombo

OLD KINGDOM: UPPER AND LOWER EGYPT

Qubbet el Hawa
Aswân

NUBIA
Lake Nasser

MAP KEY

• Selected Old Kingdom and First Intermediate Period site

• Present-day city

Fertile area

0   50   100 kilometers
0   50   100 miles

Present-day drainage, coastlines, and country boundaries are represented. Modern names appear in parentheses.

Toshka Lakes

Abram went down to Egypt to reside there as an alien,
for the famine was severe in the land.

GENESIS 12:10

This wall painting from the New Kingdom tomb of Nebamun, dated around 1356 B.C.E., shows a group of women enjoying a lavish banquet.

SARAH ENTERS THE ROYAL HAREM

It would have fallen on Abraham to talk his way past the border controls, but as he approached the Egyptian frontier, he became apprehensive. With their high living standard, Egyptians were known to be a sensuous, pleasure-loving people, and Abraham was well aware that his wife, Sarah, was a beautiful woman. He began to imagine that the Egyptians might get so besotted with her that they would kill him and do with Sarah what they wished. How Abraham arrived at this amazing conclusion is not explained, but his apprehensions became so acute that he urged his wife to "say that you are my sister, so that it may go well with me because of you" (Genesis 12:13).

And indeed, the officials of Pharaoh did not fail to report Sarah's beauty to Pharaoh, who promptly ordered her to be "taken into Pharaoh's house." The episode brings to mind the Egyptian Governor Labaya, who served the kings of the 18th Dynasty from his base in the southern hills of Samaria. In one of his letters to the crown, preserved in the Amarna correspondence, he said, "If the king wrote for my wife, how could I hold her back?"

As for Abraham, he did quite well in the exchange, being compensated with "sheep, oxen, male donkeys, male and female slaves, female donkeys, and camels" (Genesis 12:16).

Genesis gives us no information that would help us to identify this particular pharaoh, and perhaps no specific king is intended. In the sixth century B.C.E., when many scholars believe the Torah reached its current form, Egypt may no longer have been the superpower it once was, but under the kings of the 26th Dynasty, it did recover some of its erstwhile prosperity on the strength of its primary export surplus: papyrus and grain. The conquest of Judah and the subsequent Babylonian exile took place during the reign of King Apries (589-570 B.C.E.), who, like his predecessors, considered Judah an ally in the war against Neo-Babylonia, and even allowed a large group of Jewish refugees to settle in Elephantine. The generally favorable treatment of Pharaoh in Genesis (in contrast to the king of Exodus) may reflect this.

If indeed there is a historical basis for the story of Abraham in Egypt, then the episode arguably took place during the Middle Kingdom (2040-1640 B.C.E.). Some authors have suggested the reign of Senwosret I (1971-1926 B.C.E.) or Senwosret II (1897-1878 B.C.E.), but no literary or archaeological evidence supports such. What we do know is that Amenemhat I, the first king of the 12th Dynasty, moved the kingdom's capital from Thebes back to the Memphis region, where he established a new city, Amenemhat-itj-tawy, or simply Itjtawy, meaning "[Amenemhat]

the seizer of two lands." This is where Sarah would have joined the royal seraglio. The precise location of this city has never been identified, though its primary mortuary centers at Lisht and el-Lahun have yielded several pyramids and mastaba tombs, including the pyramid of Amenemhat I himself.

The next centuries of the Middle Kingdom saw an era of great artistic revival, as attested by its surviving sculpture and literature. Most striking is the realism from this period, which shows kings such as Senwosret III with visible lines of fatigue and age, as if illustrating the great burdens of kingship.

ABRAHAM'S WEALTH

In the Abraham story, however, the king knows how to enjoy his leisure pursuits. Sarah becomes his concubine, whereupon God, in a prelude to the Ten Plagues from the Book of Exodus, afflicts the

In a mural from the tomb of Khnumhotep in Beni-Hasan, members of a Semitic tribe who served Pharaoh Amenemhat II ask permission to enter Egypt (1876 to 1842 B.C.E.).

house of Pharaoh with great plagues. It does not take long for the king to figure out why his house must suffer these visitations. He summons Abraham and asks, "Why did you not tell me that she was your wife?" A very good question, but Abraham's response is not recorded. Pharaoh then tells Abraham, "Now then, here is your wife, take her, and be gone" (Genesis 12:18-19)—a surprisingly lenient response. The king even allows Abraham to leave Egypt with all of the gifts that he has amassed to date.

This may be an important clue to the purpose of the Egyptian interlude, because Abraham has now become a man of consequence and great wealth, "rich in livestock, in silver, and in gold" (Genesis 13:1).

With these funds, he is able to acquire many lands and thus lay the foundation for his future descendants and the tribes of Israel. But the vast increase of his herds inevitably leads to conflict over the scarce water sources in the area. Abraham knows he has no choice but to split his livestock from that of Lot, the son of his brother, so that each can go his separate way. With the casual selfishness that comes naturally to the young, Lot picks the best part of Abraham's lands: the well-watered plain of Jordan to the east. Abraham has no choice but to return to the hill country and pitch his tents by the oaks of Mamre, near the Canaanite city of Hebron, from whence his journey started. ∎

This simple but moving sculpture depicts an Egyptian couple, Dersenedji and Nofretka, from the period of the Old Kingdom, circa 2400 B.C.E.

ca 2000
Trade routes carry amber between
Greece and northern Europe

ca 2000
Wheeled plow is adopted
in Europe

ca 2000
Growing trade between Indus
Valley and Mesopotamia

ca 1991
King Amenemhat I launches
economic revival in Egypt

THE SONS OF ABRAHAM

The Conflict Between Ishmael and Isaac

Hebron is one of the oldest cities in the southern part of Samaria. Perched on a lovely mountain ridge of vineyards and olive and fruit trees, it is located about 3,000 feet above sea level at a distance of some 20 miles south of Jerusalem in today's West Bank. Some archaeologists believe that the biblical Hebron should be identified with an excavated area of about 15 acres on the eastern slope of Jebel Rumeida. Originally uncovered in the 1960s, Jewish settlers in the politically contested area of Hebron began a new dig here in 2014 so as to bolster their case for expanding the existing Jewish settlement in Hebron, which may be the reason that several Israeli archaeologists have distanced themselves from the project. Nevertheless, the remains excavated by Philip Hammond in the 1960s suggest that Hebron was a flourishing community around 2300 B.C.E., only to be largely abandoned near the end of the third millennium, possibly because of the climate change already noted. But during the Middle Bronze II Period, it was rebuilt using cyclopean walls similar to the ones built at Shechem. The city gate was particularly impressive, built with huge, uncut stones to a height of 20 feet.

Later in the Genesis story, Abraham asked Ephron the Hittite to sell him the Cave of Machpelah, located in Hebron, as a future burial tomb for his wife, Sarah. This conversation took place, says Genesis, in earshot "of all who went in at the gate of the city" (Genesis 23:10). Hammond theorized that the biblical author may have this particular gate in mind because it was still a prominent feature of the city well into the sixth century B.C.E. Excavators also found a cuneiform text from the late 17th century B.C.E. that suggests that the settlement was largely pastoral. This seems to be in character with the biblical depiction of Abraham settling in these pastures, "under the oaks of Mamre," with his extended herd.

The decision to separate from Lot had one important consequence: It left Abraham without an heir. Since Sarah was barren, this raised the question of who would succeed Abraham as head of the clan and become heir to God's covenant. One option was to divorce Sarah and marry a woman from a local tribe, for God had told him that "no one but your very own issue shall be your heir,"

A stormy evening on the western shore of the Dead Sea evokes the story of the destruction of Sodom and Gomorrah.

ca 1980
Palace of Knossos in Crete features baths fed by water channels

ca 1971
Reign of King Senwosret I in Egypt begins

ca 1960
Egypt extends borders to Nile's Second Cataract

ca 1950
Egyptian army subjugates Canaan

This partial reconstruction of a Bronze Age well stood outside the city gate of ancient Beersheba in today's Negev.

thus disqualifying Lot or any other adoptees (Genesis 15:4). The prevailing laws in Mesopotamia, including the Code of Hammurabi, certainly considered infertility a sufficient cause to divorce a wife. All a husband needed to do in these circumstances was to return "the full amount of her marriage-price and … the dowry which she brought from her father's house."

But there was also a second option: to engage a surrogate mother. Here, too, prevailing laws were explicit. An Assyrian marriage contract from the 19th century B.C.E., for example, stipulates that if a wife cannot bear children within two years of the wedding, she must purchase a slave woman for the specific purpose of conceiving her husband's child. Many of these customs had their roots in older codes, such as the Sumerian Code of Lipit-Ishtar (circa 1860 B.C.E.), the Code of Ur-Nammu (21st century B.C.E.), or the oldest known legal document, drafted by Urukagina, king of Lagash (2350 B.C.E.).

THE BIRTH OF ISHMAEL

As a true daughter of Mesopotamia, Sarah knew what was expected of her. She took one of her slave girls, whose name was Hagar, and told Abraham, "Go in to my slave-girl; it may be that I shall obtain children by her." Abraham agreed, whereupon Sarah took Hagar to her husband's tent "as a wife" (*'ishshâ*, a term that can mean either "wife" or "concubine"). Genesis is careful to note that Hagar was not a Hebrew woman but an Egyptian slave girl, whom Pharaoh gave to Abraham in exchange for Sarah's favors. Just as Sarah once served as "surrogate wife" to the Egyptian king, this Egyptian slave will now serve in that same capacity for Abraham (Genesis 16:1).

But Hagar was young, and as soon as she knew she was pregnant, she began to take on airs and "looked with contempt on her mistress." Naturally Sarah vented her wrath on her husband. "I gave my slave-girl to your embrace," she scolded him, "and when she saw that she had conceived, she looked on me with contempt!" Like any other man in such a difficult position, Abraham equivocated. "Your slave-girl is in your power," he said, "do to her as you please."

But here was the rub. Sarah *could not* do as she pleased, for the same Code of Hammurabi, anticipating this situation, stipulated that "if a female slave has claimed equality with her mistress because she bore children, her mistress may not sell her" (Hammurabi, §146). All she could do was to "put the girl in her place," which is exactly what Sarah did. She "dealt harshly" with Hagar, whereupon the pregnant girl ran away into the desert and collapsed near an oasis "on the way to Shur" (Genesis 16:4-7). The Way of Shur, as we will see, ran from Canaan straight across Sinai to the Egyptian border. Hagar was trying to run home, but she was clearly not equipped for a long desert journey. According to Genesis, an angel found her at the oasis and comforted her by saying that she would bear a son. She should name him "Ishmael." *Yišmā'ē* means "God hears [me]" in Hebrew, for God had given heed to Sarah's affliction. Moreover, said the angel, "I will so greatly multiply your offspring that they cannot be counted for multitude"—a prophecy similar to the one that God would soon give to another son also.

THE BIRTH OF ISAAC

Then something incredible happened: At 90 years, Sarah (still known as Sarai) became pregnant with a son. When God first told Abraham about it, Abraham "fell on his face and laughed" (Genesis 17:17). That is why the boy would be named *Yishāq*, meaning "he will laugh." To seal his covenant, God gave the husband and wife new names. Abram was henceforth known as Abraham, from *abh* ("father") and *raham* ("multitude"), meaning "father of a multitude (of nations)." Sarai would be renamed Sarah, rooted in the Akkadian word *sharratu*, which means "princess." And second, as a sign of the promise of fertility for Abraham and his descendants and as a token of their covenantal relationship with God, every male descendant would from now on be circumcised, beginning with Abraham and Ishmael. "So shall my covenant be in your flesh," God explained (Genesis 17:13).

Meanwhile, things were not going well for Abraham's adopted son, Lot. It had come to God's attention that evil things were happening in the plain of Jordan, north of the Dead Sea. Particularly in the cities of Sodom and Gomorrah, men were doing unspeakable things. God resolved to destroy this evil, just as he had destroyed the wickedness of humankind with the Flood.

Abraham was aghast, for he knew that his nephew Lot lived in Sodom. Whatever misdeeds these people had committed, he knew that Lot could not be one of them. And so, as a true tribal chieftain, he started to negotiate with God, to the point where God agreed that if just ten righteous men could be found in Sodom, "I will not destroy it" (Genesis 18:32).

According to archaeologist Steven Collins, a violent conflagration destroyed the settlement of Tall el-Hammam near the Dead Sea, scorching its foundation stones and leaving several feet of ash.

Hagar bore Abram a son; and Abram named his son, whom Hagar bore, Ishmael.

GENESIS 16:15

"Abraham Turning Away Hagar" was painted by the French artist Emile Jean Horace Vernet (1789-1865) in 1837.

THE DESTRUCTION OF SODOM AND GOMORRAH

But matters took their own course. Two angels that God sent to investigate were physically attacked by men of Sodom, which sealed the city's fate. The angels were able to rescue Lot and his family in the nick of time, after which God rained sulfur and fire from heaven, destroying everything on the plain.

The next morning, the angels bundled Lot and his family out of the city. Lot had urged his sons-in-law to leave as well, but they didn't take the threat seriously and decided to remain. Lot and his wife, as well as his two unmarried daughters, then fled to a nearby township of Zoar. As dawn broke, God rained down "sulfur and fire" from heaven; both cities and the surrounding countryside were destroyed (Genesis 19:25). Lot's family had nearly reached safety when Lot's wife, unable to contain her curiosity, decided to turn. She "looked back, and she became a pillar of salt," says Genesis (19:26). Today visitors can still see a 65-foot pillar of salt on the southern shore of the Dead Sea, jutting out from Mount Sedom, named after the biblical Sodom.

As in the case of the Great Flood, archaeologists have searched for evidence attesting this great cataclysm. One theory holds that the cities were destroyed by a great earthquake between 2100 and 1900 B.C.E. The excavations at Bab edh-Dhra, located on the south bank of Wadi Kerak on the Jordanian side of the Dead Sea, appear to bear this out and offer some evidence of a massive fire.

Another possibility stems from the dig begun in 2006 at Tall el-Hammam, located some nine miles northeast of the Dead Sea. This site is located in the heart of an area some scholars have identified as the plain of Jordan *(ha-kikkar)* described in Genesis. Inhabited as early as the Chalcolithic Age (4500-3150 B.C.E.), the settlement grew into a large city with a monumental gateway complex, which rose as high as 50 feet. But apparently the city experienced a major disruption in the Middle Bronze Age, around 1600 B.C.E., and remained abandoned for the next six centuries.

Some excavators believe they have identified evidence of a meteoric burst, or perhaps a meteor impact, of such intense heat that it melted pottery and even fused sand into glass. In 2013, Steven Collins of Trinity Southwest University wrote in *Biblical Archaeology Review* that some artifacts "bubbled up like 'frothy' magma, indicating they were burned in a flash heat event far exceeding 2,000 degrees Fahrenheit." Eric Cline, an archaeologist at George Washington University, disputes these claims, citing the paucity of evidence.

Whatever the cause of this catastrophic event, it seems plausible to suggest some correlation with the story of Sodom and Gomorrah. Even today, visitors can still find plenty of tar along the Dead Sea shore and recall the note in Genesis that the valley of Sodom was "full of bitumen pits" (Genesis 14:10). ■

The Choice Between Ishmael and Isaac

As the father of two sons, Abraham faced the question of who would become his heir—a concern that runs throughout Genesis and returns in the conflict between Isaac and Esau. Ishmael had perhaps the stronger case: He was Abraham's firstborn, already 13 years of age, and soon mature enough to succeed his father. But Genesis cannot countenance this because it would give the tribes of Israel a foreign ancestor. The Code of Hammurabi stipulated that the children of the first wife could be entitled to preferential treatment, as did the Code of Lipit-Ishtar, which decreed that "the children of the slave shall not divide the estate with the children of their former master" (Lipit-Ishtar, §25). Thus Isaac was chosen. "My own covenant I will establish with Isaac," God said, but Ishmael would become the ancestor of many Arab tribes, including the Nebaioth (later known as Nabataeans) (Genesis 17:20; 25:13-15). This is why the Qur'an, the Holy Book of Islam, considers Ishmael the true son and heir of God's covenant.

These cones contain excerpts from the Code of Lipit-Ishtar (circa 1860 B.C.E.), a legal code that predates the more famous Code of Hammurabi by a hundred years.

THE STORY OF ISAAC

The Conflict Over the Covenantal Birthright Continues

Once God chose to designate Isaac as the heir of his covenant, Ishmael's position became tenuous, and Sarah felt emboldened to urge her husband to "cast out this slave woman with her son." Abraham, much advanced in age, could not resist his wife's entreaties. He gave Hagar some bread and a "skin of water" and sent her on her way (Genesis 21:10). The question of why Abraham did not give Ishmael his own fields and a share of the herd, as he had done with his nephew, Lot, is not explained. To send the child with his young mother into the desert was tantamount to a death sentence. True enough, after several days of aimless wandering in the Negev, Hagar was hopelessly lost. She collapsed near some shrubs while Ishmael lay dying.

Fortunately, says Genesis, God took pity on her. "Come, lift up the boy and hold him fast with your hand," said an angel, "for I will make a great nation of him" (Genesis 21:17-18). God then opened Hagar's eyes, and she saw a well nearby. They were saved. Hagar and Ishmael moved to the "wilderness of Paran," usually identified as the northeastern part of the Sinai near the oasis of Qadesh-Barnea. Here, the boy "became an expert with the bow" and eventually married an Egyptian woman.

The Muslim tradition picks up the story from this point. As the ancestor of Arabian tribes, Ishmael (Ismail in Arabic) moved south toward the region of the Hejaz, in southern Arabia. Here, the scene from Genesis repeats itself as Ishmael lay dying of thirst. Deeply distraught, Hagar went in search of water, running between the mountains of Al-Safa and Al-Marwa seven times. This ritual, known as the sa'y, is reenacted by Muslims to this day during the annual hajj, or pilgrimage, to Mecca.

Hagar was rewarded with her efforts when suddenly the ground opened up and a spring burst forth. This was the Well of Zamzam, around which the

This geometric vase with a tall neck and handle depicting a bird on its body is typical of the Late Helladic I pottery from Mycenae.

city of Mecca would arise. Here, Abraham and Ishmael built a square temple, known as the Ka'bah, which today is the holiest site in Islam.

THE SACRIFICE OF ISAAC

Isaac's heritage now seemed assured, but God decided to put Abraham to a test. He told Abraham to take his son, "whom you love, and go to the land of Moriah, and offer him there as a burnt offering on one of the mountains that I shall show you" (Genesis 22:2). With a heavy heart, Abraham complied. Genesis doesn't provide any specifics, but the second Book of Chronicles equates Moriah with Jerusalem (II Chronicles 3:1). Here, Abraham built a pyre, bound his son, and placed him on top of the kindling. Just before he could strike with his blade, an angel intervened. Relieved beyond words, Abraham offered a ram instead.

The sacrifice of Isaac, known as the *Akedát Yitzhák* ("Binding of Isaac") in Judaism and remembered in the Muslim festival of Eid al-Adha (in which the son to be sacrificed is Ishmael), has given rise to much debate. Why would God ask Abraham to do such a horrible thing? How could anyone ask a father to sacrifice his own son? One traditional view is that the episode is a test of Abraham's obedience, to validate his bona fides as the progenitor of God's covenantal nation. Another view holds that Abraham was being punished for his transgressions—specifically, his decision to send his other son, Ishmael, into the desert and certain death.

The most persuasive interpretation, perhaps, is that the episode illustrates God's utter rejection of human sacrifice. In the seventh and sixth centuries B.C.E., this may not have been a theoretical matter. While archaeologists have as yet failed to uncover any hard evidence of child sacrifice for deities such as the Phoenician god Moloch, the second Book of Kings states that such

ca 1950
Development of wheel with spokes

ca 1900
Ur enters its final period of decline

ca 1900
Elamites migrate from Persia to southern Mesopotamia

ca 1900
Assyrians develop trading centers throughout the Near East

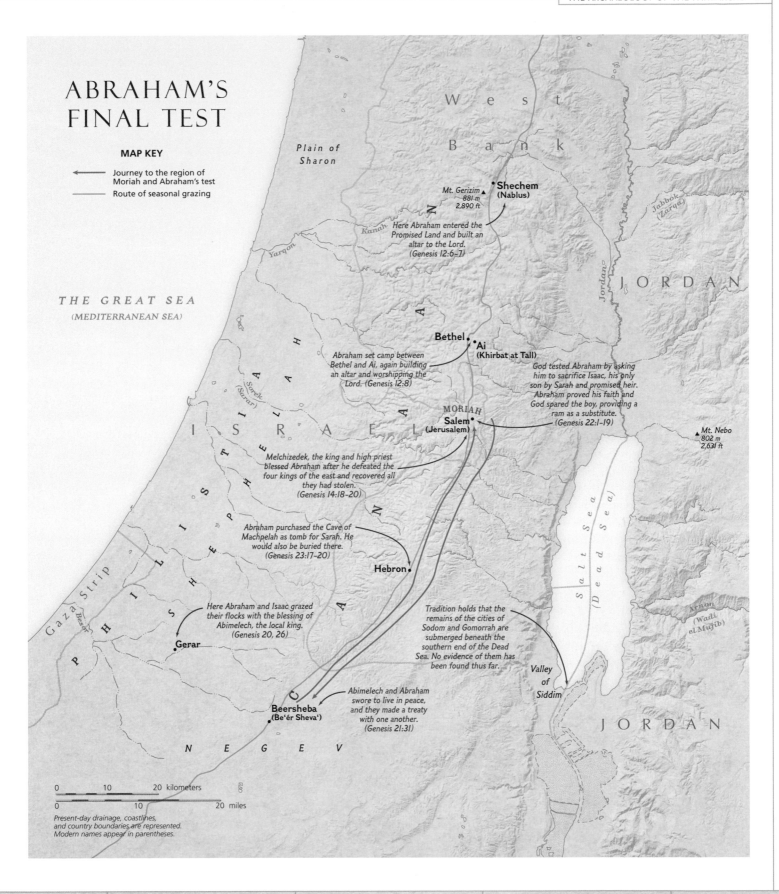

ABRAHAM'S FINAL TEST

MAP KEY

⟵ Journey to the region of Moriah and Abraham's test

— Route of seasonal grazing

Plain of Sharon

W e s t

B a n k

Mt. Gerizim ▲
881 m
2,890 ft

•**Shechem**
(Nablus)

Kanah

Yarqon

Jabbok (Zarqa)

J O R D A N

Jordan

Here Abraham entered the Promised Land and built an altar to the Lord. (Genesis 12:6–7)

THE GREAT SEA
(MEDITERRANEAN SEA)

Bethel •**Ai**
(Khirbat at Tall)

Abraham set camp between Bethel and Ai, again building an altar and worshipping the Lord. (Genesis 12:8)

God tested Abraham by asking him to sacrifice Isaac, his only son by Sarah and promised heir. Abraham proved his faith and God spared the boy, providing a ram as a substitute. (Genesis 22:1–19)

I S R A E L

S H E P H E L A H

Sorek (Sarar)

MORIAH
Salem
(Jerusalem)

▲ *Mt. Nebo*
802 m
2,631 ft

Melchizedek, the king and high priest blessed Abraham after he defeated the four kings of the east and recovered all they had stolen. (Genesis 14:18–20)

C A N A A N

S a l t   S e a
(D e a d   S e a)

Abraham purchased the Cave of Machpelah as tomb for Sarah. He would also be buried there. (Genesis 23:17–20)

Hebron •

Arnon (Wadi el Mujib)

P H I L I S T I A

Here Abraham and Isaac grazed their flocks with the blessing of Abimelech, the local king. (Genesis 20, 26)

Tradition holds that the remains of the cities of Sodom and Gomorrah are submerged beneath the southern end of the Dead Sea. No evidence of them has been found thus far.

Gaza Strip

Besor

•**Gerar**

Valley of Siddim

Abimelech and Abraham swore to live in peace, and they made a treaty with one another. (Genesis 21:31)

Beersheba
•(Be'ér Sheva')

J O R D A N

N E G E V

0   10   20 kilometers

0   10   20 miles

Present-day drainage, coastlines, and country boundaries are represented. Modern names appear in parentheses.

---

ca 1900
Cuneiform script is streamlined into 600 characters

ca 1894
Sumu-Abum establishes new dynasty at Babylon

ca 1860
Legendary founding date of Babylon by Amorites

ca 1860
The Code of Lipit-Ishtar is recorded

sacrifices were practiced during the reign of King Ahaz of Judah, who even "made his son pass through fire" (II Kings 16:3).

ISAAC MARRIES REBEKAH

Once Isaac came of age, Abraham sent a servant to find a suitable wife for him from among his kin, the family he had left behind in Harran. The servant came back with a comely young woman named Rebekah, and according to Genesis, it was love on first sight. Eventually they settled in a valley near a well that Isaac called Shibah. "Therefore," says Genesis, "the name of the city is Beer-sheba to this day" (Genesis 26:33).

Beersheba is usually identified as the site in the southern Negev known as Tel es-Sheba, on the Wadi Be'er Sheva, excavated in the 1970s by Yohanan Aharoni. What he found was an Iron Age Israelite city, built around 1100 B.C.E., though there was some evidence of occupation going back to the fourth millennium. During the subsequent period of the Judges (circa 11th century B.C.E.), Beersheba formed the southernmost point of Israelite territory (Judges 20:1). This may explain the remains of a small stronghold that appeared to have been fortified at a later period, perhaps during the reign of King David, only to be destroyed during the Egyptian invasion of 925 B.C.E. On his list of captured cities in the Temple of Karnak, King Shishak included a town called Fort Abram, which may refer to this citadel.

What made Beersheba so attractive was its access to a number of wells, each fed by a large underground aquifer. This appears to resonate with the Genesis story that Isaac's servants dug a well here and told Isaac excitedly, "We have found water!" (Genesis 26:32), and with the putative origin of the name Beersheba as "the well of seven" (Genesis 21:29).

Like Abraham and Sarah, Isaac and Rebekah remained childless for a long time. Eventually she conceived twins, but the children struggled inside her womb. God warned her that her twins would become ancestors of nations that would be frequently at loggerheads. Indeed, when she gave birth, the two boys were very different. Esau, the firstborn, became a renowned hunter covered in red hair— '*Ēśāw* means "hairy"—and the forefather of Edom, the land below the Dead Sea. Jacob was a gentle lad who preferred to stay in his tent or tend to his father's

Ancient Beersheba, excavated near Tel es-Sheba in the southern Negev, yielded the remains of city dwellings from the Middle Iron Age (1000-900 B.C.E.). Inset: Mycenaean pottery such as this vessel with loop handles and splayed top illustrates the trade between the Mycenaean civilization and Syria-Canaan in this period.

"The Sacrifice of Isaac" is believed to have been painted by Italian Renaissance artist Michelangelo Caravaggio (1571-1610) around 1598. Right: A copper dagger from Elam, circa 2400 B.C.E., closely resembles similar daggers excavated from the Royal Tombs of Ur.

flocks. The tension between the boys may be another reflection of the typical Stone Age rivalry between hunter-gatherers and shepherds.

Jacob was also his mother's favorite, and she soon began to plot how Jacob could inherit the covenantal birthright—the *bekorah*—even though he was second-born. For God had made a prophecy, while her children were still in her womb, that "the elder shall serve the younger" (Genesis 25:23).

One day, when Jacob was cooking a tasty stew, Esau came in from the field without any game in his bag. Smelling the aroma of his brother's bubbling red stew, he eagerly ran to the tent to partake of the meal and said, "Let me eat some of that red stuff, for I am famished." This is another example of Genesis' double entendres, for Edom, "red stuff," is also Esau's nickname and the name of the land where he will dwell in the future. Jacob, sensing a sudden advantage, offered his brother a deal. "First sell me your birthright," he said. Esau, ruled by the rumbling in his belly, agreed (Genesis 25:30-33).

Of course, such an arrangement would never have held up in the eyes of Isaac. It is the father, not the son, who decides who

Sarah saw the son of Hagar the Egyptian,
whom she had borne to Abraham, playing with her son Isaac.

GENESIS 21:9

The Ka'bah in Mecca, Saudi Arabia, is an ancient shrine that today is revered as the holiest place in Islam.

inherits the birthright and the leadership of the clan. What is remarkable about this story, however, is that Jacob resorts to deception—a theme that will run throughout the Jacob story as well as the journey of Joseph.

Rebekah then came up with a ruse. She cooked her husband's favorite stew of meat and told Jacob to give it to his father, pretending to be Esau. Since Jacob was smooth-skinned, she covered his hands and neck with fleece from sheep and gave him one of Esau's coats. Isaac, who was nearly blind, touched Jacob's arms, smelled Esau's scent on his coat, and readily gave Jacob his blessing, granting him his birthright (Genesis 27:27-29).

Naturally, as soon as Esau found out, he was furious. But Rebekah quickly sent Jacob away to Harran, to safety. In retaliation, Esau—who had already taken three wives outside his clan—now took another, Mahalath, who was none other than the daughter of his father's rival, Ishmael. Nevertheless, after many years had passed and Jacob had returned from Harran with his wives and children, the brothers reconciled, close to the spot where the Jabbok River joins the Jordan (Genesis 33:4). Still, in the centuries to come, Edom and Israel would often be at war. ∎

The Epic of Aqhat

There are some parallels between the saga of Ishmael and Isaac, and an Ugaritic text known as the Aqhat Epic, dating from the 14th century B.C.E. It tells the story of an elderly king named Danel (or Dn'il, meaning "El is judge"), who is left without a son and heir. He fervently prays for his wife to conceive, and Baal, the god of storms and rain, pleads to El, the supreme god of Canaan, on his behalf. El responds, "Let him kiss his wife, and she will conceive; in her embracing she will become pregnant." And indeed, Danel's wife conceives and in due course gives birth to a son, who is named Aqhat. When he has grown into a young man, he is presented with a bow, and soon he becomes an expert archer.

Similarly, Abraham's son by a slave girl named Hagar, a young boy named Ishmael, is cast out into the desert with his mother. An angel leads them to a well. Thus fortified, Genesis tells us, "The boy lived in the wilderness and became an expert with the bow. He lived in the wilderness of Paran" (Genesis 21:20-21). Paran is a name associated with the northeastern part of the Sinai Peninsula, a region centered on the oasis of Qadesh-Barnea.

A terra-cotta figure showing a boy with a quiver from Myrina, Asia Minor, is dated between 50 B.C.E. and 30 C.E.

JACOB AND HIS SONS

The Origins of the Twelve Tribes of Israel

E sau's wrath over the loss of his birthright forced Jacob to flee. He decided to go up north to Paddan-Aram, literally the "road of Aram," which led to Harran, the town of his mother, Rebekah. It was the same road that Jacob's grandfather Abraham had used to travel to Canaan so many years before. The distance to Harran was around 700 miles and took him north through Hebron, Salem (later associated with Jerusalem), and Ai. One night, Jacob fell asleep and dreamed of a ladder going up into heaven. At the top stood God, reaffirming his covenant with Abraham that had now passed on to Jacob: "The land on which you lie I will give to you and to your offspring" (Genesis 28:13). When he woke up, Jacob anointed the stone on which he had slept with oil and called the altar *bet'el,* or Bethel ("the House of God").

As we saw, the identity of Bethel is uncertain. The 19th-century scholar Edward Robinson believed it was located near the West Bank village of Beitin. According to Genesis, the place was originally called Luz (Genesis 28:19), a name that has been associated with the nearby remains of a Canaanite town from the Middle Bronze Age (circa 1750 B.C.E.). Whether Bethel and Luz were one and the same is a matter of considerable debate.

Jacob continued on his journey, traveling from Shechem through the Jezreel Valley to Hazor, Damascus, the great caravan city of Carchemish, before reaching Harran. Here, he fell in love with the "beautiful and lovely" Rachel, who was the daughter of his uncle Laban (Genesis 29:17). But Laban insisted that Jacob should first work for him as a shepherd, for no less than seven years, before he was allowed to marry Rachel. When that time was fulfilled at last, Jacob entered his tent for the wedding night, only to discover at dawn that it wasn't Rachel but her elder sister Leah whom Laban had placed in his bed. Thus, Jacob himself

A rocky outcropping near the old city of Samaria offers a stunning view of the valley through which ran the ancient road from Jerusalem to Harran. Inset: A gypsum head of an unknown ruler was probably carved circa 2140 B.C.E.

ca 1850
Egyptians develop irrigation projects in Faiyum

ca 1822
With King Rim-Sin, Sumerian rule comes to an end

ca 1800
Hebrew clans begin migrating to Egypt

ca 1800
Egyptian texts list Jerusalem as one of Canaan's city-states

ca 1800
More than 3,000 menhirs are
erected in Carnac, France

ca 1800
Babylonians adopt
lunar calendar

ca 1792
Code of Hammurabi is
recorded on numerous stelae

ca 1790
Rise of the Hittites
in Asia Minor

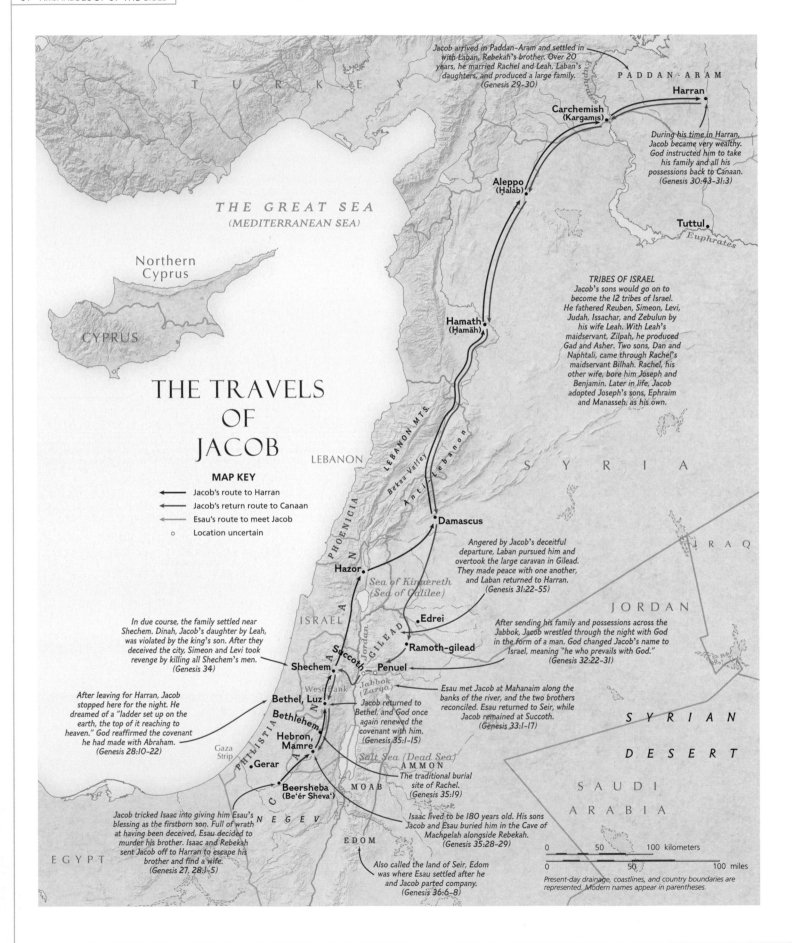

Jacob arrived in Paddan-Aram and settled in with Laban, Rebekah's brother. Over 20 years, he married Rachel and Leah, Laban's daughters, and produced a large family. (Genesis 29–30)

PADDAN-ARAM

Harran

Carchemish
(Kargamış)

During his time in Harran, Jacob became very wealthy. God instructed him to take his family and all his possessions back to Canaan. (Genesis 30:43–31:3)

Aleppo
(Ḥalab)

THE GREAT SEA
(MEDITERRANEAN SEA)

Northern
Cyprus

Tuttul
Euphrates

CYPRUS

TRIBES OF ISRAEL
Jacob's sons would go on to become the 12 tribes of Israel. He fathered Reuben, Simeon, Levi, Judah, Issachar, and Zebulun by his wife Leah. With Leah's maidservant, Zilpah, he produced Gad and Asher. Two sons, Dan and Naphtali, came through Rachel's maidservant Bilhah. Rachel, his other wife, bore him Joseph and Benjamin. Later in life, Jacob adopted Joseph's sons, Ephraim and Manasseh, as his own.

Hamath
(Ḥamāh)

THE TRAVELS
OF
JACOB

LEBANON

S Y R I A

MAP KEY

→ Jacob's route to Harran
← Jacob's return route to Canaan
← Esau's route to meet Jacob
○ Location uncertain

Lebanon Mts.
Beqaa Valley
Anti-Lebanon

I R A Q

Damascus

Angered by Jacob's deceitful departure, Laban pursued him and overtook the large caravan in Gilead. They made peace with one another, and Laban returned to Harran. (Genesis 31:22–55)

J O R D A N

Hazor

Sea of Kinnereth
(Sea of Galilee)

ISRAEL

Edrei

GILEAD

Jordan

After sending his family and possessions across the Jabbok, Jacob wrestled through the night with God in the form of a man. God changed Jacob's name to Israel, meaning "he who prevails with God." (Genesis 32:22–31)

In due course, the family settled near Shechem. Dinah, Jacob's daughter by Leah, was violated by the king's son. After they deceived the city, Simeon and Levi took revenge by killing all Shechem's men. (Genesis 34)

Succoth

Ramoth-gilead

Shechem

Penuel

West Bank
Jabbok
(Zarqa)

Esau met Jacob at Mahanaim along the banks of the river, and the two brothers reconciled. Esau returned to Seir, while Jacob remained at Succoth. (Genesis 33:1–17)

After leaving for Harran, Jacob stopped here for the night. He dreamed of a "ladder set up on the earth, the top of it reaching to heaven." God reaffirmed the covenant he had made with Abraham. (Genesis 28:10–22)

Bethel, Luz

Jacob returned to Bethel, and God once again renewed the covenant with him. (Genesis 35:1–15)

Bethlehem

Hebron,
Mamre

S Y R I A N

D E S E R T

Gaza
Strip

Salt Sea (Dead Sea)

AMMON

The traditional burial site of Rachel. (Genesis 35:19)

Gerar

MOAB

S A U D I

A R A B I A

Beersheba
(Be'ér Shéva')

N E G E V

Jacob tricked Isaac into giving him Esau's blessing as the firstborn son. Full of wrath at having been deceived, Esau decided to murder his brother. Isaac and Rebekah sent Jacob off to Harran to escape his brother and find a wife. (Genesis 27, 28:1–5)

Isaac lived to be 180 years old. His sons Jacob and Esau buried him in the Cave of Machpelah alongside Rebekah. (Genesis 35:28–29)

E D O M

0   50   100 kilometers
0   50   100 miles

EGYPT

Also called the land of Seir, Edom was where Esau settled after he and Jacob parted company. (Genesis 36:6–8)

Present-day drainage, coastlines, and country boundaries are represented. Modern names appear in parentheses.

*Jacob settled in the land where his father
had lived as an alien, the land of Canaan.*

GENESIS 37:1

*A Bedouin shepherd grazes his flock in the hills of the Negev, not far from
ancient Beersheba.*

became the victim of the same type of identity switch by which he
had obtained his father's birthright.

Laban was unapologetic, since tribal custom demanded that the
oldest daughter be married first. "This is not done in our country—
giving the younger before the firstborn," he said (Genesis 29:26).
If Jacob wanted to marry Rachel as well, he simply had to tend
Laban's flocks for another seven years.

As the husband of two wives, Jacob returned to his labors and
worked as a shepherd for another seven years.

THE RETURN TO CANAAN

The upshot of these years in Harran, however, was that Jacob could
now claim a large share of the herd, even though the ever calculating
Laban was trying to cheat him out of the best of the flock. Thus,
when Jacob finally decided to return to Canaan, he traveled with a
large entourage. This included his two wives, Leah and Rachel, as
well as their handmaidens, Zilpah and Bilhah, who also served as
Jacob's concubines. In all, these women presented him with eleven
sons and one daughter. The "unloved" Leah bore seven of Jacob's
children—six sons (Reuben, Simeon, Levi, Judah, Issachar, and
Zebulun) and a daughter, Dinah. Bilhah gave birth to Dan and
Naphtali (Genesis 30:3-8), while Zilpah gave him Gad and Asher
(Genesis 30:9-13). Only Rachel's womb remained closed, but eventually "God heeded her and opened her womb" (Genesis 29:22). She
gave birth to a boy named Joseph, who inevitably became Jacob's
favorite, as well as a second son, named Benjamin. Together with the
sons of Joseph, Manasseh and Ephraim, these men would become
the ancestors of the 12 tribes of Israel, sealing God's covenant.

Laban was not pleased with Jacob's sudden departure and went after
him. Jacob had anticipated this, however, and had taken a different
route into the Transjordan, to a land later known as Edom. But Laban

"Jacob Receives the Bloody Coat of Joseph" by the Spanish painter Diego Rodríguez de Silva y Velázquez (1599-1660) was painted around 1630.

was able to track him down, and an angry exchange ensued in a place called "Galeed," which is probably Gilead. But once tempers cooled, Laban and his son-in-law decided to make peace and built a heap of stones as a primitive stela to mark their reconciliation (Genesis 31:46).

WRESTLING WITH A STRANGER

While traveling south, close to the Jabbok River, Jacob came upon a stranger who challenged him to a struggle. The two wrestled all night; the word "wrestled" (*ye'abeq*) is another Genesis wordplay, using Jacob's name (*ya'aqov*) and that of the river (*yabboq*). The fight lasted through the night and continued even after Jacob's thigh was injured. At long last, the stranger—an angel of the Lord, or perhaps God himself—relented, declaring that henceforth Jacob would be

known as Israel ("he who prevails with God") (Genesis 31:28). Just as Jacob had struggled with God, so too would the nation of Israel wrestle for centuries with their obedience to the Lord. Jacob decided to call the place Peniel ("God's face"), saying, "I have seen God face to face" (Genesis 31:30).

Upon his return to Canaan, the land that God had promised him, Jacob asked everyone in his entourage to get rid of the idols that they'd brought from Harran. In response, says Genesis, "they gave to Jacob all the foreign gods that they had, and the rings that were in their ears; and Jacob hid them under the oak that was near Shechem" (Genesis 35:4). Why the earrings? What form of idolatry could be attached to a simple earring? The answer, as Israeli scholar Victor Hurowitz has shown, is that earrings were a prominent attribute for some Canaanite and Assyrian deities. A prayer dedicated to King Shalmaneser III of Assyria states, "They placed earrings of fine gold on [the deity's] ears." Genesis may therefore not be referring to human earrings but to the adornments of the pagan idols.

THE DEATH OF RACHEL

Jacob's family was exhausted from the long journey, so Jacob built a temporary house for them, with sheds for his cattle, near the village of Succoth. The name is a wordplay on *Sukkot*, or "booths," which would later become one of the three principal Jewish festivals, also known as the Feast of Tabernacles. Succoth is usually associated with a high mound known as Tell Deir 'Alla, located in Balqa, Jordan.

Jacob then traveled to Shechem and settled there. But one day, his daughter Dinah was seized and raped by the son of the local ruler, King Hamor. The boy, also named Shechem, was deeply penitent and offered to marry the girl. The king gave his consent. "Give your daughters to us," the king said, "and take our daughters for yourselves" (Genesis 34:9). Jacob agreed on the condition that all of the local males be circumcised. This was not a pleasant procedure for adults in Antiquity, and so it isn't surprising that three days later, most of the males in Shechem were "still in pain" (Genesis 34:26). This is when two of Dinah's brothers, Simeon and Levi, entered the city and killed all the men so as to avenge the rape of their sister.

Here, for the first time, Jacob's sons reveal their rebellious nature. They do not share their forefathers' sense of loyalty and obedience. When Jacob denounces the massacre in Shechem, they retort, "Should our sister be treated like a whore?" (Genesis 34:31). Soon these brothers will have another reason to challenge and deceive their father.

In the wake of the mass murder at Shechem, Jacob had little choice but to move on and settle in Bethel. During this journey, however, another tragedy befell him: his beloved wife, Rachel, who was pregnant with Benjamin, went into labor and died in childbirth; the baby survived. This sad event took place near a village that, many centuries later, would be associated with another birth: the hamlet of Bethlehem.

The name Bethlehem, or Bēṯ Leḥem, literally means "house of bread," but its original name may be Beit Lachama, since a temple to the Canaanite god Lachama (or Lakhmu') stood here as early as the third millennium B.C.E. By the seventh century B.C.E. Bethlehem had become a regional center for the shipment of grain, olive oil, or wine, to judge by a *bulla,* or "clay seal," found in 2012 during excavations at the City of David in Jerusalem. The bulla, which confirmed the tax payment on a shipment of agricultural produce, reads, "From the town of Bethlehem to the King"—the oldest object to attest the existence of this famous town.

A geometric stirrup jar with two loop handles and spout, found in central Israel, betrays the influence of Mycenaean models in the Late Bronze Age (1550-1200 B.C.E.).

JOSEPH IS SOLD

Now that Rachel was gone, Jacob turned his affections toward her son Joseph. This naturally raised the ire of his brothers, including the sons of the "unloved" wife, Leah. They deeply resented the way Jacob pampered Rachel's son, especially when he presented Joseph with a beautiful coat "with long sleeves" (erroneously translated in the King James Bible as a "coat of many colors"). Their envy was further inflamed when Joseph told them about his dreams in which he seemed to be set above his brothers (Genesis 37:6-8).

The brothers took the fateful decision of getting rid of Joseph. They set the stage by taking their flock far up north, away from the home fields in Shechem. Predictably, Jacob became worried and asked Joseph to check on them. The unsuspecting Joseph left right away and caught up with his brothers near the town of Dothan, located some 65 miles north of Hebron. "Here comes this dreamer," the brothers said when they spotted him. "Come now, let us kill him and throw him into one of the pits" (Genesis 37:20). But Reuben, Jacob's eldest son by Leah, did not want to shed his half-brother's blood. As it happened, Dothan was perched on one of the main trade routes from Syria to the Mediterranean. Looking at a passing caravan of Ishmaelites, the brothers hatched a plan to sell Joseph as a slave. The next caravan happened to be a group of Arab traders from Midian heading for Egypt, and it was to them that Joseph was sold "for twenty pieces of silver," the going rate for a healthy male slave (Genesis 37:28; Leviticus 27:5).

To cover their tracks, they took Joseph's clothes and spilled goat's blood on them. When Jacob saw the torn and bloody garments, he was inconsolable. "I shall go down to Sheol to my son, mourning," he said, referring to the concept of the underworld in ancient Judaism (Genesis 37:35). ■

When [Joseph's] brothers saw that their father loved him more than all his brothers, they hated him, and could not speak peaceably to him.

GENESIS 37:4

THE ART OF THE BRONZE AGE

The Emergence of Human Civilization

Tʜᴇ Eᴀʀʟʏ Bʀᴏɴᴢᴇ Aɢᴇ (3300-2100 ʙ.ᴄ.ᴇ.) ᴡɪᴛɴᴇssᴇᴅ ᴛʜᴇ ʀɪsᴇ ᴏꜰ ʜᴜᴍᴀɴᴋɪɴᴅ's ꜰɪʀsᴛ ɢʀᴇᴀᴛ ᴄɪᴠɪʟɪᴢᴀᴛɪᴏɴs, beginning with the culture of Sumer in Mesopotamia. Leading centers were the city-state of Uruk, known as Erech in the Bible, and that of Ur. The Sumerian civilization would eventually be absorbed in the Akkadian Empire and, subsequently, the Babylonian Empire founded by King Hammurabi around 1760 ʙ.ᴄ.ᴇ. At the same time, another civilization was rising along the banks of the Nile, producing the Old Kingdom of ancient Egypt. ∎

An Early Cypriot bowl, dated around 2300 ʙ.ᴄ.ᴇ., features images of cattle and a vulture.

This painted clay figure of a Babylonian god, dated around 1800 ʙ.ᴄ.ᴇ., wears a sheepskin garment and is seated on a black throne.

A clay vessel of almost deceptive simplicity was probably created in the Middle Bronze Age around 2350 ʙ.ᴄ.ᴇ.

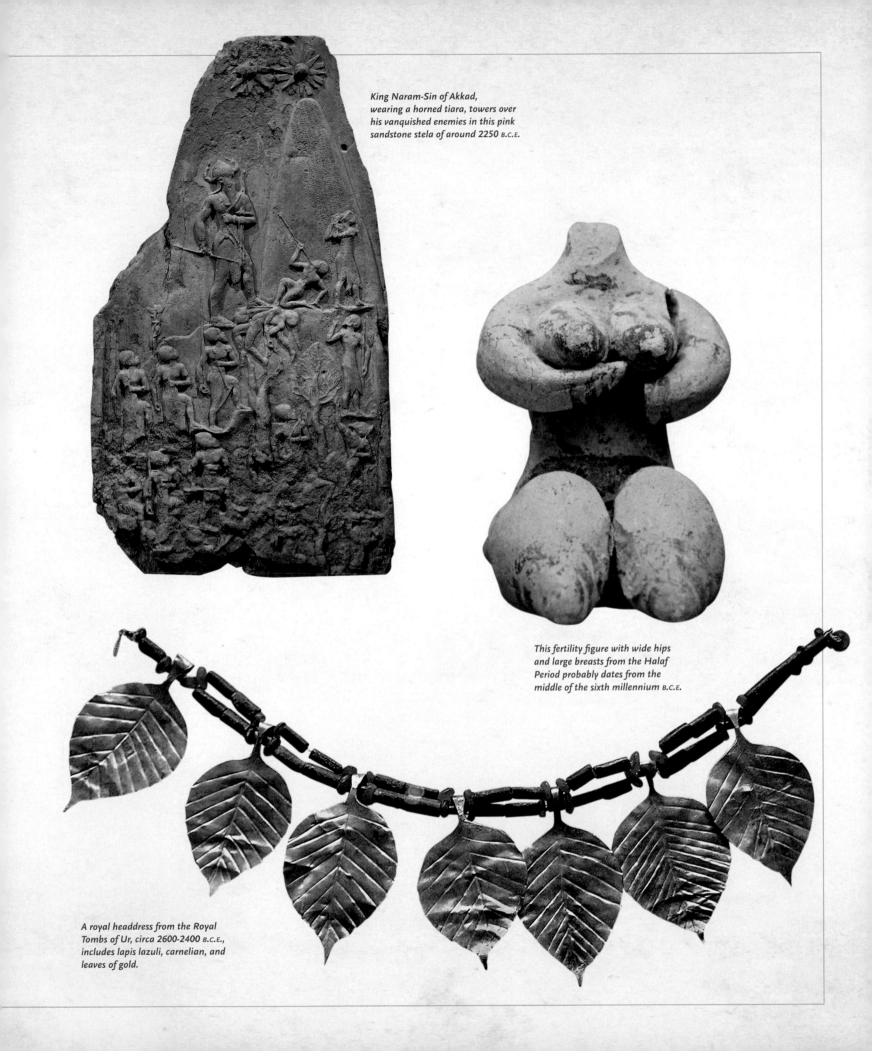

King Naram-Sin of Akkad, wearing a horned tiara, towers over his vanquished enemies in this pink sandstone stela of around 2250 B.C.E.

This fertility figure with wide hips and large breasts from the Halaf Period probably dates from the middle of the sixth millennium B.C.E.

A royal headdress from the Royal Tombs of Ur, circa 2600-2400 B.C.E., includes lapis lazuli, carnelian, and leaves of gold.

THE ARCHAEOLOGY OF THE EXODUS

From Genesis to Deuteronomy

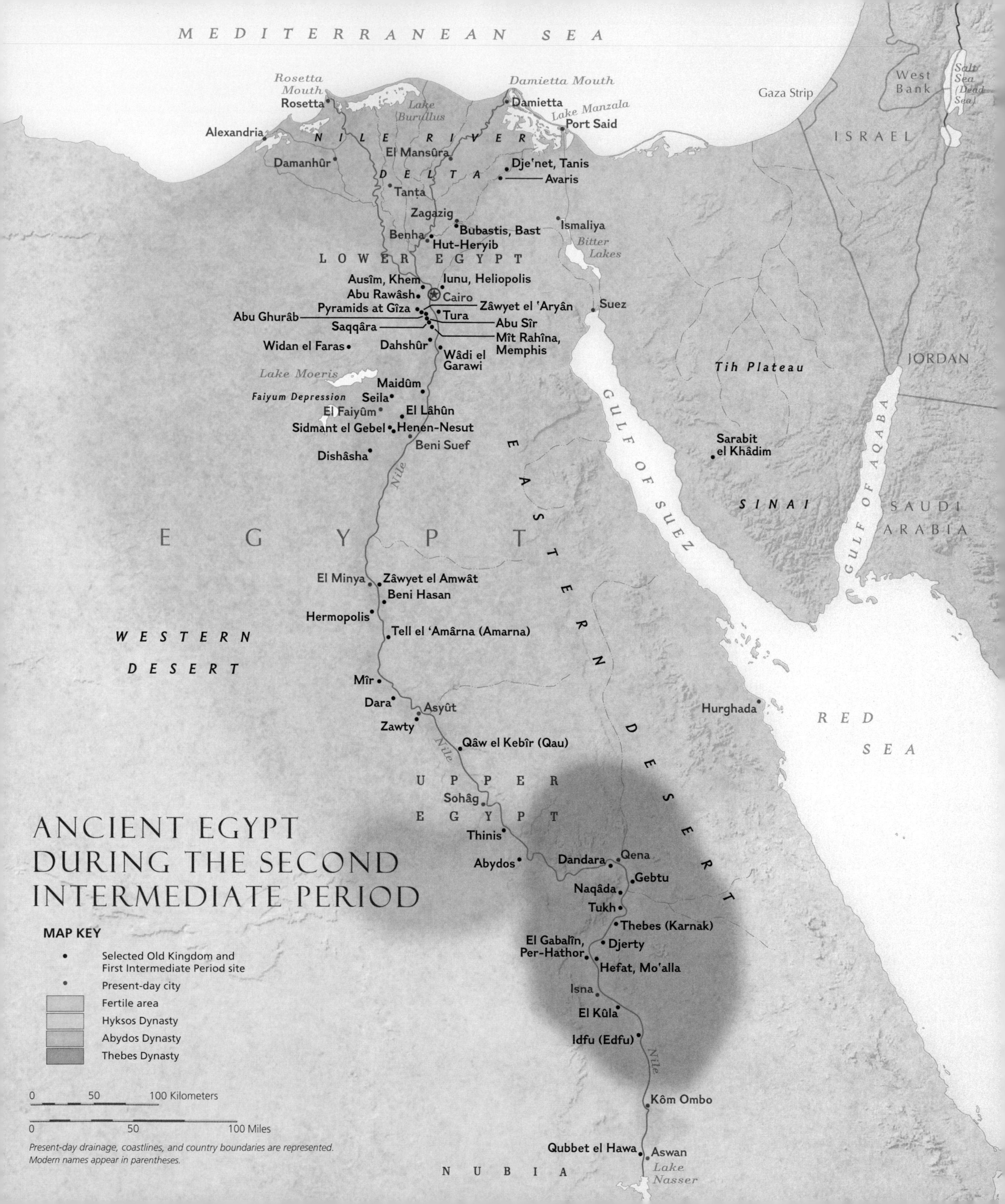

MEDITERRANEAN SEA

Rosetta
Mouth
Rosetta

Alexandria

Damanhûr

NILE RIVER

El Mansûra

DELTA

Tanta

Zagazig

Benha

Ausîm, Khem

Abu Rawâsh

Pyramids at Gîza

Abu Ghurâb

Saqqâra

Widan el Faras

LOWER EGYPT

Damietta Mouth

Damietta

Port Said

Dje'net, Tanis

Avaris

Bubastis, Bast

Hut-Heryib

Iunu, Heliopolis

Cairo

Zâwyet el 'Aryân

Tura

Abu Sîr

Dahshûr

Mît Rahîna,
Memphis

Wâdi el
Garawi

Lake Moeris

Maidûm

Faiyum Depression

Seila

El Faiyûm

El Lâhûn

Sidmant el Gebel

Henen-Nesut

Beni Suef

Dishâsha

Lake
Burullus

Ismaliya

Bitter
Lakes

Lake Manzala

Suez

GULF OF SUEZ

Gaza Strip

ISRAEL

West
Bank

Salt
Sea
(Dead
Sea)

JORDAN

Tih Plateau

Sarabit
el Khâdim

SINAI

GULF OF AQABA

SAUDI
ARABIA

E   G   Y   P   T

WESTERN

DESERT

El Minya

Hermopolis

Zâwyet el Amwât

Beni Hasan

Tell el 'Amârna (Amarna)

Mîr

Dara

Zawty

Asyût

Qâw el Kebîr (Qau)

EASTERN   DESERT

Nile

Hurghada

RED

SEA

UPPER

Sohâg

EGYPT

Thinis

ANCIENT EGYPT
DURING THE SECOND
INTERMEDIATE PERIOD

Abydos

Dandara

Qena

Naqâda

Gebtu

Tukh

Thebes (Karnak)

El Gabalîn,
Per-Hathor

Djerty

Hefat, Mo'alla

Isna

El Kûla

Idfu (Edfu)

MAP KEY

• Selected Old Kingdom and
First Intermediate Period site

• Present-day city

Fertile area

Hyksos Dynasty

Abydos Dynasty

Thebes Dynasty

0   50   100 Kilometers

0   50   100 Miles

Present-day drainage, coastlines, and country boundaries are represented.
Modern names appear in parentheses.

Kôm Ombo

Qubbet el Hawa

Aswan

Lake
Nasser

NUBIA

Now a new king arose over Egypt, who did not know Joseph.
He said to his people, "Look, the Israelite people
are more numerous and more powerful than we."

EXODUS 1:8-9

THE WORLD IN 1640 B.C.E.

Egypt's Second Intermediate Period, Circa 1640-1542 B.C.E.

FOR MORE THAN A THOUSAND YEARS, EGYPT HAD RULED AS THE DOMINANT POWER OF THE Near East, with its trade and cultural influences stretching as far as Syria-Canaan and beyond. But near the end of the Middle Kingdom (circa 2040-1640 B.C.E.), after the reign of Pharaoh Sobeknefru (a female king also known as Neferusobek), the unity of the realm began to crumble. This was partly due to the poor governance by the kings of the subsequent 13th Dynasty, who lacked the energy and initiative of previous kings. Another factor was a series of poor harvests, caused by insufficient flooding of the Nile River, which further destabilized the kingdom's economy. As a result, arts and crafts went into a steady decline, as did Egypt's former prowess in monumental architecture. The pyramids from the 13th Dynasty at Saqqara, including the tomb of King Khendjer (or Userkare), are small affairs built of brick with just a thin limestone casing—a mere shadow of the grand pyramids of Khufu and Khafre in Giza, which at that time were already more than 800 years old.

The disintegration of a strong, central authority provoked a wave of immigration from the east, including a large number of tribes from Canaan, Syria, and Anatolia. To be sure, the wealth and prosperity of Egypt had always been a powerful magnet for people in the East. At first, Egypt's response was to

Preceding pages: *The sun rises over marshland of the Nile River, near the famed Valley of the Kings, burial ground of the kings of the New Kingdom.* Right: *This figure of a man named Djehutera is one of the few examples of figurative art from the Second Intermediate Period (1640-1532 B.C.E.).*

A scarab or beetle-shaped seal refers to Y'qb-HR, possibly an Egyptian transposition of the name Yaqub, or "Jacob."

One of several upright markers, or stelae, at the ancient Egyptian turquoise mine in Serabit el-Khadem, Sinai.

deter these immigrants by building a string of forts along the eastern delta. But eventually Egypt's kings changed their mind and welcomed Syro-Canaanite immigrants. Perhaps they were motivated by a growing labor shortage. During the 12th Dynasty (1991-1793 B.C.E.), Egypt's kings vastly expanded their operations at gold mines in the eastern desert, as well as the turquoise mines of southern Sinai. They even built cities to house their workers. Today's visitors can still see a number of upright monuments or stelae at Serabit el-Khadem, in the heart of the Sinai, inscribed with names and devotional messages from Egyptian officials and countless foreign workers.

But the advent of the weak 13th Dynasty saw an overwhelming number of refugees pressing against Egypt's borders, fleeing the instability and famines of their native lands. Since Egypt's kings were powerless to stop them, these Syro-Canaanite immigrants were free to settle in the Nile Delta as they liked. In time, their Semitic chieftains began to dominate the trade, cultivation, and governance of local communities, gradually replacing Egyptian control of the area. The third-century Egyptian historian Manetho refers to these Semitic tribes as Hikau-khoswet (Hyksos in Greek), which means "desert princes." Manetho also claims that these foreign tribes took control of Egypt's Lower Kingdom as the result of a military invasion, but modern research has shown that their domination of the region was a gradual process that took nearly a century.

Nevertheless, by 1640 B.C.E., the Hyksos had effectively replaced the old Egyptian monarchy with a dynasty of their own: the 15th Dynasty. The Egyptian nobility was forced to abandon the Middle Kingdom capital of el-Lisht and move southward to Thebes, the former capital of the 11th Dynasty. Here, they would establish a court-in-exile and plot their eventual restoration.

The Hyksos kings then built a capital city of their own, known as Avaris. The excavations by archaeologist Manfred Bietak have conclusively established that Avaris was located at Tell el-Dahba in the eastern Nile Delta. Very little remains, however, since most of the Hyksos palaces were built in mud-brick, only to be washed away by flooding over the subsequent centuries. Nonetheless, Bietak's team was able to excavate the foundations of a 200-foot mud-brick palace, arguably the largest Hyksos structure ever found in the delta, probably built during the reign of King Khayan around 1600 B.C.E.

Craving the legitimacy of the ancient monarchy they had ousted, the Hyksos kings worked hard to imitate them. In the few portraits and statuettes that have survived, they have the same traditional attributes as the pharaohs of old. As it was, the Hyksos Dynasty lasted only a single century, spanning the reign of six kings. We know their foreign-sounding names from the so-called Turin King List papyrus, probably composed during the reign of Ramesses II. Among them is a king called Y'qb-Hr (or Yaqub-Her), a name that bears an obvious resemblance to the Semitic name of Jacob from Genesis.

It is plausible to imagine that the story of Joseph in Genesis is set in the Lower Egypt kingdom of the Hyksos pharaohs rather any other place and time in Egypt's history. The idea that an immigrant from Canaan could rise to the post of grand

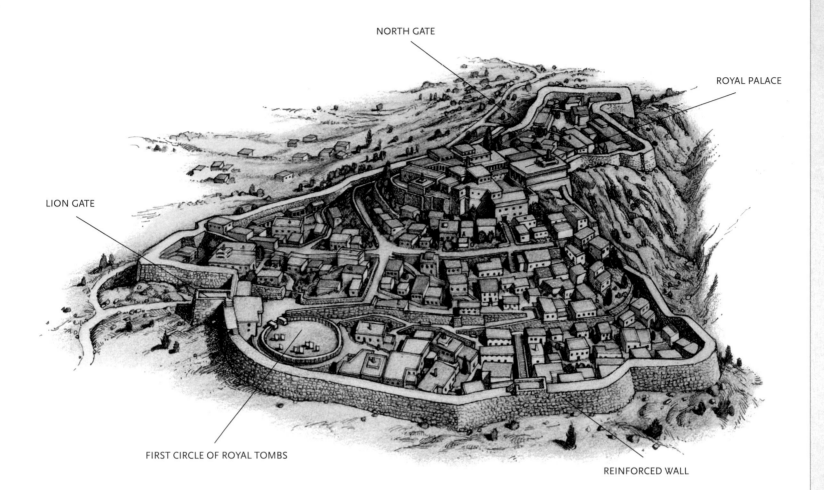

NORTH GATE

ROYAL PALACE

LION GATE

FIRST CIRCLE OF ROYAL TOMBS

REINFORCED WALL

A reconstruction of the ancient citadel of Mycenae in the northeastern Peloponnese in Greece shows the city in its heyday, circa 1300 B.C.E.

vizier of Egypt, which some scholars have dismissed as preposterous, is less astonishing when we consider that most other officials at the court of Avaris would have hailed from Syria-Canaan as well. If it is true that the story of Joseph is somehow correlated with the reign of a Hyksos king, then his descendants would have lived under kings with Canaanite names such as Khyan, Apophis, and Khamudi. Indeed, a stela in Karnak refers to Apophis as "the Prince of Retenu," the Egyptian name for the greater region of Syria-Canaan.

Meanwhile, in the southern capital of Thebes, the disenfranchised 17th Dynasty of Egypt continued to plan the reconquest of Lower Egypt. Sometime around 1570 B.C.E., Pharaoh Seqenenre cast off his battle fleet and floated down toward the Nile Delta to invade the North. Years of hard fighting would follow, led on the Theban side by Seqenenre's successor, Kamose, and the first king of the new 18th Dynasty, Ahmose I.

By then, a cataclysmic event in the Aegean Sea had thrown the Mediterranean in disarray. Around 1600 B.C.E., the volcano on the Cycladic island of Thera (today's Santorini) erupted, casting a large cloud of ash as far as Egypt and Greenland. Even crops in China were affected. Soon after, the Minoan civilization went into decline. This allowed a new culture to flourish, that of Mycenae on the Greek mainland, which would soon expand its influence on trading partners throughout the eastern Mediterranean, including Canaan. ■

JOSEPH'S JOURNEY TO EGYPT

Jacob's Son Is Imprisoned in Egypt's Capital City

The distance from Dothan to the Nile Delta in Egypt was well over 300 miles. It was a long and arduous journey fraught with danger—particularly from marauding bands of raiders and thieves. That is why the road was mostly used by caravans, which traveled in groups for mutual protection. As a slave, however, Joseph would not have been given a mount to ride. He would have been forced to stumble along, tied to one of the Ishmaelite traders riding on donkeys. Genesis claims that the Ishmaelite caravan rode camels, but that is probably the imagination of the scribes who compiled the final version of the Torah in the sixth or fifth century B.C.E. Archaeological evidence has shown that camels were not domesticated in the Near East until around 1200 B.C.E., and became the standard mode of long-distance transport only well after the tenth century.

It is also likely that Joseph traveled in a group of slaves, corralled by the traders for sale in Egypt. In the past, Egypt had obtained its slaves during military campaigns in Nubia or Canaan, but the turmoil of the Second Intermediate Period had made any such foreign expeditions impossible. Still, like other ancient civilizations, Egypt depended on slaves to maintain its upper-class households and its temples and to work in the fields and construction pits. Its slave markets therefore relied on private contractors to procure healthy slave stock from foreign territory.

There were two major routes from Canaan to Egypt: one that cut straight through the Sinai Desert, known as the Way of Shur, and one that ran along the Mediterranean coast. Since the journey started in Dothan, it is likely that the traders chose the latter. During the

"Joseph Explaining Pharaoh's Dreams" was painted by the French artist Jean Adrien Guignet (1816-1854). Dreams play a large role in the story of Joseph.

New Kingdom, this route would become the highway of Egyptian military campaigns against Canaan, Syria, and Hittite territory and eventually become known as the Way of the Philistines. Even in the best of times, during the New Kingdom, the route was dangerous, since its watering holes often ran dry. In 1270 B.C.E., a high official of one of Egypt's desert mines reported regretfully that "only half of the caravans arrive safely, for they die of thirst on the road, together with the asses they drive before them."

In the case of Joseph, however, the caravan reached Egypt's border at Pelusium (now Tell el-Farama) in safety. Genesis says that upon their arrival, the merchants sold Joseph to Potiphar, a captain of Pharaoh's guard. This would imply that Joseph was directly taken to the capital city—in the case of the Hyksos kings of the 15th Dynasty, the city of Avaris.

A visitor to Potiphar's house would no doubt have encountered many foreign slaves and "guest workers." An 18th-century B.C.E. inventory of an upper-class household from Thebes lists 80 servants, half of them clearly of Semitic origin, with such names as Aqaba, Haiimmi, and Menahem. In most cases, however, foreign slaves would have been given an Egyptian name. The Egyptian upper classes were notoriously chauvinistic and would never stoop so low as to try to pronounce a foreign name. "Their tongues are separate in speech, and their natures as well," reads a 14th-century hymn to the Egyptian god Aten, referring to Asiatic slaves; "their skins are distinguished … [Yet everyone] has his food, and his time of life is reckoned." It was therefore up to every slave to quickly learn enough Egyptian to understand his master's commands.

ca 1780
Multiplication tables
appear in Babylonia

ca 1750
Egyptian geometry calculates
volume of a truncated pyramid

ca 1720
The Hyksos, Semitic nomads,
penetrate Egypt's Middle Kingdom

ca 1700
The Phoenicians develop
the 22-letter alphabet

JOSEPH'S JOURNEYS

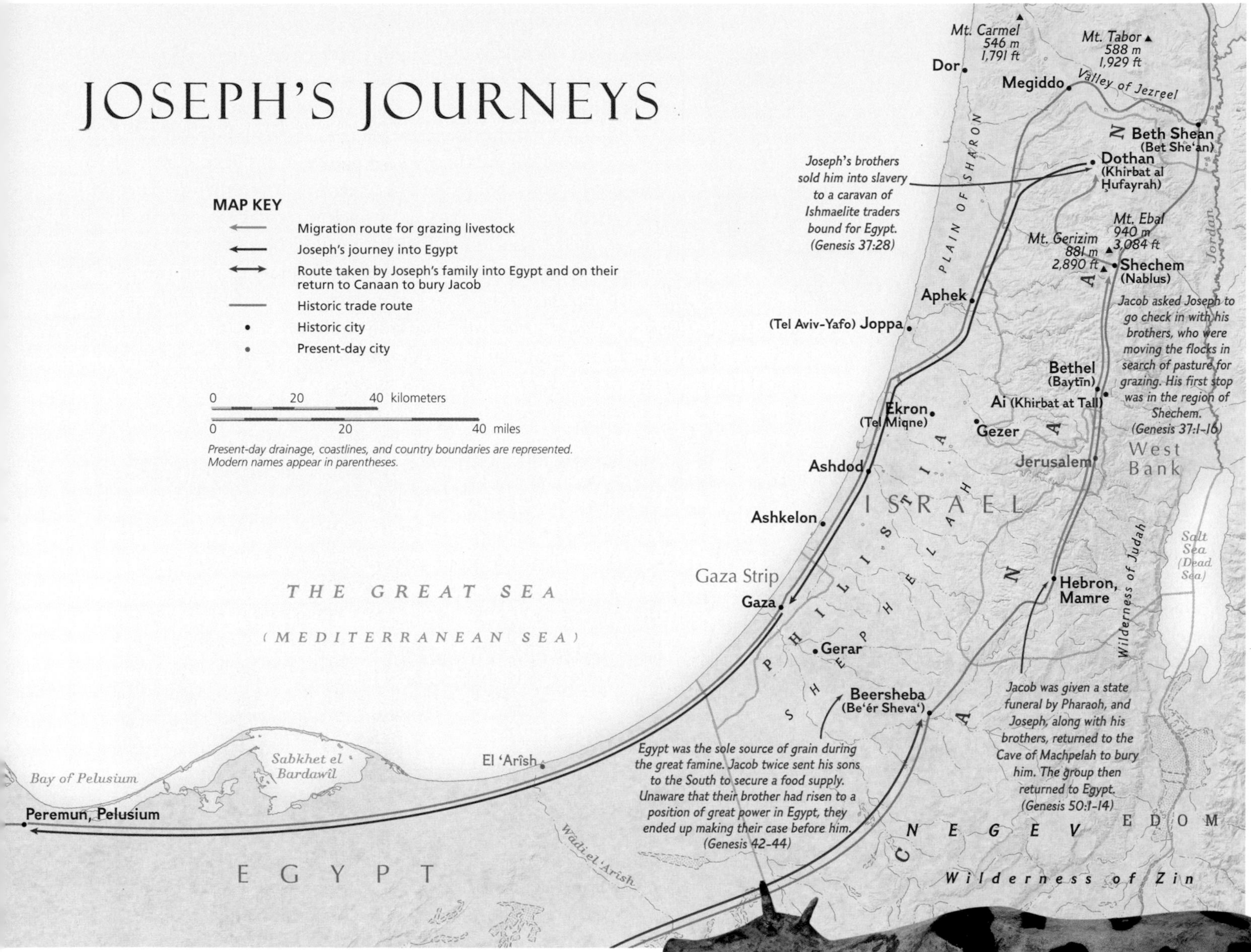

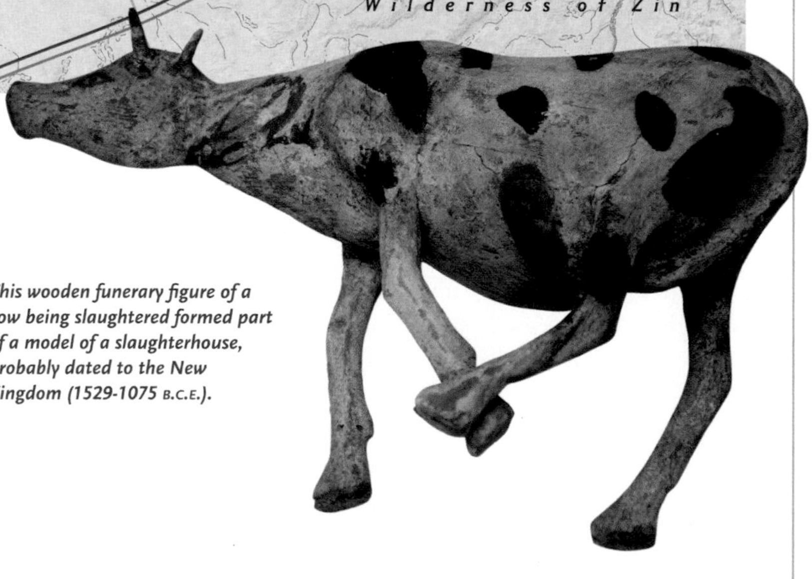

MAP KEY
Migration route for grazing livestock
Joseph's journey into Egypt
Route taken by Joseph's family into Egypt and on their return to Canaan to bury Jacob
Historic trade route
Historic city
Present-day city
0 20 40 kilometers
0 20 40 miles
Present-day drainage, coastlines, and country boundaries are represented. Modern names appear in parentheses.
Joseph's brothers sold him into slavery to a caravan of Ishmaelite traders bound for Egypt. (Genesis 37:28)
Jacob asked Joseph to go check in with his brothers, who were moving the flocks in search of pasture for grazing. His first stop was in the region of Shechem. (Genesis 37:1-16)
Egypt was the sole source of grain during the great famine. Jacob twice sent his sons to the South to secure a food supply. Unaware that their brother had risen to a position of great power in Egypt, they ended up making their case before him. (Genesis 42-44)
Jacob was given a state funeral by Pharaoh, and Joseph, along with his brothers, returned to the Cave of Machpelah to bury him. The group then returned to Egypt. (Genesis 50:1-14)
Mt. Carmel 546 m 1,791 ft
Mt. Tabor 588 m 1,929 ft
Dor
Megiddo
Valley of Jezreel
Beth Shean (Bet She'an)
Dothan (Khirbat al Ḥufayrah)
PLAIN OF SHARON
Mt. Ebal 940 m 3,084 ft
Mt. Gerizim 881 m 2,890 ft
Shechem (Nablus)
Jordan
Aphek
(Tel Aviv-Yafo) Joppa
Bethel (Baytīn)
Ai (Khirbat at Tall)
Ekron (Tel Miqne)
Gezer
Jerusalem
West Bank
Ashdod
ISRAEL
Ashkelon
SHEPHELAH
Wilderness of Judah
Salt Sea (Dead Sea)
Gaza Strip
Gaza
Hebron, Mamre
CANAAN
THE GREAT SEA
(MEDITERRANEAN SEA)
PHILISTIA
Gerar
Beersheba (Be'ér Sheva')
Sabkhet el Bardawil
Bay of Pelusium
El 'Arîsh
Peremun, Pelusium
NEGEV
EDOM
Wadi el 'Arish
EGYPT
Wilderness of Zin

This wooden funerary figure of a cow being slaughtered formed part of a model of a slaughterhouse, probably dated to the New Kingdom (1529-1075 B.C.E.).

Now Joseph was taken down to Egypt, and Potiphar, an officer of Pharaoh, the captain of the guard, an Egyptian, bought him from the Ishmaelites who had brought him down there.

GENESIS 39:1

ca 1650
Rhind papyrus reveals the extent of Egyptian mathematics

ca 1650
The Babylonians record appearances of the planet Venus

ca 1600
Volcano of Thera erupts, covering the Mediterranean in ash

ca 1595
The Hittites sack Babylon, ending the Old Babylonian Kingdom

A lovely young woman in a sheer white dress fans herself in this painted relief from the New Kingdom, 18th Dynasty (circa 1570-1292).

book from the Middle Kingdom, entitled *Teaching for Merykara* and written shortly before the Hyksos period, warns that dreams typically mean the exact opposite of what they seem to convey.

And so it is not surprising that when Pharaoh himself had a distressing dream, all the court was in uproar. In his dream the king saw seven fat cows coming out of the river, which were then devoured by seven thin cows. The sages and magicians at court were mystified; no one could explain its meaning. Fortunately, the cupbearer remembered Joseph's gift for divining dreams. Summoned from prison, Joseph explained the dream as a warning of great famine: Egypt's seven years of plenty would be followed by seven years of drought. His audience must have been speechless. Seven years of unrelenting famine was a harsh prophecy that threatened Egypt's law and order—its *maat*. Many a royal house had fallen because of such prolonged

But in the case of Joseph, that did not appear to be a problem. In fact, Joseph soon impressed his master with his diligence. As a result, says Genesis, Potiphar "made him overseer of his house and put him in charge of all that he had"—a foreshadowing of his future role of grand vizier over all of Egypt (Genesis 39:4). As it happened, Joseph was also remarkably "handsome and good-looking." Potiphar's wife—Genesis does not give us her name, but in the Qur'an she is called Zuleikha—was attracted to him and even tried to seduce him (Genesis 39:6). When Joseph declined her advances, she covered her tracks by denouncing him to her husband. Joseph was promptly thrown in prison.

Here, he was joined by two prominent figures from Pharaoh's court who had fallen from favor: the royal baker and the cupbearer. One night, these men had disturbing dreams. The cupbearer saw three branches: "Pharaoh's cup was in my hand; and I took the grapes and pressed them into Pharaoh's cup." The baker, meanwhile, dreamed of three cake baskets poised on his head, and birds were eating from them. Joseph accurately explained their meaning: The baker would be put to death, but the cupbearer would be restored to his position (Genesis 40:10-14).

Dreams play a very large role in the story of Joseph. While back in Dothan, Joseph's own dreams had prompted his brothers to get rid of him, it was now the dream of Pharaoh that would lead to his rehabilitation. This is why several scholars have opined that the Joseph story is a stand-alone novella in Hebrew Scripture, bracketed by the ancient preoccupation with dreams. In ancient Egypt—and elsewhere in Antiquity—dreams were believed to be harbingers of change. The interpretation of dreams was therefore an important discipline, practiced by soothsayers as well as highly placed savants at court. Scores of "dream books" were written, claiming to help readers unlock the meaning of their sleep-induced visions. One

These Roman breastworks once marked the Egyptian border at Pelusium, now known as Tell el-Farama.

famines. "Now therefore," Joseph concluded, "let Pharaoh look for a man discreet and wise, and set him and let him appoint officers over the land, and ... [let] them gather all the food of these good years that are coming" (Genesis 41:33-35).

Pharaoh pondered the young man in front of him. "You shall be over my house," the king replied, "and all my people shall order themselves as you command; only with regard to the throne will I

This vivid wall painting of a boy leading cows from the tomb of Nebamun in western Thebes is dated around 1356 B.C.E. (New Kingdom, 18th Dynasty).

be greater than you" (Genesis 41:40). With one stroke Pharaoh appointed Joseph the Hebrew slave, the son of Jacob, to grand vizier, a powerful position akin to that of prime minister, second only to Pharaoh himself. ∎

After two whole years, Pharaoh dreamed that he was standing by the Nile, and there came up out of the Nile seven sleek and fat cows, and they grazed in the reed grass.

GENESIS 41:1-2

A GRAND VIZIER IN AVARIS

Joseph Rises to High Office in Hyksos-Occupied Lower Egypt

Historians have searched in vain for documentation of Joseph's elevation to grand vizier, Pharaoh's second-in-command, a title that is perhaps comparable to the modern position of prime minister. This is why many scholars have dismissed the historicity of the Joseph story. Others caution, however, that most of the records from the Hyksos period were destroyed during Ahmose's vengeful destruction of their capital city. During his excavations at Tell el-Dahba, Manfred Bietak uncovered a layer of burned earth—mute testimony to the fury of King Ahmose's wrath. Indeed, scholars such as Israel Finkelstein have argued that the Joseph story should be seen as a glorious legend from Israel's prehistory. It reminded Israelites that their forefathers had once ruled as Hyksos lords in Egypt, in anticipation of the establishment of Israel in Canaan.

In fact, the idea that a foreigner could rise to high office in Egypt is not without precedent. Historian James Hoffmeier cites the example of a Canaanite individual named Bay, who after the death of Pharaoh Seti II in 1204 B.C.E. was elevated to the position of "great chancellor of the entire land," possibly because the new king, Siptah, had a Canaanite mother named Sutailja. Another Semite served as vizier during the reign of the female Pharaoh Hatshepsut. And as recently as the 1980s, French Egyptologist Alain Zivie uncovered a tomb at Saqqara belonging to a man named 'pr-el or Aper-El. Aper is a common name in the Hyksos period, and El is the name of God in both Canaanite and Hebrew texts. Aper, who like many other Egyptians had a theophoric name honoring his patron god, most likely descended from a family in Canaan. And the inscriptions in his tomb leave no doubt about his position at court: He served as vizier to Amenhotep III as well as Akhenaten.

AUTHENTIC CLUES IN THE JOSEPH STORY

In addition, a number of details in the Joseph story appear to be authentic. The use of "seven years" as a unit of reckoning is found in several Egyptian texts. A decree from the Ptolemaic period referring to King Djoser states that "all in the palace were afflicted by a great evil, since the Nile had not come [inundated the land] in my time for seven years." The method of Joseph's installation as grand vizier rings true as well. Pharaoh, says Genesis, "put a gold chain

ca 1640
The 15th Dynasty of the Hyksos
begins (1640-1532 B.C.E.)

ca 1640
Hyksos King Salitis
rules in Lower Egypt

ca 1626 (?)
Salitis is succeeded
by Maaibre Sheshi

ca 1620 (?)
Sheshi is succeeded
by Yakubher Meruserre

"Joseph, Overseer of the Pharaohs" was painted by the British artist Sir Lawrence Alma-Tadema (1836-1912) in 1874.

This seated figure depicts the Egyptian overseer Chertihotep, carved during the Middle Kingdom, 12th Dynasty, around 1800 B.C.E.

ca 1610
Khyan Seuserenre ascends
the throne in Lower Egypt

ca 1575
Seuserenre is succeeded by
Apophis (or Apepi I) Awoserre

ca 1542
Khamudi Aqenenre,
last Hyksos king in Lower Egypt

ca 1550
King Seqenenre launches
an invasion of Lower Egypt

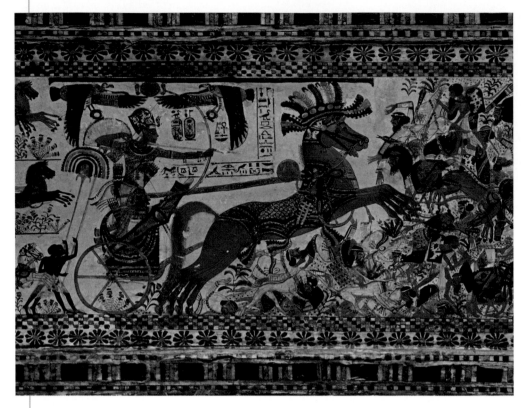

King Tutankhamun (1332-1322 B.C.E.) is shown in full battle gear, riding his war chariot while leading an attack against his enemies.

the nobility against Joseph's extraordinary powers. Indeed, says Genesis, "Thus Joseph gained authority over the land of Egypt" (Genesis 41:45).

JOSEPH'S RESPONSIBILITIES

As grand vizier of the realm, Joseph's duties, in addition to the staggering responsibility of preparing the land for a seven-year famine, would have been manifold. A text describing the daily schedule of Rekhmire, vizier to Thutmose III, notes that "the overseers of hundreds ... shall report to him their affairs." Historian William Ward has noted that if indeed it was Joseph's task to store up supplies throughout the land, his responsibilities would involve those of the overseer of the granaries, the royal seal bearer, the great steward, and the chief of the land—a staggering array of titles. Countless large beehive-type granaries would have been built in each of the key cities. Many such granaries have survived, in miniature form, in tombs throughout Egypt.

around his neck" to denote his high position (Genesis 41:42). Many such fine collars of office, sometimes capped with two falcon heads, can be found in archaeological collections around the world.

But the most intriguing reference in Genesis is the one where Pharaoh allowed Joseph to "ride in the chariot of his second-in-command" (Genesis 41:43). Before the advent of the Hyksos, no one in Egypt had ever ridden in a chariot. This iron conveyance with spoked wheels, pulled by two fast horses, was introduced during the Hyksos period, possibly inspired by Hittite war chariots.

Another intriguing detail is Pharaoh's decision to give Joseph a new Egyptian name. Joseph was henceforth to be known as Zaphenath-Paneah. Similarly, the Syrian vizier, Bay, was named Ramesse-Khamenteru. And in order to cement Joseph's position in Egypt's upper elite, Pharaoh gave him the hand of Asenath, the daughter of Potiphera, who served as the priest of On. This was a calculated move, because even during the Hyksos period, priests continued to exert considerable influence on public policy. By marrying Joseph into a priestly family, Pharaoh may have preempted whatever resistance might have risen among the clergy or

the land—a staggering array of titles. Countless large beehive-type granaries would have been built in each of the key cities. Many such granaries have survived, in miniature form, in tombs throughout Egypt.

The reference in Genesis to the city of On is probably no accident. On became a major population center during the Middle Kingdom, when it served as an important destination for the worship of Egypt's most ancient god, Atum. It also happened to be located at the apex of the Nile Delta, a natural place from which to supervise the collection of grain. From On, Joseph could travel on any of the tributaries north to oversee the harvesting of grain, or south across the Nile to supervise the gathering of dates, figs, and other fruits from the nearby fields of the Faiyum. In Book of the Dead, On is described as the place of "multiplying bread," based on an ancient myth by which the god Horus fed mummy spirits with only seven loaves of bread, a metaphor for the seven souls of the god Ra.

Thus, Joseph prepared Lower Egypt for the great cataclysm to come. And when it did arrive, says Genesis, "There was famine in every country, but throughout the land of Egypt there was bread"

The seven years of plenty that prevailed in the land of Egypt came to an end; and the seven years of famine began to come, just as Joseph had said.

GENESIS 41:53-54

HEARTLAND OF THE HYKSOS

Rosetta Mouth

Rosetta

Lake Burullus

Damietta Mouth

Damietta

Lake Manzala

THE GREAT SEA (MEDITERRANEAN SEA)

Kôm el-Qolsoum • Port Said

Diospolis Inferior (Tell el-Balamûn)

NILE RIVER DELTA

Bay of Pelusium

El Manṣûra

Pelusium (Tell el-Farâma)

El Manhalla el Kúbra

Sân el Hagar • Tanis

Tell Hebua

Way of the Philistines (Way of Horus)

Mendes (Tell el-Rub')

GOSHEN

Tell el-Ginn

Tell el-Her

Tell el-Borg

Ṭanta

Daphnai (Kôm Dafana)

Sile (Tell Abu Sefeh)

Pi-Ramesses (Tell el Dab'a) Avaris

Nabasha, Imet (Tell Fara'ûn)

Fâqûs

Zagazig

Pithom (Tell el-Ratabah)

Succoth (Tell el-Maskhuta)

Ismâ'ilîya

Wilderness of Shur

Shibîn el Kôm

Bubastis

Wâdi el Tumîlat

Tell el-Sahaba

Lake Timsah

Way of Shur

Benha

E G Y P T

Great Bitter Lake

Leontopolis

Little Bitter Lake

Gebel Abu Hassa

Migdol (Miktol)

On, Heliopolis

Gebel Murr

SUEZ CANAL

Nile

Cairo

Suez

Saqqâra

Memphis • Helwân

Eastern Desert

GULF OF SUEZ

MAP KEY
— Historic travel route
• Historic site
• Present-day city
○ Location uncertain

0   20   40 kilometers
0   20   40 miles

Present-day drainage, coastlines, and country boundaries are represented. Modern names appear in parentheses.

(Genesis 41:54). People from all over the Levant streamed to Egypt to buy food. Among them were Joseph's brothers. They met with Joseph but did not recognize him. Joseph then put his brothers to a test: He gave them all the food they could carry, but secretly hid a precious goblet in the bag belonging to Benjamin, his youngest brother. As they approached the frontier, the goblet was discovered; Benjamin was arrested and brought back to the capital. Judah, the same brother who had sold Joseph to the merchants, pleaded with the grand vizier for Benjamin's life, not knowing that this

This golden collar in the form of the vulture goddess Nekhbet was found in Tutankhamun's tomb (1332-1322 B.C.E.).

powerful man was Joseph. Hearing Judah's plea, Joseph could no longer restrain himself. He cried, "I am *your brother*, Joseph, whom you sold into Egypt. But don't be distressed, or angry with yourselves, because you sold me here; for God sent me before you to preserve life" (Genesis 45:5).

Soon after, Jacob, their father, and all their wives, servants, and livestock were brought from Canaan. Pharaoh granted them land in the region of Goshen, "the best part of the land" east of the Nile Delta, there to live in peace (Genesis 47:11). With their settlement in Egypt, the story of Genesis comes to a close. ■

ca 1550
Beginning of the Late Bronze Age
(1550-1200 B.C.E.)

ca 1550
Pharaoh Ahmose steadily ousts
the Hyksos from Egypt

ca 1504
Thutmose I becomes
king of Egypt

ca 1500
Growing conflicts between
Egypt and Hittites in Canaan

SETTLEMENT IN THE LAND OF GOSHEN

The Looming Conflict Between Lower and Upper Egypt

Pharaoh's decision to settle Joseph's tribal family in the land of Goshen was an inspired choice. Goshen (or Qosem, as it is called in a 12th Dynasty papyrus) was a highly fertile region located in the northeastern part of the Nile Delta near Wadi Tumeilat, between the easternmost tributary of the Nile and the Bitter Lakes. Well irrigated, it not only offered excellent soil for tilling but also plenty of grazing fields for large herds. Following the construction of the Aswan Dam in the 1960s, many of the Nile branches that existed in Joseph's day have disappeared, but the region is still among the most fertile in all of Egypt. It is therefore no accident that the Hyksos capital of Avaris was established close to this territory, in the eastern Nile Delta, since it was here that the Hyksos had first taken power. Joseph, too, may have moved here from On, since Joseph assured his family that they "shall be close" to his house.

According to the Book of Exodus, which picks up the story where Genesis left off, Joseph's family prospered in the lands of Goshen. While their herds ate their fill in the lush and moist fields of the delta, the Hebrews themselves followed the example of their Egyptian neighbors and began to cultivate the land. They began to assimilate because, as Joseph once said, "every shepherd is an abomination to the Egyptians" (Genesis 46:34).

In due course they would have learned to wait for the Nile to rise and inundate the land, and plant their seeds only after the floods receded and the soil was plump with fertile nitrates. Other than dates and fruits, the two principal crops grown in the Nile Delta were emmer wheat and barley, used to bake bread and brew beer—both staples of the average Egyptian's diet. This was complemented with lentils, beans, cabbage, and occasionally fish. Only wealthy families were able to eat meat on a regular basis, principally chicken and oxen beef.

Goshen was also surrounded by rich forests and marshland where the Egyptian nobility went to hunt for big game and farmers

The region of Goshen, in the eastern Nile Delta, is the setting for the enslavement of the Israelites as described in the Book of Exodus.

ca 1500
The cult of Amurra, god of nomads, flourishes in Babylon

ca 1500
Ugaritic sailors worship the god Baal

ca 1492
Thutmose II ascends as Pharaoh of Egypt

ca 1473
Hatshepsut, Thutmose's wife, becomes Pharaoh

An Egyptian nobleman fowling in the marshes, from the tomb of Nebamun at Western Thebes, dates from around 1356 B.C.E., New Kingdom, 18th Dynasty.

complemented their diet with fish caught in the countless lagoons and waterways. "The pools are filled with fish, the lagoons are thick with birds, the meadows are covered with succulent grass," writes a 13th-century author named Pai-Bes; "the fruits from the cultivated fields all taste like honey … people are glad to be living here." A fresco from the tomb of Nebamun, dated around 1356 B.C.E., shows this nobleman disporting himself during the hunt in the marshes, surrounded by the rich fowl of the region.

For 17 years, says Genesis, Jacob lived in this pastoral land of Goshen surrounded by his family. When he died, Joseph had him embalmed according to Egyptian custom, and Joseph too would be embalmed—the only biblical figures whose bodies would undergo the procedure (Genesis 50:2). Usually Egyptian embalmers required 70 days, but Genesis tells us that it only took 40 days to prepare the body of Jacob, possibly because the primary purpose of the mummification was to preserve the body during the long journey to Canaan. Obeying his father's wishes, Joseph arranged for the body to be taken back to Hebron, where it was buried in the Cave of Machpelah, alongside Jacob's father, Isaac, and his grandfather Abraham.

THE EGYPTIAN COURT IN THEBES

Meanwhile, things were not going well for the Egyptian court that had fled to the relative security of Thebes in Upper Egypt. The 17th Dynasty that ruled the region during this period also had to contend with foreign invaders from the Kingdom of Kush, who did not hesitate to exploit the much diminished power of Egypt's kings. The Kush invaders conquered many of Egypt's colonial possessions in Nubia (today's Sudan), thus robbing Thebes of a primary source of income as well as slaves. To make matters worse, its own control of Upper Egypt was contested by a group of breakaway noblemen who ruled part of the region as the short-lived Abydos Dynasty, from around 1640 to 1600 B.C.E. The existence of this mysterious dynasty, which had long been contested in scholarly circles, was dramatically proved in January 2014 with the discovery of the tomb of King Seneb Kay, the last of the four ruling kings, near Abydos.

The sad state of affairs in Upper Egypt during this period is reflected in the statue of the Theban king Sobekemsaf II, carved around 1570 B.C.E. The poor execution of the king's face and torso, including the awkward inversion of the waist, is a far cry from the virtuosity of Middle Kingdom artists. Equally unusual is the appearance of the hippopotamus goddess Ipi on the back of the throne. Ironically, a papyrus fragment known as Sallier I claims that the war between the North and South, between the kings of Avaris and Thebes, was precipitated by a hippopotamus in the private pool of King Seqenenre. The loud bellowing of this animal had disturbed the sleep of King Apepi's ambassador at the court of Thebes. According to the papyrus record, the ambassador lodged a complaint, whereupon King Seqenenre, deeply aggrieved, summoned his war council. The war fleet of Thebes sailed shortly after.

THE WAR BEGINS

King Seqenenre did not fare well during the initial battles. When in 1881, excavators discovered his mummified body in a tomb near Deir el-Bahari, they found that his head had been slashed with swords and spears. But the war was pursued with vigor by his successors, including King Ahmose I, founder of the 18th Dynasty, who is traditionally credited with defeating the Hyksos rule in the north.

But the Israelites were fruitful and prolific;
they multiplied and grew exceedingly strong,
so that the land was filled with them.

EXODUS 1:7

As Ahmose's forces entered Avaris, they gave no quarter. In 2012, Manfred Bietak announced the discovery of 16 severed right hands, found during the ongoing excavations at Tell el-Dahba, the site of ancient Avaris. This correlates with an inscription in King Ahmose's tomb, which states that after each battle against the Hyksos, soldiers who presented the king with the right hand of their foe were rewarded with the "gold of valor." This gruesome practice is also corroborated by the account of a captain of one of the Theban war galleys named Ahmose, who claimed, "I captured a man, and carried off with his hand." Apparently this was the custom by which Egyptian officers could determine the body count of their enemy.

Today, the fields of Avaris, just outside the village of Qantir, are still planted with the grain that Joseph's brothers once traveled from Canaan to obtain. But hardly anything remains. The last monuments of the Hyksos capital were left to crumble until the Nile tributary that was Avaris's lifeline silted up. By then, the name of Joseph was only a memory. ■

Pharaoh Ahmose I (circa 1560-1546) is the founder of the 18th Dynasty and the king credited with ousting the Hyksos from Egypt.

The mummy of Ramesses II, the most powerful king of the 19th Dynasty, is on display in the Egyptian Museum in Cairo, Egypt.

Egypt's Funeral Cult

Since the earliest beginnings of Egyptian civilization, the funerary cult played a central role. The embalming of the deceased was believed to preserve the integrity of a man's soul and body, his *ka* and *ba*. The secret of the embalming procedure was to remove all moisture from the body, thus eliminating the principal promoter of decay. Scholars believe that Egyptians may have arrived at this solution by observing the natural desiccation of corpses after burial in Egypt's dry desert sands. To imitate this process, Egyptian embalmers created a compound called natron, including sodium carbonate, bicarbonate, sodium chloride, and sulfa. Internal organs, always the first to decay, were removed and stored in so-called canopic jars, the lids of which were often shaped in the forms of the divinity to whom protection of the organs was consigned.

THE RISE OF THE NEW KINGDOM

The 18th Dynasty Restores the Empire of Egypt

How did the Theban invasion affect the farmers and fishermen of the Nile Delta, including the Hebrew descendants of Jacob and Joseph? For nearly a century they had thought themselves secure in this earthly paradise of Goshen: free to harvest, herd their sheep, and worship as they saw fit. A hundred years earlier, the advent of war might have prompted them to simply pull the pegs of their tents and move away to safer pastures. But they were no longer nomadic pastoralists; they were settlers who built their lives around the mud-brick homes that sheltered their families. It is possible that the Hebrews were left undisturbed at first, as the armies of the South vented their ire on Avaris and all who had served the Hyksos nobility. The Nile Delta was the breadbasket of Egypt; it would have served no purpose to destroy the fields on which the conquerors would depend for their food supply. But, as the Book of Exodus tells us, in time this would change.

Meanwhile, King Ahmose I was not content with merely evicting the Hyksos forces from the Nile Delta. He ordered a hot pursuit, determined not only to drive this foreign threat from Egypt's borders but to push them back from whence they came. Battling a fighting retreat, the Hyksos were steadily forced out across the Sinai Peninsula and finally into the region of Canaan, where they formed a defensive line at Sharuhen, today identified as Tell el-Far'ah, in the northwestern tip of the Negev. Only then did Ahmose turn around and take his armies back to Egypt—there to plot a new war, this time to recover the lost Nubian colonies.

A MILITANT DYNASTY

The Hyksos episode would continue to haunt the kings of the new 18th Dynasty,

at the beginning of the period known as Egypt's New Kingdom. Vowing never again to suffer the humiliation of foreign control of their territory, they became warrior kings who maintained extensive buffer zones around the Egyptian homeland. Large standing armies were raised, and strongholds were built all along the eastern border, the Upper Nile, and the frontiers with Nubia.

The militancy of Egypt's New Kingdom at the dawn of the Late Bronze Age also had a deep impact on Canaan. At the time, the region was organized into several loose confederacies: one centered around Megiddo, one anchored in Qadesh, and one located around Hazor in the north. The Hyksos period had spurred strong economic and political bonds between the Nile Delta and the Canaanite motherland. It had also boosted the region's role as the nexus of trade among the delta, Anatolia, and the Aegean world, including Cyprus. This is the time when the slender, double-handed clay amphora makes its appearance as a container for precious substances, such as olive oil and wine, during long sea voyages. The prominent role of Mycenae in this Mediterranean commerce, located on the mainland of Greece, is attested by numerous pottery samples found in Canaan. Most of these goods entered Canaan through its port of Tell el-Ajjul, which has been identified with the biblical city of Sharuhen, while Hazor was a main conduit for trade with Syria, Anatolia, and even Mesopotamia. The trade activity also spurred a new form of simplified writing, so that merchants could document who owed what to whom. Largely under influence of Mycenae, the first syllabic signs of the Linear B alphabet, the first attested form of written Greek, began to emerge.

But Canaan's prosperity receded after the rulers of Egypt's New Kingdom

A copper amulet bearing the image of Astarte testifies to the enduring popularity of this fertility goddess well into the days of the Israelite monarchy.

ca 1455
Thutmose III leads the first
of 16 campaigns into Canaan

ca 1450
First appearance
of water clocks in Egypt

ca 1400
Olmec influence expands from
the Gulf of Mexico to the Pacific

ca 1400
Tyre, Byblos, and Sidon emerge
as leading centers of trade

EGYPTIAN CAMPAIGNS

0   50   100   150 kilometers

0   50   100   150 miles

Present-day drainage, coastlines, and country boundaries are represented. Modern names appear in parentheses.

The second campaign of Amenhotep II pressed his sovereignty to the north beyond the territory conquered in his first campaign. He traveled north to the vicinity of Qatna. From there he made a circuit through the cities of the region before heading back overland to Egypt.

Thutmose III traveled to the vicinity of Byblos to begin his eighth campaign, where he had a small fleet of boats constructed. They were transported by cart to the Euphrates, where the vessels were used to cross and engage the forces of Mitanni. Ultimately a success, the pharaoh placed a stela on the east bank to commemorate the victory.

The fifth and seventh campaigns of Thutmose III dealt with subduing the area around Ardata, Simyra, and Ullaza. The subjugation of the coast was critical to support the inland conquest of his later efforts.

During Thutmose III's sixth campaign, the pharaoh destroyed the strategic city of Kadesh, which commanded the Orontes River Valley and the Kabir River Valley.

Located at a major crossroads of the region, Megiddo was the objective of Thutmose III's first campaign. After a seven-month siege the fortress fell. From this new base, the pharaoh sent forces into present-day Lebanon.

The second, third, and fourth campaigns of Thutmose III appear to have been incursions to collect tribute and solidify Egypt's control of southern Canaan.

The third offensive of Amenhotep II dealt with the cities of Canaan. He arrived at the town of Aphek, then moved on past Socoh and Yaham. The drive ended near Anaharath.

An Egyptian border fortress, where Thutmose III gathered his forces in response to the Syro-Canaanite coalition gathering at Megiddo.

"Retenu" was an ancient Egyptian name for the Levant region. The region extended from the Negev north to the Orontes River.

Amenhotep II's first campaign objective was to bring the local rulers of the Retenu and the region of Takhsi under Egyptian control. Once victorious, the pharaoh displayed the corpses of the vanquished rulers to emphasize the penalty for opposing Amenhotep's authority.

Thutmose III led as many as 17 military campaigns, over nearly two decades, to expand and maintain Egyptian control of the Levant. Many of his latter campaigns dealt with halting the ambitions of rival kingdoms, subduing revolts, and steadying the flow of tribute.

MAP KEY

— Campaigns of Thutmose III

— Campaigns of Amenhotep II

• Historic city

○ Location uncertain

▨ Maximum extent of Egyptian control ca 1420 B.C.E.

Modern names appear in parentheses.

This ancient Egyptian game board was used to play senet, the "game of passing," often depicted on funerary art for it endowed the winner with the protection of the gods Ra and Osiris.

How manifold it is, you have made! They are hidden from the face (of man). O sole god, like whom there is no other!

GREAT HYMN TO THE GOD ATEN

ca 1400	ca 1400	ca 1400	ca 1400
Evidence of alphabetic writing in Ugarit	Stonehenge in Britain assumes the form it has today	Egyptians develop water clocks, later known as clepsydras	India's Aryans establish the foundation of Hinduism

The so-called kiosk of Taharqa forms the first courtyard of the Temple at Karnak, built by King Seti I (1290-1279 B.C.E.).

A clay rhyton, or drinking cup, in the shape of a human head from Jericho dates from the Middle Bronze Age IIB (1750-1550 B.C.E.).

THE MONOTHEISM OF AKHENATEN

From that point on, Canaan became a vassal province of Egypt and would remain so for many centuries, except during the brief rule of one of Egypt's most enigmatic pharaohs: King Amenhotep IV. Shortly after assuming power in 1353 B.C.E., Amenhotep declared that his people's faith in the ancient Egyptian pantheon was misguided. It had been revealed to him that there was only one god to be worshipped, and that was Egypt's most ancient deity, the sun god Aten. The king changed his name to Akhenaten ("effective for Aten") and moved his court from Thebes to a city in central Egypt, which he named Akhetaten ("the horizon of Aten"), now identified with Amarna. There, he and his wife, Nefertiti, spent Egypt's treasure in the construction of temples and devotional statues to the sun god. Stylistically, the art of the period changed as well. The painting and sculpture from the period depict the king and his family in strange pear-shaped bodies with protruding stomach, heavy eyelids, and elongated skull. The exception, perhaps, is the breathtaking polychrome bust of Nefertiti that today is the pride of Berlin.

The king's almost complete dedication to religious affairs led to his neglect of Egypt's vassal states in the east. The Hittites did not fail to take notice, and their king, Suppiluliuma I, soon began to probe into Egypt's Eastern Empire. The much-reduced Egyptian garrisons stationed in Canaan and Syria, particularly Amurru, were powerless to resist them, as shown in a series of cuneiform tablets known as the Amarna Letters. "Please, my King," writes the Egyptian governor of Jerusalem, Abdiheba, in

reasserted their control of the region, particularly when it became a growing conflict zone between Egyptian and Hittite spheres of influence. During the reign of King Thutmose III, several tribal kingdoms, notably the Mitanni and the Hittites (located in today's Turkey and Syria), began to challenge Egypt's control of Syria and Canaan. According to Thutmose's stone inscriptions in Karnak, the king gathered his armies and around 1468 B.C.E. met the rebellious Hittites near the Canaanite battleground of Megiddo in the Jezreel Valley. Riding "in a chariot of fine gold, adorned with his accoutrements of combat," the pharaoh and his troops executed a pincer movement around the ancient Megiddo fortress that confused and ultimately routed the enemy. "Thou hast smitten the Sand-dwellers as living captives!" exult the king's inscriptions in Karnak, carved around 1460 B.C.E. "Thou has made captive the heads of the Asiatics of [Canaan]."

Now a new king arose over Egypt, who did not know Joseph.

EXODUS 1:8

An aerial view shows the excavations of the ancient Canaanite fortress Megiddo, which guarded the Jezreel Valley, as well as later additions by King Ahab (874-853 B.C.E.).

one such tablet, "send archers against the men who are committing these crimes … The Habiru are taking the cities of the king!" The apparent resemblance between *Habiru* (or *Apiru*) and the word *'Ibriyyîm,* or "Hebrews," has led some authors to suggest that these letters are actually referring to the conquest of Canaan by Joshua, as documented in the Book of Exodus. Most scholars now dismiss this notion. Recent research indicates that the use of the term "Habiru" refers to a number of Hurrian, Syrian, and Canaanite warlords who used the reduced Egyptian presence in the area as an opportunity to expand their power base.

Around 1336 B.C.E., Egypt's experiment with monotheism came to an end. Akhenaten died, little mourned, and soon after the boy-king Tutankhaten moved the court back to Thebes. He changed his name to the now-famous Tutankhamun ("the living image of Amun"), and thus the traditional worship of Amun and other deities was reinstated. ■

THE TREASURE CITIES OF RAMESSES II

The Ramessides Expand the Power of Egypt

Notwithstanding his great celebrity today, fired by the discovery of his treasure-filled tomb in 1922, King Tutankhamun's nine-year reign was of little consequence. Egypt's grip on its eastern territories continued to crumble under the relentless pressure of foreign invaders and local warlords, and the Egyptian economy suffered accordingly. These conditions would probably have led to another intermediate period of political and social turmoil were it not for the arrival of a new and even more warrior-like group of kings, the 19th Dynasty. It was established by a vizier named Paramessu. King Horemheb, who was childless, appointed him as his successor because of his evident military skills, for Horemheb realized that Egypt would need such talents in the years to come. But when Horemheb died in 1307, Paramessu was already advanced in age. Ascending the throne as Ramesses I, his reign was brief—no more than two years, by some calculations. He was succeeded by his son Seti (or Sethos) I, who was thoroughly indoctrinated by his father that only a massive new military effort would restore Egypt to its former power and glory.

As a result, soon after his ascension, Seti impulsively launched a campaign into Canaan, pushing as far as Tyre in Phoenicia. But the expedition exposed many shortcomings, particularly with regard to Egypt's infrastructure and the readiness of its military. The highway garrisons were poorly staffed or abandoned, many of the wells were dry, and morale among the garrison troops was low. If Egypt was to remain an empire, Seti realized, it would have to restore its buffer states, fortify its border with the East, and maintain extensive garrisons in the North, in Lower Egypt, rather than in Thebes.

A head depicts King Thutmose I (circa 1506-1493 B.C.E.), who extended the reach of the Egyptian empire and was arguably the first to be buried in the Valley of the Kings.

PI-RAMESSES OR "RAMESSES"

The ideal place, as the Hyksos kings had found, was the eastern Nile Delta. The Hyksos capital, Avaris, however, had fallen into ruin after the Nile tributary that had sustained it had silted up. A new city in the North was therefore needed: a city to house and train recruits, raise horses, and manufacture arms. This, then, became the city that in later years was known as Pi-Ramesses or Per-Ramesses-Aa-nakhtu ("the house of Ramesses, great in victory") and that the Book of Exodus refers to as "Ramesses." It was probably built on the remains of an old royal summer palace near one of the Pelusiac branches of the Nile.

Pi-Ramesses has been identified today as the large field bordered by palm trees near the village of Qantir, just north of the provincial capital of Faqus, some 70 miles north of Cairo. Since much of the land here is privately owned by local farmers, archaeologists are required to fill in their excavations with earth once their work is done and return the land to the farmers for cultivation. Therefore, all that is visible here is a mound, not far from the place where archaeologist Manfred Bietak discovered the remains of the Hyksos-era city of Avaris. Perhaps this close proximity enabled Seti's builders to reuse the *spolia* of the Hyksos capital—masonry, columns, and decorative remains—to expedite the construction of the new one.

Nevertheless, excavations aided by modern ground-penetrating radar have shown that once Pi-Ramesses was completed, it was one of the largest cities in Lower Egypt, with a population of more than 300,000 spread over seven square miles. The city plan

The Temple of Karnak—and its 134 columns of the Hypostyle Hall—was built by Seti I and completed by his successor, Ramesses II (1279-1213 B.C.E.).

ca 1380
Amenhotep III commissions the Great Temple at Luxor dedicated to Amun

ca 1365
Glass is invented simultaneously in Egypt and Mesopotamia

ca 1348
King Akhenaten shifts the capital of Egypt to Amarna

ca 1345
The Amarna Letters, a group of cuneiform tablets, are written

ca 1335
Akhenaten is succeeded
by Smenkhkare (Neferneferuaten?)

ca 1330
Tutankhaten ends the worship
of Aten, returns to Thebes

ca 1330
Tutankhaten adopts
name of Tutankhamun,
"living image of Amun"

ca 1320
A ship sinks off the coast
of Uluburun, Turkey's oldest
known shipwreck

This modern reconstruction of the interior courtyard of the mortuary temple of Ramesses III at Medinet Habu shows the polychrome ornamentation of Egyptian temples.

Inset: *This richly decorated ax was found in the tomb of Ahhotep in Thebes, New Kingdom, 18th Dynasty, 16th century B.C.E.*

consisted of a grid pattern radiating from a royal center filled with palaces and a large central temple, perhaps devoted to the worship of Amun. Workshops and artisan houses, as well as a series of cisterns with tether points for nearly 500 horses, underscore the military character of the city. The Bible calls Pi-Ramesses a "supply city," and that was indeed its purpose: to serve as a central depot and military barracks for the rapid-deployment divisions of Egyptian cavalry and infantry. While its location was far removed from the splendor of the royal court in Thebes, its close proximity to Egypt's vassal states in Syria-Canaan held obvious advantages, for it afforded Seti far swifter communications with his colonial governors while shortening his response time to any foreign incursions.

THE ISRAELITES BECOME SLAVE LABOR

What kind of labor would have built this city? When not working in the fields, most young Egyptians were either serving in Seti's expanded armed forces or being dispatched to large construction projects down south. This included the design of no fewer than three new temples in Abydos, several new mortuary temples in Thebes, as well as the famous Hypostyle Hall in the Temple of Amun in Karnak, which stands to this day. Where, then, to find the manpower for the construction of Pi-Ramesses in the North?

The Book of Exodus offers an answer. According to the Bible, the king observed the Israelite tribes herding their sheep and cattle in the Nile Delta and marveled at their sheer numbers. While some were

*Therefore they set taskmasters over them to oppress
them with forced labor. They built supply cities,
Pithom and Rameses, for Pharaoh.*

EXODUS 1:11

farmers, many others were shepherds just like their forefathers—and therefore not critical to the Egyptian economy. "Come," says Pharaoh in Exodus, "let us deal shrewdly with them." Given the urgent manpower problem in Egypt, the king decided to "set taskmasters over them to oppress them with forced labor" (Exodus 1:10-11).

Exodus intimates that even after some 400 years of settlement in Goshen, the Israelites were still considered a separate community with distinct Asiatic roots. "Look," the king says, "the Israelite people are more numerous and more powerful than we." Quite apart from their putative association with the despised Hyksos period, almost every pharaoh since Ahmose I had found himself fighting one "Asiatic" incursion after another. If indeed Egypt's kings still considered the Canaanite settlements in Goshen as foreign colonies, close in language and customs to the tribes that they routinely battled in the East, then the animosity toward the Hebrews during the 19th Dynasty certainly seems quite plausible. And given the labor shortages of Seti's reign, the decision to force them into indenture, as forced labor, would be a logical next step. Even in Roman times, whenever a magistrate wanted to build a new monument or city, it was standard practice to recruit forced labor *ad opus publicum* ("for public works") as letters by Pliny attest. "I have fed these *Habiru* tribes with bread, beer and every good thing," reads an inscription in the tomb of grand vizier Rekhmire in Thebes; "but the rod is in my hand; be not idle."

THE BUILDING OF PER ATUM OR "PITHOM"

King Seti I died in 1290 and was succeeded by his son Ramesses II, then still in his teens. There are indications that Ramesses may have served as prince

regent from age 14, which would have enabled him to become thoroughly acquainted with his father's projects before assuming power himself. Blessed with a long reign—as long as 66 years by some estimates—Ramesses II would become the most powerful king of the 19th Dynasty. Not only did he continue to build the supply city begun by his father—now modestly named after himself, as Pi-Ramesses—but also he started the construction of a second city

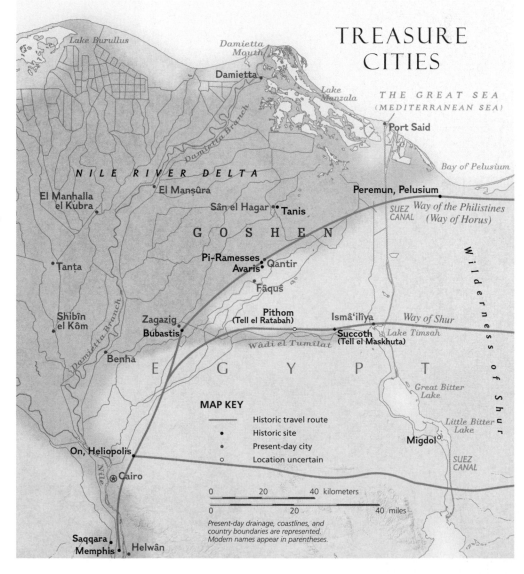

TREASURE CITIES

The Royal Capital of Thebes

With the advent of the 18th Dynasty, Thebes became a true royal city. Instead of pyramids, Egypt's kings now focused on building elaborate tombs and mortuary temples in the Valley of the Kings. One of the most spectacular of these projects was initiated by the spouse and co-regent of Thutmose II, the mysterious Queen Hatshepsut, near the towering cliffs of Deir el-Bahari. Designed by her brilliant court architect and senior adviser, Senenmut, Hatshepsut's mortuary temple, now undergoing extensive restoration, is a magnificent three-floor esplanade leading to a sanctuary cut deep into the rock. Its bold angular lines are strangely reminiscent of Modernist architecture from the 1920s. This feat of engineering was carefully aligned with the Great Temple of Amun in Karnak on the opposite bank of the Nile. Thutmose III himself claimed that his campaign to extend the borders of Imperial Egypt was "at the command of his divine father Amun-Re," a sentiment soon echoed by Ramesses II.

A relief shows King Akhenaten (1353-1336 B.C.E.) and his family during worship of the god Aten, shown as a sun disc bathing the royal couple with its rays.

in the eastern delta, dedicated to the patron god of his family and dynasty, Atum. Thus rose Per Atum, "house of Atum," or "Pithom" as the Bible calls it. Atum, the first god of the Egyptian pantheon, was considered the creator of life and father to Egypt's kings, who were deities themselves. Ramesses' close association with his towering figure no doubt enhanced his own personality cult, as witnessed by scores of statues that have been recovered from this period.

According to Exodus, the Israelite slaves were deployed in the work pits of both Pi-Ramesses and Per Atum under ever more oppressive

Sunset dapples the tranquil waters of the Nile River near Luxor, Egypt, the source of the ancient kingdom's fertility and prosperity.

The famous bust of Queen Nefertiti, the royal consort of King Akhenaten, today forms part of the collection of the Neues Museum in Berlin.

conditions. "The Egyptians became ruthless in imposing tasks on the Israelites," says Exodus, "and made their lives bitter with hard service in mortar and brick and in every kind of field labor" (Exodus 1:13). The Bible also states that "the more they were oppressed, the more they multiplied and spread, so that the Egyptians came to dread the Israelites" (Exodus 1:12). At first glance, this argument seems to defy logic. If Pharaoh needed so many workers, why would he be concerned over the rapid growth of his labor pool? Indeed, why would he want the male issue of his slaves killed, as he orders the midwives to do later in the story? Perhaps the answer is twofold. On the one hand, the specter of another Hyksos-type revolt among these Hebrew tribes may never have been far from Pharaoh's mind. And on the other, the episode of the Hebrew infanticide will, in a later Exodus chapter, justify the terrible retribution of the Tenth Plague, when it is the Egyptian firstborns who are slain.

This, then, sets the stage for the story of a young babe, a son of a Hebrew couple, who is set adrift on the river in a basket made of papyrus, sealed with bitumen and pitch. ∎

MOSES IN MIDIAN

The Origins of the Moses Saga in Egypt

As in the case of Joseph, there are no Egyptian records attesting the life of Moses, the man who according to the Bible was raised by Pharaoh's daughter "as her own son" (Exodus 2:10). If the story of the Exodus is set during the reign of Ramesses II, as many authors suggest, then the story of his birth would have taken place during the rule of his predecessor, King Seti I. According to Egyptian records, Seti was married to Queen Tuy, who presented him with two children: a son and heir named Ramesses and a daughter named Tia. This princess, in turn, had two daughters but no son. Some scholars believe that Seti and Tuy may have had another girl named Henutmire, who could have been the "Pharaoh's daughter" described in Exodus, but recent data suggest she was actually a daughter of Ramesses himself. There is therefore no record of a man, such as Moses, who was raised by Seti's daughter. The first Book of Chronicles, as well as the rabbinic midrash, refer to Moses' adoptive mother as Bithiah (literally, "daughter of Yah," meaning YHWH), but this name does not appear in Egyptian annals (I Chronicles 4:18).

Some historians have argued that this is not surprising, given that the New Kingdom was not in the habit of recording its defeats—and if the Exodus story has some historical roots, the loss of a large part of Egypt's active workforce must surely have ranked as a major setback. Others see Moses as a composite figure, the result of multiple traditions, which is not unusual for the Torah. For example, Exodus depicts him as the son of a Hebrew couple, but one who is raised at the royal court as an Egyptian prince. He feels a strong affinity with the Israelites of Goshen, his "kinsfolk," but the Hebrews rebuff him; as one Israelite cries, "Who made you a ruler and judge over us?" (Exodus 2:11,14). And even though he is a coddled prince at Pharaoh's court, with no experience in desert survival, Moses is somehow able to travel through the Sinai and across the Gulf of Aqaba to the region of Midian (today's southern Jordan).

A BASKET OF REEDS AND PITCH

The Book of Exodus introduces Moses in the midst of a grave crisis among the Israelite slaves, who are toiling away in the work pits of

"The Finding of Moses" was painted by the British painter Sir Lawrence Alma-Tadema (1836-1912) in 1904 on the occasion of the opening of the Aswan Dam.

ca 1300
Mycenae is the dominant
power in the Aegean

ca 1300
First evidence of Chinese
characters on oracle bones

ca 1300
Use of iron to make arms
becomes widespread

ca 1300
Ashur rises as the dominant
deity in Babylon

"Moses Before the Burning Bush" was painted by the Italian artist Domenico Fetti (1588-1623) around 1614. Opposite: The summit of Mount Sinai (Jebel Musa in Arabic) is traditionally associated with Mount Sinai in the Bible, where Moses received the Tablets of the Law from YHWH.

Pithom and Pi-Ramesses. Pharaoh has decreed that all newborn boys among the Hebrews should be cast into the river. One of these is the baby of a young couple from the tribe of Levi, Amram, and Jochebed. In order to save their child, Jochebed "got a papyrus basket for him, and plastered it with bitumen and pitch," then set the baby afloat on the river (Exodus 2:3).

Eventually the basket was discovered by Pharaoh's daughter, who took the baby in. In due course, this princess adopted the child and named him Moses, "because I drew him out of the water" (Exodus 2:10). The Hebrew verb *moshe* means "to draw out." However, *moshe* or *moses* was also a common theophoric patronymic in Egypt, as in Thutmose, meaning "son of Tut," meant to invoke the blessings

> *But Moses fled from Pharaoh.*
> *He settled in the land of Midian,*
> *and sat down by a well.*

EXODUS 2:15

of the deity. Later traditions may have omitted the name of the Egyptian god, leaving us with the name "(blank)-Moses."

As in the case of Genesis, Exodus doesn't hesitate to borrow literary motifs that would have been familiar to its audience. Just as the story of the attempted seduction of Joseph by Potiphar's wife may have been modeled on a popular Egyptian novella, *The Tale of Two Brothers*, so too is the image of Moses drifting down in a basket perhaps inspired by the saga of Sargon I, founder of the Akkadian Empire. As an infant, Sargon was reportedly placed "in a box made of reeds," smeared with bitumen for buoyancy, and cast on the river so as to escape his enemies. These and other literary parallels followed the convention in ancient literature to attend the birth of great leaders with miraculous portents and events, which underscored the supernatural origins and divine sanction of their lives.

One day, after Moses had become an adult, he was visiting the Hebrews in their work pits. There he was witness to an Egyptian overseer beating one of the Israelite slaves. In a fit of rage, Moses jumped in and killed the taskmaster, hiding him in the sand so that no one would discover the deed (Exodus 2:12). Moses was concerned what Pharaoh's reaction would be. Mercy was a prized virtue in ancient Egypt, especially in those destined to lead. "Guard yourself from preying on the oppressed," says the Instruction of Amenemopet, an 11th-century papyrus manuscript written for young princes, "or against overbearing those who are powerless." But this was not a sentiment that Pharaoh shared. The Bible says that as soon as word of this murder spread, Pharaoh vowed to kill Moses, so he fled into the desert.

THE MYSTERY OF MIDIAN

Why would the king so rashly condemn his adopted grandson? The answer to this question may lie in the region that Moses chose to flee to. This was not Canaan, as we might expect, but Midian—which required him to take a far longer and more perilous journey. At the time, Midian was one of the vassal regions subjugated by the 18th Dynasty as one of the buffer zones around his borders. Midian was therefore administered by vassal chieftains under Egyptian supervision. It was sometimes the custom to require these chieftains to send their sons to Egypt, where as "hostage princes" they would be raised and indoctrinated at Pharaoh's court. The intent was clear: If the vassal ruler ever did anything to displease the king in Thebes, his sons would instantly be put to death.

[The priest] gave Moses his daughter Zipporah in marriage.
She bore a son, and he named him Gershom; for he said,
"I have been an alien residing in a foreign land."

EXODUS 2:21-22

What we may see here, in other words, is an oral tradition about a Midianite prince in Thebes. It may explain why Pharaoh was moved to condemn Moses and why Moses was able to find his way to Midian—for the simple reason that this was his native region. It also explains why Moses would feel a kinship with the Israelites in the Nile Delta. According to Genesis, the ancestor of the tribe of the Midianites was a son of Abraham's second wife, Keturah, whom he married after Sarah's death (Genesis 25:1-2). As scholar Frank Cross has argued, it is reasonable to think that the people of Midian had remained faithful to the worship of El, the Abrahamaic God. Their customs, their songs, and their prayers would not have been dissimilar to those that Moses observed among the Israelites in Goshen.

Indeed, the father of the young woman whom Moses fell in love with, Jethro, is described by Exodus as a "priest." The Book of Judges goes as far as to identify Jethro as a Midianite priest of YHWH (Judges 1:16; 4:11). And it is only after meeting Jethro that Moses would come face to face with God. ∎

Chariots of War

The war chariot was possibly developed by the Hittites in their home territory of Anatolia (modern Turkey) and subsequently introduced in the Near East. During the Hyksos Period, the exiled royals in Thebes began to build chariots of their own. These horse-drawn chariots figured prominently in the story of the Exodus, as well as in the climactic Battle of Qadesh, where Ramesses II deployed thousands of his chariots against an equal number in the Hittite army. The battle, dated around 1274 B.C.E., ended in a draw, and Ramesses and Hittite King Hattusilis III entered into a nonaggression pact, the first in recorded history.

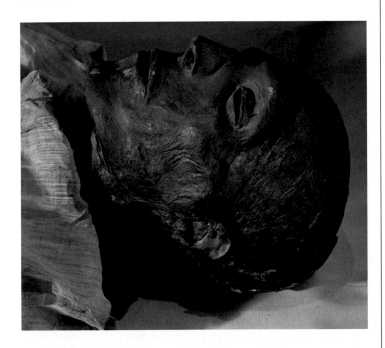

A detail of the mummy of Pharaoh Seti I of the 19th Dynasty shows his well-preserved head.

The magnificent desert wasteland of Wadi Rum, in today's Jordan, is close to the biblical Midian.

This tablet documents the peace treaty, believed to be the first in history, concluded between the Egyptians and the Hittites in 1259 B.C.E. after the Battle of Qadesh.

ca 1290
City of Troy is destroyed
by Mycenaeans

ca 1285
Assyrian Empire begins under
King Adad-nirari I

ca 1285
Oral traditions of the Trojan War
begin to circulate

ca 1280
First books are produced
in China

THE TEN PLAGUES

Scientific Sources of the Great Trials of Egypt

In Midian, Moses not only comes to terms with his origins as a Hebrew; he is also charged by God to deliver the Israelite slaves from Egypt. "I have observed the misery of my people who are in Egypt," God's voice calls out to him from a burning bush on Mount Horeb. "I have heard their cry on account of their taskmasters" (Exodus 3:1-7). Moses' response, however, suggests that the Hebrews in Egypt may no longer recognize God as the deity of their ancestors, "the God of Abraham, the God of Isaac, and the God of Jacob." What if, Moses asks, "they ask me, 'What is his name?' What shall I say to them?" (Exodus 3:13).

The question underscores the theme of alienation that runs through the story of the Exodus. The Israelites are alienated from their ancestral God, possibly as the result of their long assimilation to Egyptian customs and Egyptian culture. Moses is alienated from the Egyptian court that raised him, but he is also struggling to be accepted by the people he's destined to save. This triangular relationship is a tenuous one, and throughout the Exodus saga, we hear of the people abandoning their faith in either God or Moses.

God tells Moses, "I am who I am … Thus you shall say to the Israelites, 'I am has sent me to you.'" *Ehyeh asher ehyeh*: Until the Second Temple Period, God will be called by the tetragrammaton, the four Hebrew characters of YHWH (biblical Hebrew was written only in consonants), usually pronounced "Yahweh."

Thus Moses returns to the court of Pharaoh, accompanied by his brother Aaron, to negotiate with the Egyptian king for the release of the Israelites. But their pleas fall on deaf ears. In fact, Pharaoh orders his taskmasters to "no longer give the people straw to make bricks, as before," but to let them "gather straw for themselves," though the daily quota of finished bricks remains the same (Exodus 5:7-8). Naturally, the Hebrew slaves are none too pleased with the outcome from this botched rescue attempt.

THE SEQUENCE OF THE PLAGUES

In retaliation, God sends Egypt a series of plagues, each more terrible than the previous one, to bend Pharaoh to his will and project

The British painter Sir Lawrence Alma-Tadema (1836-1912) painted "The Death of the First Born" in 1874.

ca 1279
Reign of Ramesses II
begins

ca 1275
Hittite forces invade Canaan
and Syria

ca 1274
Ramesses II battles Hittites
near Qadesh to a draw

ca 1269
Two new Ramesses temples
are built at Abu Simbel

the awesome power of the Hebrew God. First, the water of the Nile turns to blood, making its waters undrinkable and causing the fish to die. Next, huge hordes of frogs overrun the land. The third plague brings an infestation of *kinim*, usually translated as "gnats" or "lice," followed by a monstrous swarm (*'arov*) of animals that most sources interpret as "flies." Fortunately, this fourth plague affects only the Egyptians, not the Hebrews in Goshen, just as they will be spared from all subsequent tribulations. A pestilence then sweeps over the land, killing the livestock, after which the Egyptians themselves are struck with an outbreak of *šehin*, usually translated as "boils."

Several authors see a logical progression in these first six plagues, informed by Egypt's unique desert climate, lashed by hot, dusty winds known as *khamsanin*. There are, for example, several explanations for the Nile running red. Some authorities claim this can happen in extremely hot conditions, when the muddy waters favor the excess breeding of freshwater algae, which tend to color red when they die. The mud itself can turn a bright ochre-brown. Under these conditions, the water would become toxic, leading to the poisoning of the river's fish population. Other river animals such as frogs would inevitably crawl out and plunge into the hinterland in a desperate search for water.

Meanwhile, the decomposing carcasses of dead fish would become natural breeding grounds for all sorts of bacteria, as well as gnats and flies. These insects then serve as natural carriers of disease, spreading pestilence among both livestock and humans. A poem known as the Admonitions of Ipuwer, written on a papyrus now in Leiden, the Netherlands, describes several natural disasters, including the reference that "the river is blood and one drinks from it." Significantly, the papyrus document dates from the 19th Dynasty, the period in which the ten plagues are reputed to have taken place, although some authors believe it was written much later. Most scholars, however, reject the idea that this poem and the Exodus account could have the same historical origin.

Nevertheless, the next sequence of plagues is also closely related to the unique conditions of the Nile Delta. After the pestilence, a hailstorm lashed the land, "such heavy hail as had never fallen in all the land of Egypt since it became a nation" (Exodus 9:24). Though this may seem surprising, severe winter weather is quite common in the Middle East. In February 2004, a vast winter storm dumped more than two feet of snow on large areas in Jordan and Israel.

Such unusually high levels of hail and rain can then encourage the breeding of a variety of insects, including locusts, which Exodus

A colored tablet from the New Kingdom shows a young Egyptian woman with her son, holding a goose, surrounded by the wealth of her household.

*I will send all my plagues upon you yourself,
and upon your officials, and upon your people, so that you
may know that there is no one like me in all the earth.*

EXODUS 9:14

identifies as the eighth plague (Exodus 10:12-15). Desert locusts *(Schistocerca gregaria)* are very common in Egypt and the Sudan. Egyptian records refer to a devastating locust plague around 1250 B.C.E., which destroyed crops throughout the Nile Valley.

Desert locusts, like this swarm photographed in Africa, can completely denude a field of its crops in a matter of days, recalling the Eighth Plague of the Book of Exodus.

THE DESERT KHAMSANIN

When Pharaoh still refused to let the Hebrews go, the eighth plague was followed by "a very strong west wind," most likely one of the region's *khamsanin,* which brought a period of darkness to all of Egypt. Blowing from the southwest across the Sahara, a *khamsin* can travel from Libya across Egypt toward the Arabian Peninsula while reaching temperatures of well over 100 degrees Fahrenheit. The large amounts of sand and dust particles carried by this storm can literally turn day into dusk, or even night. The Arabic name *khamsin* means "50"—the number of days that this Sahara wind can torment the land. Other authors have linked the ninth plague to the eruption of Thera, which all but destroyed the Minoan Civilization and probably darkened the skies throughout the eastern Mediterranean. But that eruption took place in either 1600 or 1500

B.C.E., several centuries before the putative date of the Moses story.

It is the tenth and final plague that finally breaks Pharaoh's will. All of Egypt's firstborn males are slain by God's angels, from the "firstborn of Pharaoh" to the firstborn of the lowliest prisoners in the dungeons (Exodus 12:29). To ensure that the angels will bypass the Hebrew homes, each family is told to slaughter a lamb, roast it, and brush its blood on the doorposts. This moment, says God, should henceforth be celebrated as "the Lord's Passover" (Exodus 12:11).

Ramesses had many sons, to judge by the processions of his offspring that are found on temples throughout Egypt, including the Ramesseum. Egyptologists calculate that Ramesses had around 100 children from multiple wives, including some 48 sons and more than 50 daughters. But apparently, Pharaoh's oldest son by his wife, Nefertiry, Crown Prince Amenhirkopshef, died in the 25th year of the king's reign. His tomb was not discovered until 1995. ∎

THE ESCAPE FROM EGYPT

The Great Israelite Migration to Canaan Begins

This deep canyon in the Sinai Desert, accessible via a camel footpath, leads to the Bedouin settlement of Hudheira, associated by some with the biblical Hazeroth.

Take your flocks and your herds," Pharaoh tells Moses and Aaron, "and be gone" (Exodus 12:31-32). And so, the Israelites are freed at last—their freedom paid in blood, the blood of the innocent firstborn children slain by the angels of the Lord. Now it is the Egyptians who urge the Hebrews to "hasten their departure from the land." The natives are heartily sick of all the terrible plagues that have been inflicted on them, and fear that unless the Israelites get out of Egypt soon, "We shall all be dead" (Exodus 12:33).

By the same token, many Hebrews are probably just as eager to get away before Pharaoh can change his mind—as in due course he will. It is dawn, and all over the Hebrew neighborhoods, women are beginning to prepare the dough for their daily bread. But the haste of preparing for the journey does not allow them to wait for the dough to be leavened and allowed to rise. As a result, they bake bread from unleavened bread, producing the hard, cracker-like wafers known as matzo, an integral part of the Passover celebrations to this day. Another reason for baking matzo bread is that it lasts longer. As Ze'ev Meshel has observed, the Bedouin of the Sinai still bake their version of matzo, known as *libeh,* two or three times a day.

The staging point for the great exodus from Egypt is Pi-Ramesses, or "Ramesses" as the Bible calls it. From there, the Israelites journey to "Succoth, about six hundred thousand men on foot, besides children," as well as their livestock (Exodus 12:37-28). The precise location of Succoth is uncertain. Some authors believe it is another name for Per-Atum (or "Pithom" in biblical parlance), sometimes identified as today's Tell el-Retabeh, while others believe it was located at Tell el-Mashkuta. Either way, both places are close to Wadi Tumeilat, a highly fertile strip of land adjoining the Nile that served as a natural transit point from Egypt to Canaan. It is here that the great caravan route known as the Way of Shur began its long path across the Sinai Desert. And indeed, this is the direction that Moses appears to take, ending the march at Etham. Had he continued on this road, he would have reached Beersheba, the doorstep of the Promised Land in Canaan, in just a matter of weeks.

But then something strange happens. God tells Moses to backtrack, to "turn back and camp in front of Pi-hahiroth, between Migdol and the sea" (Exodus 14:2). As it turns out, this is a calculated maneuver to deceive and confuse the Egyptians, for Pharaoh has indeed changed his mind. Six hundred chariots, aided by ancillary units from all over Egypt, are in hot pursuit of the Hebrew fugitives. This is when Moses lifts his staff and the sea divides itself, allowing the Israelites to pass on dry ground. When the last Hebrew is safely on the opposite bank, Moses stretches his hand once more and the waters close, burying the Egyptians in a watery grave.

Where did this magnificent spectacle take place? The Bible describes the location merely as "the sea," though previously it refers to the Red Sea (*yam suph,* which actually means the "sea of reeds") (Exodus 13:18). There are no reeds on the shores of the Red Sea. But shallow sandbanks, sometimes covered with brush or reeds, are found near the marshes of the Bitter Lakes to this day. Depending on the season, these sandbanks could be sufficiently exposed to allow a person to cross. The obvious place is the narrow point between the

ca 1259
Hittites and Ramesses II conclude a peace treaty, the first in history

ca 1255
Ramesses' Queen Nefertari dies; Istnofret is chief queen

ca 1249
Earthquake damages temples at Abu Simbel

ca 1250
Earthquake in Nineveh damages the Temple of Ishtar

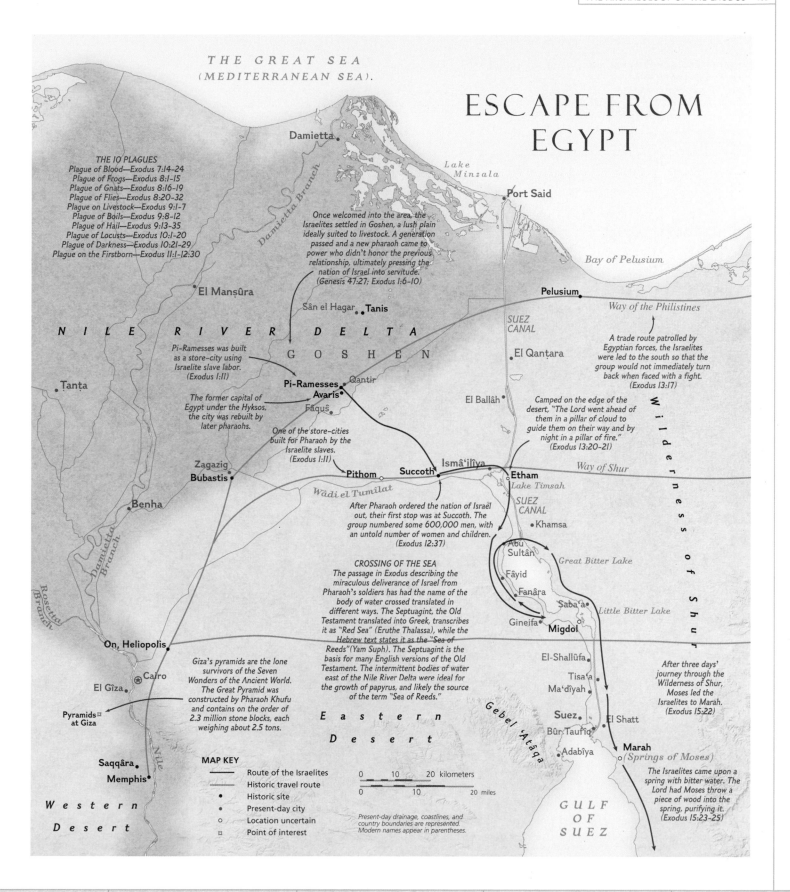

ESCAPE FROM EGYPT

THE GREAT SEA
(MEDITERRANEAN SEA).

THE 10 PLAGUES
Plague of Blood—Exodus 7:14-24
Plague of Frogs—Exodus 8:1-15
Plague of Gnats—Exodus 8:16-19
Plague of Flies—Exodus 8:20-32
Plague on Livestock—Exodus 9:1-7
Plague of Boils—Exodus 9:8-12
Plague of Hail—Exodus 9:13-35
Plague of Locusts—Exodus 10:1-20
Plague of Darkness—Exodus 10:21-29
Plague on the Firstborn—Exodus 11:1-12:30

Once welcomed into the area, the Israelites settled in Goshen, a lush plain ideally suited to livestock. A generation passed and a new pharaoh came to power who didn't honor the previous relationship, ultimately pressing the nation of Israel into servitude. (Genesis 47:27; Exodus 1:6-10)

Pi-Ramesses was built as a store-city using Israelite slave labor. (Exodus 1:11)

The former capital of Egypt under the Hyksos, the city was rebuilt by later pharaohs.

A trade route patrolled by Egyptian forces, the Israelites were led to the south so that the group would not immediately turn back when faced with a fight. (Exodus 13:17)

Camped on the edge of the desert, "The Lord went ahead of them in a pillar of cloud to guide them on their way and by night in a pillar of fire." (Exodus 13:20-21)

One of the store-cities built for Pharaoh by the Israelite slaves. (Exodus 1:11)

After Pharaoh ordered the nation of Israel out, their first stop was at Succoth. The group numbered some 600,000 men, with an untold number of women and children. (Exodus 12:37)

CROSSING OF THE SEA
The passage in Exodus describing the miraculous deliverance of Israel from Pharaoh's soldiers has had the name of the body of water crossed translated in different ways. The Septuagint, the Old Testament translated into Greek, transcribes it as "Red Sea" (Eruthe Thalassa), while the Hebrew text states it as the "Sea of Reeds"(Yam Suph). The Septuagint is the basis for many English versions of the Old Testament. The intermittent bodies of water east of the Nile River Delta were ideal for the growth of papyrus, and likely the source of the term "Sea of Reeds."

Giza's pyramids are the lone survivors of the Seven Wonders of the Ancient World. The Great Pyramid was constructed by Pharaoh Khufu and contains on the order of 2.3 million stone blocks, each weighing about 2.5 tons.

After three days' journey through the Wilderness of Shur, Moses led the Israelites to Marah. (Exodus 15:22)

The Israelites came upon a spring with bitter water. The Lord had Moses throw a piece of wood into the spring, purifying it. (Exodus 15:23-25)

NILE RIVER DELTA
GOSHEN
SUEZ CANAL
Way of the Philistines
Way of Shur
Wilderness of Shur
Wādi el Tumilat
SUEZ CANAL
Eastern Desert
Western Desert
Gebel 'Atāqa
GULF OF SUEZ
Lake Minzala
Bay of Pelusium
Lake Timsah
Great Bitter Lake
Little Bitter Lake
Damietta Branch
Rosetta Branch
Nile

Damietta
Port Said
Pelusium
El Mansûra
El Qantara
Sân el Hagar · **Tanis**
El Ballâh
Pi-Ramesses · Qantir
Avaris
Fâqûs
Tanta
On, Heliopolis
Zagazig
Bubastis
Benha
El Gîza ⊛ Cairo
Pithom **Succoth** Ismâ'ilîya **Etham**
Khamsa
Abu Sultân
Fâyid
Fanâra
Saba'a
Gineifa **Migdol**
El-Shallûfa
Tisa'a
Ma'dîyah
Suez
Bûr Taufîq El Shatt
Adabîya
Marah (Springs of Moses)
Pyramids at Giza
Saqqâra
Memphis

MAP KEY
—— Route of the Israelites
—— Historic travel route
• Historic site
• Present-day city
○ Location uncertain
⊡ Point of interest

0   10   20 kilometers
0   10   20 miles

Present-day drainage, coastlines, and country boundaries are represented. Modern names appear in parentheses.

ca 1250
Swarms of locusts destroy crops in the Nile Valley

ca 1244
Tukulti-Ninurta becomes king of Assyria

ca 1236
Ramesses leads raid into Nubia

ca 1225
Ramesses' son and heir dies; Merneptah is new heir

The Book of Exodus places the vast, moonlike surface of the Wilderness of Sin "between Elim and Sinai."

A pair of fashionable children's sandals attests to the high standard of living in ancient Egypt during the New Kingdom.

Great Bitter Lake and the Little Bitter Lake, located just above the site of Migdol near today's Abu Hasan—where, as Exodus tells us, the Israelites were encamped. These sandbanks would just be firm enough to support a man or woman, but Pharaoh's heavy armored chariots would certainly have gotten stuck in the sands or sucked under altogether.

With their deliverance now secure, the question is, Where to go next? North of Etham ran the coastal road along the Mediterranean, later known as the Way of the Philistines. Eastward ran the Way of Shur across the Sinai Desert. Which route should Moses take?

As the next chapters of Exodus reveal, Moses chose neither. Instead, he decided to head south, along the coast of what is today the Gulf of Suez, retracing his steps as a fugitive so many years ago. His destination is the southern tip of the Sinai Peninsula, close to the mountain where he once herded the sheep of his father-in-law, Jethro. Quite simply, it is the only path through the desert he was familiar with.

Exodus offers a somewhat different explanation. "God did not lead them by way of the land of the Philistines, although that was

The Bounty of Ancient Egypt

The reality of daily survival in the Sinai Desert came as a shock to the Israelites. They nostalgically remembered the bounty of Egypt, "where we sat by the fleshpots and ate our fill of bread" (Exodus 17:3;16:3). The Hebrews had good reason to miss their former life in the Nile Delta. As the Rekhmire inscription states, even slaves received their allotment of "bread, beer and every good thing." A 19th Dynasty poem extolling the city of Pi-Ramesses, where the Hebrews reportedly lived, speaks of fields that are "full of supplies and food every day, its ponds with fish, and its lakes with birds." Here, there are "pomegranates, apples, and olives, figs of the orchard" in abundance. This variety would stand in sharp contrast to the Israelite diet during the early settlement in Canaan, when they eked out a living from the soil of the highlands, where the cultivation of wheat, vegetables, and fruits was far more difficult.

This depiction of Earth's bounty shows the wealth of Nebamun, a grain official from Thebes during the New Kingdom, 18th Dynasty.

nearer," the Bible says, "for God thought, 'If the people face war, they may change their minds and return to Egypt'" (Exodus 13:17). This suggests that on the coastal road, the fugitives would have run afoul of border patrols or units of the Egyptian army—not an unreasonable suggestion, given that this road was indeed Egypt's principal military artery to its vassal states up north.

Notwithstanding the questions about its historical roots, reconstructing the route of the Exodus as a literary exercise is fraught with challenges, principally because the place-names that the Bible gives us seldom correlate with sites on the ground. We must therefore look for other evidence to pinpoint the movement of the Israelites, at least as the seventh- and sixth-century scribes of the Book of Exodus envisioned it—possibly with the hindsight of many centuries later.

For example, the next stop on the march was the oasis of Marah, where the water was "bitter," but Moses made the water sweet (Exodus 15:22-23). The most likely location is the oasis of Uyun Musa ("springs of Moses" in Arabic), located some 25 miles from the Bitter Lakes. Even today, it still has a thermal well so rich in minerals that its water is flavored with a slight metallic taste. Another possible location is the cluster of hot springs at Hammam Fara'un Malun ("baths of the cursed pharaoh"), some three miles from Uyun Musa. From here, a trail leads through the Wadi Matalla and across the soft limestone plateau of Debbet el-Qerai to the ancient mining complex of Serabit el-Khadem, where Canaanite guest workers labored during Egypt's Middle Kingdom. Nearby is another large mining area, that of Wadi Maghareh ("valley of caves"), where malachite, copper, and turquoise had

been extracted since the days of Khufu, builder of the Great Pyramid in Giza. Discovered in 1809 and excavated by Harvard University in 1932, Wadi Maghareh has yielded tablets and inscriptions going back as far as the reign of King Djoser and King Sanakht of the 3rd Dynasty, as well as several monuments from the 12th Dynasty.

In other words, Moses chose the ancient Egyptian route to the principal mine centers of the Sinai. This is perhaps not surprising when we remember that the Midianites, also known as Kenites (a name that is perhaps related to the word *qain,* or "coppersmith," in Arabic) were renowned for their skills in copper (Numbers 24:21).

Paramount for the Hebrews' survival in the Sinai wilderness was the availability of water. According to Exodus, the Hebrews eventually found their way to "*Elim*, where there were 12 springs of water and 70 palm trees; and they camped there by the water" (Exodus 15:27). Quite possibly, Elim is the small grove known as

"Early Morning in the Wilderness of Shur" was painted by the British artist Frederick Goodall (1822-1904) in 1860. The site is on the western shore of the Red Sea.

Then he summoned Moses and Aaron in the night, and said,
"Rise up, go away from my people, both you and the Israelites!"

EXODUS 12:31

Wadi Gharandel, located some five miles from Serabit el-Khadem. "Elim" is a word that means "tamarisks," and even today the oasis is surrounded by a copse of date palms and tamarisks, the principal trees of the Sinai Desert.

Now that they had quenched their thirst, the Hebrews began to complain of hunger. In response, God promised Moses that he would "rain bread from heaven for you"; and indeed, "in the evening quails came up and covered the camp," ready for the taking, while in the morning there "was a fine flaky substance, as fine as frost on the ground" (Exodus 16:4;13-14). At first, the bewildered Israelites called it "manna," which may mean, "What is it?" But soon, some enterprising souls rolled it into dough and were able to bake bread.

What is remarkable about this story is that both quails and manna are known to the Bedouins of today. Manna *(Tamarix mannifera)* is the secretion of a small-scale insect that feeds off the sap from tamarisks. The sweet substance trickles to the ground where it can be collected and used as a sweetener or made into wafers. Even more astonishing is the presence of quail in the heart of the desert. As it happens, the Sinai Peninsula is positioned on the path of migrating birds, including quail, during their annual spring trek from Africa to cooler regions in the North. To this day, Bedouins in northern Sinai set up nets to capture them. By the early 2000s, the slaughter of quail became so widespread that the Egyptian government required Bedouins to obtain a quail hunting license. ■

ca 1224
Ramesses II dies
at age 90

ca 1224
Ramesses' son Merneptah
ascends the throne
in Egypt

ca 1214
The Merneptah Stele
is the first monument
to refer to "Israel"

ca 1214
Sethi, or Sethos II,
ascends the throne in Egypt

MOSES ON THE MOUNT

The Traditional Origin of the Torah—the Laws of Moses

After the sojourn in Elim, Moses turned away from the coastal region to plunge into the Wilderness of Sin, one of the most desolate places on the planet. Here, the ancient path leading into the Sinai first coils around the towering escarpments of the Jebel Serbal and the Jebel Tarfa before running down the pass of Watia. Along the way is a rock that the local Gabaly Bedouin call Hesi el-Khattatin ("spring hidden by the scribes"). In Bedouin lore, the scribes are Moses and Aaron.

Shortly after, the Israelites were confronted with the first military threat since escaping the clutches of Pharaoh. According to Exodus, this situation developed—not surprisingly—at one of the largest oases in all of Sinai, that of Rephidim. Today, it is known as Wadi Feiran (or El Hesweh), a large and fertile wadi about three miles in length, bordered by deep rows of palm trees. Although the oasis produces corn, barley, wheat, and tobacco, it is chiefly known for the quality of its dates, rumored to be the sweetest in all of the Near East. This is where, according to Exodus, Moses struck a rock and caused water to come from it (Exodus 17:6).

Wadi Feiran's fame goes back many thousands of years. Local inscriptions indicate the presence of passing caravans as early as the eighth and seventh centuries B.C.E. So the staging of Israel's first military clash in this stunning locale, surrounded on all sides by the Sinai massif, was an inspired choice.

Naturally, the local tribes took offense at seeing this multitude of people with their livestock overrunning their precious water wells, and they rushed to arms. The identification of these tribes as "Amalekites" is somewhat mysterious, however (Exodus 17:8). The descendants of Amalek, grandson of Esau, were a nomadic people who usually dwelled with their flocks in the southern Negev or near the great oasis of Qadesh-Barnea up north. But they defended the oasis with vigor.

Moses designated a man named Joshua as the commander of the Hebrew militia and then withdrew with Aaron to the top of the nearby hill. As Joshua led his men into battle, Moses discovered that whenever he "held up his hand, Israel prevailed; and whenever he

Pilgrims worship on the summit of Mount Sinai—the site, according to the Bible, where God spoke to Moses.

ca 1204
Siptah, son of Canaanite royal concubine, is king of Egypt

ca 1200
First use of flax to make linen in Egypt

ca 1200
First signs of raiders, the Sea Peoples, in the eastern Mediterranean

ca 1150
Mycenae's power is challenged by invading Dorian Greeks

Tall date palms mark the spot of the Wadi Feiran oasis in the Sinai, believed to be the location of Rephidim in the account of Exodus.

lowered his hand, Amalek prevailed" (Exodus 17:11). Aaron and another companion named Hur were quickly pressed into service to hold up both of Moses' arms, so that Joshua could continue battling the Amalekite host until sunset, when at last he defeated them.

JETHRO THE PRIEST

Immediately after this resounding victory, Jethro the priest arrived in the Israelite camp. This is the second time in the Exodus story that an encounter between Moses and God is preceded by Jethro's appearance. Jethro, says Exodus, had "heard of all that God had done for Moses and for his people Israel," which underscores the close relationship between this priest and the God of Abraham and Jacob—especially since Jethro then proceeded to bring "a burnt offering and sacrifices to God" (Exodus 18:12). A happy reunion followed, as "Moses bowed down and kissed him." Better yet, Jethro had also brought along Moses' wife, Zipporah, and their two sons, Gershom and Eliezer (Exodus 18:27).

The next day, Jethro sat down with Moses and advised him to create a proper organization, ruled by laws, to manage the unruly Israelites. "You must teach them ordinances and laws," he said. "Moreover, you must select out of all these people able men, who worship God, men of truth ... to rule over them as officers and judges" (Exodus 18:20-21).

Thus, Jethro prepared Moses for the great climax of the Exodus drama: the moment when God would hand him the laws that would govern the nation of Israel for all time. According to the Bible, this moment took place at a five-day march from Rephidim,

*When God finished speaking with Moses on Mount Sinai,
he gave him the two tablets of the covenant, tablets of stone,
written with the finger of God.*

EXODUS 31:18

in a place called Mount Sinai (also known as Mount Horeb, the place where God spoke to Moses from the burning bush). It has been traditionally identified with Jebel Musa, a rather forbidding mass of gray and pink granite that rises some 7,500 feet into the deep blue sky. This mountain is surrounded by several peaks of even greater height, including Jebel Katerin (8,651 feet) and Jebel Umm Shomar (8,482 feet), but Jebel Musa, "the Mount of Moses" in Arabic, has consistently remained the favorite identification for the place where Moses received the Ten Commandments. The only way to reach its summit is to climb a camel path from St. Catherine's Monastery, located at the foot of the mountain, which is usually undertaken in the hours before dawn. As the sun rises over this wild and craggy plateau, the visitor is presented with a breathtaking panorama of hills and desert, bathed in a golden light and stretching as far as the Gulf of Aqaba.

THE LAWS OF MOSES

Here, on this summit, God's covenant with Abraham, Isaac, and Jacob was ratified in a formal treaty between YHWH and his people. It stipulated that as long as the Hebrews remained faithful to their God and obeyed his laws, God would dwell in their land and protect them. This would become the dominant motif of the next division of Hebrew Scripture, the Books of the Prophets that document the history of ancient Israel.

The remainder of the Book of Exodus as well as the Books of Leviticus, Numbers, and Deuteronomy, spell out these laws in detail. Such legislation was not unique in the Bronze Age. The Babylonian Code of Hammurabi, one of the oldest written documents, predates the earliest origins of the Mosaic Laws by at least 500 years. In 282 entries, the Hammurabi Code prescribes a great variety of punishments and inducements for all members of society, from slave to nobleman, on the principle of "an eye for an eye, a tooth for a tooth."

The Laws of Moses, however, go well beyond the judicial measures of a centralized state. They specified, in great detail, a form of conduct by which humanity would be able to prosper, not only as a family and a community but also as a nation under the benevolent guidance of God. While much of the Mosaic Law, particularly Leviticus, is concerned with the Holiness Code governing the worship of YHWH, its sacrificial rites and the rules of ritual purity, its concern for social justice, makes the Torah stand out

among all of the legislative efforts of ancient prehistory. "You shall not strip your vineyard bare, or gather the fallen grapes of your vineyard," warns Leviticus. "[You] shall leave them for the poor and the alien" (Leviticus 19:10). Deuteronomy urges merchants and traders to be fair and just: "You shall have only a full and honest measure" (Deuteronomy 25:15). And judges and high

The Merneptah Stele (1213-1204 B.C.E.), from the pharaoh's funerary temple in Thebes, contains the only reference to Israel in ancient Egyptian sources.

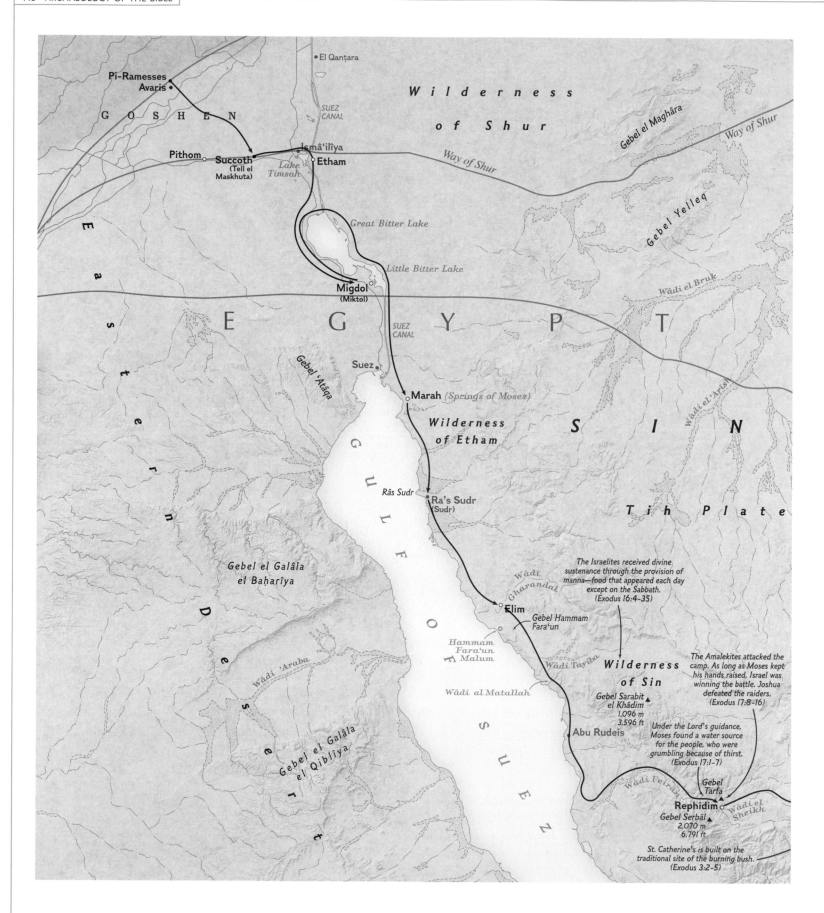

• El Qantara

Pi-Ramesses
Avaris •

GOSHEN

Wilderness

of Shur

Gebel el Maghâra

*SUEZ
CANAL*

Ismâ'ilîya

Pithom   Succoth   Etham

(Tell el
Maskhuta)

*Lake
Timsah*

Way of Shur

Gebel Yelleq

Great Bitter Lake

Little Bitter Lake

E a s t e r n

Migdol
(Miktol)

Wâdi el Bruk

E   G   Y   P   T

*SUEZ
CANAL*

Suez •

Marah *(Springs of Moses)*

Gebel 'Atâqa

Wilderness

of Etham

S   I   N

Râs Sudr   Ra's Sudr
(Sudr)

Tih Plate

G

*Gebel el Galâla
el Bahârîya*

U

*Wâdi
Gharandal*

The Israelites received divine
sustenance through the provision of
manna—food that appeared each day
except on the Sabbath.
(Exodus 16:4–35)

L

F

Elim

*Gebel Hammam
Fara'un*

*Hammam
Fara'un
Malum*

Wâdi Tayiba

Wilderness

of Sin

The Amalekites attacked the
camp. As long as Moses kept
his hands raised, Israel was
winning the battle. Joshua
defeated the raiders.
(Exodus 17:8–16)

D

Wâdi 'Araba

O

Wâdi al Matallah

*Gebel Sarabit
el Khâdim*
1,096 m
3,596 ft

Under the Lord's guidance,
Moses found a water source
for the people, who were
grumbling because of thirst.
(Exodus 17:1–7)

e

F

Abu Rudeis

*Gebel el Galâla
el Qiblîya*

S

Wâdi Feirân

*Gebel
Tarfa*

s

U

Rephidim   *Wâdi el
Sheikh*

Gebel Serbâl
2,070 m
6,791 ft

e

E

r

Z

St. Catherine's is built on the
traditional site of the burning bush.
(Exodus 3:2–5)

t

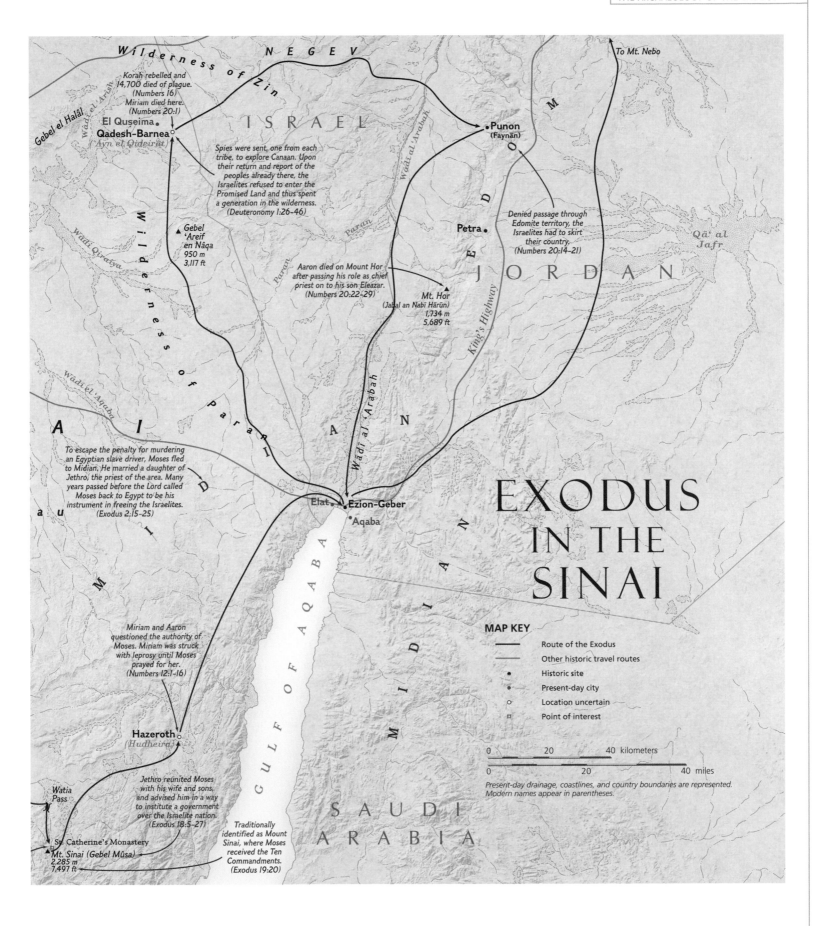

To Mt. Nebo

Wilderness of Zin N E G E V

Korah rebelled and 14,700 died of plague. (Numbers 16) Miriam died here. (Numbers 20:1)

I S R A E L

El Quṣeima
Qadesh-Barnea
('Ayn el Qideirāt)

Gebel el Halāl

Wādī el Arīsh

Spies were sent, one from each tribe, to explore Canaan. Upon their return and report of the peoples already there, the Israelites refused to enter the Promised Land and thus spent a generation in the wilderness. (Deuteronomy 1:26–46)

▲ *Gebel 'Areif en Nâqa 950 m 3,117 ft*

Punon
(Faynān)

E D O M

Petra •

Denied passage through Edomite territory, the Israelites had to skirt their country. (Numbers 20:14–21)

Qā' al Jafr

J O R D A N

Wādī al Arabah

Aaron died on Mount Hor after passing his role as chief priest on to his son Eleazar. (Numbers 20:22–29)

Wilderness of Paran

Wādī Qirațya

Paran

Paran

▲ *Mt. Hor (Jabal an Nabī Hārūn) 1,734 m 5,689 ft*

King's Highway

Wādī el Aqaba

A I I D

a u

To escape the penalty for murdering an Egyptian slave driver, Moses fled to Midian. He married a daughter of Jethro, the priest of the area. Many years passed before the Lord called Moses back to Egypt to be his instrument in freeing the Israelites. (Exodus 2:15–25)

P A R A N

Wādī al Arabah

N

Elat • • **Ezion-Geber**

• **Aqaba**

M I D I A N

EXODUS
IN THE
SINAI

M
I
D
I
a
N

Miriam and Aaron questioned the authority of Moses. Miriam was struck with leprosy until Moses prayed for her. (Numbers 12:1–16)

G U L F   O F   A Q A B A

MAP KEY

—————— Route of the Exodus

—————— Other historic travel routes

•———— Historic site

•———— Present-day city

○———— Location uncertain

▢———— Point of interest

Hazeroth
(Hudheira) ○

0   20   40 kilometers
0   20   40 miles

Present-day drainage, coastlines, and country boundaries are represented. Modern names appear in parentheses.

Watia Pass

Jethro reunited Moses with his wife and sons, and advised him in a way to institute a government over the Israelite nation. (Exodus 18:5–27)

▲ *St. Catherine's Monastery*
▲ *Mt. Sinai (Gebel Mûsa) 2,285 m 7,497 ft*

Traditionally identified as Mount Sinai, where Moses received the Ten Commandments. (Exodus 19:20)

S A U D I
A R A B I A

The Timna Valley in southern Israel has been the location of copper mines since the fifth millennium B.C.E. and has yielded the earliest evidence of camel bones from around the tenth century B.C.E.

deity El, and this type of idolatry would persist well into the period of the divided monarchy. King Jeroboam I of the Northern Kingdom of Israel, for example, commissioned two golden calves for the sanctuaries of YHWH in Bethel and Dan, to serve as the Lord's attendants. Some scholars have argued that Aaron's golden calf was not meant to displace God but to make him more tangible to the Israelites by drawing from Canaanite models.

When Moses descended from Mount Sinai, however, he was so incensed by this pagan image that he smashed the stone tablets of the Law and ordered 3,000 men to be put to death. Moses had to ascend Mount Sinai again so that the stone tablets could be written once more (Exodus 34:2).

Before long, the people of Israel were once again on the move. They were now headed for another Egyptian mining center, Ezion-Geber, near today's Eilat, led by guides from Midian. These guides moved the caravan from one major oasis to another, including the oasis of Hazeroth and the great oasis of Qadesh-Barnea.

The location of Hazeroth has been identified with the Bedouin oasis of Hudheira. It is the only oasis of note in this part of Sinai, so remote that even today a traveler can reach it only by camel. From here to Qadesh-Barnea, on the threshold of Canaan, is a mere 60 miles. But Moses realized that his exhausted people were not ready to enter the Promised Land. They would have to build an army first. Only then could the great conquest of Canaan begin. ■

officials are warned not to "distort justice; you must not show partiality" (Deuteronomy 16:19).

For as the Torah reminds its people, once "you were strangers in the land of Egypt" (Deuteronomy 10:19).

THE GOLDEN CALF

While Moses tarried on Mount Sinai, the Israelites grew impatient. According to Exodus, they "gathered around Aaron and said to him: 'Come, make gods for us, who shall go before us'" (Exodus 32:1). Rather than remaining steadfast in his faith, Aaron gave in. He told the people to collect all the gold in their possession and used it to create a golden calf for worship. He ordered a great feast, and all the Israelites "rose up to play" (Exodus 32:6).

The choice of a calf for this idol was no accident. A calf or bull, symbol of virility and strength, is associated with the Canaanite

The ancient Nabataean city of Avdat (or Obodat) was once a key stop on the incense route from today's Oman to the temples of the Near East and beyond.

Remember the long way that the Lord your God has led you these forty years in the wilderness, in order to humble you, testing you to know what was in your heart, whether or not you would keep his commandments.

DEUTERONOMY 8:2

THE ART OF THE NEW KINGDOM

Egyptian Art Flourishes Under the Kings of the 18th and 19th Dynasties

THE ROUGHLY 500-YEAR PERIOD OF EGYPT's NEW KINGDOM (CIRCA 1570-1292) SAW THE ANCIENT EMPIRE AT THE peak of its power and wealth. In an effort to forestall a repeat of the Hyksos disaster or other foreign invasions, these kings created buffer zones of vassal states, including Canaan, Edom, Moab, and Syria, in the Northeast and Nubia in the South. Buoyed by royal patronage, the arts flourished, as did the construction of monumental projects throughout Egypt, including the building of elaborate tombs in the Valley of the Kings. ∎

A wooden funerary stela shows the priest Hor with two assistants, named Taperet and Hany, worshipping the god Ra.

This elegant faience-like votive vase was dedicated to the dwarf god Bes, protector of pregnant women.

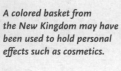

A colored basket from the New Kingdom may have been used to hold personal effects such as cosmetics.

A royal couple walks in the garden in this colored relief from the New Kingdom, 18th Dynasty (circa 1539-1292).

A beautiful polychrome vase with palmetto ornamentation and wide splayed orifice dates from the 19th Dynasty of the New Kingdom.

This temple-shaped funerary pendant of gilt wood with painted sacred symbols was believed to grant the deceased divine protection in the afterlife.

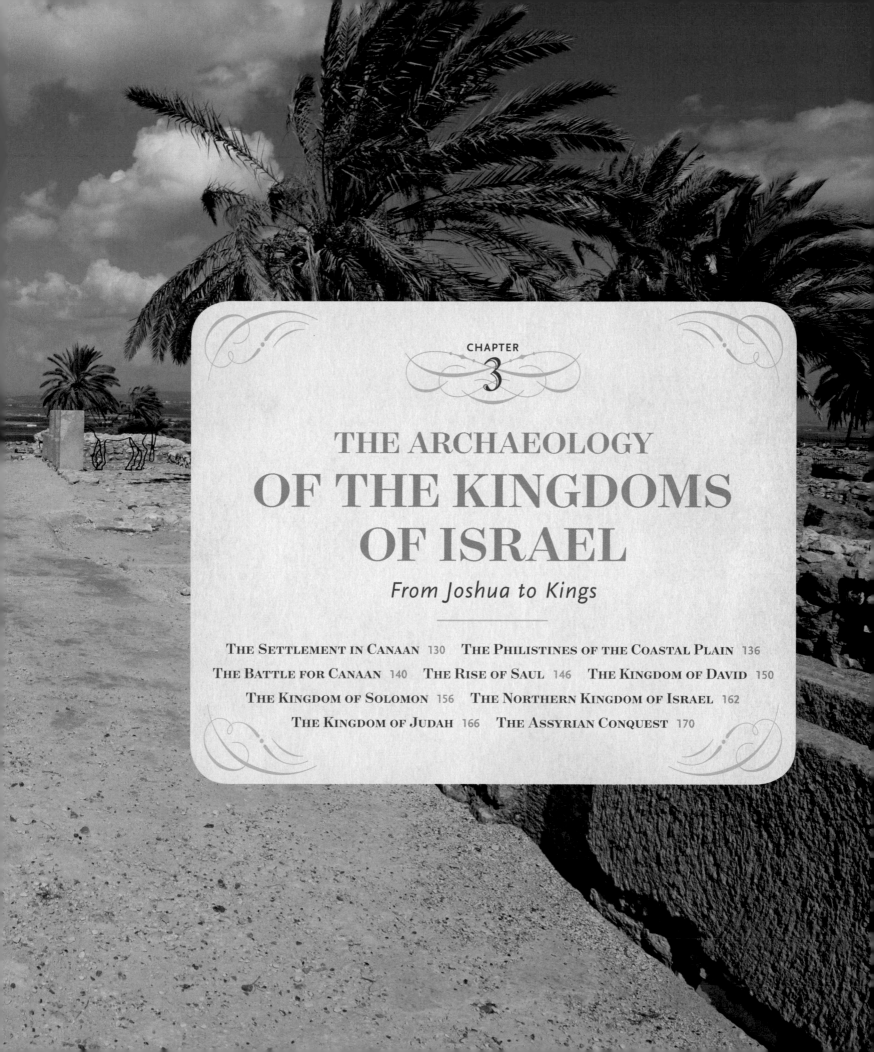

CHAPTER

3

THE ARCHAEOLOGY OF THE KINGDOMS OF ISRAEL

From Joshua to Kings

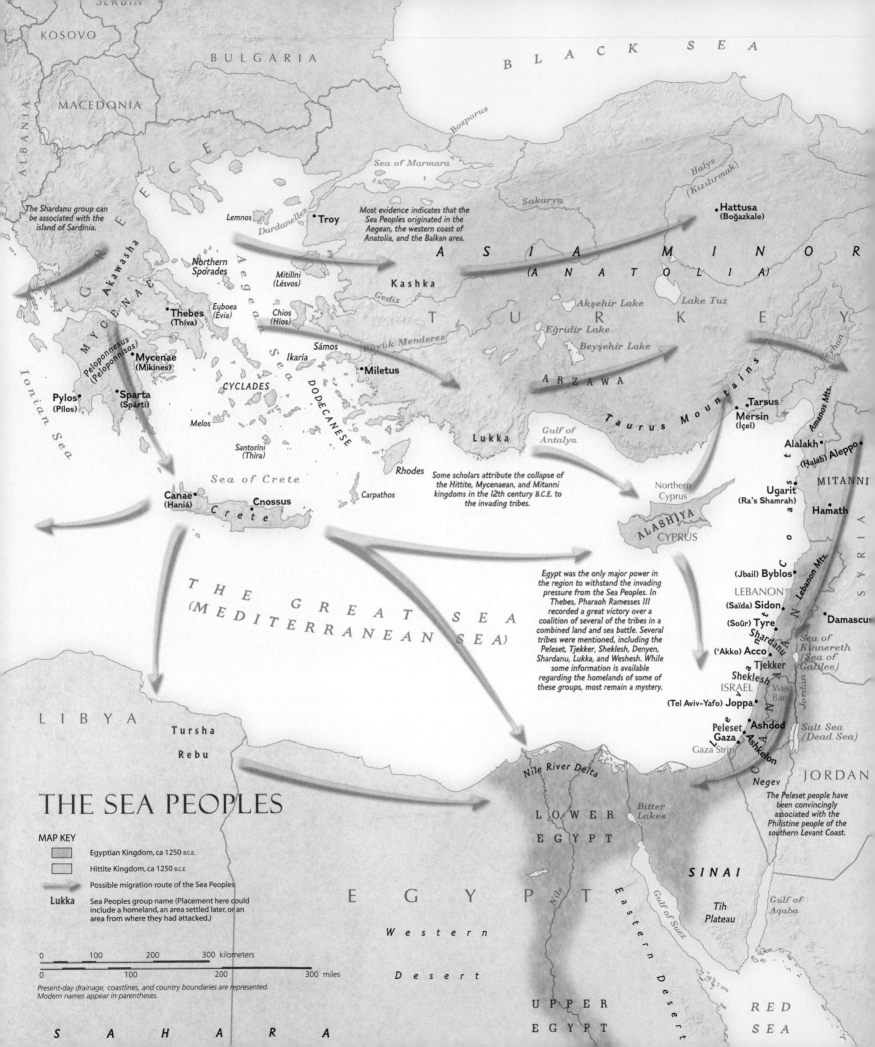

KOSOVO

BULGARIA

BLACK SEA

MACEDONIA

ALBANIA

SERBIA

Sea of Marmara

Bosporus

Dardanelles

The Shardanu group can be associated with the island of Sardinia.

Lemnos

Troy

Most evidence indicates that the Sea Peoples originated in the Aegean, the western coast of Anatolia, and the Balkan area.

A S I A   M I N O R

(A N A T O L I A)

Hattusa
(Boğazkale)

*Halys
(Kızılırmak)*

Sakarya

Akawasha

Northern
Sporades

Mitilíni
(Lésvos)

Kashka

Gediz

T U R K E Y

Akşehir Lake

Lake Tuz

G R E E C E

Thebes
(Thíva)

Euboea
(Évia)

Chios
(Híos)

Aegean Sea

Eğridir Lake

Beyşehir Lake

MYCENAE

Sámos

Ikaría

Büyük Menderes

A R Z A W A

Taurus Mountains

Amanos Mts.

Tarsus

Ceyhan

Peloponnesus
(Pelopónnisos)

Mycenae
(Mikínes)

Miletus

CYCLADES

Mersin
(İçel)

Ionian Sea

Pylos
(Pílos)

Sparta
(Spárti)

Melos

DODECANESE

Lukka

Gulf of Antalya

Alalakh

(Halab) **Aleppo**

MITANNI

Santoríni
(Thíra)

Rhodes

Some scholars attribute the collapse of the Hittite, Mycenaean, and Mitanni kingdoms in the 12th century B.C.E. to the invading tribes.

Northern
Cyprus

Ugarit
(Ra's Shamrah)

Hamath

Canae
(Haniá)

Cnossus

Sea of Crete

Carpathos

C r e t e

ALASHIYA

CYPRUS

(Jbail) **Byblos**

Egypt was the only major power in the region to withstand the invading pressure from the Sea Peoples. In Thebes, Pharaoh Ramesses III recorded a great victory over a coalition of several of the tribes in a combined land and sea battle. Several tribes were mentioned, including the Peleset, Tjekker, Sheklesh, Denyen, Shardanu, Lukka, and Weshesh. While some information is available regarding the homelands of some of these groups, most remain a mystery.

LEBANON

T H E   G R E A T   S E A

(M E D I T E R R A N E A N   S E A)

(Saïda) **Sidon**

(Soûr) **Tyre**

Damascus

Shardanu

Sea of Kinnereth (Sea of Galilee)

('Akko) **Acco**

Tjekker

Sheklesh

SYRIA

ISRAEL

West
Bank

L I B Y A

(Tel Aviv-Yafo) **Joppa**

Tursha

Peleset

Ashdod

Salt Sea (Dead Sea)

Rebu

Gaza

Ashkelon

Gaza Strip

JORDAN

Negev

THE SEA PEOPLES

Nile River Delta

L O W E R

E G Y P T

*Bitter
Lakes*

The Peleset people have been convincingly associated with the Philistine people of the southern Levant Coast.

MAP KEY

Egyptian Kingdom, ca 1250 B.C.E.

Hittite Kingdom, ca 1250 B.C.E.

Possible migration route of the Sea Peoples

Lukka Sea Peoples group name (Placement here could include a homeland, an area settled later, or an area from where they had attacked.)

S I N A I

*Gulf of
Aqaba*

0   100   200   300 kilometers

0   100   200   300 miles

Present-day drainage, coastlines, and country boundaries are represented. Modern names appear in parentheses.

E G Y P T

Nile

W e s t e r n

Eastern Desert

Gulf of Suez

Tih
Plateau

D e s e r t

U P P E R

E G Y P T

R E D

S E A

S A H A R A

*In those days the Philistines mustered
for war against Israel, and Israel went out
to battle against them.*

I SAMUEL 4:1

THE WORLD IN 1200 B.C.E.

The Beginning of the Iron Age, From 1250 B.C.E. to 582 B.C.E.

THE WORLD EXPERIENCED A NUMBER OF TRANSFORMATIVE CHANGES IN THE 13TH century B.C.E., which scholars have tried to encapsulate in the term "Iron Age." Although the growing sophistication of iron metallurgy was certainly a key feature of this new era, this development did not occur simultaneously in all of the major world cultures of the time. But most historians accept that in the Near East at least, the replacement of bronze with iron tools accelerated between 1300 and 1100 B.C.E. The idea that it was the Hittites who perfected ironwork in Anatolia before introducing it throughout the Near East has now been abandoned by most archaeologists, particularly since similar developments took place elsewhere in the world. The adoption of iron tools in Europe, for example, was almost simultaneous with the introduction in the Near East. In China, by contrast, the Iron Age did not begin until after the tenth century B.C.E., although in India, iron metallurgy was first practiced as early as the 16th century B.C.E., as evidenced by objects from Hyderabad and Lahuradewa. In Africa, where bronze was hardly ever used (with the exception of the Egyptian colony of Nubia, today's Sudan), the introduction of iron came only around 550 B.C.E. after a long period in which stone remained the primary material for tools.

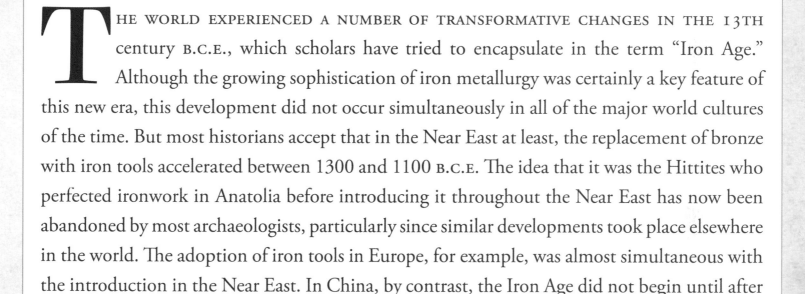

Preceding pages: *This structure near the courtyard of the fortress of Megiddo has been identified by some scholars as stables and stone troughs, built by either King Solomon or ninth-century King Ahab.* **Right:** *A cover of a cosmetic box from Ugarit shows a fertility goddess, possibly Asherah, with rams, carved from elephantine ivory and dated around 1200 B.C.E.*

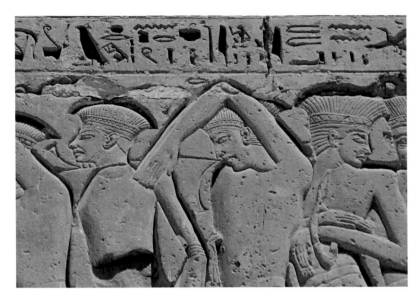

This detail of captured Sea Peoples or Peleset prisoners appears on the mortuary temple of Ramesses III at Medinet Habu.

Another, and perhaps even more important, innovation of this era was the emergence of linear alphabets—in contrast to the pictographic and cuneiform writing of the Bronze Age—that produced three distinct variations: (1) the Phoenician alphabet, which took form in the 11th century B.C.E.; (2) the Hebrew alphabet, which emerged in the tenth century B.C.E.; and (3) distinct Aramaic alphabets that would become widespread after the sixth century B.C.E. under the influence of both the Phoenician and Hebrew models. Because of Phoenicia's extensive trade contacts with the Mediterranean world, the Phoenician alphabet would strongly influence the emergence of the Greek alphabet, which is the basis for our modern Latin-based style of writing. Tantalizing clues of early Hebrew, meanwhile, can be glimpsed on several tenth-century pottery sherds, or *ostraca*; seals stamped on the handles of vessels prior to transportation; inscriptions on arrowheads, the metal tip of an arrow; and early tablets, such as the remarkable Gezer Tablet, believed to be a writing exercise for children in the form of a calendar for planting and harvesting.

Politically, the beginning of the Iron Age was also a time of great instability and turmoil, caused by the wholesale movement of different peoples throughout the Near East—including, conceivably, the Hebrew refugees from Egypt. An inscription in the Great Temple of Karnak from 1200 B.C.E. is one of the first to alert the nation to this development, citing the influx of five distinct groups of migrants. The name "Peleset" (*P-r-s-t* in Egyptian hieroglyphics), which would play such a disruptive role in Canaan and early Israel, is not mentioned until some ten years later, in the mortuary Temple of Ramesses III at Medinet Habu. But these inscriptions inspired the 19th-century Louvre Egyptologist Emmanuel de Rougé to coin the phrase *les peuples de la mer* (Sea Peoples), and this name has stuck. Their rise is also attested by contemporary Assyrian records, which refer to the Sea Peoples as *Ahhlamu* or "Wanderers."

Who were these seaborne migrants, and what drove them to invade parts of Anatolia, Syria, Canaan, and Egypt? A variety of theories have been offered, most recently in Eric Cline's book *1177 B.C.: The Year Civilization Collapsed*. Some of these include the decline of the Mycenaean civilization, the collapse of the Hittite Empire, and the attendant rupture in trade across the Aegean Sea. Some historians also suspect that the after-effects of the great eruption of the volcano at Thera may have played a role, though this would require a redating of this cataclysmic event by at least 200 years (an idea that is not corroborated by carbon-dating tests). According to the Bible, the Philistines came from "Caphtor" (either Crete or Cyprus), which may not be far from the truth (Amos 9:7, Jeremiah 47:4).

What is clear, however, is that the vast migration of Sea Peoples and other migrant communities caused a major realignment of the Near East. In the words of Hittitologist Gary Beckman, "no land could stand before their arms." The great city of Ugarit was utterly destroyed; one of the last Ugaritic letters, addressed to the king of Alasiya (modern Cyprus), reads: "My father, behold, the enemy's ships came here; my cities were burned, and they did evil things in my country."

A 13th-century terra-cotta sieve jug in Mycenaean style includes a strainer built in the vessel's spout to retain sediment from the bottom of the vessel.

Even Egypt came close to being torn asunder by the Peleset steamroller, as we will see shortly. When these migrant peoples finally suspended their campaigns to settle along the coast of Canaan, only the kingdoms of Sidon, Byblos, and Carchemish (northern Phoenicia and Syria) emerged relatively unscathed from the ordeal.

It was perhaps the misfortune—or good fortune, depending on one's point of view—of the early Israelites that their settlement in Canaan, the Promised Land, would coincide with these transformative changes in the Near East. On the one hand, the threat of the Peleset—the Philistines—would distract native Canaanite forces as well as the Egyptian military, which still considered Canaan a vassal territory. This gave the Hebrews in the highlands the necessary breathing room to consolidate their settlements. But on the other hand, once Canaan's military strength was exhausted, the Philistines became a major existential threat to the nascent nation of Israel, as documented in the Books of Joshua, Judges, and Kings. The federation of Philistine coastal cities, known as Philistia, would remain a potent force in the centuries to come, when the region fell victim to Assyrian aggression. One stela by the eighth century B.C.E. Assyrian king Adad-nirari reads: "I ordered the numerous army of Assyria to march against Palestine [Pa-la-áš-tu]," which may show that the term "Philistia" was already being mutated to "Palestine."

Perhaps most significant, the Iron Age is a period in which biblical stories are increasingly attested by archaeological evidence. For the first time, we see that certain figures in the Bible—including some kings of Israel and Judah—are documented in nonbiblical sources as well. ■

The explosion of the volcano at Thera (modern Santorini) in Greece left a large caldera or crater, now a large lagoon, still visible today.

THE SETTLEMENT IN CANAAN

Israelites Establish Communities in the Canaanite Highlands

U p to this point, our narrative has of necessity been based on hypothesis, largely informed by circumstantial evidence. By and large, the author(s) of the Five Books of Moses were not so much interested in writing history as in making a strong argument for the theological underpinnings of Israel's prehistory and specifying the conditions under which a future nation of Israel should honor its covenantal relationship with God. For example, the suggestion that the pharaoh described in the Book of Exodus could be Ramesses II is largely based on the reference in the biblical text to the cities of Pithom and Pi-Ramesses, which were built during the king's reign, though any of his immediate successors might fit that role as well.

The speculative nature of our quest changes considerably when we turn to the second division of the Hebrew Bible, referred to as *Nevi'im*, or "the Prophets." This includes the books of the so-called former prophets (Joshua, Judges, Samuel, and Kings), with stories of prophets such as Samuel, Nathan, Elijah, and Elisha, and the latter prophets (including Isaiah, Jeremiah, Ezekiel, and the 12 Minor Prophets). With these books, the biblical narrative shifts to a clear chronological saga that aims to record the rise of the kingdoms of Israel and its eventual fall to Assyrian and Babylonian aggression.

A majority of scholars have embraced the idea, first proposed by German scholar Martin Noth, that the Book of Deuteronomy originally formed part of the group of former prophets (Joshua, Judges, Samuel, and Kings) rather than the Torah. The reason is that the author(s) of these books see Israel's history through a consistent prism of covenant theology—of judging the nation by its ability (or failure) to abide by God's covenant. That is why this grouping is often called the Deuteronomist history. Recent research, pioneered by American scholar Frank Moore Cross, suggests that the Deuteronomist collection was compiled during and after the reign of King Josiah in the seventh century B.C.E., probably based on both oral and written traditions that were circulating about the history of ancient Israel, and that this canon was completed after the Babylonian exile (586-537 C.E.).

If this is true, then it is immediately clear that the span of time between these scribes and the events they wrote about is much shorter than with regard to the saga of the Patriarchs. It is therefore more plausible to create a historical framework for the stories in this grouping than for the narrative of Genesis and Exodus.

ca 1230	ca 1207	ca 1200	ca 1200
Israelites destroy Hazor	**Merneptah Stele refers to Israel**	**A four-room house appears in Canaan**	**Beginning of Iron Age I in the Near East**

Pictured is a reconstruction of the Shrine of the Steles, a Canaanite temple believed to have been destroyed around 1230 C.E., as it was found on Hazor by Yigael Yadin in 1955.

A large krater or mixing vessel with Mycenaean geometric motifs, dated around the 13th century B.C.E., was excavated in northern Israel.

ca 1185
Reign of Ramesses III
begins in Egypt

ca 1177
Invasion of Egypt by
the Sea Peoples is repulsed

ca 1150
Philistines consolidate
their territory in Canaan

ca 1150
Dark Age of
Greece begins

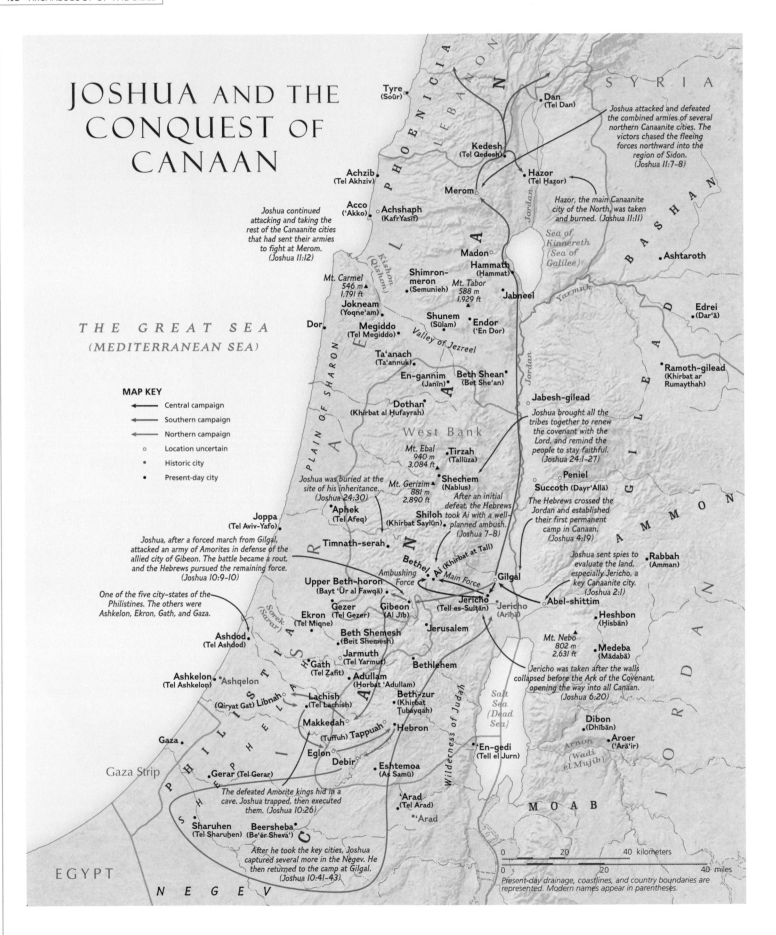

JOSHUA AND THE CONQUEST OF CANAAN

Tyre
(Soûr)

PHOENICIA

Dan
(Tel Dan)

Joshua attacked and defeated
the combined armies of several
northern Canaanite cities. The
victors chased the fleeing
forces northward into the
region of Sidon.
(Joshua 11:7-8)

Kedesh
(Tel Qedesh)

Achzib
(Tel Akhziv)

Hazor
(Tel Hazor)

Merom

Hazor, the main Canaanite
city of the North, was taken
and burned. (Joshua 11:11)

Joshua continued
attacking and taking the
rest of the Canaanite cities
that had sent their armies
to fight at Merom.
(Joshua 11:12)

Acco
('Akko)

Achshaph
(KafrYasîf)

Sea of
Kinnereth
(Sea of
Galilee)

Ashtaroth

Madon

Hammath
(Hammat)

BASHAN

Mt. Carmel
546 m ▲
1,791 ft

Shimron-
meron
(Semunieh)

Mt. Tabor
588 m
1,929 ft ▲

Jabneel

Jokneam
(Yoqne'am)

Dor

Megiddo
(Tel Megiddo)

Shunem
(Sûlam)

Endor
('En Dor)

Edrei
(Dar'ā)

THE GREAT SEA
(MEDITERRANEAN SEA)

Valley of Jezreel

Yarmuk

Ta'anach
(Ta'annuk)

En-gannim
(Janîn)

Beth Shean
(Bet She'an)

Ramoth-gilead
(Khirbat ar
Rumaythah)

PLAIN OF SHARON

Dothan
(Khirbat al Ḥufayrah)

Jabesh-gilead

MAP KEY

◄─── Central campaign
◄─── Southern campaign
◄─── Northern campaign
○ Location uncertain
• Historic city
● Present-day city

West Bank

Mt. Ebal
940 m
3,084 ft

Tirzah
(Tallūza)

Joshua brought all the
tribes together to renew
the covenant with the
Lord, and remind the
people to stay faithful.
(Joshua 24:1-27)

Peniel

Joshua was buried at the
site of his inheritance.
(Joshua 24:30)

Mt. Gerizim ▲
881 m
2,890 ft

Shechem
(Nablus)

Succoth (Dayr'Allā)

The Hebrews crossed the
Jordan and established
their first permanent
camp in Canaan.
(Joshua 4:19)

Shiloh
(Khirbat Saylūn)

After an initial
defeat, the Hebrews
took Ai with a well-
planned ambush.
(Joshua 7-8)

Joppa
(Tel Aviv-Yafo)

Aphek
(Tel Afeq)

Joshua, after a forced march from Gilgal,
attacked an army of Amorites in defense of the
allied city of Gibeon. The battle became a rout,
and the Hebrews pursued the remaining force.
(Joshua 10:9-10)

Timnath-serah

Bethel

Ai (Khirbat at Tall)

Gilgal

Joshua sent spies to
evaluate the land,
especially Jericho, a
key Canaanite city.
(Joshua 2:1)

Rabbah
(Amman)

One of the five city-states of the
Philistines. The others were
Ashkelon, Ekron, Gath, and Gaza.

Ambushing
Force

Main Force

Upper Beth-horon
(Bayt 'Ûr al Fawqā)

Jericho
(Tell es-Sultān)

Jericho
(Arīḥā)

Abel-shittim

Heshbon
(Ḥisbān)

Ekron
(Tel Miqne)

Gezer
(Tel Gezer)

Gibeon
(Al Jîb)

Ashdod
(Tel Ashdod)

Beth Shemesh
(Beit Shemesh)

Jerusalem

Mt. Nebo
802 m
2,631 ft

Medeba
(Mādabā)

Jarmuth
(Tel Yarmut)

Bethlehem

Ashkelon
(Tel Ashkelon)

Ashqelon

Gath
(Tel Zafit)

Adullam
(Horbat 'Adullam)

Beth-zur
(Khirbat
Ṭubāyqah)

Jericho was taken after the walls
collapsed before the Ark of the Covenant,
opening the way into all Canaan.
(Joshua 6:20)

Lachish
(Tel Lachish)

Libnah

(Qiryat Gat)

Makkedah

Tappuah
(Tuffuh)

Hebron

Salt
Sea
(Dead
Sea)

Dibon
(Dhībān)

Gaza

Eglon

Debir

Eshtemoa
(As Samū)

En-gedi
(Tell el Jurn)

Aroer
('Arā'ir)

Gaza Strip

Gerar
(Tel Gerar)

The defeated Amorite kings hid in a
cave. Joshua trapped, then executed
them. (Joshua 10:26)

'Arad
(Tel Arad)

Arnon
(Wadi
el Mujib)

MOAB

Wilderness of Judah

EGYPT

Sharuhen
(Tel Sharuhen)

Beersheba
(Be'ér Sheva')

After he took the key cities, Joshua
captured several more in the Negev. He
then returned to the camp at Gilgal.
(Joshua 10:41-43)

'Arad

NEGEV

0   20   40 kilometers
0   20   40 miles

Present-day drainage, coastlines, and country boundaries are
represented. Modern names appear in parentheses.

SYRIA

LEBANON

GILEAD

AMMON

JORDAN

PHILISTIA

Kishon
(Qishon)

Jordan

Jordan

Sorek
(Sarar)

This tower and surrounding fortifications in ancient Jericho date from the Middle Bronze Age IIA and IIB (1950-1550 B.C.E.).

Many historians are prepared to accept, for example, that the story of Joshua's "conquest" is set in the second half of the 13th century B.C.E., given that by 1207—the date of the Merneptah Stele—an entity known as Israel must have existed in the Canaan region.

Another factor that will favor us in exploring the archaeological context of these stories is that their location, the land of Israel, is much smaller and more accessible than the wide expanses of Mesopotamia, Egypt, and Sinai. In addition, this narrow strip of land has seen an unprecedented level of excavation activity that began in the 19th century and accelerated substantially after the Six Day War of 1967, when the West Bank and the Old City of Jerusalem came under Israeli control. These excavations, which in many places are ongoing, have yielded a rich harvest of data that can help us to put the biblical stories in a historical context—though this doesn't always yield the results we might expect.

THE CONQUEST OF JERICHO

A case in point is the first major campaign for the conquest of Canaan: the Battle of Jericho. As described in Deuteronomy, Moses did not live to see that day. On the eve of the Hebrews' crossing of the Jordan, the great leader went up Mount Nebo, where God showed him the hills of the Promised Land. And there he died and was buried in an unmarked grave (Deuteronomy 34:6).

Joshua was designated as the leader to take the Israelites into Canaan. He had previously shown his mettle in the battle against the Amalekites at Rephidim, and he later formed part of the reconnaissance team sent to explore the lay of the land (Exodus 17:9; Numbers 13:17). His elevation showed that the Israelites now needed a bold and imaginative military commander rather than a spiritual guide and prophet.

What follows next is undoubtedly one of the most famous passages in the Bible. For six days, Joshua and his troops marched around the walls of Jericho. In the middle of their column was the Ark of the Covenant containing the sacred tablets of Moses, accompanied by seven priests blasting away on their war horns. On the

seventh day, the Book of Joshua says, the Israelite army repeated the military parade, but as the soldiers finished their seventh turn, with the priests blowing the rams' horns, Joshua rallied his people to a mighty war cry. The walls "fell down flat" (Joshua 6:20).

As we saw, Jericho is one of the oldest continuously inhabited cities on Earth. Digging through the tell (a mound of successive layers of habitation) of Tell es-Sultan, archaeologists have identified no fewer than 20 successive settlements. This revealed that Jericho was indeed a flourishing city during the Middle Bronze Age, but that its destruction occurred much earlier, in either 1400 or even 1550 B.C.E. (the actual date is still the subject of debate). What's more, British archaeologist Kathleen Kenyon did find massive, six-foot-thick walls, but these were demolished sometime before the sixth millennium B.C.E., most likely as a result of an earthquake. When the city was later rebuilt, it surrounded itself with a rampart of packed mud walls—not much of a defense against a determined enemy. Here again, as Eric Cline has suggested, the biblical narrative may have been inspired by an ancient saga—that of the Ugaritic Legend of Keret of the 14th century B.C.E. According to this legend, King Keret besieged the city of Udum for six days, then attacked with his forces amid a huge blast of noise. The city promptly surrendered.

The Lord spoke to Joshua son of Nun ... "Now proceed to cross the Jordan, you and all this people, into the land that I am giving to them, to the Israelites."

JOSHUA 1:1-2

A Military Disadvantage

If the Israelites had indeed tried to conquer Canaan by military means, they would have faced a number of disadvantages. To begin with, they were a hardscrabble force, raised in the desert, without any military experience—unlike the Canaanite warriors who had been bloodied in decades past by battles with Egyptians, Hittites, and other rival cities. Worse, the Israelites lacked the implements of modern Iron Age warfare—such as composite bows, chariots, or battering rams—that the Assyrians would use to great effect when it was their turn to invade this territory. The composite bow was a particularly effective weapon. Developed during the 13th century, it used laminated layers of wood to create a bow of tremendous propellant strength that could outrange traditional bows by far. All this may have motivated Joshua's strategy of attacking the sparsely populated Jordan Valley, with Jericho as its first major objective.

This situation is repeated when we follow the exploits of Joshua through the Bible. Harvard archaeologist Lawrence Stager, who made a study of Joshua's campaign, has shown that of the 31 cities said to be taken by Joshua and the Israelites, 20 have been identified by excavation sites. Of these, the vast majority show no evidence of violent destruction in the late 13th century B.C.E. For example, despite extensive excavations at the site identified as Ai, the next city said to be destroyed by Joshua, there is no evidence of any occupation between 2400 and 1200 B.C.E.

The exception may be the cities of Lachish and Hazor. Lachish was a key center of Egyptian occupation forces during the 18th Dynasty and became sufficiently prominent to merit a description in the Amarna Letters as Lakisha-Lakiša. The Bible states that Joshua "smote it with the edge of the sword, and every person in it" (Joshua 10:32). And indeed the site, known as Tel Lachish, shows clear signs of violent destruction during the Early Iron Age. New excavations by archaeologist David Ussishkin, however, show that the city was actually destroyed after 1150 B.C.E., which puts it outside the putative time frame of Joshua's conquest. That still leaves open the possibility that Lachish was destroyed at a later date as the result of clashes between Canaanite and Israelite forces. What's more, a recent article has revealed the discovery of another layer at Tel Lachish (Level VII), which may indeed have been destroyed in the latter part of the 13th century.

The only city that shows clear and unambiguous evidence of destruction during the putative period of Joshua's campaign was one of the most powerful cities of Upper Canaan—the royal acropolis of Hazor. At its peak, Hazor had a population of more than 15,000, with active trade links throughout Egypt, Anatolia, and Syria. It also boasted one of the most sophisticated courts in Canaan, with singers and musicians whose excellence was praised in some of the Mari tablets. Not surprisingly, the Bible calls the ruler of Hazor the king of "all Canaan" (Judges 4:2). Indeed, this king is said to have formed an alliance of Canaanite cities to defeat the Israelites. One of the tablets found at Hazor refers to a king named Ibni-Addu, while the Amarna Letters mention a king called 'Abdi-Tirshi. These names are etymologically similar to the name

French painter and illustrator James Tissot (1836-1902) painted "The Seven Trumpets of Jericho" around 1900.

A cuneiform tablet found in the excavations of Hazor and dated to the 18th century B.C.E. appears to be a description of a lawsuit.

"King Jabin" described in the Book of Joshua (Joshua 11:1). Perhaps "Ibni/'Abdi" or "Jabin" was a dynastic name adopted by all of Hazor's kings.

According to the Book of Joshua, the Israelites succeeded in defeating and burning the city (Joshua 11:1-12). In the 1950s, renowned archaeologist Yigael Yadin discovered physical traces of soot and burned stone among the excavated remains of Jabin's palace, which he identified as evidence of the biblical account. Recent attempts to ascribe this destruction to Egyptian or Philistine forces, or perhaps an internal uprising, are compelling but have as yet failed to identify any substantive evidence.

Even if we accept that Hazor was destroyed by Joshua, we are still left with the problem that most other cities cited in his conquest were not. As a result, most scholars believe that the emergence of Israelite settlement in Canaan was probably a gradual process of infiltration that only occasionally resulted in armed conflict. As noted before, this was a period of great instability. The Israelites happened to be one of several migrating peoples passing in and out of the region—thus weakening the ability of local Canaanite cities to respond. One could thus imagine that the story of the settlement was later telescoped into a hero saga, buttressed by great military victories, in order to affirm the legitimacy of Israelite settlement in this volatile region. ∎

THE PHILISTINES OF THE COASTAL PLAIN

The Sea Peoples Invade the Lands of the Fertile Crescent

If anyone had asked a Canaanite farmer at the beginning of the 12th century B.C.E. to identify the greatest threat to his family and property, chances are that his answer would not have been "the Israelites" but rather "the Philistines." Unlike the Israelite settlers, the Philistines, or Peleset, were a potent, battle-hardened, and highly experienced military force that was plowing through the Near East like a scythe.

Such was their reputation that even the kings of Egypt's 20th Dynasty became alarmed. It wasn't just the Philistines who threatened the Egyptian Empire, but a veritable confederacy of several Sea Peoples, including such foreign-sounding tribes as the Shekelesh, the Teresh, and the Weshesh. The master plan of this coalition was to undertake a brilliant two-pronged invasion of Lower Egypt using both land and seaborne forces. Most likely, Egypt had been their ultimate objective all along as they fought their way down south through Anatolia, Syria, and Canaan, for behind the troops came a long baggage train of women, children, and livestock.

As evidenced by reliefs on the mortuary Temple of Ramesses III in Medinet Habu, the Philistines and their allied forces were well equipped. Protected by body armor and wielding spears and swords, they hurtled down the plain toward the Egyptian border on their fast chariots, each pulled by two horses. At the same time, the Teresh landed their amphibious forces along the Mediterranean coast in an attempt to confuse and split the Egyptian defenses. "They came with fire prepared before them, forward to Egypt," the hieroglyphics at Medinet Habu declare breathlessly.

A mighty battle ensued. The reliefs of Medinet Habu's Second Pylon indicate

King Ramesses III appears before the triad of Memphis: Ptah; his consort, the goddess Sekhmet; and Nefertum, god of the lotus in the Great Harris Papyrus; dated around 1150 B.C.E.

that Ramesses III established a defensive line at Djahy, the Egyptian name for the southern coastal region of Canaan. From here, his defenses ran all the way to the "mouths of the river," the Nile Delta. Ramesses was determined to stop the invaders on the beaches, before they could disperse into the dense network of the Nile tributaries and take control of the orchards and wheat fields of the delta. At first, it looked like he might have succeeded; the enemy land forces were cut to pieces and scattered in all directions. But the Egyptians were land warriors, not a seafaring people. Egypt had never fought a naval battle in home waters, and Ramesses' foes were numerically superior. But Ramesses had wisely crewed his river galleys "from bow to stern with valiant warriors bearing their arms, soldiers of the choicest of Egypt, being like lions roaring upon the mountain-tops." By posting his best archers on the ships, Ramesses had turned his weakest asset into a formidable attack formation. As soon as the enemy ships came within range, clouds of Egyptian arrows rained down on them. The Sea Peoples withdrew. The king had halted the Sea Peoples and pushed them back toward the coast of Canaan, where they would settle at last.

Thus ends the triumphant account of the king's exploits on the panels at Medinet Habu. Elated, Ramesses posted monuments of his spectacular victory throughout his realm; one even found its way to the residence of the Egyptian governor in Beth Shean. But Egyptian kings tended to overstate their glorious achievements. The Great Harris Papyrus found in a tomb at Medinet Habu boasts that the Philistines "were reduced to ashes," but clearly they were not; some archaeologists estimate that the first Philistine settlement in Canaan

ca 1125
Israelites and Canaanites clash near Megiddo

ca 1100
Phoenicians modify Proto-Canaanite alphabetic script

ca 1075
Egyptian New Kingdom ends

ca 1025
Samuel anoints Saul as king of Israel

The excavation of the mortuary temple of Ramesses III in the 19th century revealed the rich polychrome decoration of Egyptian temples.

This is the land that still remains: all the regions of the Philistines ... there are five rulers of the Philistines, those of Gaza, Ashdod, Ashkelon, Gath, and Ekron.

JOSHUA 13:2-3

A large Philistine krater or mixing vessel with handles and wide-open orifice betrays the influence of Aegean pottery.

ca 1000
Hebrew alphabet
emerges

ca 1000
Beginning
of Iron Age II

ca 1000
Phoenicians establish colonies
in Mediterranean

ca 1000
King David conquers
Jebusite city of Jerusalem

A Philistine Temple

The Book of Judges relates how a man named Samson, who possessed almost superhuman strength, was captured by the Philistines and brought into their Temple of Dagon. Standing between the "two middle pillars" of the hall, Samson pushed the stone columns and brought down the roof, killing every last soul (Judges 16:29-30). In 1971, a team of excavators led by Israeli archaeologist Amihai Mazar uncovered the remains of three Philistine temples on Tell Qasile, north of modern Tel Aviv. Mazar determined that one temple, measuring 46 by 26 feet, was destroyed by fire around 980 B.C.E. Interestingly, its roof rested on a huge crossbeam that in turn was supported by two large pillars of cedarwood, each planted on a round limestone base.

numbered around 25,000 and eventually grew to 30,000. Equally remarkable is the fact that Ramesses did not pursue the fleeing enemy forces, as standard Egyptian doctrine would have required him to do. Rather than ousting them from the Egyptian Empire, the king watched helplessly as they settled on his doorstep.

A more realistic assessment, as some scholars have argued, is that the Philistines simply chose to settle on the southern coast of Canaan on their own accord. One scenario even suggests that Ramesses III actually gave them this strip of land—which technically was still within the Egyptian sphere of influence—as part of the negotiations to keep them out of Egypt proper.

THE BIRTH OF PHILISTIA

Thus was born the confederacy of Philistine cities that in the years to come would wreak such havoc on Canaan and the Israelites. As attested by both the Bible and archaeological evidence, the cities in the region of Philistia were Ashdod, Ashkelon, Ekron, Gaza, and Gath, each ruled by a local king. Of these five (also known as the Philistine "Pentapolis"), all have been excavated except Gaza, because its ancient tell is covered by modern buildings and the Gaza Strip has been controlled by the militant Palestinian group Hamas since 2003.

Virtually all of these cities were conquered by force. For example, the excavations at Tel Miqne, site of ancient Ekron, showed that after its founding before the Early Bronze Age, the town experienced rapid growth around 1600 B.C.E. before its destruction during the Sea Peoples' invasions of the late 13th century B.C.E. The Philistines

Burial using ceramic anthropoid coffins has long been associated with the Philistines, but new research shows it was widespread in Egypt and Canaan as well.

During the Bronze Age, Ashkelon was an important seaport for Canaanites and later, for the population of Philistia. Inset: This fragment with an inscription in Hebrew was discovered in Ashkelon but probably dates to a much later era.

then settled there around 1180 B.C.E. and fortified the city in the years to come, no doubt because Ekron sat on the highly volatile border between Philistia and Judah (Joshua 13:3).

Modern excavations have shown that all of the early Philistine settlements shared a strong cultural tradition with Cyprus and Aegean regions under influence from Mycenae, as witnessed by the bichrome, red and black geometric style of their pottery (known as Mycenaean IIIC). But the Philistines also introduced innovations of their own, such as the use of unperforated loom weights in their looms; a fondness for the Greek custom of mixing water with wine; the worship of a number of foreign female deities; and a diet heavily dependent on pork, supplied by large herds of swine. As Penn State's Ann E. Killebrew has noted, at both Tel Miqne/Ekron and Ashkelon, excavators have identified a 15 percent increase in pig bones at the expense of sheep and goats during Iron Age I. No such increase in pig consumption has been observed anywhere else in Canaan.

Another unique feature of Philistine life was its funerary cult. The Philistines buried their deceased in clay anthropoid coffins, several samples of which have survived. They may betray an influence from Egyptian models. In ancient Egypt, a clay coffin engraved with basic humanoid features was the preferred burial for the working classes, who could not afford the expense of full Egyptian embalmment and interment. Some scholars have challenged this assessment, however, since no large Philistine cemeteries have as yet been uncovered, and most anthropoid coffins were found in border regions with Egypt.

And so, by the middle of the 12th century B.C.E., a third group other than the local Canaanites and Israelites began to compete for the scarce water and land resources of Canaan. It was only a matter of time before these headstrong people would come into conflict with the equally headstrong and determined Israelite settlers. ■

THE BATTLE FOR CANAAN

Israelites Clash With Rival Groups Over the Region's Resources

For the next two centuries, says the Bible, Canaan would witness a dramatic series of pitched battles over control of the region. In the first phase, the clashes between Israelite and Canaanite forces centered on the highly fertile Jezreel Valley, center of Canaan's agricultural production. In the second, the continuing turmoil invited adjoining groups and nations, including the Midianites, Amalekites, Moab, and Ammon, to plunge into the melee to try to grab what they could. And in the last and climactic phase, the Israelites confronted the growing power of Philistia, producing a vicious war of attrition that nearly brought the young Israelite commonwealth to its knees.

These wars are the subject of the Book of Judges, which covers the period from the death of Joshua to a critical peak in the battles for Canaan, roughly from 1200 to 1020 B.C.E., the period known as Iron Age I. Its narrative reveals that the distribution of the Hebrew tribes, as seen through the theological lens of a later period, had placed a number of these communities in acute danger of being overrun. As described in the Book of Joshua, the tribes of Reuben and Gad were allocated to the former Amorite possession of Sihon, on the Transjordan plateau (Joshua 13:15-28). One part of the large Manasseh tribe was given half the land of Gilead, between the Jabbok and Yarmuk Rivers (Joshua 13:29-32), while the other Manasseh clans went to the foothills between Shechem and the Jezreel Valley. The tribe of Joseph's other son, Ephraim, was settled in the hills south of Shechem, while Judah was given the land south of Jerusalem, centered on Hebron, though Hebron itself became the possession of Caleb (Joshua 14-15).

The remaining seven tribes drew lots for the remaining territory. Benjamin's tribe moved to the hill country north of Jerusalem (Joshua 18:11-28). The tribe of Dan received the coastal plain (Joshua 19:40-48). Simeon's tribe was sent south, to the Negev region around Beersheba (Joshua 19:1-9). The tribe of Issachar was moved to the valley between Beth Shean and the Jezreel (Joshua 19:17-23).

That left the Galilee, one of the most desirable regions of Canaan due to the abundance of its fields and orchards. Asher received western Galilee (Joshua 19:24-31), Zebulun was settled in central Galilee (Joshua 19:10-16), and Naphtali went to eastern Galilee (Joshua 19:32-39). That is why Matthew would later write, "[Jesus]

ca 1000
Putative date of the unified kingdom of Israel

ca 978
Reign of King Siamun of Egypt begins

ca 970
Solomon succeeds David

ca 945
Pharaoh Shoshenq I founds 22nd Dynasty

Chariots, such as the one shown here in a stela from Tell el-Amarna, provided the Canaanites with a major military advantage.

A view from the central highlands of Samaria reveals the fertile terraced hills of the valley below, which today forms part of the West Bank.

ca 931	ca 931	ca 931	ca 925
Solomon's kingdom splits into two	Jeroboam is king of the Northern Kingdom	Rehoboam's kingdom shrinks to that of Judah	Shoshenq I invades Judah and Israel

The Italian artist Michelangelo Merisi da Caravaggio (1571-1610) painted this impression of "Samson and Delilah."

admits, "[but he] could not drive out the inhabitants of the plain, because they had chariots of iron" (Judges 1:19). And although these judges were effective leaders, their allegiance was principally to the tribe they were sworn to defend. The appointment of a supreme unified commander still lay far in the future.

One of the most prominent judges was a woman, a prophet from the tribe of Issachar named Deborah. Issachar had been settled near the Jezreel, but the adjoining Canaanites kept them oppressed and forced to pay tribute by virtue of their superior military strength—including the chariots of iron, the Iron Age version of the tank (Judges 1:19). Deborah decided to remove the Canaanite threat by conquering the Jezreel Valley once and for all. But to do so, she needed help from all the tribes. Ephraim, Benjamin, and east Manasseh rallied to her side, but other tribes turned a blind eye. Undeterred, Deborah marshaled her forces, led by her commander Barak, and rode out into battle—to Mount Tabor. Here, the Canaanite General Sisera had arrayed his forces in the Wadi Kishon, the river that runs through the plain of Megiddo—fatefully, as it turned out.

left Nazareth and made his home in Capernaum by the sea, in the territory of Zebulun and Naphtali" (Matthew 4:13). As a priestly caste, the tribe of Levi was placed in various towns throughout the land so as to serve all the nation of Israel (Joshua 21). This allocation of the 12 tribes does not always correspond to other lists, or the archaeological record for that matter, and may therefore reflect the particular theological view of the Bible's redactors.

THE SONG OF DEBORAH

The Book of Judges relates how the tribes adjoining the kingdoms of Moab and Edom, such as Reuben and Gad, lived in constant fear of invasion, while many others found themselves living in the shadow of heavily fortified cities such as Beth Shean, Megiddo, and Jerusalem, which remained firmly in Canaanite hands. Meanwhile, the tribe of Dan could never take full control of the coastal region, which was challenged by the Philistines.

In keeping with the underlying Deuteronomist theme, the Bible depicts these foes as enemies sent by God to punish the tribes for their transgressions and disobedience to the Law. But God also sustained the Hebrew tribes in their trials. He did so by fostering certain ad hoc military commanders, who could rally the community in times of war. The Bible tells the story of 12 of these leaders, known as judges, who often faced impossible odds. "The Lord was with Judah," the Book of Judges

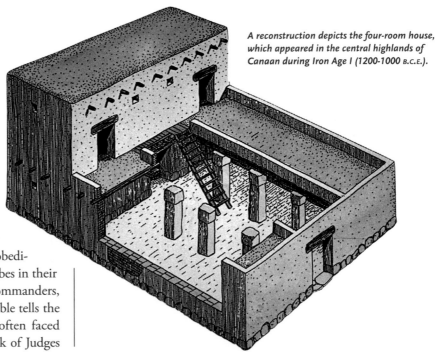

A reconstruction depicts the four-room house, which appeared in the central highlands of Canaan during Iron Age I (1200-1000 B.C.E.).

Then the Lord raised up judges, who delivered them out of the power of those who plundered them.

JUDGES 2:16

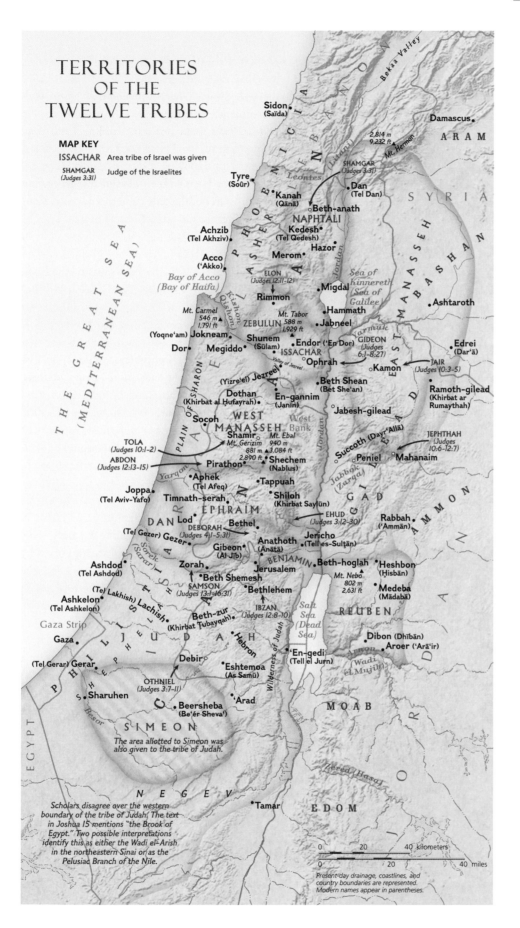

TERRITORIES OF THE TWELVE TRIBES

MAP KEY

ISSACHAR Area tribe of Israel was given

SHAMGAR
(Judges 3:31) Judge of the Israelites

Sidon
(Saïda)

Damascus

Bekaa Valley

LEBANON

PHOENICIA

2,814 m
9,232 ft
Mt. Hermon

ARAM

SHAMGAR
(Judges 3:31)

Tyre
(Soûr)

Leontes

Litani

Dan
(Tel Dan)

SYRIA

Kanah
(Qānā)

Beth-anath

NAPHTALI

Achzib
(Tel Akhziv)

Kedesh
(Tel Qedesh)

Acco
('Akko)

Merom

Hazor

BASHAN

MANASSEH

Bay of Acco
(Bay of Haifa)

ELON
(Judges 12:11-12)

Rimmon

Sea of
Kinnereth
Sea of
Galilee

Migdal

Ashtaroth

Mt. Carmel
546 m
1,791 ft

Mt. Tabor
588 m
1,929 ft

ZEBULUN

Hammath

Jabneel

Jordan

Yarmuk

THE GREAT SEA (MEDITERRANEAN SEA)

Kishon (Qishon)

(Yoqne'am) Jokneam

Shunem
(Sūlam)

Endor
('En Dor)

GIDEON
(Judges
6:1-8:27)

Edrei
(Dar'ā)

Dor

Megiddo

ISSACHAR

Ophrah

Kamon

JAIR
(Judges 10:3-5)

EAST MANASSEH

(Yizre'el) Jezreel

Beth Shean
(Bet She'an)

Ramoth-gilead
(Khirbat ar
Rumaythah)

Plain of Sharon

Dothan
(Khirbat al Ḥufayrah)

Valley of Jezreel

En-gannim
(Janin)

Jabesh-gilead

Socoh

WEST
MANASSEH

West
Bank

TOLA
(Judges 10:1-2)

Shamir

Mt. Gerizim
881 m ▲3,084 ft
2,890 ft

Mt. Ebal
940 m

Succoth (Dayr 'Allā)

JEPHTHAH
(Judges
10:6-12:7)

ABDON
(Judges 12:13-15)

Pirathon

Shechem
(Nablus)

Peniel

Mahanaim

Yarqon

Aphek
(Tel Afeq)

Tappuah

Jabbok (Zarqa)

GILEAD

GAD

Joppa
(Tel Aviv-Yafo)

Timnath-serah

Shiloh
(Khirbat Saylūn)

AMMON

EPHRAIM

DAN

Lod

DEBORAH
(Judges 4:1-5:31)

Bethel

EHUD
(Judges 3:12-30)

Rabbah
('Ammān)

(Tel Gezer) Gezer

Gibeon
(Al Jīb)

Anathoth
(Anāta)

Jericho
(Tell es-Sulṭān)

Sorek (Sarar)

Ashdod
(Tel Ashdod)

Zorah

Jerusalem

BENJAMIN

Beth-hoglah

Heshbon
(Ḥisbān)

(Tel Lakhish) Lachish

SAMSON
(Judges 13:1-16:31)

Beth Shemesh

Bethlehem

Mt. Nebo
802 m
2,631 ft

Medeba
(Mādabā)

Ashkelon
(Tel Ashkelon)

Beth-zur
(Khirbat Ṭubayqah)

IBZAN
(Judges 12:8-10)

Salt
Sea
(Dead
Sea)

REUBEN

Gaza Strip

Gaza

Hebron

Dibon (Dhībān)

Aroer ('Arā'ir)

JUDAH

Arnon

Wadi
el Mujīb

(Tel Gerar) Gerar

Debir

En-gedi
(Tell el Jurn)

PHILISTIA

SHEPHELAH

Eshtemoa
(As Samū)

Wilderness of Judah

OTHNIEL
(Judges 3:7-11)

Sharuhen

'Arad

MOAB

EGYPT

Besor

Beersheba
(Be'ér Sheva')

SIMEON

The area allotted to Simeon was
also given to the tribe of Judah.

NEGEV

Zered (Ḥasal)

Tamar

EDOM

Scholars disagree over the western
boundary of the tribe of Judah. The text
in Joshua 15 mentions "the Brook of
Egypt." Two possible interpretations
identify this as either the Wadi el-Arish
in the northeastern Sinai or as the
Pelusiac Branch of the Nile.

0   20   40 kilometers
0   20   40 miles

Present-day drainage, coastlines, and
country boundaries are represented.
Modern names appear in parentheses.

An elegant calcite jug with handle and beaked spout is dated around 1150 B.C.E.

The richly decorated hilt of a Philistine sword illustrates the military prowess of the Sea Peoples and their associated tribes.

The Emergence of Hebrew Writing

Around 1100 B.C.E., evidence of ancient (or "Old") Hebrew began to emerge in Canaan. Its source was a common northwestern Semitic root that, by varying degrees, was also spoken in Phoenician, Ugaritic, Moabite, and Edomite dialects. Some historians suggest that Old Hebrew crystallized after the settlement in Canaan, but others believe that Old Hebrew must have originated earlier. Scholarly analysis has shown that the oldest written texts in the Bible are a few select poetic passages in the books of Genesis, Exodus, and Judges. No doubt the growth of Israelite communities in Canaan accelerated the development of indigenous Hebrew. The new language used neither cuneiform script nor the Egyptian hieroglyphic or hieratic (cursive) systems. Instead it adapted the first truly alphabetic script, known as the Phoenician alphabet, documented in a royal monument from Byblos around 1050 B.C.E. One of the oldest examples of written Hebrew may be a small tablet from Gezer, dated around 925 B.C.E., describing a calendar of agricultural seasons.

The Gezer calendar, discovered at Tell el-Jazari, is believed to be the one of the oldest examples of Hebrew writing, dated to the late tenth century B.C.E.

As soon as Sisera's 900 chariots were given the order to advance, God unleashed a torrential rainstorm that flooded the Jezreel Valley and stranded the chariots in the mud. Barak's soldiers made short work of them. Deborah commemorated the victory in a rousing song: "Hear, O kings; give ear, O princes; to the Lord I will sing, I will make melody to the Lord, the God of Israel" (Judges 5:3). Some scholars believe that this song is one of the oldest texts in Hebrew Scripture, dating back to the 12th century B.C.E.; biblical scholar George Foot Moore wrote that the song may be "the only contemporaneous monument of Hebrew history" before the time of Israel's monarchy.

THE ARCHAEOLOGICAL EVIDENCE

Is there any evidence that can support the hero sagas of the Book of Judges? Though inevitably this is the subject of debate, a majority of scholars agree that the highlands of Canaan show a substantial population increase in Iron Age I, between 1200 and 1000 B.C.E.— the time span of the Book of Judges. Lawrence Stager wrote that excavations have identified a population increase from 27 to 211 sites, almost an eightfold increase. What's more, many of these settlements were only 2 acres in size, compared to the 12 acre spread of older, established Canaanite communities. All this points to the growth of new settlers with a primary focus on farming rather than the steady expansion of existing communities. This would corroborate the biblical account of tribes such as Ephraim and Manasseh, who bitterly complained of their being restricted to the highlands (with its poor terra rossa topsoil), while the better-armed Canaanites controlled the far more fertile lowland valleys (Joshua 17:16). In response, Stager argues, the highland tribes turned to terracing—the artificial creation of flat, arable plots in the hillside, supported by retaining walls of boulders and dry-laid stones. Terraced soil was not suitable for cereals like wheat, but perfectly fine for the production of olive oil and grapes. These terraces may be the *meromei sadeh*, the "heights of the field" of the Naphtali extolled in the Song of Deborah (Judges 5:18); similar terracing can still be seen today in parts of the West Bank. At the same time, the diversity of animal bones found at these sites indicates that the new settlements also raised sheep, goats, and cattle.

Tribes located in other parts of Canaan, such as the tribe of Dan, also came under pressure from their hostile neighbors. Because of the growing Philistine strength, Dan could never take control of the coastal region allotted to them—a situation that forms the framework for the story of Samson. Instead, the tribe moved up north. According to the Book of Judges, the Danites "came to Laish, to a people quiet and unsuspecting, put them to the sword, and burned down the city" (Judges 18:27). Working at the ancient site of Tel Dan, Avraham Biran may have found some evidence of this event. Over the ruins of a once-flourishing city from the Late Bronze Age lay the remains of a more recent and rather primitive rural settlement. Significantly, this layer

This monumental eastern gate of ancient Tel Dan may be one of the first examples of a brick arch, some 1,500 years before the Roman era.

contained none of the bichrome Philistine-style pottery that was amply present in the preceding layer—clear evidence, in Biran's opinion, that the city was destroyed by Israelites rather than Philistines or Canaanites.

Two other archaeological phenomena are often cited as proof of the growth of Israelite settlements. One is the introduction of lime-plastered cisterns as water catchment systems, first identified by the archaeologist William F. Albright. Living predominantly in the highland regions, the Hebrew settlers did not have access to the wells or streams in the valleys. Therefore it made sense to think that the cisterns found in this region must have been invented by the ever resourceful Israelites, putting their iron implements to good use. But recent research has cast doubt on this hypothesis. Several similarly lined cisterns, found at Taanach (today's northern West Bank) and Hazor, date from the Late Bronze Age. Furthermore, iron tools of the strength and size needed to create large cisterns did not appear in any large quantity until the tenth century B.C.E. The Israelites may not have developed the plaster-lined cistern, but they may well have adopted it using whatever bronze tools they had available, given their urgent need to catch and preserve water.

Another phenomenon associated with the early Hebrew settlement is the so-called four-room house. This simple design used pillars supporting roof beams to divide the house into four separate functions—sleeping, eating, storage, and animal husbandry—all grouped around a small central courtyard for air and light. Soon after their discovery in Iron Age settlements of the highlands, scholars such as Yigal Shiloh pronounced this dwelling type "an original Israelite concept." But this idea has also been questioned in recent years. Manfred Bietak, the excavator of the Hyksos structures in Egypt, noted that the same four-room design can be seen in the remains of 12th-century B.C.E. workers' villages at Medinet Habu. Other similar dwellings have been found in Philistine settlements such as Tell Qasile, or at Tel Masos in the Negev, reportedly populated by Amalekites.

What we may deduce from these discoveries is that a new and distinct culture was emerging in the highlands during Iron Age I, even though some of the features of this culture were not as original or exclusively Israelite as was previously thought. ■

THE RISE OF SAUL

The 12 Tribes Coalesce Around a Supreme Commander

By the end of the 12th century, the Canaanites had ceased to exist as a major threat to the Israelite settlement. The growth of commercial and social contacts between adjoining villages allowed Israelites and Canaanites to find a modus vivendi that no longer involved a conflict over sparse resources. At the same time, Israelite settlements in the highlands and other outlying regions continued to grow. Some archaeologists have estimated that during the 11th century B.C.E., the Hebrew population grew from 45,000 to around 150,000. This, then, is the time when a far more potent threat emerged, prompted by the urgent desire of the Philistine Pentapolis to break out of their coastal enclave and take possession of the fertile valleys inland. A great clash between the Israelite and Philistine spheres was inevitable.

This era of escalating warfare forms the subject of the Books of Samuel. The son of Hannah, a woman from the hill country of Ephraim, Samuel (or Shmu'el, which means "God heard [me]") is the first major prophet of ancient Israel. Samuel was at the shrine of Shiloh when the Philistines and Israelites clashed near the city of Aphek, which resulted in a stunning Hebrew defeat. The Philistines were even able to capture the Ark of the Covenant.

Aphek has been identified with a site just east of modern Tel Aviv, near Tell Ras el-Ain on the Yarkon River (*aphik* means "riverbed"). Since it straddled the Via Maris, the Way of the Sea, it was destined to become a battleground between Philistine and Israelite spheres of influence. Excavated by Moshe Kochavi between 1972 and 1985, Aphek is one of the largest ancient settlements found to date, spread over 30 acres. Once a powerful Late Bronze Age city, it boasted no fewer than three palaces for local Egyptian administrators. Aphek then went into a steep period of decline, only to be resettled by Philistines in the 11th century as attested by numerous pottery sherds—thus confirming the biblical account.

*Inset: **The famous Qeiyafa Ostracon, discovered in 2008, has prompted an intense debate over the nature of its inscription, which is either Proto-Phoenician or early Hebrew.***

The remains of the Egyptian fort at Tel Afeq, the biblical Aphek, probably date to the Late Bronze Age, before the influence of Egypt in Canaan began to wane.

ca 909
Baasha succeeds
King Nadab in Israel

ca 900
Assyria is the dominant
power in Mesopotamia

ca 890
Adad-nirari II of Assyria
is succeeded by Tukulti-Ninurta II

ca 886
Elah succeeds
King Baasha in Israel

After the capture of the Ark, says the Bible, God intervened; every Philistine city in which the Ark was placed as war booty was promptly struck by the plague. Exasperated, the Philistines put the Ark on a cart pulled by cows, which took it to the Hebrew settlement of Beth Shemesh (I Samuel 6:1-12). Named after the Canaanite sun god Shamash, the seven-acre mound of Beit Shemesh was excavated by archaeologist Claire Epstein in the 1970s and subsequently by Shlomo Bunimovitz and Zvi Lederman in the 1990s. These campaigns revealed an Iron Age I settlement from which pig bones are conspicuously missing—evidence of the emerging dietary practices of Israelite communities.

The near loss of the Ark convinced the tribes that they needed a unified command to counter the highly disciplined Philistine forces. They also realized that only Samuel had the wisdom and impartiality to choose such an individual from their midst and appoint him as their *melekh*—a word that can mean "king" or "commander." But the Bible depicts Samuel as reluctant to do so, possibly because of the presence of two different narrative strands. The monarchic source believes that the creation of Israel's monarchy was the will of YHWH, while another strand argues that the kingship was imposed by tribal elders on Samuel against his will (I Samuel 8:4-6). "[A king] will take the best of your fields," this version warns. "He will take your male and female slaves, and the best of your cattle and donkeys, and put them to his work" (I Samuel 8:14-16).

The fields of ancient Beit Shemesh are where, according to the Bible, the Philistines returned the Ark of the Covenant on a cart pulled by cows.

THE REIGN OF SAUL

In the end, a young man from the tribe of Benjamin named Saul was chosen as the first *nagid*, or "leader," of the people of Israel. Though it is difficult to date this pivotal event, many scholars accept a date near the end of the 11th century B.C.E. A potsherd discovered in 2008, known as the Qeiyafa Ostracon, may shed light on the matter. Though scholars do not agree on the interpretation of its five lines of text, French epigrapher Émile Puech believes it should be read as follows:

- Do not oppress, and serve God … despoiled him/her
- The judge and the widow wept; he had the power over the resident alien and the child, he eliminated them together
- The men and the chiefs/officers have established a king
- He marked 60 [?] servants among the communities/ habitations/generation

If Puech is correct, then the line "The men and the chiefs/officers have established a king" could refer to the decision by tribal leaders to anoint Saul (and not King David, as others have suggested) as Israel's first monarch. Puech dates the ostracon to 1000 B.C.E. If true, it would provide a clear marker for Saul's ascension, while making the Qeiyafa Ostracon the oldest known Hebrew text. Other scholars, however, including Christopher Rollston, have argued that there are insufficient linguistic data to classify the text as Old Hebrew.

According to the Books of Samuel, Saul soon proved his mettle as a military leader. He mobilized the tribal militias and rushed north to defeat the invading forces of the king of Ammon, Nahash (I Samuel 11:11). Flushed with victory, the young general led his army southward to attack the Philistines in the highlands. The Philistines withdrew, and the Hebrew army continued to score impressive triumphs at the Battle of Bozez and Michmash. Unfortunately none of these battles was decisive, so that the war soon developed into an attritional stalemate that drained manpower and resources. "I regret that I made Saul king," God told Samuel, "for he has turned back from following me, and has not carried out my commands" (I Samuel 15:11).

Another military confrontation soon loomed at a place "between Socoh and Azekah, in Ephes-dammim," possibly today's Khirbet 'Abbad, west of Bethlehem (I Samuel 17:1). Here the Philistines fielded a new weapon of mass destruction: the giant Goliath, who challenged the Israelites to a duel. The Israelite army was paralyzed with fear—except for Saul's young armor bearer, a humble shepherd from Bethlehem called David. The boy took his sling, grabbed a stone

When Samuel saw Saul, the Lord told him, "Here is the man of whom I spoke to you. He it is who shall rule over my people."

I SAMUEL 9:17

"David Victorious Over Goliath" was painted by Michelangelo Merisi da Caravaggio (1571-1610) around 1600.

from his bag, and fired it straight into Goliath's forehead, whereupon the giant thudded to the ground. David quickly dispatched him with his sword (I Samuel 17:49-51). The Israelites were jubilant. Saul was compelled to place David at the head of his army—thus igniting an intense rivalry between the shepherd and the king. The purpose of the story is to show David's mettle as a courageous and imaginative leader, thus proving his qualifications as the future king of Israel.

But Saul's days were numbered. When he led his army to meet the Philistine forces at Mount Gilboa, he saw all of his sons being killed in battle. Badly wounded, Saul fell upon his own sword (I Samuel 31:1-7). His corpse, and those of his sons, were dragged by the Philistines to Beth Shean and hung from the city's walls.

Beth Shean is one of Israel's most important archaeological sites, since it also includes the

This clay figure from Tell Duweir, near the ancient city of Lachish, probably represents a Canaanite fertility deity.

Greco-Roman city of Scythopolis at the foot of its mound. Excavated by G. M. Fitzgerald in the 1930s and by Amihai Mazar from 1989 onward, the huge tell yielded seven principal strata ranging from the Neolithic (New Stone Age) to the Late Bronze Age, when Beth Shean was the site of the principal Egyptian garrison. It appears that these Egyptian dwellings were destroyed by fire around 1130 B.C.E., after which the mound once again became a Canaanite stronghold. However, Mazar found no evidence of any Philistine occupation at all. If indeed the bodies of Saul and his sons had been displayed there so as to further demoralize the defeated Israelite forces, it did not result in the Philistines' actually taking control of the city. ■

THE KINGDOM OF DAVID

The Controversy Over the Legendary Davidic Kingdom

No other biblical figure would become so prominent in the history of ancient Israel as King David. Particularly after the fall of Judah, when Israel would suffer under the boot of Assyria, Persia, Egypt, Syria, and Rome, the specter of a Davidic restoration shone as never before. So dominant is this theme of David as the embodiment of God's covenantal promise that it would color the history of ancient Israel itself. Scholars have identified several strands running through the Books of Kings, now divided in two volumes, which, together with the Books of Samuel, form the primary source for the biblical David. In addition to the Deuteronomist strand, which interprets Israel's misfortunes as God's punishment for its lack of faith and pagan aberrations, a strand associated with the seventh-century King Josiah emulates the Davidic model as justification for the king's expansionist policies and religious centralization. A smaller strand, possibly linked to the Northern Kingdom of King Jehu, projects a uniquely northern perspective that is often at odds with the view of its southern neighbor Judah, while a postexilic tradition interprets the events through a pro-Judah prism.

Given the immense importance of the Davidic monarchy for the identity and political aspirations of Judaism, in both ancient times and today, the modern archaeologist faces an acute quandary. In the mid-20th century, scholars such as William Albright and Yigael Yadin tended to generously identify archaeological discoveries as corroborative evidence of David's kingdom. In recent decades, however, the pendulum has swung to a more critical stance. Historians Neil Silberman, Israel Finkelstein, Jacob Wright, and Donald Redford, among others, do not believe that the data from Iron Age II (Iron IIA) support the biblical idea of an expansive kingdom or the claim of a united monarchy. Instead, they see the gradual emergence of two rival entities, Judah and Israel, which later authors

Inset, top: *This portrait of King David was painted by Dutch painter Aert de Gelder (1645-1727), a pupil of Rembrandt, around 1680.*

A modern reconstruction of the City of David depicts a modest terraced and walled community running south from Temple Mount toward the Valley of Hinnom.

Inset: *This stepped stone structure is believed by some to date to the tenth-century Davidic era, possibly as part of a large Israelite palace, though others question this conclusion.*

ca 885
The usurper Zimri
takes power in Israel

ca 885
Zimri is toppled by
King Omri of Israel

ca 880
Omri builds the new capital
of Samaria

ca 883
The reign of Ashurnasirpal II
begins in Assyria

ca 874
Omri is succeeded
by his son King Ahab

ca 870
Ashurnasirpal II invades
Syria and Israel

ca 870
King Asa is succeeded
by Jehoshaphat of Judah

ca 870
Beginning of the ministry
of Elijah in the North

So all the elders of Israel came to the king at Hebron;
and King David made a covenant with them at Hebron
before the Lord, and they anointed David king over Israel.

II SAMUEL 5:3

conflated into an ideal monarchy, as a model for the future restoration of an independent Jewish state.

As I stated at the beginning, this book does not favor one perspective over another; it merely aims to present the archaeological evidence for the reader's consideration. Indeed, the discoveries from the Davidic era are too complex to warrant a unilateral choice for one position or another.

THE BIBLICAL KING DAVID

The Bible presents David as a wise and resourceful leader, but also as a tormented and morally flawed character. His rise to power was overshadowed by the dire military situation that the Hebrew tribes faced after the great Philistine victory at Mount Gilboa. Philistine forces were flooding over the Hebrew highlands, threatening every

Israelite settlement. Worse, the tribes faced an incipient split in their ranks when the northern tribes designated Saul's only surviving son, Ishbaal (or Ishbosheth, "man of shame" as he is known in later traditions), as Saul's heir, while the southern tribes chose David as king "over the house of Judah" (II Samuel 2:4). Fortunately, a dispute over one of Saul's concubines eroded Ishbaal's support, whereupon the northern tribes reluctantly pledged their submission to David—thus producing a unified kingdom.

Remarkably, David did not exploit this moment to rally the tribal forces in the fight against the Philistines. Instead, he marched on Jerusalem, the city of the Jebusites, even though the Jebusites no

An aerial photograph of Khirbet Qeiyafa offers an overview of the citadel that some archaeologists believe dates from the Davidic era, circa tenth century B.C.E.

JERUSALEM IN THE OLD TESTAMENT

Northeastern Hill

MAP KEY

Original Jebusite city captured by David
Attributed to Solomon's construction
8th-7th century B.C.E. construction
Postexilic construction
Wall from the Old Testament period
Modern walls (16th century C.E.)
City gate

Central Valley

Northwestern Hill

Tower of Hananel (?) (Hasmonean Baris)

Fish Gate

Sheep Gate

Muster Gate

This section was not occupied by the Hasmoneans.

T E M P L E
Temple
Altar

East Gate

Bridge (Wilson's Arch)

Royal Palace Complex

M O U N T

M I S H N E H

Horse Gate

Ephraim Gate

Hasmonean Palace

Gareb

Central Valley

Southwestern Hill

Valley Gate

Millo

Gate of the Spring

Warren's Shaft

Gihon Spring

M A K T E S H

Central Valley

Southeastern Hill (Zion)

Hezekiah's Tunnel

Siloam Channel

K I D R O N   V A L L E Y

Mount of Olives

Water Gate (Fountain Gate)

Valley Gate

Pool of Siloam

Dung Gate

Mount of Offence

Valley of Hinnom

Contour interval: 10 meters

0   .1   .2 kilometers

0   .1   .2 miles

According to I Samuel 24:1-2, David found refuge in this lush oasis from King Saul and his "three thousand chosen men."

The ninth-century B.C.E. Mesha Stela, also known as the Moabite Stone, was discovered in Dhiban, Jordan, in 1868 and is one of the first nonbiblical attestations of Israel's kings.

longer posed a threat to the Israelite commonwealth (II Samuel 5:6). David wanted to anchor the newly unified nation in a national shrine dedicated to the worship of YHWH, preferably located in neutral territory not associated with any one tribe. He proceeded to conquer the city by stealth, sending his soldiers up "the water shaft," arguably a tunnel that connected the spring of Gihon with the Jerusalem citadel (II Samuel 5:8). The city fell into his lap.

Thoroughly alarmed, the Philistines sped their army to Jerusalem, determined to crush David before his new polity became too powerful, but they were repulsed. From that point on, says the second Book of Samuel, David's forces gradually evicted the Philistines from Israelite territory until they were safely pushed back into the coastal enclaves of Philistia. How David was able to accomplish such a stunning turn in Israel's military fortunes without any fresh influx of troops or weaponry is an open question.

THE CITY OF DAVID

With the state secure at last, David turned to building a proper capital in Jerusalem. This putative "city of David" is today identified with a large complex of excavations beneath the southern city walls of Jerusalem, in the predominantly Arab neighborhood of Silwan in East Jerusalem. First identified by Charles Warren in

The Ark of the Covenant

The Ark of the Covenant was a sacred gold-plated chest of acacia wood that contained the stone tablets of the Ten Commandments handed by God to Moses. The Ark was kept in various places held by the Israelite tribes until its capture by the Philistines. This convinced King David of the need to build a permanent tabernacle on neutral ground: the Jebusite citadel known as Jerusalem. After its capture by the Babylonian army, the Ark disappeared, though the Ethiopian Church claims to possess it in its chapel in Axum.

as well as a collection of *bullae,* or clay seal impressions, found in a nearby dwelling, suggest a date in the tenth century B.C.E., which would put the building in the putative time frame of David's reign. Other Israeli archaeologists have questioned her findings, however. Since then, other pieces of evidence have been found, including a bone that has been radiocarbon-dated to between 1050 and 780 B.C.E., and a seal, discovered in 2015, that some claim was a royal seal issued during the Jebusite or Davidic period.

DID THE DAVIDIC KINGDOM EXIST?

Although the dates of these and other excavations continue to be debated, the historicity of David himself is supported by several other discoveries. An Aramean victory stela discovered at Tel Dan in 1993, dated around 850 B.C.E., includes the phrase *bytdwd,* which most probably means "house of David." The so-called Mesha Stele, also known as the Moabite Stone and dating from the same period, has an inscription in Phoenician script that refers to the Northern Kingdom ("house of Omri") and, as some believe, a fragmentary reference to the "house of David" as well. Furthermore, in 2007, Yosef Garfinkel and Saar Ganor discovered an ancient citadel, known as Khirbet Qeiyafa, close to the ancient site of Beth Shemesh. The archaeologists have posited that a large structure inside the citadel could be a palace from the time of King David. The fortress, which straddled the boundary between the Philistine territory of Philistia and the Israelite region of Judah, was certainly strategically placed.

In sum, what the current archaeological record appears to show is that the kingdom of Judah might indeed have existed as a political entity in the tenth century B.C.E., possibly under David's leadership, but that evidence for the large unified monarchy as described in the Bible is as yet still elusive. ■

1867, the site has yielded a number of large structures as well as several tunnels and shafts that linked the ancient city to the Gihon Spring, its primary source of water. The size of the excavations suggests a modest settlement, and some of its features—such as the water shafts—may confirm the biblical narrative. The question confronted by archaeologists is, Can the site indeed be associated with one man: the biblical figure of King David?

This debate sharpened in 2005 when Israeli archaeologist Eilat Mazar discovered a large stone structure that she identified as the palace of David described in the Books of Samuel. Artifacts found within the structure, including two Phoenician-style ivory inlays,

THE KINGDOM OF SOLOMON

The First Temple to YHWH Is Built in Jerusalem

The story of Solomon's rise to power is one of the most dramatic and riveting passages in the Bible. It unfolds against the backdrop of several intrigues that swirled around David's throne, not only because of ongoing tribal conflicts but also because of the extended family that the king surrounded himself with. According to the second Book of Samuel, David took a wife from almost every tribe in order to balance competing tribal interests and safeguard the legitimacy of his throne. Many of these wives bore the king sons, who then saw themselves as potential heirs to the throne.

Polygamy is, of course, a frequent motif in the Bible. The patriarchs of Genesis took several wives so as to produce enough children to herd the flock, or till and reap the fields. Childbirth was fraught with danger, and many infants were carried off by disease. Some women, like Sarah and Rebekah, turned out to be barren. Polygamy, then, was a practice that ensured a sufficiently large offspring to sustain a tribe.

In the case of David, however, the decision to take on many wives and concubines was motivated by political considerations—both to balance the influence of the 12 tribes at his court and seal important treaties with foreign rulers. This was bound to produce an intensive rivalry among the wives and their sons.

A tragic example is the story of David's third son, Absalom, by his wife Maacah. Absalom's sister Tamar had been raped by her half-brother, Ammon, David's firstborn son by his wife Ahinoam. The incident infuriated David, but he couldn't bring himself to punish Ammon "because he loved him, for he was his firstborn" (II Samuel 13:21). Two years later, Absalom took his own revenge by having Ammon killed during a sheep-shearing festival. David was incensed, and his relationship with Absalom rapidly deteriorated—to the point that Absalom sought to initiate a revolt. The king was able to defeat his rebellious army in the forest of Ephraim, prompting Absalom to flee, but as the young man raced through the forest, his hair got caught in the branches of a low-hanging oak. The "forest of Ephraim" has sometimes been identified as a wooded grove east of the Jordan River, near Jabbok, which at the time formed part of the great forest of Gilead. When David's senior general, Joab, saw Absalom hanging from the tree, he promptly killed him, in violation of David's strict orders not to harm his son (II Samuel 18:5). On hearing the news, David was inconsolable. "O my son Absalom, my son, my son Absalom!" he cried; "Would I had died instead of you, O Absalom, my son, my son!" (II Samuel 18:33).

THE INTRIGUE AT COURT

Absalom's revolt had exposed the sharp fissures within the unified monarchy. Soon another revolt erupted, this one led by a member of the Benjamite tribe named Sheba. It too was bloodily suppressed.

Meanwhile, the intrigue at David's court flourished unchecked. As the king grew older, a number of factions began to align themselves with potential pretenders. David's oldest surviving son was now Adonijah, but David himself seemed to favor the son by his lovely beloved wife (and former paramour) Bathsheba.

Here, the Books of Samuel end and the first Book of Kings takes over. This is also the first time that the Bible refers to a number of historical sources underlying its narrative, perhaps to bolster its authenticity. Thus we hear of sources known as Acts of Solomon (I Kings 11:41), the Annals of the Kings of Judah (I Kings 14:29), and the Annals of the Kings of Israel (I Kings 15:31), but, regrettably, none of these sources has survived.

At the beginning of the first Book of Kings, the narrative returns to Jerusalem to find King David "old and advanced in years," and unable to get warm (I Kings 1:1). This is when the heir apparent, Adonijah, decides to prepare for his ascension to the throne, which he believes is imminent, by throwing a party. As the revelry is in progress, the prophet Nathan urges Bathsheba to slip into the king's bedroom and warn him that an attempted coup is in progress. David then orders Bathsheba's son to be taken to the spring of Gihon, in the

This clay figurine of the Canaanite goddess Asherah was found near the City of David and is dated to the ninth to eighth centuries B.C.E.

ca 858
Ashurnasirpal II is succeeded by Shalmaneser III

ca 853
Battle of Qarqar pits Assyria against Egypt, Syria, and Israel

ca 853
King Ahab of Israel is succeeded by Ahaziah

ca 852
Ahaziah of Israel is replaced by King Jehoram

*The casemate portal of Megiddo bears a close resemblance
to a similar gate in Hazor and is dated by some to the era of Solomon.*

*Solomon was sovereign over
all the kingdoms from the Euphrates
to the land of the Philistines,
even to the border of Egypt.*

I KINGS 4:21

*An elaborate base of lions
and griffins is tentatively dated
to Iron Age II (1000-586 B.C.E.).*

ca 850
Greek city-states coalesce,
ending Dark Age

ca 850
Shalmaneser III
invades Israel

ca 848
Jehoshaphat of Judah is succeeded
by King Jehoram

ca 845
Ministry of Elisha
begins in Israel

valley of Kidron, where Zadok the priest should anoint him king without delay (I Kings 1:34).

THE REIGN OF SOLOMON

Thus begins the reign of King Solomon, whose legendary exploits form the subject of the first 11 chapters of the first Book of Kings. Though dating is difficult, some scholars calculate his reign from 970 to 931 B.C.E. And almost from the beginning, the Bible shows that Solomon's character is the very antithesis of his father, David. Where David is a cunning and brave, though intemperate,

character, Solomon is depicted as a cool and dispassionate intellectual—an aloof figure whose elegant exterior hides a sharp brain and ruthless ambition.

True to form, Solomon moved quickly to consolidate his power. His chief rival, his half-brother Adonijah, was put to death. Other prominent figures of the Adonijah faction, including General Joab, were either banished or put to the sword.

The first Book of Kings depicts Solomon as an energetic, hands-on leader. He reorganized the kingdom into 12 districts led by professional administrators, rather than tribal chieftains, so as to centralize

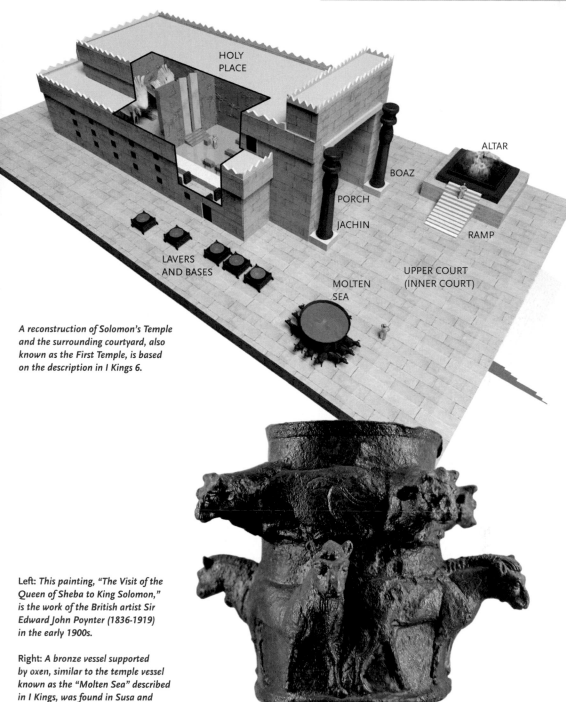

A reconstruction of Solomon's Temple and the surrounding courtyard, also known as the First Temple, is based on the description in I Kings 6.

Left: *This painting, "The Visit of the Queen of Sheba to King Solomon," is the work of the British artist Sir Edward John Poynter (1836-1919) in the early 1900s.*

Right: *A bronze vessel supported by oxen, similar to the temple vessel known as the "Molten Sea" described in I Kings, was found in Susa and dates to around 1500 B.C.E.*

his control of the kingdom and vastly improve the collection of taxes. Next, he reached out to bordering states to foster greater trade across the region, leveraging Israel's strategic position on the nexus between Egypt in the south and Mesopotamia in the north. One of these alliances involved a treaty with King Hiram of Tyre to build copies of the famous Phoenician galley, which enabled Solomon to ship cargo across the Mediterranean and even down to the eastern coast of Africa. Here, Solomon was busy mining gold from the rich ores of Ophir, which produced revenues of 666 talents, roughly the equivalent of 50,000 pounds of gold (I Kings 10:14).

To seal these economic ties, Solomon continued David's practice of concluding political marriages, so that his palaces eventually accommodated no fewer than 700 princesses and 300 concubines, including "many foreign women" (I Kings 11:3).

THE ARCHAEOLOGICAL EVIDENCE

If evidence for David's reign is sparse, the archaeological data for Solomon's 60-year rule are even more difficult to ascertain. If Solomon's kingdom was indeed so flush with wealth and prosperity, some scholars ask, why then is there so little evidence of it in royal cities

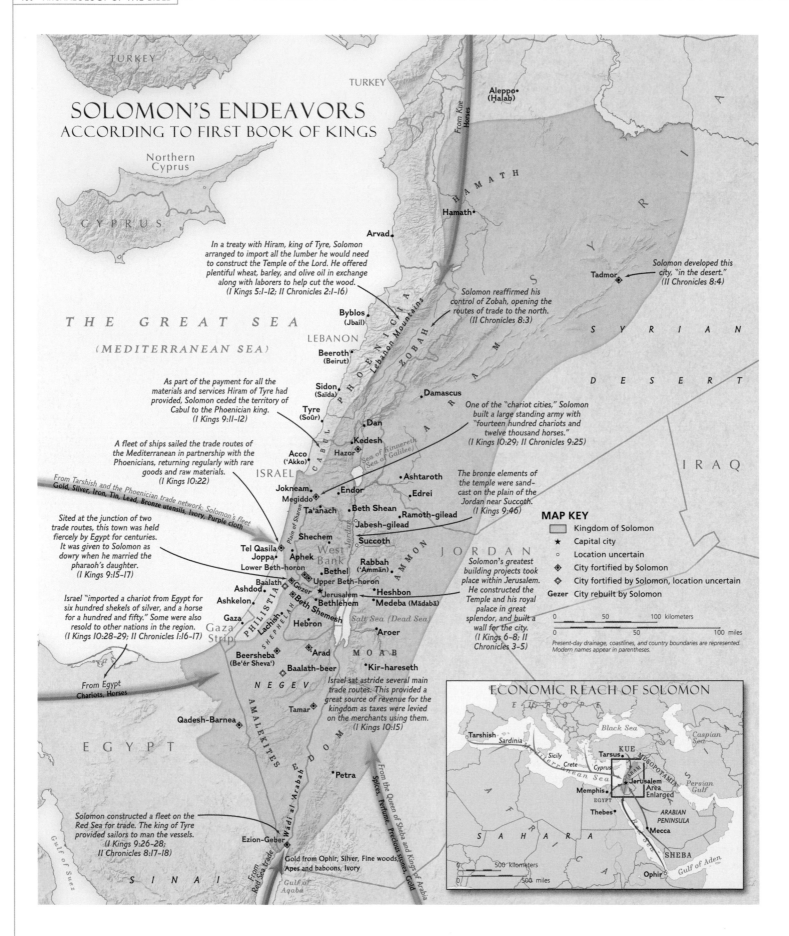

SOLOMON'S ENDEAVORS
ACCORDING TO FIRST BOOK OF KINGS

Northern
Cyprus

TURKEY

TURKEY

C Y P R U S

Aleppo•
(Ḥalab)

From Kue
Horses

HAMATH

Hamath•

Arvad•

In a treaty with Hiram, king of Tyre, Solomon arranged to import all the lumber he would need to construct the Temple of the Lord. He offered plentiful wheat, barley, and olive oil in exchange along with laborers to help cut the wood.
(I Kings 5:1-12; II Chronicles 2:1-16)

Solomon reaffirmed his control of Zobah, opening the routes of trade to the north.
(II Chronicles 8:3)

Solomon developed this city, "in the desert."
(II Chronicles 8:4)

Tadmor•

S Y R I A

T H E   G R E A T   S E A

(MEDITERRANEAN SEA)

Byblos•
(Jbail)

LEBANON

Beeroth•
(Beirut)

Lebanon Mountains

ZOBAH

D E S E R T

As part of the payment for all the materials and services Hiram of Tyre had provided, Solomon ceded the territory of Cabul to the Phoenician king.
(I Kings 9:11-12)

Sidon•
(Saïda)

Tyre•
(Soûr)

Damascus•

ARAM

S Y R I A N

One of the "chariot cities," Solomon built a large standing army with "fourteen hundred chariots and twelve thousand horses."
(I Kings 10:29; II Chronicles 9:25)

I R A Q

Dan•

•Kedesh

A fleet of ships sailed the trade routes of the Mediterranean in partnership with the Phoenicians, returning regularly with rare goods and raw materials.
(I Kings 10:22)

Acco•
('Akko)

Hazor•

Sea of Kinnereth
(Sea of Galilee)

ISRAEL

Jokneam•

Megiddo•

•Endor

•Ashtaroth

•Edrei

The bronze elements of the temple were sand-cast on the plain of the Jordan near Succoth.
(I Kings 9:46)

From Tarshish and the Phoenician trade network; Solomon's fleet
Gold, Silver, Iron, Tin, Lead, Bronze utensils, Ivory, Purple cloth

•Ta'anach

•Beth Shean

•Ramoth-gilead

Jabesh-gilead•

Plain of Sharon

•Shechem

•Succoth

Jordan

Sited at the junction of two trade routes, this town was held fiercely by Egypt for centuries. It was given to Solomon as dowry when he married the pharaoh's daughter.
(I Kings 9:15-17)

Tel Qasila•
Joppa•

•Aphek

West
Bank

•Rabbah
('Ammān)

AMMON

J O R D A N

Lower Beth-horon

Baalath•

Gezer•

Upper Beth-horon

•Bethel

Solomon's greatest building projects took place within Jerusalem. He constructed the Temple and his royal palace in great splendor, and built a wall for the city.
(I Kings 6-8; II Chronicles 3-5)

Ashdod•

Ashkelon•

Beth Shemesh•

Jerusalem★

•Heshbon

•Medeba (Mādabā)

Israel "imported a chariot from Egypt for six hundred shekels of silver, and a horse for a hundred and fifty." Some were also resold to other nations in the region.
(I Kings 10:28-29; II Chronicles 1:16-17)

Gaza•

Bethlehem•

PHILISTIA

Lachish•

Hebron•

Salt Sea (Dead Sea)

Gaza
Strip

SHEPHELAH

•Aroer

From Egypt
Chariots, Horses

Beersheba•
(Be'ér Sheva')

•Arad

M O A B

Baalath-beer•

•Kir-hareseth

N E G E V

Israel sat astride several main trade routes. This provided a great source of revenue for the kingdom as taxes were levied on the merchants using them.
(I Kings 10:15)

AMALEKITES

•Tamar

Qadesh-Barnea•

E G Y P T

E D O M

Wādi al-'Arabah

•Petra

Solomon constructed a fleet on the Red Sea for trade. The king of Tyre provided sailors to man the vessels.
(I Kings 9:26-28; II Chronicles 8:17-18)

Gulf of Suez

S I N A I

Ezion-Geber•

From the Queen of Sheba and Kings of Arabia
Spices, Perfume, Precious stones, Gold

From Red Sea trade

Gold from Ophir, Silver, Fine woods
Apes and baboons, Ivory

Gulf of Aqaba

MAP KEY

▭ Kingdom of Solomon
★ Capital city
○ Location uncertain
◈ City fortified by Solomon
◇ City fortified by Solomon, location uncertain
Gezer City rebuilt by Solomon

| 0 | 50 | 100 kilometers |
| 0 | 50 | 100 miles |

Present-day drainage, coastlines, and country boundaries are represented. Modern names appear in parentheses.

ECONOMIC REACH OF SOLOMON

E U R O P E

Black Sea

Caspian Sea

Tarshish•

Sardinia

Sicily

Crete

Cyprus

Tarsus•

KUE

ARAM

MESOPOTAMIA

S

Jerusalem★
Area
Enlarged

Persian Gulf

Memphis•

EGYPT

A

F

R

I

C

A

Thebes•

S A H A R A

ARABIAN
PENINSULA

•Mecca

Mediterranean Sea

SHEBA

Ophir•

Gulf of Aden

| 0 | 500 kilometers |
| 0 | 500 miles |

like Jerusalem, Hazor, Megiddo, and Gezer, which Solomon reportedly fortified? In fact, they say, these settlements actually show a *decline,* rather than a renaissance, during Iron Age II compared to the Late Bronze Age. Other scholars have countered that argument by pointing to the destructive impact of successive waves of invaders, from Assyrian rulers on down. Whatever Solomon may have been built, they argue, was probably erased by Israel's vengeful enemies.

Perhaps the truth lies somewhere in between. Although it is true that archaeologists have found few monuments attributed to Solomon's reign, there are some exceptions. In both Megiddo and Hazor, for example, excavators have identified nearly identical casemate portals: large, fortified gateways built with ashlar masonry and flanked by storerooms that quite possibly sheltered guards with their weaponry. Inside Megiddo proper, Yigael Yadin laid bare a vast exercise yard that once may have served as the training ground for some of Solomon's 4,000 chariots. Next to the yard are rows of stalls with troughs, possibly stables for the horses. The first Book of Kings says that "Solomon also had forty thousand stalls of horses for his chariots, and twelve thousand horsemen" (I Kings 4:26). It would have made sense for Solomon to station such mounted divisions in strategic garrisons like Megiddo.

Among the regions that Solomon's ships visited was the legendary land of Sheba, which scholars have identified as Saba on the southern coast of Yemen. Its queen was intrigued by stories of Solomon's wealth and "came to test him with hard questions" (II Chronicles 9:1). The queen presented the king with gold, gems, and spices and interrogated him at length. Solomon indulged her and "gave to the queen of Sheba every desire that she expressed" (I Kings 10:1, 13). Though impossible to attest, the story would later be taken up by both the Qur'an and rabbinic literature, with many more details and embellishments.

THE FIRST TEMPLE

The Bible says that the greatest monument Solomon built was the First Temple in Jerusalem, which replaced the tentlike tabernacle set up by King David to house the Ark of the Covenant. The first Book of Kings provides detailed specifications of this structure, which seems to closely resemble the Syrian archetype of a *megaron*: a large rectangular nave (*hekal*), flanked by lower aisles (*yasia*) and preceded by a ceremonial portal (*ulam*). In front of the Temple stood an altar and a large bronze vessel for sacrificial rituals; inside, at the very end of the nave, was an inner sanctuary (*debir*) to hold the Ark. As the late Victor Hurowitz, a biblical scholar at Ben-Gurion University, has shown, this type is found at other temples in the Near East, notably at Tell Tayinat in southeastern Turkey and Ain Dara in Syria. Another prototype of Solomon's Temple can be seen in the acropolis of Tel Arad, excavated during a series of campaigns from 1962 to 1984. Though repeatedly destroyed and rebuilt, the Arad temple may be the oldest surviving Israelite sanctuary from Iron Age II, with a courtyard surrounded by administrative rooms and an altar for burnt offerings, just as in Solomon's Temple in Jerusalem. ■

Solomon's Temple

The Temple erected by Solomon on Temple Mount in Jerusalem was probably the most impressive structure ever built in Canaan. Measuring some 120 feet in length and 55 feet in width, its exterior was adorned with "carved engravings of cherubim, palm trees, and open flowers" (I Kings 6:29). The Temple was fronted by a spacious courtyard that contained a sacrificial altar and a bronze vessel, known as the Sea of Bronze. This vessel rested on 12 bronze oxen, each group of three facing the four points of the compass. For the next 400 years, the Temple was repeatedly plundered, possibly by Pharaoh Shishak or Shoshenq, then by King Jehoash of the Northern Kingdom, as well as King Ahaz of Judah, so as to obtain the ransom needed to placate the Assyrian king Tiglath-Pileser. The temple was destroyed in 586 B.C.E. by the Babylonian king Nebuchadnezzar (II Kings 24:13).

Jerusalem's Temple Mount, where the Temple once stood, is today occupied by the Dome of the Rock (top) and the Al Aqsa Mosque (bottom).

THE NORTHERN KINGDOM OF ISRAEL

Ancient Israel Reaches Its Apogee During the Reign of King Omri

For roughly 200 years, from around 930 to 720 B.C.E., there flourished a Hebrew monarchy in the northern part of what was once the Egyptian vassal region of Canaan. It stretched from the ancient sanctuary of Bethel, just north of Jerusalem at its southern border, to another sanctuary, that of Dan, in the North. As various inscriptions show, this Northern Kingdom was referred to as "Israel" by its surrounding states. It encompassed all of the Hebrew tribes except for Judah and Benjamin, thus becoming the most important Israelite entity of its time. In both size and economic activity, this kingdom dwarfed the other Israelite monarchy, the kingdom of Judah, in the south. Much of the North's economic and political activity was centered in the highlands of Shomron, the Samarian Mountains, including Shechem, Tirzah, and the city of Samaria itself.

How the Northern Kingdom came about is the subject of intense debate, which in recent years has taken on distinct political overtones. According to the first Book of Kings, the kingdom was formed when the northern tribes split from the Unified Kingdom after the death of King Solomon. Reading between the lines, one can see several reasons that these tribes would withdraw their pledge of fealty to the Davidic Kingdom. To begin, there was widespread dissatisfaction over Solomon's use of forced labor for his construction projects, as well as the "heavy yoke" that his taxes had imposed on the tribal territories (I Kings 12:4). This had denuded the fields of able-bodied men and put a severe strain on the tribal economy, while making the North increasingly dependent on Jerusalem's public works program.

Second, the concentration of YHWH worship in the Temple of Jerusalem had effectively put the sanctuaries in the North out of business, even though such ancient shrines as Bethel, Shechem, and Shiloh could claim a pedigree going back to the days

of the Patriarchs. And last, the idea of a royal dynasty rooted exclusively in the house of David had never gained full support among the chieftains, who saw the control of their tribes gradually being usurped by the central authority in Jerusalem.

And so the North broke away. According to Kings, this sequence of events was set in motion after the defection of Solomon's minister for forced labor, Jeroboam, to Egypt. Apparently Jeroboam had been plotting with the northern tribes to create a breakaway kingdom, but Solomon found out about it and condemned him to death. Once in Egypt, Jeroboam was granted asylum by Pharaoh Shishak, who most likely is King Shoshenq I, the founder of the 22nd Dynasty (945-715 B.C.E.).

Meanwhile in Israel, things were coming to a head. Solomon's successor, a rather weak and vacillating man named Rehoboam, summoned the tribal leaders to Shechem to renew the treaty of unification. When the elders insisted on a reduction in taxes and forced labor, Rehoboam refused, and the tribes broke away with the cry, "To your tents, O Israel!" (I Kings 12:14-16). Jeroboam returned from Egypt to become king of Israel, while Rehoboam suddenly saw his kingdom reduced to the small footprint of Judah.

To make matters worse, King Shoshenq used the political chaos to invade Judah and threaten to take Jerusalem. Deprived of any meaningful force to combat Pharaoh's "twelve hundred chariots and sixty thousand cavalry," Rehoboam sued for terms, which allowed Shoshenq to make off with "the treasures of the house of the Lord" (II Chronicles 12:3; I Kings 14:25). For Rehoboam, there was only one small comfort: Not content with raiding Jerusalem, Shoshenq continued north and invaded the kingdom of his erstwhile guest Jeroboam, plundering all the way to the North's mightiest fortress, that of Ma-ke-thu, or Megiddo.

Most scholars do not contest the existence of two Hebrew kingdoms, which

This stela fragment of Sargon II of circa 720 B.C.E. records the suppression of revolt in Syria and Israel by the Assyrian king Sargon.

ca 841
King Ahazia begins
his short reign in Judah

ca 841
Ahazia is succeeded
by King Athalia of Judah

ca 841
King Jehu ascends
the throne of Israel

ca 835
Jehoash succeeds Athalia
as king of Judah

King Jehu of Israel prostrates before King Shalmaneser III of Assyria in a detail from the Black Obelisk of Shalmaneser III.

So [Jeroboam] took counsel, and made two calves of gold. He said to the people, "You have gone up to Jerusalem long enough. Here are your gods, O Israel."

I KINGS 12:28

The remains of the palace of King Omri at the acropolis of ancient Samaria, the capital of the Northern Kingdom

ca 823
Assyrian astronomers
first record a solar eclipse

ca 782
Shalmaneser IV ascends
the throne of Assyria

ca 781
King Uzziah ascends
the throne in Judah

ca 745
Shalmaneser IV is succeeded
by Tiglath-Pileser III

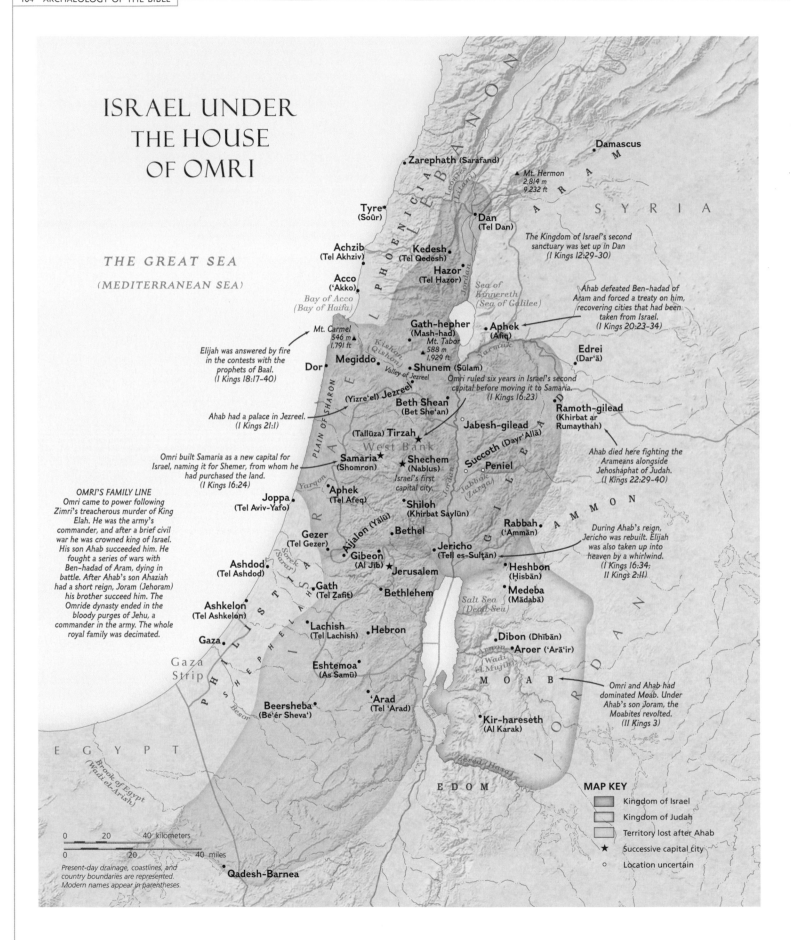

ISRAEL UNDER THE HOUSE OF OMRI

THE GREAT SEA

(MEDITERRANEAN SEA)

Damascus

▲ Mt. Hermon
2,814 m
9,232 ft

Zarephath (Sarafand)

Tyre
(Soûr)

Dan
(Tel Dan)

S Y R I A

The Kingdom of Israel's second
sanctuary was set up in Dan
(I Kings 12:29-30)

Achzib
(Tel Akhziv)

Kedesh
(Tel Qedesh)

Acco
('Akko)

Hazor
(Tel Hazor)

Bay of Acco
(Bay of Haifa)

Sea of
Kinnereth
(Sea of Galilee)

Ahab defeated Ben-hadad of
Aram and forced a treaty on him,
recovering cities that had been
taken from Israel.
(I Kings 20:23-34)

Mt. Carmel
546 m ▲
1,791 ft

Gath-hepher
(Mash-had)

Aphek
(Afiq)

Edrei
(Dar'ā)

Elijah was answered by fire
in the contests with the
prophets of Baal.
(I Kings 18:17-40)

Dor

Megiddo

Mt. Tabor
588 m
1,929 ft

Shunem (Sūlam)

Valley of Jezreel

Omri ruled six years in Israel's second
capital before moving it to Samaria.
(I Kings 16:23)

(Yizre'el) Jezreel

Beth Shean
(Bet She'an)

Ramoth-gilead
(Khirbat ar
Rumaythah)

Ahab had a palace in Jezreel.
(I Kings 21:1)

(Tallūza) Tirzah

Jabesh-gilead

West Bank

Omri built Samaria as a new capital for
Israel, naming it for Shemer, from whom he
had purchased the land.
(I Kings 16:24)

Samaria
(Shomron)

Shechem
(Nablus)

Succoth (Dayr 'Allā)

Peniel

Ahab died here fighting the
Arameans alongside
Jehoshaphat of Judah.
(I Kings 22:29-40)

Israel's first
capital city.

OMRI'S FAMILY LINE
Omri came to power following
Zimri's treacherous murder of King
Elah. He was the army's
commander, and after a brief civil
war he was crowned king of Israel.
His son Ahab succeeded him. He
fought a series of wars with
Ben-hadad of Aram, dying in
battle. After Ahab's son Ahaziah
had a short reign, Joram (Jehoram)
his brother succeed him. The
Omride dynasty ended in the
bloody purges of Jehu, a
commander in the army. The
whole royal family was decimated.

Joppa
(Tel Aviv-Yafo)

Aphek
(Tel Afeq)

Shiloh
(Khirbat Saylūn)

Rabbah
('Ammān)

A M M O N

During Ahab's reign,
Jericho was rebuilt. Elijah
was also taken up into
heaven by a whirlwind.
(I Kings 16:34;
II Kings 2:11)

Gezer
(Tel Gezer)

Aijalon (Yālū)

Bethel

Ashdod
(Tel Ashdod)

Gibeon
(Al Jīb)

Jericho
(Tell es-Sulṭān)

Jerusalem

Heshbon
(Ḥisbān)

Gath
(Tel Zafit)

Bethlehem

Medeba
(Mādabā)

Ashkelon
(Tel Ashkelon)

Salt Sea
(Dead Sea)

Gaza

Lachish
(Tel Lachish)

Hebron

Dibon (Dhībān)

Aroer ('Arā'ir)

Gaza
Strip

Eshtemoa
(As Samū)

M O A B

Omri and Ahab had
dominated Moab. Under
Ahab's son Joram, the
Moabites revolted.
(II Kings 3)

Beersheba
(Be'ér Sheva')

'Arad
(Tel 'Arad)

Kir-hareseth
(Al Karak)

E G Y P T

E D O M

MAP KEY

▮	Kingdom of Israel
▮	Kingdom of Judah
▮	Territory lost after Ahab
★	Successive capital city
○	Location uncertain

0   20   40 kilometers
0   20   40 miles

Present-day drainage, coastlines, and
country boundaries are represented.
Modern names appear in parentheses.

Qadesh-Barnea

The tribute of Jehu, son of Omri: I received from him silver, gold,
a golden bowl, a golden vase with pointed bottom, golden tumblers,
golden buckets, tin, a staff for a king [and] spears.

BLACK OBELISK OF SHALMANESER III

are probably the first political entities in the Bible attested by archaeological evidence. But many question the idea of a split, arguing that these kingdoms emerged as separate entities from the beginning and that the Unified Monarchy is probably a utopian concept from later times.

THE HOUSE OF OMRI

The North would enter a period of cultural and economic growth that culminated in the reign of King Omri. Aware of the ever present threat on his borders, Omri ended the long-simmering tensions with Judah and concluded a peace treaty with King Ittobaal of Phoenicia. The deal was sealed, fatefully, when Omri's son Ahab married the Phoenician princess Jezebel. Omri then defeated his hostile neighbor to the east, Aram-Damascus, bringing peace to his kingdom. His military prowess is acknowledged by the Moabite Stone, which admits that "Omri humbled Moab for many years." So prominent was Omri's reign that even after the king's death, Assyrian texts would refer to Israel as *bit humri*, "the house of Omri."

Having secured the peace, the king began to build a new capital city that could rival the splendor of Jerusalem (I Kings 16:23-24). This new acropolis rose on a summit in the hills of Ephraim, close to Shechem, known as Samaria. During excavations by Harvard's Clarence Fisher in the early 20th century, excavators uncovered a monumental palace that was much enlarged in later years. Amid the ruins, fragments of the original ivory ornamentation, crafted by Phoenician artisans, were found in situ. In a 2007 article, archaeologist Norma Franklin theorized that caverns underneath this structure may have been the tombs of Omri and his descendants, but others have challenged this idea.

RELIGIOUS ACTIVITY

Cut off from the Temple in Jerusalem, the Northern Kingdom struggled to develop an indigenous religious tradition. The first Book of Kings describes how the veneration of YHWH was increasingly challenged by Syro-Phoenician practices, including the worship of Baal Melkart and Asherah (or Astarte), and historians agree that this is probably what happened. Jeroboam reactivated the ancient shrines of Dan and Bethel for YHWH worship, and even developed religious festivals to compete with the ones in Jerusalem. But it is not clear how closely these sanctuaries hew to Yahwist liturgy. In both Dan and Bethel, Jeroboam installed gold calves, the

These two ninth-century ivories in the Phoenician style from the Assyrian palace of Nimrud may have been war loot, possibly from Syria, Israel, or Judah.

traditional Canaanite idol of El. When the Dan sanctuary was discovered by chance in 1992, archaeologists found a stone platform that may be the *bamah,* or "high place," where the gold calf could have been placed.

Omri's successor, King Ahab, seems to have abetted the growing syncretism of farmers worshipping both YHWH and important fertility deities such as Baal. According to the first Book of Kings, this incurred the wrath of the prophet Elijah ("Eliyahu" means "My God is Yahu"), the first of many prominent prophets who would minister during the Divided Monarchy. Elijah challenged the "four hundred and fifty prophets of Baal" who, not surprisingly, ate "at the table" of Ahab's wife, the Phoenician princess Jezebel (I Kings 18:19). A test was conducted on Mount Carmel, which Elijah won (I Kings 18:38-40). The Bible claims that the priests of Baal were summarily put to death, but as excavations have shown, the use of fertility figures and amulets bearing the image of Astarte continued unabated.

For the Deuteronomist scribes of the Books of Kings, it was this policy of pagan tolerance and open idolatry that ultimately doomed the kingdom. For in the North, a new superpower was emerging on the banks of the Tigris and Euphrates Rivers: the Assyrian Empire. ■

THE KINGDOM OF JUDAH

The Rise and Fall of the Southern Monarchy

Though much smaller than the Northern Kingdom and bereft of the ample resources of Israel's valleys, the Southern Kingdom of Judah was nevertheless able to survive for two centuries after the fall of the North. One reason may be that Judah's kings were more deft in international diplomacy during a time of growing conflict among foreign states, particularly Assyria. Another factor could be that Judah was simply too small and insignificant to play a major role in international affairs. And while Judah's agricultural economy was far more modest than that of the North and largely limited to the Shephelah Valley, it did find a way to exploit a native form of dry farming on the southern highlands, using iron tools to optimize the plowing and planting of topsoil. Part of this strategy involved the careful husbandry of rainfall. The second Book of Chronicles, a parallel history to the Books of Kings, claims that in the eighth century, King Uzzia "hewed out many cisterns … both in the Shephelah and in the plain, and he had farmers and vinedressers in the hills and in the fertile lands, for he loved the soil" (II Chronicles 26:10).

As in the case of the Northern Kingdom, historians have found little evidence for the biblical claim that Judah came about as a result of a split in the Unified Monarchy after the death of King Solomon. That doesn't rule out the sequence of events as the Bible depicts them. What it does say is that from a strictly historical perspective, Judah's statehood may have emerged more slowly, becoming a true independent polity only by the late tenth or ninth century B.C.E.

The Bible reserves harsh judgment for many of Judah's kings, as it did for the kings of the North, blaming them for the continuing practice of idolatry and pagan worship in parallel to the official veneration of YHWH. Despite the fact that some of these kings, notably Mannaseh, were able and successful rulers, many are denounced by the Books of Kings for their "abominable practices."

A bulla, or clay seal, is inscribed with the legend "To Hezekiah [son of] Ahaz King [of] Judah" and is dated by some to the seventh century B.C.E.

The eighth and seventh centuries also saw the rise of many prominent prophets in Judah, including Amos, Micah, and Jeremiah, but remarkably their ministry was not primarily targeted against any pagan idolatry. By contrast, these prophets directed their scorn on the growing gap between rich and poor, which violated the Torah's commandments of social justice and compassion. Amos, a shepherd from Tekoa near Bethlehem, saw how the growth in agricultural yields led to land speculation and the rise of a wealthy landowner class, at the expense of small subsistence farmers. "Because you trample on the poor and take from them levies of grain," the prophet inveighed, "you have built houses of hewn stone, but you shall not live in them"—a prophesy that may have inspired Jesus' parable about the rich man storing up his grain in barns (Amos 5:11; Luke 12:18-20). Similarly, Jeremiah would castigate those who "amass wealth unjustly; in mid-life it will leave them, and at their end they will prove to be fools" (Jeremiah 17:10-11).

THE ARCHAEOLOGICAL EVIDENCE

The first mention of the name "Judah" outside the Bible appears on the Nimrud Tablet, discovered by British excavator George Smith during the excavations of Nimrud in 1873. Written around 733 B.C.E. during the reign of the great Assyrian warlord Tiglath-Pileser III, it describes the foreign tribute flowing into the imperial coffers as a result of the king's conquests. One of these vassal kings is "Jehoahaz of the land Judah (Yaudaya)," also known (without the theophoric Jeho or YHWH) as King Ahaz. One of the most prominent and controversial kings of Judah, Ahaz probably ascended the throne around 736, after serving as co-regent with his father, Jotham, for four years, and then faced an immediate international crisis. King Pekah of Israel had entered into a defensive alliance with Aram-Damascus (Syria), Ashkelon, and Tyre to try to stop the Assyrian aggression, and he pressed Ahaz to join this coalition as well.

ca 745
Tiglath-Pileser III conquers the Northern Kingdom

ca 765
Birth of the prophet Isaiah

ca 743
Ministry of the prophets Amos and Hosea begin

ca 737
King Pekah is king of Israel

Ahaz sent messengers to King Tiglath-Pileser of Assyria, saying ... "Come up, and rescue me from the hand of the king of Aram and from the hand of the king of Israel, who are attacking me."

II KINGS 16:7

Lachish's defenders (left) fight to stem the Assyrian onslaught and (right) are impaled by Assyrian soldiers in tableaux from Sennacherib's palace at Nineveh, around 700 B.C.E.

A modern reconstruction of Jerusalem during the reign of King Hezekiah shows how the original City of David expanded westward toward the Central Valley.

ca 732
Judah is vassal
state of Assyria

ca 726
Shalmaneser V is succeeded
by King Sargon II

ca 721
Rump state of Samaria
falls to King Sargon II

ca 716
Hezekiah is
king of Judah

THE KINGDOMS OF ISRAEL AND JUDAH

MAP KEY

- Kingdom of Israel
- Kingdom of Judah
- ★ Successive capital city
- ○ Location uncertain
- ■ Royal sanctuary of Israel

Note: The boundaries of Israel and Judah changed repeatedly throughout their history.

Sidon
(Saïda)

Damascus

*The capital of Aram. Ahab defeated Ben-hadad their king, forcing a treaty.
(I Kings 20:1-34)*

▲ Mt. Hermon
2,814 m
9,232 ft

Tyre
(Soûr)

Leontes

Kanah
(Qānā)

Dan
(Tel Dan)

S Y R I A

Kedesh
(Tel Qedesh)

*The Kingdom of Israel's second sanctuary was set up in Dan.
(I Kings 12:29-30)*

Achzib
(Tel Akhziv)

Hazor

Merom

Acco
('Akko)

Gath-hepher
(Mash-had)

Migdal

*Bay of Acco
(Bay of Haifa)*

Sea of Kinnereth
(Sea of Galilee)

Ashtaroth

Hammath

Mt. Carmel
546 m ▲
1,791 ft

▲ Mt. Tabor
588 m
1,929 ft

Edrei
(Dar'ā)

Dor

Megiddo

Valley of Jezreel

Shunem (Sūlam)

*Hit by a randomly shot arrow in battle, King Ahab died here fighting the Arameans.
(I Kings 22:29-40)*

THE GREAT SEA

(MEDITERRANEAN SEA)

(Yizre'el) Jezreel

Beth Shean
(Bet She'an)

(Janīn) En-gannim

Abel-meholah

Jabesh-gilead

Ramoth-gilead
(Khirbat ar Rumaythah)

*Omri founded this city as Israel's third capital.
(I Kings 16:24)*

Tishbe

(Tallūza) Tirzah ★

Israel's second capital

Succoth (Dayr 'Allā)

Gerasa
(Jerash)

Mt. Ebal
940 m
3,084 ft

*The royal sanctuary of Israel was constructed in about 920 B.C.E. to rival the temple in Jerusalem.
(I Kings 12:28-33)*

Samaria ★
(Shomron)

Shechem
(Nablus)

Peniel

*Jeroboam, the first ruler of the northern Kingdom of Israel, chose Shechem as his capital. He had been an exiled district governor under Solomon.
(I Kings 12:25)*

Mt. Gerizim
881 m, 890 ft

Aphek (Tel Afeq)

Joppa
(Tel Aviv-Yafo)

Shiloh
(Khirbat Saylūn)

West Bank

Rabbah
('Ammān)

A M M O N

(Tel Gezer)
Gezer

Ajalon (Yālū)

Bethel

Jericho
(Tell es-Sultān)

Gibeon
(Al Jib)

Anathoth
(Anātā)

Beth-hoglah

Heshbon
(Ḥisbān)

*Dibon was the one-time capital of the Moabites, whose King Mesha about 835 B.C.E. had the Moabite Stone carved as a record of his battles against the Israelites.
(II Kings 3)*

Ashdod
(Tel Ashdod)

Zorah

Jerusalem ★

Beth Shemesh

Mt. Nebo
802 m
2,631 ft

Medeba
(Mādabā)

Bethlehem

Ashkelon
(Tel Ashkelon)

Gath
(Tel Zafit)

Moresheth-gath

Tekoa (Tuqū')

Salt Sea
(Dead Sea)

Mareshah

Beth-zur
(Khirbat Tubayqah)

Gaza Strip

Lachish

Hebron

Dibon (Dhībān)

Gaza

Lachish (Tel Lakhish)

Eshtemoa
(As Samū)

'En-gedi
(Tell el Jurn)

Aroer ('Arā'ir)

(Tel Gerar) Gerar

M O A B

Sharuhen
(Tel Sharuhen)

Arad
(Tel 'Arad)

Beersheba
(Be'ér Sheva')

Kir-hareseth
(Al Karak)

N E G E V

Tamar

E G Y P T

*Brook of Egypt
(Wadi el Arish)*

Zered (Ḥasā)

0   20   40 kilometers

0   20   40 miles

Present-day drainage, coastlines, and country boundaries are represented. Modern names appear in parentheses.

Qadesh-Barnea

E D O M

But Ahaz demurred. Perhaps he understood that it would be futile to try to resist Assyria's vast military superiority. Instead, Ahaz made the fateful decision of allying himself with Assyria at the cost of making Judah a vassal state—and incurring the wrath of the prophet Isaiah. But the gamble paid off; Tiglath-Pileser easily defeated both Israel and Syria, thus eliminating any further foreign threat to Judah for the remainder of Ahaz's reign. A rather impressionable man, King Ahaz welcomed the influx of Assyrian culture. He imported Assyrian rituals into temple worship, built a Babylonian-type observatory for astrological observations, and, as we saw earlier, possibly condoned child sacrifice for the Phoenician god Moloch, to the point of even sacrificing his own son. For this he is roundly condemned in the Bible (II Kings 16:2-3).

In 1998, a *bulla,* or clay impression used to seal a papyrus, emerged on the market. It bore the inscription "Belonging to Ahaz (son of) Yehotam, King of Judah." If it is genuine, it could provide a strong historical attestation of this king.

In 2002, epigrapher and archaeologist Robert Deutsch published three other recently discovered bullae that all include the reference "servant of Hezekiah," possibly referring to high officials at the court of King Hezekiah, who succeeded King Ahaz around 716 B.C.E. However, as in the case of the Ahaz seal, a provenance for these bullae is lacking.

According to the Book of Kings, Hezekiah immediately initiated sweeping religious reforms and razed all the "high places" of pagan worship, including the removal of an Assyrian-style altar from the temple. But Hezekiah also faced a rapidly declining economy, which had suffered badly from the ongoing encroachment of Assyrian territory. Thus, the king was all ears when one of Assyria's other vassal kings, Merodach-Baladan, approached him about staging a revolt, given that the Assyrian king Sargon II was facing rebellion in many other parts of his empire.

To prepare for these hostilities, Hezekiah rebuilt the walls facing the western approaches to Jerusalem; evidence of this extension was discovered by Nahman Avigad in the late 1960s, including an 80-foot stretch with a width of 23 feet. Hezekiah also ordered a 1,600-foot tunnel dug to secure Jerusalem's access to the waters of Gihon in the event of a long siege.

Even so, Hezekiah's revolt came to naught. The new Assyrian king, Sennacherib, knew all about the plotting in the South and defeated Merodach-Baladan with ease. According to his clay prism, the king rolled up all the other parties in the conspiracy, including Sidon, Joppa, and Ashkelon, before invading Judah and destroying 46 Judean cities. One city located just 30 miles southwest of Jerusalem, Lachish, resisted. As Sennacherib

The 590-yard Tunnel of Hezekiah ran from the Gihon Spring to the pool of Siloam, thus providing Jerusalem with access to water in times of a siege.

brought up his siegeworks, Lachish's archers let loose clouds of arrows on the Assyrian attackers. At first, it seemed that the city might be saved. Among several pieces of inscribed pottery sherds, used to convey military orders, excavators found one ostracon that reads: "May Yahweh cause my lord to hear news of peace, even now, even now …" But it was not to be. The Assyrians breached the walls with their engines, and the city was taken. The male defenders were impaled on wooden stakes and the women and children led away in captivity. Nevertheless, Lachish must have made an impression on Sennacherib, because the king commissioned a series of large tableaux for his palace in Nineveh that provide a frame-by-frame reconstruction of this terrible siege.

Aghast, King Hezekiah sent a message to the Assyrian king while he was still encamped at Lachish: "I have done wrong; withdraw from me; whatever you impose on me I will bear" (II Kings 18:14). Sennacherib agreed, provided Hezekiah paid him a ransom of 300 talents of silver and 30 talents of gold. To pay this outrageous indemnity, Hezekiah was forced to strip the temple of all its gold and ornaments (II Kings 18:15). ■

A seventh-century B.C.E. statue shows Padihor, a general of the Egyptian King Psammetichus I, who succeeded in securing Egypt's independence from the Assyrian Empire.

THE ASSYRIAN CONQUEST

Assyrian Militarism Subjugates Much of the Near East

What doomed the dual kingdoms of Israel and Judah was the aggressive policy of a militaristic empire that pursued its conquests on a scale never seen before. For the Deuteronomist strand of the Books of Kings, Assyria's aggression served an important role in God's plan—as "the rod of my anger—the club in their hands in my fury!" (Isaiah 10:5). Although Assyria was a "godless nation" itself, its conquest was God's punishment for Israel's and Judah's social and religious ills. "Jerusalem shall become a heap of ruins," Micah foretold ominously (Micah 3:12).

Having first secured control over the Assyrian heartland, King Adad-nirari II launched the first war of conquest around 900 B.C.E., subjugating both the Hittite and Hurrian homelands while also taking large parts of the Babylonian kingdom. His successor, Tukulti-Ninurta II, then took the war to the East as far as the Zagros Mountains, subjugating much of today's Iran in the process.

Up to this point, Israel and Judah had been spared, but that changed with the ascension of King Ashurnasirpal II, the first to lead the Assyrian armies down south. Finding little opposition to his overwhelming firepower, the king plowed through Aram-Damascus, Phrygia, Phoenicia, and northern Israel, levying heavy tribute on his conquered vassals. Vast wealth poured into the Assyrian coffers. Ashurnasirpal put it to good use by restoring ancient Babylonian temples and ziggurats and by building a vast new palace complex in the city of Kalhu or Nimrud (known as Calah in the Bible), which he made his capital. Soon the new city became the nucleus of an Assyrian culture that flourished with lavish spending on science, architecture,

The Taylor Prism, a six-sided baked clay document dated to 691 B.C.E., provides a detailed record of the Assyrian King Sennacherib's military operations in Judah.

and the arts. Excavated in 1845 by British explorer Austen Henry Layard, the king's palace at Nimrud yielded huge interior walls covered from top to bottom with sculpted reliefs depicting the king's victories. This set a trend that would be emulated by nearly all of Ashurnasirpal's successors.

The death of the king around 858 B.C.E. and the succession by Shalmaneser III led to a dozen revolts among Assyria's restless subjects. Among the rebels was King Ahab of the Northern Kingdom of Israel, which had allied itself with Syria and Egypt in a desperate attempt to shake off the Assyrian yoke. These coalition forces met Shalmaneser's army in the Battle of Qarqar around 853 B.C.E. According to Shalmaneser's impressive stela, discovered in 1861 and now in the British Museum, the coalition fielded more than 4,000 chariots, half of them supplied by "Ahabbu" or Ahab. No doubt the figures are exaggerated, but there is little doubt that the battle was one of the largest armored clashes to date. Nor was the outcome ever in any doubt. Shalmaneser's Black Obelisk, excavated in 1846, shows Ahab's successor, King Jehu, kneeling before the Assyrian king and his patron, the winged god Ashur.

THE DEPORTATIONS

In the eighth century B.C.E., Assyria's policy toward its subject peoples changed. Whereas before the kings had been satisfied with collecting tribute from its vassal states, the rapid population growth in the Assyrian plateau demanded an outright colonization of its outlying empire. This task fell on King Tiglath-Pileser III, who ascended the throne in 745 B.C.E. and promptly mobilized his troops. It is this threat that had compelled King Pekah of

ca 704	ca 687	ca 640	ca 622
King Sennacherib ascends the throne in Assyria	**Hezekiah is succeeded by King Manasseh**	**Reign of King Josiah of Judah**	**Hilkiah discovers Book of the Law**

An artist's reconstruction shows the interior of Tiglath-Pileser III's palace in Nimrud, late seventh century B.C.E.

An Assyrian siege engine batters the walls of a city, while defending archers loosen a volley of arrows in a tableau from the Northwest Palace in Nimrud, about 860 B.C.E.

The king of Assyria carried the Israelites away to Assyria, settled them in Halah, on the Habor, the river of Gozan, and in the cities of the Medes.

II KINGS 18:11

ca 612	ca 609	ca 605	ca 586
Medes and Babylonians sack Nineveh	Pharaoh Necho II defeats Josiah at Megiddo	Babylonians defeat Egyptians and Assyrians at Carchemish	Nebuchadnezzar destroys Jerusalem

Israel to ally himself with Aram-Damascus in an anti-Assyrian coalition, which in turn led King Ahaz of Judah to choose the side of Assyria instead. But Tiglath-Pileser rapidly conquered the Northern Kingdom, and this time he engaged in the wholesale deportation of the native population so as to make room for Assyrian settlers. "King Tiglath-Pileser of Assyria came," says the second Book of Kings, "and he carried the people captive to Assyria" (II Kings 15:29). Tiglath-Pileser's own account confirms it. "I carried off [to] Assyria the land of Béµt-Håumria [or *Beth Omri,* the "house of Israel"]," the king boasts in an Assyrian inscription; "its auxiliary [army], [and] all of its people." A vivid image of these deportations was captured on a stone relief from Nimrud that shows the king in his chariot, calmly observing his soldiers as they force-march their captives to an uncertain fate in Assyria.

Only the rump state of Samaria remained of what was once the proud kingdom of Israel. This region too would fall victim to deportation after King Sargon II captured the Samarian citadel in the final decade of the eighth century. According to the Bible, the prisoners were settled "in Halah, on Habor, by the river of Gozan," today identified with the Khabur River, one of the largest tributaries of the Euphrates in Syria (II Kings 17:6). Sargon's annals claim that some 27,000 Israelites were thus uprooted. In their stead, Samaria was settled with colonists from places like "Cuthah" (possibly Tell Ibrahim, northeast of Babylon). This is one reason that the Jews of the New Testament held the Samaritans, or "Cuthaeans," in such contempt, for although these foreign farmers had assimilated with the remaining Samarian population and eventually adopted Jewish practices, they possessed a Babylonian bloodline.

THE FALL OF JERUSALEM

The kingdom of Judah would fall victim to the invaders as well, but not before the nation experienced a remarkable renaissance during the reign of King Josiah. Josiah rose to the throne after the 55-year reign of King Manasseh, under whose rule Hezekiah's reforms were ignored and the local population drifted back to polytheistic idolatry—even child sacrifice in the valley of Hinnom. Nevertheless, as archaeologists Israel Finkelstein and Neil Asher Silberman have argued, Manasseh oversaw a strong recovery of Judah's agricultural economy, particularly in the export of olive oil to Assyria. They suggest that the restoration of pagan practices such as the Assyrian astral cult may have been a quid pro quo for Assyria's opening itself up as an export market. The growing prosperity also allowed Manasseh to reinforce the kingdom's

This eighth-century weight in the form of a lion, excavated at Nimrud, was equal to the Assyrian currency of a heavy mina, weighing two pounds, four ounces.

"The Flight of the Prisoners" was painted by the French artist James Tissot (1836-1902) around 1900.

The eighth-century B.C.E. stone head of an eagle once formed part of an Assyrian sculpture from Sennacherib's palace at Nineveh.

This rare glazed terra-cotta tile from Nimrud, circa 875 B.C.E., shows an Assyrian king holding a cup in one hand and a bow in another; he is accompanied by his assistants.

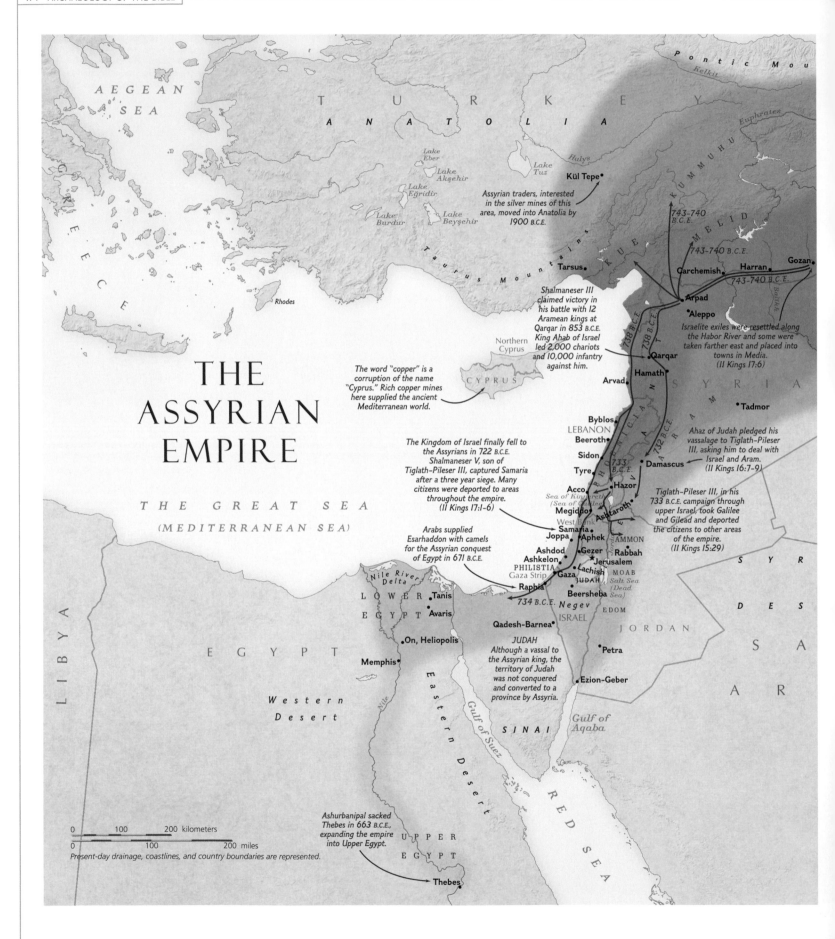

AEGEAN
SEA

TURKEY

ANATOLIA

Pontic Mou

Lake Eber

Lake Akşehir

Lake Tuz

Lake Egridir

Lake Burdur

Lake Beyşehir

Kül Tepe

Assyrian traders, interested in the silver mines of this area, moved into Anatolia by 1900 B.C.E.

743-740 B.C.E.

743-740 B.C.E.

743-740 B.C.E.

Rhodes

GREECE

Taurus Mountains

Tarsus

Gozan

Harran

Carchemish

Arpad

Aleppo

Israelite exiles were resettled along the Habor River and some were taken farther east and placed into towns in Media. (II Kings 17:6)

Shalmaneser III claimed victory in his battle with 12 Aramean kings at Qarqar in 853 B.C.E. King Ahab of Israel led 2,000 chariots and 10,000 infantry against him.

Northern
Cyprus

The word "copper" is a corruption of the name "Cyprus." Rich copper mines here supplied the ancient Mediterranean world.

CYPRUS

THE
ASSYRIAN
EMPIRE

Qarqar

Hamath

Arvad

Tadmor

SYRIA

Ahaz of Judah pledged his vassalage to Tiglath-Pileser III, asking him to deal with Israel and Aram. (II Kings 16:7-9)

Byblos

LEBANON

Beeroth

Sidon

Tyre

Damascus

The Kingdom of Israel finally fell to the Assyrians in 722 B.C.E. Shalmaneser V, son of Tiglath-Pileser III, captured Samaria after a three year siege. Many citizens were deported to areas throughout the empire. (II Kings 17:1-6)

Acco

Sea of Kinnereth (Sea of Galilee)

Hazor

Tiglath-Pileser III, in his 733 B.C.E. campaign through upper Israel, took Galilee and Gilead and deported the citizens to other areas of the empire. (II Kings 15:29)

THE GREAT SEA
(MEDITERRANEAN SEA)

Megiddo

Ashtaroth

West Bank

Samaria

Joppa

Aphek

AMMON

Arabs supplied Esarhaddon with camels for the Assyrian conquest of Egypt in 671 B.C.E.

Ashdod

Ashkelon

Gezer

Rabbah

Jerusalem

Lachish

JUDAH

MOAB

SYR

Nile River Delta

PHILISTIA

Gaza Strip

Gaza

Salt Sea (Dead Sea)

DES

Raphia

Beersheba

734 B.C.E.

Negev

EDOM

SA

LOWER

Tanis

EGYPT

Avaris

ISRAEL

JORDAN

Qadesh-Barnea

On, Heliopolis

*JUDAH
Although a vassal to the Assyrian king, the territory of Judah was not conquered and converted to a province by Assyria.*

Petra

R

Memphis

LIBYA

EGYPT

Eastern Desert

Ezion-Geber

Western Desert

Nile

Gulf of Suez

SINAI

Gulf of Aqaba

RED SEA

0   100   200 kilometers

0   100   200 miles

Present-day drainage, coastlines, and country boundaries are represented.

Ashurbanipal sacked Thebes in 663 B.C.E., expanding the empire into Upper Egypt.

UPPER
EGYPT

Thebes

KUMMUHU

MELID

KUE

Euphrates

Relkit

Hulys

Balikh

738 B.C.E.

738 B.C.E.

732 B.C.E.

733 B.C.E.

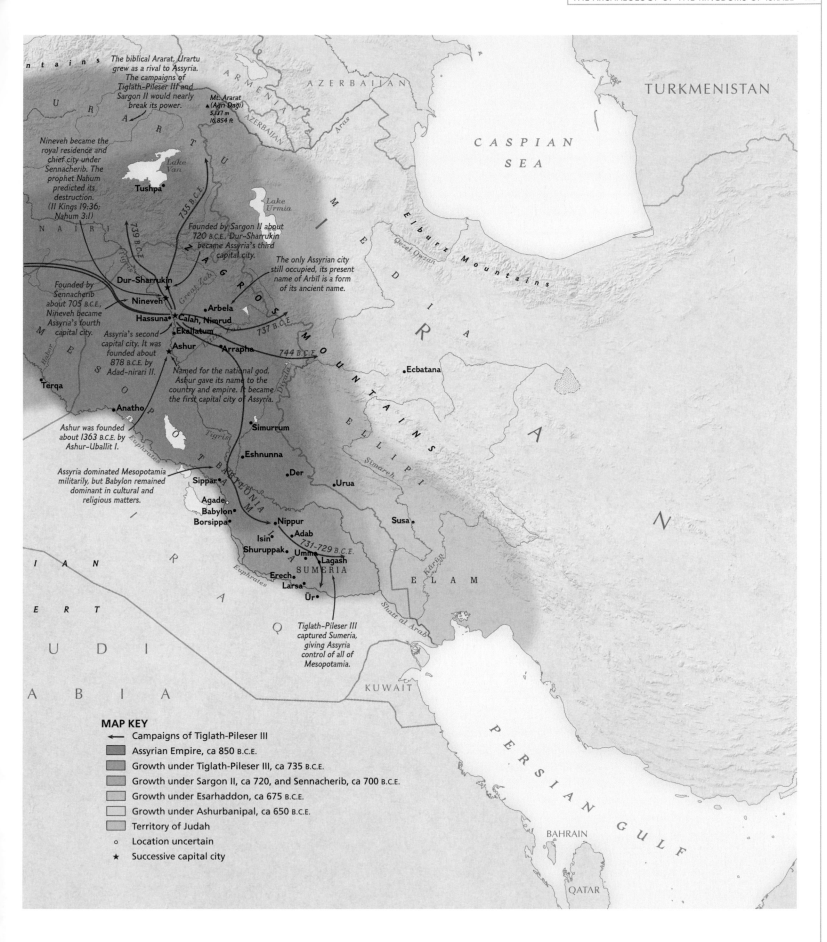

The biblical Ararat, Urartu grew as a rival to Assyria. The campaigns of Tiglath-Pileser III and Sargon II would nearly break its power.

Nineveh became the royal residence and chief city under Sennacherib. The prophet Nahum predicted its destruction. (II Kings 19:36; Nahum 3:1)

Founded by Sargon II about 720 B.C.E., Dur-Sharrukin became Assyria's third capital city.

The only Assyrian city still occupied, its present name of Arbīl is a form of its ancient name.

Founded by Sennacherib about 705 B.C.E., Nineveh became Assyria's fourth capital city.

Assyria's second capital city. It was founded about 878 B.C.E. by Adad-nirari II.

Named for the national god, Ashur gave its name to the country and empire. It became the first capital city of Assyria.

Ashur was founded about 1363 B.C.E. by Ashur-Uballit I.

Assyria dominated Mesopotamia militarily, but Babylon remained dominant in cultural and religious matters.

Tiglath-Pileser III captured Sumeria, giving Assyria control of all of Mesopotamia.

MAP KEY

→ Campaigns of Tiglath-Pileser III

Assyrian Empire, ca 850 B.C.E.

Growth under Tiglath-Pileser III, ca 735 B.C.E.

Growth under Sargon II, ca 720, and Sennacherib, ca 700 B.C.E.

Growth under Esarhaddon, ca 675 B.C.E.

Growth under Ashurbanipal, ca 650 B.C.E.

Territory of Judah

○ Location uncertain

★ Successive capital city

Map labels: TURKMENISTAN · CASPIAN SEA · AZERBAIJAN · ARMENIA · Mt. Ararat (Ağrı Dağı) 5,137 m 16,854 ft · Aras · Lake Van · Tushpa · Lake Urmia · URARTU · NAIRI · ZAGROS MOUNTAINS · Elburz Mountains · Qezel Owzan · MEDIA · Ecbatana · Dur-Sharrukin · Nineveh · Hassuna · Arbela · Calah, Nimrud · Ekallatum · Ashur · Arrapha · Terqa · Anatho · MESOPOTAMIA · Simurrum · Eshnunna · Der · Urua · Susa · ELAM · Tigris · Diyala · Euphrates · Habur · Sippar · Agade · Babylon · Borsippa · BABYLONIA · Nippur · Adab · Isin · Shuruppak · Umma · Lagash · Erech · SUMERIA · Larsa · Ūr · Kārūn · ELLIPI · Simareh · Shatt al Arab · KUWAIT · PERSIAN GULF · BAHRAIN · QATAR · ARABIA · SYRIAN DESERT

735 B.C.E. · 739 B.C.E. · 737 B.C.E. · 744 B.C.E. · 731-729 B.C.E.

Captive Judean families are sent under guard into exile in a wall panel from Sennacherib's palace at Nineveh, 701 B.C.E.

outlying fortresses facing Egypt, particularly in Arad, as evidenced by excavations there.

Thus, when around 640 B.C.E. his grandson Josiah (or Yoshi-yyáhu, "healed by Yah") succeeded him, the new king found a replenished treasury and a well-functioning economy. This allowed him to focus on two areas: religious reforms and territorial expansion, including a complete restoration of the temple that under Manasseh had been devoted to Baal and Asherah. During the renovation, the Bible tells us, the high priest Hilkiah discovered an ancient scroll in the temple archives that contained "the book of the law"—quite possibly an early version of what would become the Book of Deuteronomy (II Kings 22:8). If this is indeed what happened, Josiah and the newly reformed priesthood would have been astonished at the sheer detail of the Mosaic Laws, so far removed from the worship of their own day. Indeed, the Bible states that Josiah banned all foreign cults in order to refocus Judah on the sole worship of YHWH. All "high places"—sanctuaries for idolatry—throughout the country were destroyed, and all pagan priests were put to death. Most important, the discovery of the scroll may have spurred an attempt to create a canon of the full Pentateuch, the Five Books of Moses—a process that would not be completed until after the exile.

Meanwhile, the political situation was changing. The old Assyrian Empire was steadily crumbling, and Egypt was still recovering from Assyrian occupation. Josiah seized the ensuing power vacuum by

As for the king of Judah, Hezekiah, who had not submitted to my authority, I besieged and captured forty-six of his fortified cities, along with many smaller towns.

SENNACHERIB'S ANNALS, ALSO KNOWN AS THE "TAYLOR PRISM"

invading the Assyrian provinces in the North, thus combining Judah and Israel into a united monarchy. This conquest, as some scholars have argued, was extolled by Josiah's panegyrists as a "restoration" of the legendary Davidic Kingdom, an idea that was subsequently woven into the fabric of Deuteronomist history by Josiah's scribes.

But then the king overreached. When in 612 B.C.E., the Medes and the Babylonians rose in rebellion and sacked Assyria's capital of Nineveh, Egyptian Pharaoh (either Psammetichus I or Necho I) came to the aid of the hard-pressed Assyrian forces. This was not inspired by any love for Egypt's former oppressors, but by the realpolitik of trying to secure Egypt's trade routes at all costs. Surprisingly, Josiah decided to back the side of the rebels. In an ill-considered move, the king attacked the supply lines of the Egyptian army near the fortress of Megiddo. What motivated Josiah to turn against his southern neighbor has never been fully explained, but the fallout was considerable. Judah's forces were defeated, the king himself was fatally wounded, and the kingdom of Judah became, once more, a vassal state of Egypt, like the Canaan of old. All of Josiah's grand ambitions had come to naught.

Seven years later, the Medean-Babylonian forces defeated the Assyrian-Egyptian coalition at the Battle of Carchemish, and the last act in the history of the Israelite kingdoms began. As it turned out, the new Babylonian king, Nebuchadnezzar II, was every bit as rapacious as his Assyrian predecessors and equally determined to restore the Assyrian Empire under the rule of Babylon. This time, the conquest was not for the greater glory of Ashur but for the Babylonian deity Nabu, the god of wisdom; "Nebuchadnezzar" (or Nabû-kudurri-uṣur in Akkadian) means "God Nabu, preserve my firstborn son." All of the former vassal states were summoned to pledge their fealty to Babylon or accept the consequences.

Josiah's successor, King Jehoiakim, was also forced to pledge his submission, but soon after began to plot a rebellion, as his predecessor Hezekiah had done a century before. Jehoiakim even restored many of the pagan practices that had been outlawed by his father. The prophet Jeremiah was shocked, and like Isaiah before him, he warned that God's revenge would be swift. "This whole land," Jeremiah said, "shall become a ruin and a waste, and these nations shall serve the king of Babylon seventy years" (Jeremiah 25:9-11).

This is exactly what happened. A clay tablet from the palace of Babylon states that "in the seventh year, in the month of Kislimu [winter 598 B.C.E.], the king of Akkad (Nebuchadnezzar) mustered his troops, marched to the Hatti-Land [Syria-Canaan] and encamped against the city of Judah [Jerusalem]." Jerusalem enjoyed a brief respite while the Babylonian king rushed his troops southward to defeat a rebellion by Egyptian king Apries, but in 586 B.C.E., Nebuchadnezzar returned and captured the city after a bitter struggle. The temple was destroyed, and almost all inhabitants were killed or marched into captivity. The Israelite kingdoms were no more, and the great Babylonian exile had begun. ■

A Phoenician gold and ivory inlay of a lion attacking a Nubian shepherd was found at Nimrud and dated to the late eighth century B.C.E.

Assyrian Motives

While the Bible portrays the Assyrian conquest as God's punishment for the dual monarchy, its true motives lay elsewhere. The Assyrian kings recognized that the gradual collapse of Egyptian control in the Levant had produced a power vacuum in which all sorts of upstart kingdoms (including Israel and Judah) were trying to stake a claim, thus disrupting strategic trade contacts. What's more, Assyria's population was growing just as the kingdom of Urartu, located in today's Armenian highlands, began to challenge Assyrian access to metal ores and livestock from Anatolia. The war aims of Assyria were therefore twofold: to create a series of buffer states and to vouchsafe all of the principal trade arteries of the Levant. The Assyrians clad their aggressive wars in a pious cloak of religious observance: The need for conquest was spurred by the desire of the Assyrian god Ashur to bring all the world under his rule.

THE ART OF THE IRON AGE

New Creative Motifs Emerge in the Period of Israelite Monarchies

Many scholars would agree that the first appearance of Israelite settlements in Canaan probably took place in the Early Iron Age (1200-1000 B.C.E.), but that distinctive creative expressions would not emerge until much later, during the period of the kingdoms of Israel and Judah. Much of this creative output was still heavily influenced by surrounding cultures, predominantly the artifacts and writing systems of Phoenicia, Egypt, and Canaan proper. Indeed, the emergence of ancient (or "Old") Hebrew coincided with the development of the first truly alphabetic script, known as the Phoenician alphabet, of which it served as a branch. Old Hebrew did not assume a clearly distinct script until the seventh century—the time when, scholars believe, the Torah was first composed in its current form. ■

A stunning gold pectoral from the ancient Canaanite city at Tell Jemmeh dates from the 11th century B.C.E.

The Tel Dan inscription, discovered in 1993 and dated around 850 B.C.E., includes the phrase bytdwd, which most scholars agree refers to the "House of David."

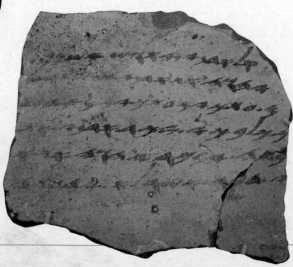

The Lachish Ostracon, which contains a message to Yaosh, the military governor of Lachish, is an example of early Hebrew script, circa 588 B.C.E.

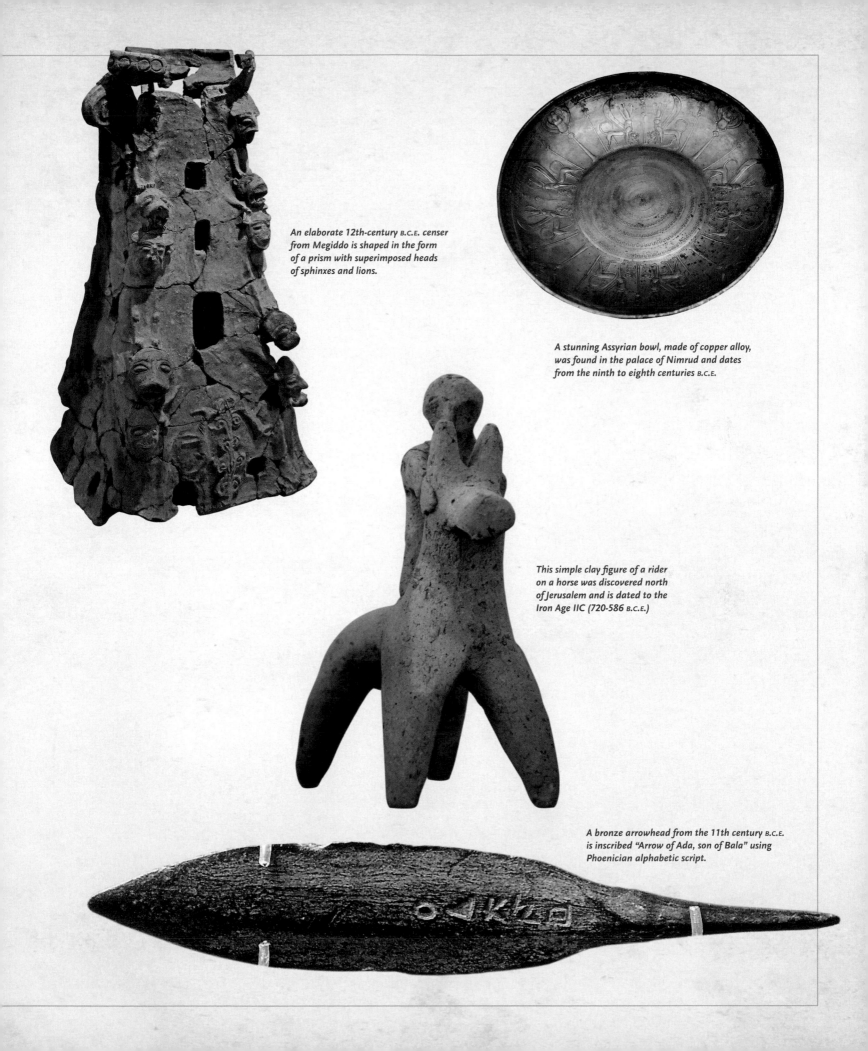

An elaborate 12th-century B.C.E. censer from Megiddo is shaped in the form of a prism with superimposed heads of sphinxes and lions.

A stunning Assyrian bowl, made of copper alloy, was found in the palace of Nimrud and dates from the ninth to eighth centuries B.C.E.

This simple clay figure of a rider on a horse was discovered north of Jerusalem and is dated to the Iron Age IIC (720-586 B.C.E.)

A bronze arrowhead from the 11th century B.C.E. is inscribed "Arrow of Ada, son of Bala" using Phoenician alphabetic script.

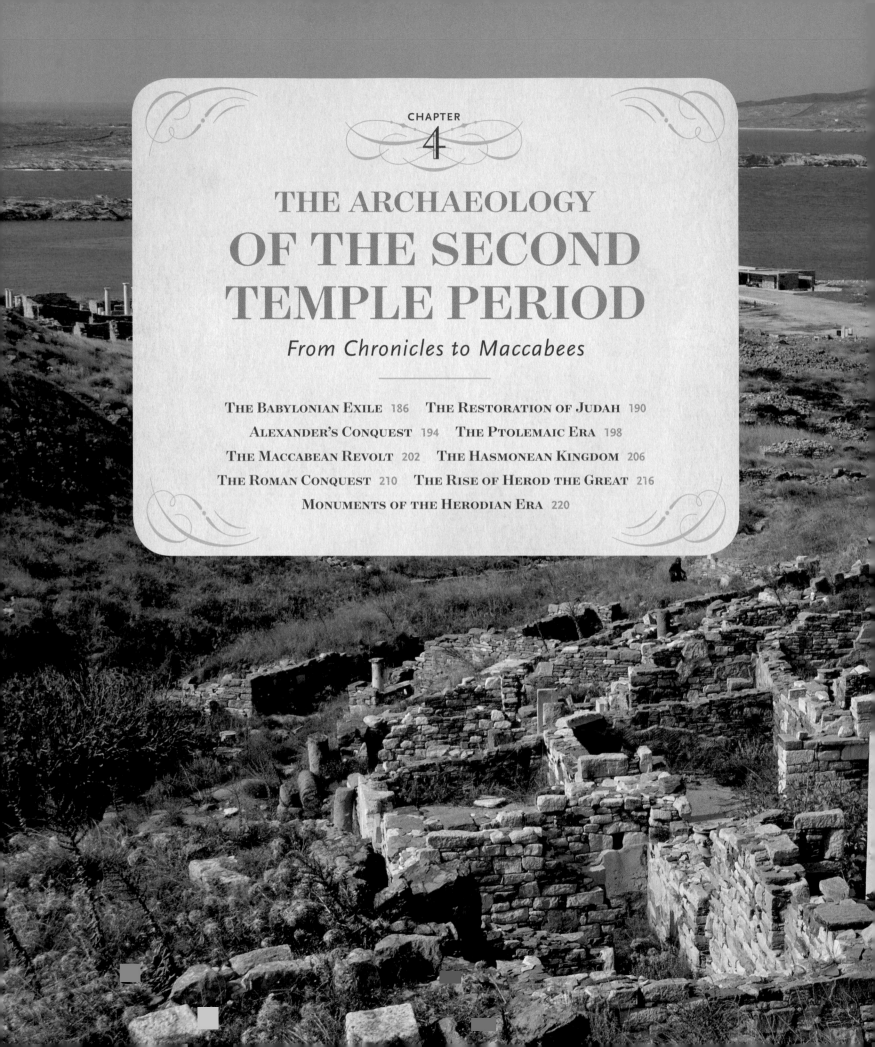

THE ARCHAEOLOGY
OF THE SECOND
TEMPLE PERIOD

From Chronicles to Maccabees

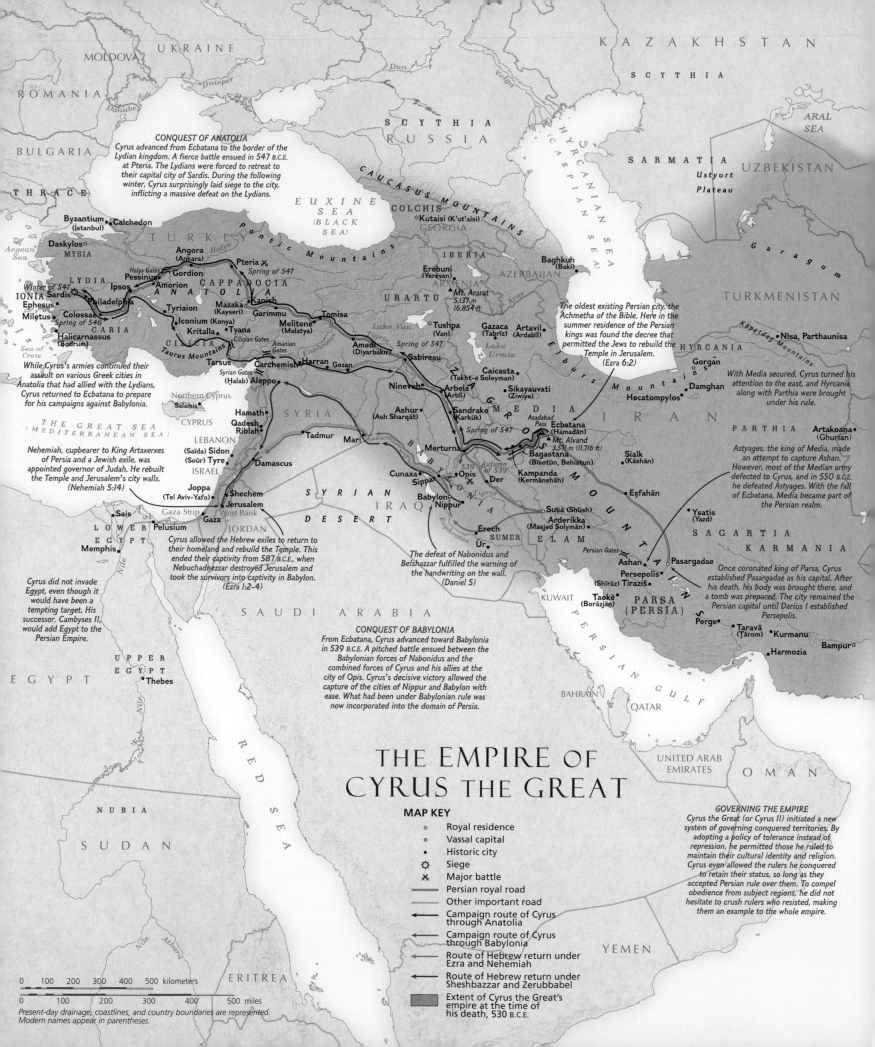

THE EMPIRE OF CYRUS THE GREAT

CONQUEST OF ANATOLIA
Cyrus advanced from Ecbatana to the border of the Lydian kingdom. A fierce battle ensued in 547 B.C.E. at Pteria. The Lydians were forced to retreat to their capital city of Sardis. During the following winter, Cyrus surprisingly laid siege to the city, inflicting a massive defeat on the Lydians.

While Cyrus's armies continued their assault on various Greek cities in Anatolia that had allied with the Lydians, Cyrus returned to Ecbatana to prepare for his campaigns against Babylonia.

Nehemiah, cupbearer to King Artaxerxes of Persia and a Jewish exile, was appointed governor of Judah. He rebuilt the Temple and Jerusalem's city walls. (Nehemiah 5:14)

Cyrus allowed the Hebrew exiles to return to their homeland and rebuild the Temple. This ended their captivity from 587 B.C.E., when Nebuchadnezzar destroyed Jerusalem and took the survivors into captivity in Babylon. (Ezra 1:2–4)

Cyrus did not invade Egypt, even though it would have been a tempting target. His successor, Cambyses II, would add Egypt to the Persian Empire.

The oldest existing Persian city, the Achmetha of the Bible. Here in the summer residence of the Persian kings was found the decree that permitted the Jews to rebuild the Temple in Jerusalem. (Ezra 6:2)

With Media secured, Cyrus turned his attention to the east, and Hyrcania along with Parthia were brought under his rule.

Astyages, the king of Media, made an attempt to capture Ashan. However, most of the Median army defected to Cyrus, and in 550 B.C.E. he defeated Astyages. With the fall of Ecbatana, Media became part of the Persian realm.

The defeat of Nabonidus and Belshazzar fulfilled the warning of the handwriting on the wall. (Daniel 5)

Once coronated king of Parsa, Cyrus established Pasargadae as his capital. After his death, his body was brought there, and a tomb was prepared. The city remained the Persian capital until Darius I established Persepolis.

CONQUEST OF BABYLONIA
From Ecbatana, Cyrus advanced toward Babylonia in 539 B.C.E. A pitched battle ensued between the Babylonian forces of Nabonidus and the combined forces of Cyrus and his allies at the city of Opis. Cyrus's decisive victory allowed the capture of the cities of Nippur and Babylon with ease. What had been under Babylonian rule was now incorporated into the domain of Persia.

MAP KEY

- ○ Royal residence
- ◎ Vassal capital
- • Historic city
- ⚙ Siege
- ✕ Major battle
- ━━ Persian royal road
- ── Other important road
- ← Campaign route of Cyrus through Anatolia
- ← Campaign route of Cyrus through Babylonia
- ← Route of Hebrew return under Ezra and Nehemiah
- ← Route of Hebrew return under Sheshbazzar and Zerubbabel
- ▓ Extent of Cyrus the Great's empire at the time of his death, 530 B.C.E.

GOVERNING THE EMPIRE
Cyrus the Great (or Cyrus II) initiated a new system of governing conquered territories. By adopting a policy of tolerance instead of repression, he permitted those he ruled to maintain their cultural identity and religion. Cyrus even allowed the rulers he conquered to retain their status, so long as they accepted Persian rule over them. To compel obedience from subject regions, he did not hesitate to crush rulers who resisted, making them an example to the whole empire.

0 100 200 300 400 500 kilometers
0 100 200 300 400 500 miles

Present-day drainage, coastlines, and country boundaries are represented. Modern names appear in parentheses.

In the first year of his reign, King Cyrus issued a decree:
Concerning the house of God at Jerusalem, let the house be rebuilt,
the place where sacrifices are offered and burnt offerings are brought.

EZRA 6:3

THE WORLD IN 550 B.C.E.

From the Persian to the Greek and Roman Empire, Circa 550 B.C.E. to 5 B.C.E.

NEBUCHADNEZZAR'S DREAM OF RE-CREATING BABYLONIA'S STORIED PAST IN A VAST Neo-Babylonian realm was surprisingly short-lived. Perhaps the king had a premonition about its short time span, because back at home in Babylon, he launched into a frenzied program to rebuild the city in a fashion that would put the Assyrian capitals of Nineveh and Ashur to shame. This new center included a huge palace precinct complete with harem facilities, which the historian Herodotus described as "the most magnificent building ever erected on earth." It was equipped with what Greek authors would later call one of the Seven Wonders of the Ancient World: a stupendous series of hanging gardens, planted on a cascade of elevated terraces, with samples of every tree and plant found in the Babylonian Empire. Each botanical garden was watered with a sophisticated system of irrigation pipes fed by mechanical pumps. According to one legend, the inspiration for this miraculous design had come from one of the king's favorite wives, named Amytis, the daughter of the vassal king of the Medes, who ached for the forests of her native Persia. Nothing remains of these gardens, which has prompted some historians to suggest that they may have been the stuff of legend, given the sheer technological difficulty of maintaining elevated gardens.

Preceding pages: The sacred island of Delos, a leading pilgrimage destination of the ancient world, was also the location of one of the earliest synagogues found to date. Right: According to its inscription, this one-mina weight was made for Assyrian King Nebuchadnezzar II, sixth century B.C.E.

That does not apply, however, to one of Nebuchadnezzar's most impressive monuments, the Ishtar Gate, which after restoration is still visible today in the Pergamon Museum in Berlin. The huge gateway was one of eight gates that led to the city's inner precinct. Begun in 575 B.C.E., the gate was covered with glazed color tiles that depicted dragons and a type of oxen known as aurochs, symbols of the Babylonian gods Marduk and Adad. Excavated by German archaeologist Robert Koldewey, the current restoration contains many of the original bricks.

Shortly after the Ishtar Gate was completed, however, the Neo-Babylonian Empire began to crumble. The trouble began in the kingdom of Ashan, today's Iran, which had been ruled by a dynasty that traced its origins to a legendary figure named Achaemenes (the later Persian dynasty would become known as the Achaemenids). In 553 B.C.E., Ashan's vassal king decided to rise up against his overlord, the king of the Medes, and in short order he proceeded to conquer all of the Median Empire. The king's name was Cyrus II.

Thus began an era that in the span of a mere four centuries would see the rise of three vast empires: those of Persia, Greece, and Rome. In 540 B.C.E. Cyrus turned his armies against the Neo-Babylonian realm, now ruled by King Nabonidus. A man who preferred to dwell in his library than in the barracks, Nabonidus had placed his son Bel-shar-usur at the head of his army. Bel-shar-usur may have inspired the character of Belshazzar in the Book of Daniel. Apparently neither king nor son inspired much confidence among the populace. According to a tablet known as the Verse Account of Nabonidus, the citizens of Babylon simply opened the gates when they saw Cyrus's army on the horizon.

For more than two centuries, the Persian or Achaemenid Empire would be ruled from its capital in Pasargadae as the largest empire in history, fostering an unprecedented level of peaceful coexistence and commercial activity in the Middle East. If projected on a modern map, the empire would have encompassed today's Turkey, Syria, Iraq, Iran, Israel, Jordan, and Lebanon, as well as Russia, Armenia, Afghanistan, and much of Central Asia, including northern India. By some estimates, this commonwealth embraced some 50 million people.

The Achaemenid period introduced a number of innovations, including a network of royal roads, a central postal system, a national army (equipped with portable pontoon bridges), and—most crucial for our story—a new degree of religious tolerance and diversity. The new empire reached its peak under King Darius I, who ascended the throne around 522 B.C.E. and built a new capital in Persepolis (today's Fars Province of Iran), as well as a stupendous new palace in Susa (the biblical Sushan), where the stories of Daniel and Esther are set. Still, Darius faced a number of revolts in virtually every corner of his empire. Worse, the growing tensions between Persia and Greece over the Persian occupation of the northern Aegean led to an all-out war, which ended in a Persian defeat at the famous Battle of Marathon in 490 B.C.E. This did not settle the argument, however. The clash between the two leading civilizations of their time continued until 466 B.C.E. when the Athenian-led Delian League liberated its Ionian colonies (on today's Turkish coast) from Persian rule. After that, hostilities petered out as the Greek city-states and Persia, exhausted by their military adventures, settled into an uneasy coexistence. Fortunately, this did not prevent an active cultural and commercial exchange, as we will see shortly.

This cuneiform tablet extols the rule of Nebuchadnezzar II (605-562 B.C.E.) as an era of greatness and justice.

Among others, this era would see one of the most important inventions of the ancient world: the struck coin. Exactly who first developed the idea of minted currency is a matter of debate, though most historians agree it first occurred in Lydia (today's north-western Turkey) during the sixth century B.C.E., possibly during the reign of King Alyattes. The first coins were struck using electrum (an alloy of silver, gold, and copper) with little more than a symbol, such as an animal, as ornamentation. From there the practice moved to the Persian interior, where it produced the gold daric and the sub-sequent adoption of coins throughout the empire. Originally called the Babylonian shekel, the daric was a gold coin of 8.4 grams. It replaced actual weights, such as the mina weighing two pounds four ounces, which had previously served as currency. The words *mene, tekel,* and *parsin,* which Daniel deciphered on the wall of Belshazzar's banqueting hall, are actually units of measure equivalent to the mina, shekel, and half-mina (Daniel 5:25).

In the fifth century, the Athenian drachma became the coin of choice throughout the Mediterranean world, usually bearing the image of an owl, symbol of the city's patron, Athena. Many cities followed suit by issuing the silver tetradrachm (four drachmas) coin, or the even larger decadrachm (ten drachmas). From the third century onward, in the wake of Alexander's conquest, coins were struck with the likeness of the local ruler, which has been a boon for archaeologists in trying to date a particular layer in excavations. This custom would become the norm during the 400-year history of the Roman Empire. ■

The Ishtar Gate with its glazed figures of bulls and dragons once towered over the Processional Way of Babylon, leading to the Temple of Marduk (sixth century B.C.E.).

THE BABYLONIAN EXILE

Captivity in Babylon Allows Work on the
Hebrew Canon to Continue

By 585 B.C.E., a large portion of the population from Judah joined their Hebrew compatriots from Israel (deported in 729 B.C.E.) and Samaria (evicted in 721 B.C.E.) in captivity. They were not the first to suffer this fate; previously, Assyrian kings had also deported other communities, including people from Urartu, the Chaldeans, and the Medeans. These deportations appeared to be organized according to some master plan. The Israelites, for example, were moved to Iran and Babylon, while Arabs and Persians were relocated to Syria-Canaan, and the Chaldeans were deported to Armenia. Judah was particularly hard hit. In the span of less than 20 years, the region suffered four deportations: during the reign of King Jehoiakim in 598, King Jehoiachin in 597, King Zedekiah in 586, and one more exile in 582.

Despite the sheer scale of these forced migrations, historians do not agree about the actual number of deportees. Excavations suggest that the total population of Judah before the Babylonian invasions was around 75,000. The second Book of Kings claims that virtually the entire populace was marched off, but studies of post-exilic settlements show that the actual number of deportees was much smaller—perhaps no more than 20 or 25 percent. According to the Book of Jeremiah, the total number of deportees amounted to no more than 4,600 (Jeremiah 52:30).

There were sound reasons for this. As we saw, Judah's economy was rooted in dry farming that required a unique skill and understanding of the climate and the soil. What's more, the principal resistance to the Babylonian occupation had come from urban centers such as Lachish and Jerusalem rather than the highlands, the valley, or

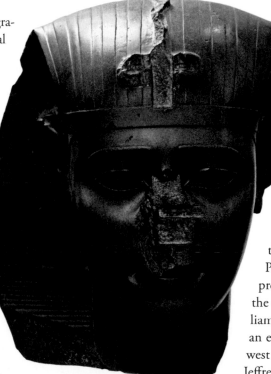

This head of the Egyptian King Nectanebo II (31st Dynasty) was deliberately mutilated, perhaps by Persian troops during Persia's conquest of Egypt.

the desert beyond. One could therefore plausibly suggest that the Babylonian ire may have been directed on the urban elites rather than the vast majority of rural workers. Two subsequent developments bear this out.

BABYLONIAN RULE IN JUDAH

According to the Book of Jeremiah, the Babylonian viceroy who had been "left in the land of Judah," Nebuzaradan, organized a redistribution of land among the poor to help rebuild the agrarian economy (Jeremiah 39:10). This suggests that the rural population had not been much affected by the deportations. Nebuzaradan then installed a provincial governor who could be trusted to do his bidding; his name was Gedaliah, of the Judean family of Shaphan (II Kings 25:22). Such was not unusual; given the vast territory they had to govern and the limited number of Babylonian officials who spoke the local language, the Babylonians often handpicked local quisling administrators to rule on their behalf. Gedaliah gathered a number of Judean officers who had survived the Babylonian invasion and set up a local government in the town of Mizpah.

Mizpah is often mentioned in the Bible. Among others, this was the place where Samuel held court (I Samuel 7:15), the Israelites mobilized to do battle with the Philistines (I Samuel 7:5), and Saul was first presented to the people (I Samuel 10:17). In the mid-1920s, American archaeologist William Badè identified Mizpah as Tell en-Nasbeh, an eight-acre plateau some seven miles northwest of Jerusalem. In a 1997 article, Professor Jeffrey Zorn argued that Badè had unwittingly discovered a layer (No. 2) above the Iron Age II stratum with structures of substantially larger size. These, he

A wall panel depicting three prisoners playing the lyre from the Southwest Palace in Nineveh (700 B.C.E.) evokes Psalm 137.

By the rivers of Babylon—
there we sat down and there
we wept when we remembered Zion.
On the willows there
we hung up our harps.

PSALM 137:1-2

This clay tablet from around 545 B.C.E., a receipt of silver for the sale of slaves, refers to Bel-shar-usur, the biblical Belshazzar, son of King Nabonidus.

ca 525	ca 520	ca 515	ca 508
King Cambyses, son of Cyrus, conquers Egypt	Haggai and Zechariah are active during the reign of Darius I	The Second Temple in Jerusalem is dedicated	The Greeks create a democratic constitution

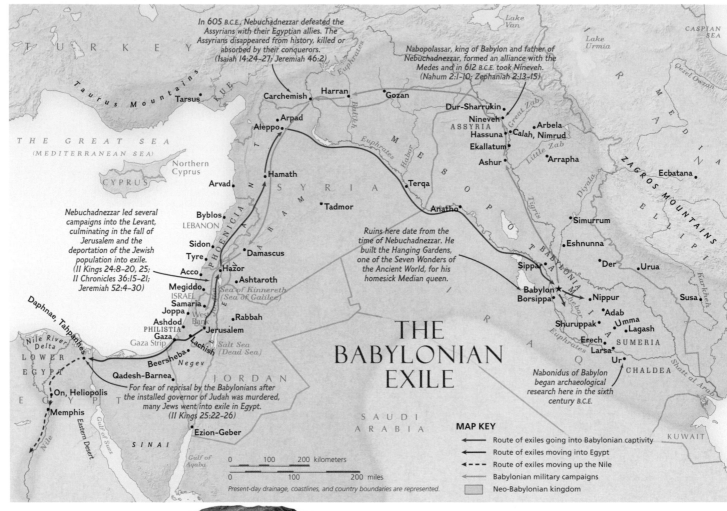

In 605 B.C.E., Nebuchadnezzar defeated the Assyrians with their Egyptian allies. The Assyrians disappeared from history, killed or absorbed by their conquerors. (Isaiah 14:24-27; Jeremiah 46:2)

Nabopolassar, king of Babylon and father of Nebuchadnezzar, formed an alliance with the Medes and in 612 B.C.E. took Nineveh. (Nahum 2:1-10; Zephaniah 2:13-15)

Nebuchadnezzar led several campaigns into the Levant, culminating in the fall of Jerusalem and the deportation of the Jewish population into exile. (II Kings 24:8-20, 25; II Chronicles 36:15-21; Jeremiah 52:4-30)

Ruins here date from the time of Nebuchadnezzar. He built the Hanging Gardens, one of the Seven Wonders of the Ancient World, for his homesick Median queen.

For fear of reprisal by the Babylonians after the installed governor of Judah was murdered, many Jews went into exile in Egypt. (II Kings 25:22-26)

Nabonidus of Babylon began archaeological research here in the sixth century B.C.E.

THE BABYLONIAN EXILE

MAP KEY

→ Route of exiles going into Babylonian captivity
← Route of exiles moving into Egypt
◄-- Route of exiles moving up the Nile
→ Babylonian military campaigns
▢ Neo-Babylonian kingdom

0   100   200 kilometers
0   100   200 miles
Present-day drainage, coastlines, and country boundaries are represented.

Two Persian guards with spears ascend the north stairs of the Apadana at Persepolis, Iran, carved around 480 B.C.E.

posited, could have been the administrative buildings of Gedaliah's government.

Naturally, Gedaliah urged all those who had stayed behind to collaborate with the occupiers as much as possible—a sentiment that Jeremiah shared. "Live in the land, serve the king of Babylon," he declared, "and it shall be well with you." But this plea was not heeded. A resistance group, led by an officer named Ishmael, staged a successful assassination attempt on Gedaliah. When news of the killing spread, many of the remaining elites, including Jeremiah, fled to Egypt, leaving the local populace to face the music. Not surprisingly, this is when another group of Judeans was forcibly marched off to an uncertain fate (II Kings 25:25-26; Jeremiah 52:30).

Other than the putative discovery at Tell en-Nasbeh, archaeological evidence of the Babylonian rule is difficult to ascertain. Jerusalem was largely despoiled; the temple lay in ruins, as did many of Judah's fortified cities. But up north, along the rivers of Babylon, the situation was noticeably different.

An artist's impression shows the hanging gardens of Babylon, considered one of the Seven Wonders of the Ancient World.

ISRAEL IN EXILE

Upon their arrival in Babylon, the deportees were not herded into camps, as some may have feared, but allowed to settle in communities as they pleased. The locations described in the Bible suggest that Babylonian planners deliberately placed their prisoners in relatively unpopulated areas so as to create a more equitable distribution of habitants in relationship to available natural resources. For example, some of the exiles were settled at Tel Abib, "by the river Chebar" (Ezekiel 3:15), which may refer to either the Khabur River in today's Syria or, more likely, the Kebar Canal near Nippur in today's Iraq. The Kebar Canal ("ka-ba-ru" in Akkadian) is attested in fifth-century records at Nippur, which suggests that the refugees were allowed to settle in areas with plentiful access to water. The Babylonians were careful not to break up families and clans, so that they were free to rebuild their communities, till the land, and practice their faith as they had done before.

The exile gave the Hebrews an opportunity to reflect on what had happened, why God had allowed this catastrophe to come about, and whether Judah would ever be restored. The prophet Ezekiel tried to address these questions by turning the tragedy of the exile into an opportunity for spiritual reflection. His visions revealed a merciful Lord whose wrath has been assuaged and once more looked forward to be the God of his people (Ezekiel 37:27). This may have spurred the exiled priests and scribes to preserve Yahwist worship and continue the work begun under King Josiah:

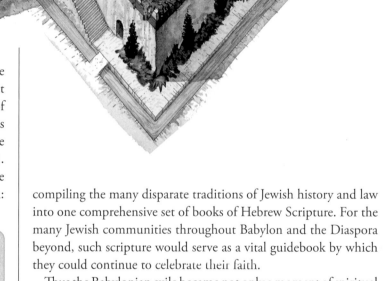

compiling the many disparate traditions of Jewish history and law into one comprehensive set of books of Hebrew Scripture. For the many Jewish communities throughout Babylon and the Diaspora beyond, such scripture would serve as a vital guidebook by which they could continue to celebrate their faith.

Thus the Babylonian exile became not only a moment of spiritual reflection, but also a unique opportunity to complete a corpus of Jewish scripture without the distractions that life in Judah would have imposed. Fittingly, the second Book of Chronicles calls the exile the "Sabbath of the Land" (II Chronicles 36:21). It is from this time forward that modern scholars speak of the Hebrew nation as "Jews" (or Yehudim, probably derived from "Judean") and refer to "Judaism" as a community in religious terms, no longer bound to a particular political entity or geographical location. Some have also argued that this is when the concept of a synagogue emerged, as a community house of assembly *(beit Knesset)* where families could gather to pray, worship, celebrate, and attend to important civic matters. ■

Prophet of the Exile

In addition to Ezekiel, an anonymous prophet referred to by scholars as "Second Isaiah" tried to sustain the grieving exiles in Babylon. "Comfort, O comfort my people, says your God," the prophet said. "Speak tenderly to Jerusalem, and cry to her that she has served her term" (Isaiah 40:1-2). By sustaining the hope for a return, the prophet inspired the people to remain true to their identity and thus preserve Judaism in its moment of peril.

THE RESTORATION OF JUDAH

The Temple in Jerusalem Is Rebuilt With Persian Assistance

King Cambyses I was the son of King Cyrus and his successor as ruler over the small nation of Ashan that today is located in the Fars Province of Iran, straddling the Zagros Mountains. Surrounded by Persians, Medeans, and Babylonians, Ashan had been governed as a vassal kingdom under the rule of the Medean king Astyages since the seventh century B.C.E. To cement the relationship, Astyages had given his daughter Mandane to Cambyses in marriage. In the first quarter of the sixth century (the record is not clear), Mandane gave birth to a son whom she named Cyrus (Kūruš in old Persian), after his grandfather.

Around 550 B.C.E., after Cyrus had succeeded his father as king of Ashan, the kingdom came to blows with its overlord, King Astyages. What caused the rupture is not known, but according to a text known as the Nabonidus Chronicle (probably written by Cyrus's rather than Nabonidus's panegyrists), Astyages was the first to attack. This set in motion a series of battles and military movements that put Cyrus at the head of not only the Medean Kingdom but of Lydia, Babylonia, and all of its vassal states as well—including a small Babylonian dependency known as Judah.

Cyrus's conquest of the Babylonian Empire was a watershed moment in history. It introduced an era in which Persian science, philosophy, literature, and the arts would spread throughout the Middle East, laying the seeds for the great flourishing of Islamo-Persian culture more than a millennium later.

THE GREAT RETURN

As the history of the Assyrian and Babylonian Empires had shown, subject states are bound to rise in revolt eventually, simply to assert and preserve their individual identity. Cyrus believed there was another way to allow his vassals to experience their autonomy: channeling their national aspirations into their native cult. The king knew that his realm encompassed many

The Nabonidus Chronicle describes the reign of Nabonidus (circa 556-539 B.C.E.), the last king of the Neo-Babylonian Empire and Babylon's conquest by Cyrus the Great.

different religions. Babylonia had its cult of Marduk (whom Cyrus quickly adopted as his patron), while the Medeans had developed a monotheistic tradition around the legendary priest named Zarathustra (or Zoroaster), and the Lydians had embraced the pantheon of Greek gods.

The king's proclamation of religious tolerance, issued around 538 B.C.E., was welcomed throughout his empire and nowhere more so than in Judah. The problem was, most of the priests, scribes, and scholars who could restore the worship of YHWH were no longer in Jerusalem but in Babylon. In response, Cyrus set the Jewish exiles free and invited them to return to their homeland.

A similar version of Cyrus's decree, which was recorded on a clay cylinder, is found in the Book of Ezra, which forms part of the third division of Hebrew Scripture known as the Ketuvim (or Kətûbîm), meaning "writings." The difference is that in the Book of Ezra, it is YHWH, the Hebrew God, who "stirred up the spirit of King Cyrus" to declare that all "are now permitted to go up to Jerusalem in Judah" (Ezra 1:1, 3). The Cyrus Cylinder, by contrast, attributes Cyrus's benevolence to the Babylonian deity Marduk.

And the king's generosity did not end there. As the Cyrus Cylinder states, the king also "returned to [the] sacred cities on the other side of the Tigris the sanctuaries which have been ruins for a long time." Among these sanctuaries was the Temple in Jerusalem. Cyrus released the funds to restore the Temple to its original condition, although this was just one of several such restoration projects. According to his cylinder, Cyrus also paid for the repair of temples dedicated to the "gods of Sumer and Akkad."

Many of the Jewish refugees joyfully prepared for the return, but many others did not. Two new generations had been born in Babylon; many of these had assimilated with the local civilization, married local Babylonians, and started families. In

Thus says King Cyrus of Persia:
the Lord, the God of heaven, has given
me all the kingdoms of the earth,
and he has charged me to build him
a house at Jerusalem in Judah.

EZRA 1:3

Persepolis in today's Iran was chosen by Cyrus the Great as the capital of the new Achaemenid Empire, although it was Darius the Great who built much of the palace complex.

The clay Cyrus Cylinder, dated to the sixth century B.C.E., describes (in Babylonian cuneiform) the conquest of Babylon by Cyrus the Great.

ca 458
Ezra undertakes
his mission to Judah

ca 444
Nehemiah, Artaxerxes' cupbearer,
travels to Judah

ca 438
The Parthenon
is completed in Athens

ca 431
Outbreak of the
Peloponnesian War

This view of Temple Mount shows the Dome of the Rock in the heart of the Old City of Jerusalem, where once the Temple was rebuilt with Persian assistance.

This sixth-century golden cup illustrates the virtuosity of the Achaemenid dynasty in precious metals.

addition, scores of scholars and scribes feared that the perilous 600-mile journey home would disrupt the work of completing the canons of Hebrew Scripture. And naturally, the living standard in Babylonia was considerably higher than that in the ravaged lands of Judah.

Thus, many refugees moved back, but many others elected to stay. These communities would eventually become leading centers of Jewish exegesis in Babylonia and serve as an important source of high priests and other priestly cadres during the Herodian era.

THE SECOND TEMPLE

The first caravan of 42,360 Jews that left for Jerusalem was led by a member of Judah's former royal house named Sheshbazzar. Before his departure, King Cyrus had given him thousands of gold and silver vessels that Nebuchadnezzar had looted from the Jerusalem Temple (Ezra 5:14). Upon his arrival, Sheshbazzar was duly installed as governor of Judah, which was then known as the subprovince of Yehud, part of the fifth Persian satrapy known as Abar-nahara ("beyond the [Euphrates] River").

The construction of the Temple was begun soon after, but the sheer magnitude of the task may have been too much. After the first blush of enthusiasm, work faltered as the people became more focused on rebuilding their homes, or their fields and trades. According to the Bible, funds were running so low that donations had to be solicited from Jewish families in Babylonia (Zechariah 6:10).

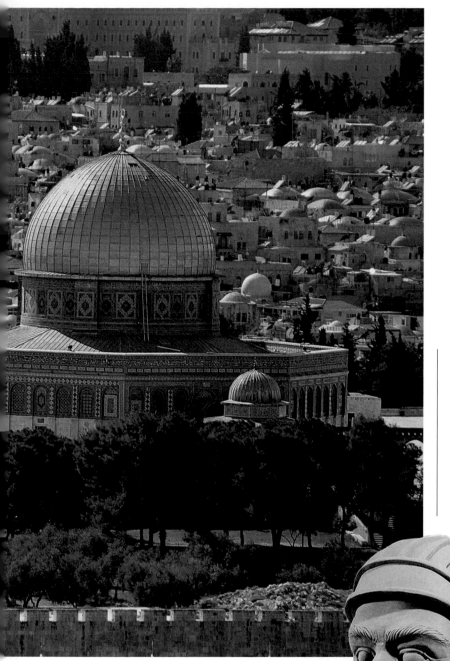

We have no visual image of what it looked like, nor are there any excavations at the location where it once stood. Following its expansion by Herod the Great, the Second Temple was destroyed during the Jewish War in 70 C.E. If indeed there are still remains, they are today buried under the Al Aqsa Mosque and the Dome of the Rock on Temple Mount, known to Muslims as the Haram al-Sharif, or "noble sanctuary."

Other archaeological evidence of the Persian period is scant, and mostly visible in outlying areas. A columned hall recently excavated at Tel Qedesh, on the Israeli-Lebanese border, may have been an administrative building of the Persian province of Tyre and Upper Galilee. And the flourishing port city of Ashkelon, which was destroyed by Nebuchadnezzar, was apparently rebuilt after an 80-year gap during the Persian period, as evidenced by some modest dwellings and storage houses—as well as a large cemetery for dogs.

The Bible suggests that in the fifth century B.C.E., during the reign of King Artaxerxes I, attendance at the Jerusalem Temple declined, as did the observance of the Torah. In response, the king sent an official of Jewish descent named Nehemiah, who restored full observance of the Law, rebuilt Jerusalem's walls, and established a priestly theocracy to rule the nation—though no archaeological evidence has to date been found. ■

Further disruption was caused by a group of Samaritans who were prevented from working on the Temple grounds. In the end, the Persian viceroy for the region wrote to the Persian king that work on the Jerusalem Temple should be abandoned (Ezra 4:1-4). According to the Bible, it was only after the prophets Haggai and Zechariah had intervened that work was resumed. It took several more years, but around 516 B.C.E., the new Temple of Jerusalem was finally consecrated.

This bust depicts Cyrus the Great (r. 559-530 B.C.E.), who liberated the Jewish exiles in Babylon and financed the rebuilding of the Temple.

ALEXANDER'S CONQUEST

A Prince of Macedon Creates a Vast Greek
Empire in the Middle East

For four centuries Greece had toiled in what historians would later call its Dark Ages, but at the beginning of the eighth century B.C.E., it was ready to emerge once more. In literature, the poet Homer had composed the twin epics of the *Iliad* and the *Odyssey* that would serve as the foundational text for the birth of Greece's civilization. In architecture, builders had begun to design their temples to the gods in stone rather than timber, although some elements (such as the column, the triglyph, and the capital) still bore the shape of their wooden precedent. Greek sculptors and painters were developing a new style, known as Archaic, that probed revolutionary ways to represent the human body. And as a nation, Greece was beginning to gather itself as well, now that wars both large and small had produced a political equilibrium among the leading city-states of Athens, Sparta, Corinth, and Thebes.

By the fifth century B.C.E. (commonly identified as the beginning of the Classical Age), Greece had become the dominant civilization of the Mediterranean, led by its cultural center, the city of Athens. The Parthenon of the Athens Acropolis, designed by the architect Ictinos to replace an older temple destroyed by the Persians, established a paradigm for classical design that would be imitated throughout Western civilization for the next two thousand years. That same temple bore sculptures by the artist Phidias; the sheer realism and plasticity of these figures would not be matched until the Italian High Renaissance.

At the same time, Greek red-figured vases and drinking cups became the fashion on affluent tables throughout the Mediterranean, including Persia, as did Greek philosophy, theater, science, and literature. So profound was the impact of Greece's imagination that long after Athens had ceased to exist as a political force,

A silver tetradrachm (worth four drachmas)
with the head of Alexander the Great was struck
sometime between 323 and 280 B.C.E.

the achievements of its artists, architects, philosophers, and mathematicians continued to reverberate throughout the ancient world.

HELLENISM IN ISRAEL

Historians refer to the spread of the Greek culture as Hellenism. Eventually these Hellenistic influences would even percolate to the Persian state of Yehud, mostly through Phoenicia, which had developed strong trade contacts with the Greek world. But for the most part, Greek pottery, coins, and figurines remained largely limited to the coastal areas, where trade and international commerce were far more important than back in the rural hinterlands. What's more, Judah had still not fully recovered from the deprivations of the Babylonian occupation and had a far lower standard of living than the more urbanized centers along the coast. The same, to some extent, was true for Jerusalem, where excavations suggest that only the eastern hill abutting Temple Mount remained inhabited. According to Mary Joan Winn Leith, the overall population of Yehud during the Persian period (I) had dropped to 10,850 from a preexilic high of 32,250. Things were somewhat better up north, at places like Tell en-Nasbeh, Gibeon, and Samaria, where excavations have yielded signs of continued habitation, perhaps because the northern regions had not resisted the Babylonian invasion as stoutly as the fortified cities farther south.

No region had been more successful in weathering the storms of invasion than Galilee. After its capture by Tiglath-Pileser III, its population had become so mixed that Isaiah would call it *galil goyim*, "Galilee of the nations" (Isaiah 9:1), and Matthew would refer to it as the "Galilee of the peoples" (Matthew 4:15). As part of the same Persian satrapy as Tyre and Sidon, Galilee saw its former Yahwist imprint weakened in favor of strong Greco-Phoenician influences, as attested by the discovery of

ca 415
The Torah (or Pentateuch)
reaches its final form

ca 406
Deaths of Euripides and Sophocles
end the great era of Greek drama

ca 366
Egypt revolts against
Persian rule

ca 359
Philip II of Macedon
assumes power

The Acropolis with the fifth-century B.C.E. Parthenon, dedicated
to Pallas Athena, looms over modern Athens by night.

*[Alexander] fought many battles,
conquered strongholds, and put to death
the kings of the earth. He advanced
to the ends of the earth,
and plundered many nations.*

I MACCABEES 2-3

A golden model chariot drawn by four horses formed part of the Oxus
treasure, a collection of 170 objects from the fifth to fourth centuries B.C.E.

ca 356	ca 342	ca 333	ca 332
Alexander is born	Persia suppresses Egyptian revolt	Alexander the Great defeats King Darius III at the Battle of Issus	Alexander the Great conquers Egypt

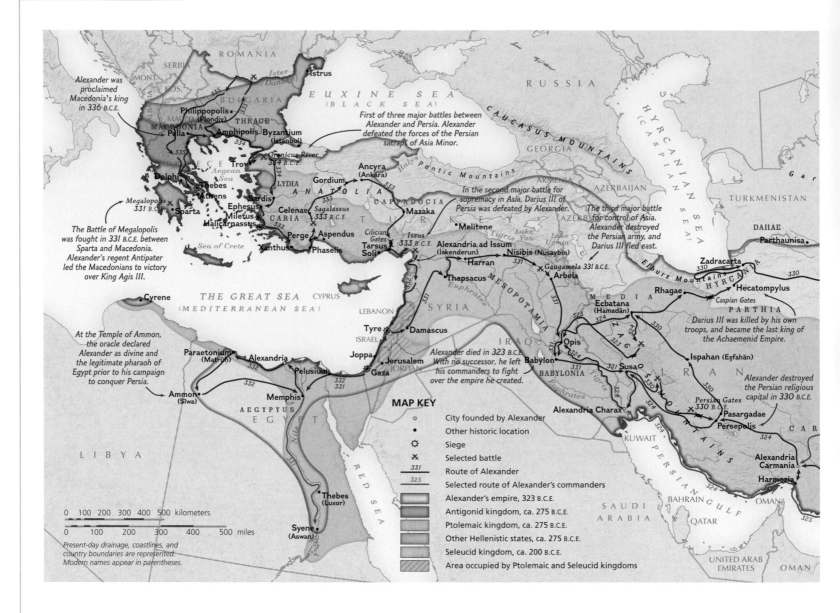

Greek pottery and cultic figurines. When Ezra and Nehemiah set out to restore Judah as an autonomous theocratic region, Galilee and Samaria were studiously omitted. Attempts by the Samaritans to become involved with the Jewish restoration were, as we saw, quickly rebuffed. While Judah would be permitted a measure of religious autonomy, the northern territories, including Galilee, would continue to be ruled as Persian colonies. As a result, Galilee became a major transit point for the Hellenization of Persian Palestine long before the arrival of Alexander of Macedon—thus deepening the estrangement between Galileans and Judeans that would form such an important backdrop for the Gospel stories.

THE AFTERMATH OF ALEXANDER'S CONQUEST

The long-simmering tensions between Greece and Persia erupted once more when in 334 B.C.E., young Alexander took his army across the Hellespont dividing Europe from Asia and went on to defeat the far superior army of Persian king Darius III at the Battle of Issus. Alexander then pushed into the Persian realm and rapidly conquered almost all of its vassal states, from Phoenicia to Egypt, and from Babylon to the Upper Indus Valley. The result was an empire even greater than its Persian precedent, covering some two million square miles.

In Persian Palestine, not everyone submitted to the young Greek warrior. The city of Tyre resisted for seven months. When the walls were finally breached, its population was either crucified or sold into slavery. According to Jewish historian Josephus, Samaria then revolted against Alexander's prefect and burned him to death. Fearing reprisals, 300 men, women, and children sought refuge in a cave near Wadi ed-Daliyeh, north of Jericho, where Alexander's army eventually found them. In 1962, several Bedouin discovered their skeletons and personal effects, including numerous papyrus fragments.

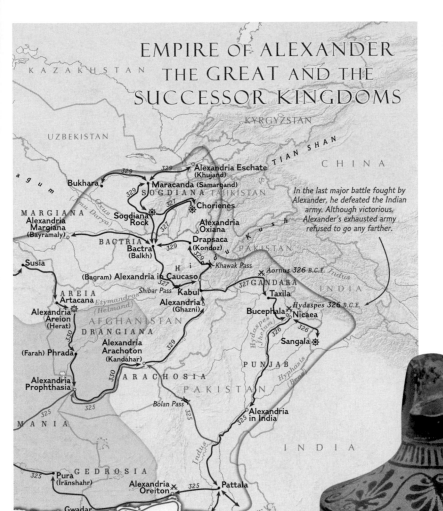

EMPIRE OF ALEXANDER THE GREAT AND THE SUCCESSOR KINGDOMS

In the last major battle fought by Alexander, he defeated the Indian army. Although victorious, Alexander's exhausted army refused to go any farther.

A Greek depiction of Alexander the Great on his horse, routing the Persians, forms part of the so-called Alexander Sarcophagus from the late fourth century B.C.E.

realms: Anatolia, headed by the Attalid Dynasty of General Lysimachus; the home territories of Greece and Macedon, ruled by the heirs of General Antigonus; the empire of Mesopotamia, led by the heirs of General Seleucus; and the empire of Egypt-Syria, wrested from the clutches of his rivals by General Ptolemy. Right on the fault line between these two kingdoms was tiny Judah, absorbed—for the moment—into the new Ptolemaic empire.

The impact of these developments on Judah—now renamed Judea—was initially rather limited. King Ptolemy and his successors recognized the unique nature of Judea as an autonomous region, ruled by its *Gerouisa*, or council of priests. Soon, trade in the Mediterranean recovered from the civil war, with the Greek drachma now serving as the coin of the realm. The Greek language (in the form of a patois known as *koiné*) slowly replaced Aramaic as the dominant language of commerce, politics, and the arts. Many Jews seized this moment to settle in the far-flung corners of the new kingdom in search of better opportunities and a higher standard of living. Thus began the first Diaspora, the first dispersal of Jews across Asia Minor and the Near East, prodded not by war or deportation but by economic opportunity. ■

As vast as Alexander's empire was, it would not outlive its founder. Just 11 years after the Battle of Issus, as Alexander was busy plotting a new campaign into the Arabian peninsula, he contracted a mysterious disease that has never been accurately diagnosed. After 14 agonizing days, he died in Darius's palace in Babylon.

His death came so suddenly that no one had prepared for an orderly succession. Alexander's son by his Bactrian wife Roxanne was not born until two months after his death. This led to a power struggle between Alexander's leading generals, known as the *Diadochi*, or "successors." A protracted civil war ensued, which by 305 B.C.E. had produced four distinct

This slender Greek lekythos vessel with red-figure decoration from the fourth century B.C.E. was found in northern Judea.

ca 331
The Persian Empire falls
to Alexander the Great

ca 323
Alexander dies; his empire
is carved up into Ptolemaic
and Seleucid realms

ca 302
Mithradates I founds
the kingdom of Pontus

ca 301
Ptolemy I defeats Antigonus
and captures Judah,
now known as Judea

THE PTOLEMAIC ERA

*Greek Rule by the Ptolemies Brings a
Measure of Peace and Prosperity*

Throughout his newly conquered realm, Alexander the Great had founded new cities, or poleis, from which Hellenistic culture could radiate into the surrounding region. These cities were usually planned on the grid pattern developed by Hippodamus of Miletus. They featured such quintessential Greek institutions as a theater; market agora; a temple dedicated to Zeus, Apollo, or other Greek gods; and a gymnasium where young men were educated and trained in sports. Sometimes existing cities were entirely rebuilt in the Greek fashion, such as Akko (renamed Ptolemais) and the Ammonite capital of Rabbath-Ammon (today's Amman in Jordan), which was refounded as "Philadelphia," both during the Ptolemaic period. After the city of Samaria rose up in rebellion against its Alexandrian governor, the young king forced the inhabitants from the city and gave it to his Macedonian veterans, who promptly fortified the old Omride walls with round towers, offering fields of fire in all directions. Today one such round tower is one of the most visible monuments of the brief Alexandrian era.

In Egypt, Alexander founded a city on the Mediterranean coast near the village of Rhakotis that would bear his name: Alexandria. Designed by his architect Dinocrates, it was designated by King Ptolemy I as the new capital of Ptolemaic Egypt, and the principal catalyst of Ptolemy's attempts to fuse both the Egyptian and Greek culture into a new syncratic civilization. Laid out in the usual grid pattern, Alexandria boasted a man-made causeway to the island of Pharos, which held the tallest lighthouse of the ancient world. It soon became the principal port in this part of the Mediterranean—assisted in no mean measure by the fact

During the successive Persian, Greek, and Syrian occupations, Galilee came under strong Greco-Phoenician influences, as attested by Greek coins, pottery, and figurines.

Inset: *A polychrome figurine of a dancer with a tambourine is typical of fourth-century Hellenistic art from Asia Minor.*

ca 285
Ptolemy II begins rule;
the Septuagint is written

ca 280
The Pharos, the famous
lighthouse of Alexandria,
is built

ca 280
The new republic of Rome
controls the Italian peninsula

ca 259
The Zenon Papyri
are written

The Origin of the Christian Old Testament

The Septuagint, the Greek translation of Hebrew Scripture, eventually included more recent Jewish works as well, including the Psalms of Solomon and the Books of the Maccabees. Since the earliest Christian Bibles were translated from the Greek rather than the Masoretic (or Hebrew) version, these extracanonical works are today found in the Christian Old Testament as well.

that its primary competitor, Tyre, had been thoroughly destroyed. Not surprisingly, this is also where Alexander's body was eventually put to rest, in a gold sarcophagus filled with honey.

THE SEPTUAGINT

By the mid-third century Alexandria had become the new Athens, the intellectual jewel of the Mediterranean, epitomized by the 400,000 volumes of the Library of Alexandria. Its population became increasingly diverse as its prosperity attracted tradesmen, bankers, scholars, and literati from throughout the former Alexandria Empire—including Judea. Naturally, the Jews of Alexandria could not routinely visit the Temple in Jerusalem except during the major festivals, if they had the means to travel. But come together for communal worship or events they did, possibly in *proseuchae*, or "private prayer houses," which became increasingly prevalent in main areas of the Diaspora. The only problem was language. The sacred scrolls of the Torah were either written in Hebrew or available in Aramaic translations known as Targumim. But in the world of Alexander, and particularly in Alexandria, people spoke Greek. By the third century, few of the Jewish expatriates could understand the ancient Hebrew texts read in the synagogue. The obvious solution was to translate the Hebrew Bible into Greek, though clearly such a

A Greek wine jug, or oenochoe, in the shape of a woman's head was produced around 490 B.C.E. by a potter named Charinos.

colossal enterprise could not be funded by the Jewish enclave of Alexandria alone.

According to a second-century B.C.E. document (possibly forged) known as the Letter of Aristeas, the community approached King Ptolemy II, who had begun to stock the great library with religious texts from around the world. The king offered the high priest Eleazar in Jerusalem an exchange: If the high priest sent him 70 (or 72) learned scholars to produce the Greek translation, the king would release any Jewish prisoners held in Alexandria. The result was a work known as the Septuagint—from the Latin word for "seventy," *septuaginta*. Most scholars see the Letter of Aristeas as an attempt to give the Septuagint the authority of Jerusalem scholarship, even though it was clearly translated into Alexandrian Greek by local scribes. But few contest the fact that this great translation project was indeed begun in Alexandria in the third century B.C.E. and completed around two centuries later.

THE ZENON AUDIT

Under Ptolemaic rule, Galilee (or Galila), Samaria, and Judah (now called Judea) became separate hyparchies in the Ptolemaic Empire. These provinces were generally left in peace as long as their taxes and agricultural tribute flowed promptly into the coffers of Alexandria. It was for this purpose that around 258 B.C.E., an official named Zenon conducted an audit of the agricultural sector in Ptolemaic Palestine on behalf of finance minister, Apollonius. His reports, which were preserved as the Zenon Papyri, offer a glimpse of the sheer variety of crops, fruits, and fish produced in Galilee and Judea during this time. Countless caravans brought Galilean and Judean oil, dates, figs, and wine to markets in Syria and Asia Minor. The region's growing prosperity encouraged the rise of a landed gentry and attracted more and more foreigners to settle in Galilee. To purists in Judea, however, this growing interaction with Gentiles made the Galileans even more suspect.

Among the places Zenon visited was Maresha (Marisa in Greek), a Judahite city that had been depopulated by Nebuchadnezzar but had since been taken over by migrants from Idumaea (an area analogous to today's Negev). Although only 10 percent of this large tell is excavated today, archaeologists

When Antiochus saw that his kingdom was established, he determined to become king of the land of Egypt, in order that he might reign over both kingdoms.

I MACCABEES 1:16

This circular watchtower was one of several built by Alexander's Macedonian veterans at the old Omride acropolis of Samaria.

have discovered a network of caves in its soft chalky soil that contain impressive burial chambers from the Ptolemaic period, with decoration inspired by Greek mythological motifs.

Another important project from the Ptolemaic era was the wholesale upgrade of the old Phoenician port of Dor to a harbor on the Greek model. Today identified as Tel Dor, some 22 miles south of Haifa and excavated during a 20-year survey by Ephraim Stern, the site yielded several important discoveries, including an underwater breakwater system and several nearby shipwrecks. However, many of the structures that were previously dated to the Ptolemaic period have now been reassessed as Roman, though portions of the city wall built by Ptolemy II using large ashlars still exist.

Near the end of the third century, international tensions threatened to disrupt the peace in Ptolemaic Palestine. Over the past century, its neighbor to the north, the Seleucid kingdom, had lost much of its territory to revolts, including its eastern provinces of Bactria, Media, and Parthia, as well as large swaths of Asia Minor. The newly crowned Seleucid king, Antiochus III, decided to bring these defectors to heel. In a series of military campaigns that lasted nearly two decades, the king recovered much of Asia Minor before pushing east, eventually leading his armies as far as Kabul in today's Afghanistan. According to the Greek historian Polybius, he then crossed the mountains of Hindu Kush and entered India, where he forced the Indian king, Subhashsena, to terms. Having thus recovered most of the original Alexandrian

empire in the east, Antiochus believed himself to be invincible, if not a reincarnation of the great Alexander himself. From this point on, his coins proclaim him as Antiochus Megas, "Antiochus the Great." Drunk with victory, he next turned his forces against the former Alexandrian possessions in the south: Ptolemaic Syria. At first he was repulsed, but in 198 B.C.E. the king succeeded in defeating Ptolemy V Epiphanes at the Battle of Paneion, close to the source of the Jordan. Syria, including Galilee and Judea, was now forcefully brought into the Seleucid Empire. ■

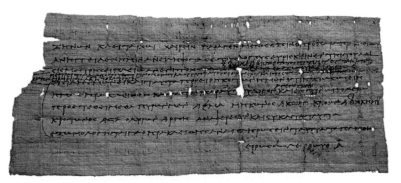

This fragment of the Zenon Papyri contains an audit of agricultural output in Ptolemaic Palestine by an official named Zenon from around 258 B.C.E.

THE MACCABEAN REVOLT

*Seleucid Oppression Sparks an
All-Out War of Independence*

The Ptolemaic Dynasty never attempted to impose its Greek culture on its subject peoples. Its Hellenizing efforts were focused on its three principal poleis in Egypt: Alexandria, Ptolemais, and Naucratis. But Greek customs, fashion, and religion nevertheless continued to seep into its realm, even in Ptolemaic Palestine. This was bound to drive a wedge in Jewish society. Many Jews, particularly the elites, were fascinated with the sophistication of Greek culture, precisely because it connected Judea, still a mostly rural and backward country, with the modern, civilized world. But most observant Jews were repelled by this paganism, particularly the Greek predilection for featuring nude men and women in its art.

Many others bridled at the idea that Greek philosophy and religion were intellectually superior. Some Jewish authors attacked this notion with books such as *The Wisdom of Solomon*. Despite its attribution, it was most likely written by a Greek-speaking author in the second century B.C.E., who argued that YHWH, not Greek philosophy, is the ultimate font of wisdom. Others, like Jewish philosopher Philo who also lived in Alexandria, tried to reconcile Greek philosophy with Judaism by arguing that to experience God is the same as recognizing Plato's divine spark within oneself.

Regardless of how Jews sought to come to terms with the Hellenistic world around them, the inner tensions between faith and reason, between YHWH and polytheism, continued to build.

THE MACCABEAN REVOLT

The Seleucid era would introduce one of the most turbulent periods in the history of Judea, although this was not apparent at first. After Judah was incorporated into the new province of Syria and Phoenicia, Antiochus III freely granted Jews the freedom to live and worship according to their Law. In Galilee, the Seleucid takeover was welcomed by the landed gentry, who fervently hoped that the

A second-century B.C.E. temple dedicated to Zeus was built in Euromos, also known as Herakleia, close to Lake Bafa in today's Turkey.

Inset: *These gold octadrachms (worth eight drachms) depict the Seleucid rulers Antiochus VII and Demetrius I.*

ca 225
Earliest known Jewish prayer
house is built in Egypt

ca 218
Hannibal invades Italy during
the Second Punic War

ca 206
The republic of Rome
conquers Spain

ca 200
Antiochus III defeats Ptolemy V;
Judea is added to Seleucid Empire

ca 190
Rome defeats Antiochus III,
extending Roman
control in Asia Minor

ca 175
Antiochus IV ascends the throne;
proscribes all non-Greek cults

ca 167
Rome conquers
Macedonia

ca 167
Mattathias, a priest in Modi'in,
launches the Maccabean Revolt

In 2015, Israeli archaeologists confirmed the discovery of what may be the family tomb of the Maccabees near the town of Modi'in.

Inset: *The Maccabee Shrine in the Sankt Andreas Kirche in Cologne, Germany, is traditionally believed to hold the relics of the Maccabee brothers.*

Seleucids would reduce their tax burden. This harmony did not last. The reason is that Antiochus made the ill-fated decision to invade mainland Greece, now a Roman dependency. Rome responded with its legions, pushing Antiochus III all the way back to the Taurus Mountains (in today's Turkey). By the time the king's son, Antiochus IV Epiphanes ("God manifest"), ascended the throne, the Seleucid military was decimated and its treasury was empty.

Judea was in turmoil as well. In Jerusalem, various factions were trying to compete for the office of the high priest, a position with tremendous political and financial benefits. One contender was Jason, the brother of high priest Onias III, who around 175 B.C.E. offered Antiochus IV the princely sum of "three hundred and sixty talents of silver." This bid was successful and enabled Jason to change Jerusalem "to the Greek way of life"—by turning it into a Greek polis named Antioch, in honor of the king (II Maccabees 4:8).

The crisis escalated when another contender, Menelaus, offered Antiochus IV a bigger bribe, even though he was not a descendant of Zadok, Solomon's high priest; until now, only Zadokites had held this high office. Jason was forced to flee to the Transjordan, where he secured the support from the wealthy Tobiad family and prepared to recapture his former post by force.

In 1950, a large tomb cut out of rock was discovered in the Jerusalem neighborhood of Rehavia. The tomb was topped by a pyramid and featured a portal supported by a single Doric column—elements that reflect the growing Hellenistic influence in this period. Inside were eight burial niches and an inscription referring to an individual named Jason, along with the depiction of ships as well as a menorah, a Jewish seven-branched candelabra. Some have suggested that it could have belonged to the family of the high priest, although "Jason" (the Greek version of Yeshua or Jesus) was a quite common name in this era.

MATTATHIAS THE PRIEST

In 168 B.C.E., Antiochus IV was in Egypt when the rumor spread that the Seleucid king had been killed. Jason thereupon launched a surprise attack on Jerusalem and evicted his rival, Menelaus. Suspecting the beginning of a major revolt, Antiochus marched back into Judea, deposed Jason, and "commanded his soldiers to cut down relentlessly everyone they met" (II Maccabees 5:12).

In an effort to forestall any further opposition, Antiochus then decreed that Jewish rites and practices would henceforth be outlawed. This was a major change in policy, because up to this point, the Ptolemaic and Seleucid regimes had been tolerant of cults other than their own Greek tradition. Antiochus's stated aim was to enforce a common culture, language, and religion in his realm, including Judea. Even the Temple was converted to a shrine dedicated to the Greek god Zeus (II Maccabees 6:4). According to the Jewish historian Josephus, those who continued to observe Jewish rites were "whipped with rods, and their bodies torn to pieces," or they were crucified on the spot.

This intimate polychrome scene of two deities embracing, found in Asia Minor, is typical of late Hellenistic mold-cast art created in Tanagra.

In towns across Judea, Seleucid officers forced the people to participate in pagan rites. In the small village of Modi'in, a *Kohen*, or "priest," named Mattathias refused to do so. He turned on the villager who was about to sacrifice, as well as the officiating Syrian official, and killed them both. The priest and his sons then fled to the hills with the cry, "Let every one who is zealous for the law and supports the covenant come out with me!" (I Maccabees 2:28).

Thus began a rebellion known as the Maccabean Revolt. It was not directed against the Syrian fondness for Greek culture—the future Hasmonean kings would themselves cloak their rule in Greek pomp—but against Antiochus's suppression of Jewish religious practice. Mattathias was killed soon after, and the leadership of the revolt was passed on to his son Judas, a skilled commander whose nom de guerre was Maccabeus (from the Aramaic word *maqqaba*, or "hammer"). Many Jewish men responded to his call to take up the torch of liberty.

THE BOOK OF DANIEL

Modern scholarship posits that it is in this difficult time of resistance that the Book of Daniel reached its final form. Among others, the book describes the great "evil" of Antiochus IV, couched as visions revealed to Daniel (Daniel 11:20-40). The book urges its audience to resist the Seleucid persecution and to have faith that God will triumph in the end, as long as the Jews remain faithful to the Torah. Some members of the rebellion abandoned the fight after the Seleucid General Lysias revoked Antiochus's edict and restored full religious freedom to the citizens of Judea (II Maccabees 11:15). For the Maccabees, however, the ultimate goal was full political independence, and so Judas persevered with the guerrilla campaign against the Seleucids. ■

People could neither keep the sabbath, nor observe the festivals of their ancestors, nor so much as confess themselves to be Jews.

II MACCABEES 6:6

THE HASMONEAN KINGDOM

The Restoration of a Jewish Monarchy Leads to Social Rifts

The history of ancient Israel described in Hebrew Scripture is filled with uprisings against foreign oppression. Most of these were destined to fail, as would the two revolts that arose during the Roman period in 70 and 135 C.E. But the Maccabean Revolt succeeded beyond all expectations. Avoiding open combat with the superior Seleucid army, Judas conducted a skilled guerrilla campaign that sought to harass the Syrian forces at every turn. The sudden death of Antiochus IV in 164 B.C.E. was a fortuitous development. Given that the king's successor, Antiochus V, was only nine years old, General Lysias sought to establish himself as regent. Knowing that several other generals were vying for the throne, he quickly sued for peace with the Jewish rebels. Thus, that same year, the Jerusalem Temple was restored to Jewish worship. It was promptly cleared of all Greek idols and solemnly restored the worship of YHWH, an event later celebrated during the Jewish festival of Hanukkah (II Maccabees 10:1-3). Judas then wisely turned to the emerging power in the West, the Republic of Rome, to secure the Senate's support for his fledgling nation. This agreement, executed in 161 B.C.E., is the first recorded treaty between Rome and the Jewish people. Unfortunately, Judas was killed one year later, during the Battle of Elasa, whereupon his brother Jonathan took over his command.

Well before then, the Lysias regency had led to a fierce contest for the Syrian throne by various heirs and usurpers in the Syrian capital of Antioch. With the Seleucid leadership thus distracted, Jonathan rapidly captured a string of cities along the Mediterranean coast. But then Jonathan made a cardinal mistake. In addition to being the de facto ruler of the liberated Jewish nation, he also assumed the position of high priest—thus combining secular and sacred authority in one individual (I Maccabees 14:41). This fateful decision would drive a deep wedge in a nation already splintered by Hellenistic alienation and the unseemly factionalism in Jerusalem. Thus the seeds were sown for the development of

A rare cameo of the Greek god Zeus was carved in sardonyx and set in gold in Alexandria around the third century B.C.E.

dissident groups, such as the Essenes and the Zealots, whose influence would extend well into the New Testament era.

After Jonathan was assassinated by a Syrian general named Trypho, his brother Simon continued the rebellion and finally achieved full independence of all Jewish-held territory in 142 B.C.E. For the first time since the fall of Israel and Judah, the Jewish nation was free once more—free to worship, free to sacrifice, free to live according to the Laws of Moses. For the next 80-odd years, Judea and its dependencies would be ruled by the Hasmonean Dynasty, the successors of Mattathias the priest, whose grandfather was called Asamoneus.

But all was not well. The Jewish Council, or Sanhedrin, that, in theory at least, was still the dominant legislative and judicial power in Judea, was increasingly contested between two parties: the conservative, priestly, aristocratic Sadducees and the more liberal brotherhood known as the Pharisees.

THE HASMONEAN DYNASTY

Simon too fell victim to Syrian intrigue; like his brother Jonathan, he and his family were assassinated in 135 B.C.E. Only his son John Hyrcanus survived and was promptly hailed as leader—and high priest. But no sooner had Hyrcanus been installed than the new Syrian king, Antiochus VII, marched into Judea to lay siege to Jerusalem. When the situation in the city became desperate, Hyrcanus was forced to sign a peace treaty that obligated the country to crushing war reparations and even compelled him to assist in Antiochus's war against the Parthians.

Fortunately, Antiochus's death in 128 B.C.E. brought an end to the restoration of Seleucid rule. Freed from the Syrian yoke, Hyrcanus embarked on an aggressive campaign to conquer buffer states around the Judean heartland. As it happened, the Seleucid Empire itself was crumbling; several former Syrian vassals, including the Ammonites in the Transjordan and the Nabataeans along the Red Sea, now broke away to pursue

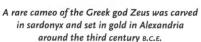

The so-called Tomb of Absalom in the Kidron Valley in Jerusalem is a rock-cut burial monument in the Hellenistic style, probably from the early first century C.E.

ca 150	ca 150	ca 142	ca 142
Jonathan is also appointed high priest by Alexander Balas	In protest, the "Righteous Priest" establishes the Essene movement	Jonathan is executed by the Seleucid commander, Trypho	Simon Maccabeus establishes an independent state in Judea

This imposing building in Petra, known as Ad Deir, or "The Monastery," was carved out of the rock by the Nabataeans in the first century C.E.

Judaism, regardless of their ethnicity. Whether this forceful Judaizing was ultimately successful in erasing all Greek influences continues to be debated. Scores of coins and pottery fragments of Greek or Hellenistic origin, brought to light in recent excavations, attest to the enduring Gentile character of many enclaves in Galilee. This may suggest that as soon as the Gentile population no longer posed an acute threat to Jewish farmers, the daily intercourse of trade between Jew and Gentile resumed as before.

Nevertheless, that such a compulsory program was even deemed necessary, less than 90 years before the birth of Jesus, may illustrate the deep suspicion harbored by conservative Jews in the South toward their Galilean brethren in the North. It also explains why Matthew still refers to the "Galilee of the Gentiles" and why, in the Gospel of John, a Judean like Nathanael can scoff, "*Nazareth?* Can any good come out of Nazareth?" (Matthew 4:15; John 1:46).

their own destiny. This is when the Nabataean city of Petra would begin its heyday of Hellenistic splendor, fueled by the growing caravan trade across the Arabian peninsula.

Around 111 B.C.E. Hyrcanus marched into Samaria, though the long and brutal campaign left many of its towns in ruins—including Shechem, the Samarian capital, and the Samaritan temple on Mount Gerizim, a rival to the Temple in Jerusalem.

THE CONQUEST OF GALILEE

Galilee, still under firm Seleucid control, was next. Over the past centuries, the region's abundant fecundity had attracted scores of Syrians, Arameans, Phoenicians, and Greeks, in addition to the Babylonian and Persian colonists who had settled there in preceding centuries. Jewish farmers had, in fact, become a minority—so much so that the outbreak of the Maccabean Revolt in the South provoked a strong anti-Jewish sentiment among Galilee's Gentile communities. According to the first Book of Maccabees, a number of these Gentiles even vowed to eradicate the Jewish presence in Galilee altogether (I Maccabees 5:15).

Thus it's not surprising that soon after Hyrcanus had brought the region under his control, he ordered the entire population to convert to

An ancient door knocker in the shape of a lion's head was a popular motif for the doors of official Roman buildings.

ROME INTERVENES

Three other rulers followed after Hyrcanus: his son Aristobulus in 104 B.C.E., the first to assume the title of *basileus*, or "king"; his other son, Alexander Jannaeus, in 103 B.C.E., who married Aristobulus's widow, Salome Alexandra; and finally, in 76 B.C.E., Salome Alexandra herself.

When Salome died, a power struggle erupted between her son and designated heir, Hyrcanus II (already serving as high priest), and her younger son, Aristobulus II. Since Hyrcanus favored the political faction of the Pharisees, the other party, the Sadducees, threw their support behind Aristobulus, who ultimately was able to capture the throne. Hyrcanus fled, but then asked King Aretas III of Nabataea to intervene. Aretas agreed, invaded Judah with his army, and laid siege to Jerusalem in 66 B.C.E. Judea was once again plunged into a messy civil war.

These developments were of great concern to Rome. The Senate feared that the turmoil could spill over into Egypt, a vital supplier of grain to Rome's growing population. And fatefully, the famous Roman general Pompeius (later known as Pompey the Great) had arrived in the region. As soon as Pompey heard of the mayhem in Judea and was invited to intervene, he mustered his troops and prepared to march. ■

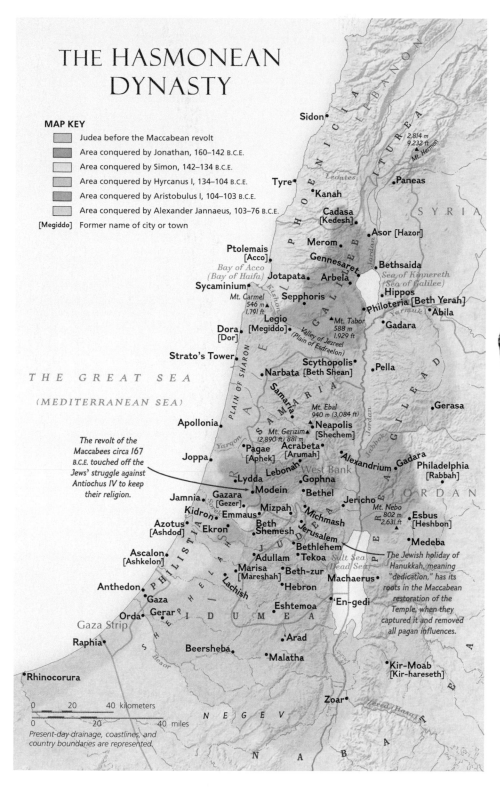

THE HASMONEAN DYNASTY

MAP KEY

- Judea before the Maccabean revolt
- Area conquered by Jonathan, 160–142 B.C.E.
- Area conquered by Simon, 142–134 B.C.E.
- Area conquered by Hyrcanus I, 134–104 B.C.E.
- Area conquered by Aristobulus I, 104–103 B.C.E.
- Area conquered by Alexander Jannaeus, 103–76 B.C.E.

[Megiddo]   Former name of city or town

The revolt of the Maccabees circa 167 B.C.E. touched off the Jews' struggle against Antiochus IV to keep their religion.

The Jewish holiday of Hanukkah, meaning "dedication," has its roots in the Maccabean restoration of the Temple, when they captured it and removed all pagan influences.

Sidon

2,814 m
9,232 ft
Mt. Hermon

Tyre
Kanah
Leontes

Paneas

SYRIA

ITUREA

Cadasa
[Kedesh]

Asor [Hazor]

Merom

Ptolemais
[Acco]
Bay of Acco
(Bay of Haifa)

Jotapata
Gennesaret
Arbela

Bethsaida

Sea of Kinnereth
(Sea of Galilee)

Sycaminium

Sepphoris

Hippos
Philoteria [Beth Yerah]
Abila

Mt. Carmel
546 m
1,791 ft

Legio
[Megiddo]

Mt. Tabor
588 m
1,929 ft

Valley of Jezreel
(Plain of Esdraelon)

Gadara

Dora
[Dor]

Strato's Tower

Scythopolis
[Beth Shean]

Pella

Narbata

THE GREAT SEA
(MEDITERRANEAN SEA)

SAMARIA

Mt. Ebal
940 m (3,084 ft)

GILEAD

Gerasa

Apollonia

Mt. Gerizim
(2,890 ft) 881 m

Neapolis
[Shechem]

Yarqon

Pagae
[Aphek]

Acrabeta
[Arumah]

Joppa

Lebonah
Gophna

Alexandrium
Gadara

Philadelphia
[Rabbah]

Lydda

Modein

Bethel

Jamnia
Gazara
[Gezer]

Mizpah

Jericho

JORDAN

Kidron
Emmaus

Michmash

Mt. Nebo
802 m
2,631 ft

Esbus
[Heshbon]

Azotus
[Ashdod]

Ekron

Beth
Shemesh

Jerusalem

Bethlehem

Medeba

Ascalon
[Ashkelon]

Adullam

Tekoa

Salt Sea
(Dead Sea)

Anthedon

Marisa
[Mareshah]

Beth-zur

Machaerus

Gaza

Lachish

Hebron

En-gedi

Orda
Gerar

IDUMEA

Eshtemoa

Gaza Strip

Raphia

Arad

Beersheba

Malatha

Kir-Moab
[Kir-hareseth]

Rhinocorura

Zoar

NEGEV

NABA

0   20   40 kilometers
0   20   40 miles

Present-day drainage, coastlines, and country boundaries are represented.

PHOENICIA   LEBANON   GALILEE   PLAIN OF SHARON   PHILISTIA   JUDEA   PEREA   MOAB

A prutah (ancient Jewish copper coin) was possibly struck during the reign of John Hyrcanus I (135-104 B.C.E.), the first Jewish ruler to issue coins in his name.

Now Judas heard of the fame of the Romans, that they were very strong and were well-disposed toward all who made an alliance with them.

I MACCABEES 8:1

THE ROMAN CONQUEST

*The Jewish Kingdom, Exhausted by Strife,
Falls Victim to Roman Expansion*

The question of how a small nation like the Roman Republic could become one of the most powerful empires in Antiquity continues to fascinate modern scholars. Few factors seemed to favor it. Rome didn't have a long historical pedigree, or abundant natural resources, or any cultural or religious foundation that could have destined it for greatness. Much of the future Roman civilization was adopted from the Greeks, not only with regard to its arts and sciences but also its polytheistic religion: gods such as Jupiter, Venus, and Saturn were amalgamated from the Greek deities Zeus, Aphrodite, and Kronos.

In fact, during the Ptolemaic era, few people had even heard of Rome. At the time, the city itself was a mere group of settlements, scattered across seven hills rising along the Tiber River. According to Rome's founding myth, the city was established by two brothers, Romulus and Remus, though archaeologists have determined that Rome's origins are more prosaic: a modest village of the Latini tribe around the eighth century B.C.E. It became a small kingdom, until—according to the Roman historian Livy—the citizens of Rome ousted their kings in 509 B.C.E. and decided to establish a republic. The concept of a republic (based on the Latin *res publica*, or "public matter") was, like its precedent in Athens, more inclusive than the monarchies of its time, but it was hardly a democracy. Most of its political power lay in the hands of a landed aristocracy that controlled its chief executive and legislative body, the Roman Senate.

During the next five centuries, the city steadily expanded its commercial and territorial influence,

An evening view highlights the Roman Forum in Rome with the Arch of Septimius Severus (center) and the Temple of Saturn (at right).

Inset: A bust of General Marcus Agrippa (62-12 B.C.E.), a close friend of Augustus, shows the penchant for realism in the Late Republican phase of Roman art.

ca 140	ca 135	ca 140	ca 140
Control of the Sanhedrin is contested between Sadducees and Pharisees	Simon dies and is succeeded by John Hyrcanus	John Hyrcanus conquers Idumea and Samaria	People in Idumea and Samaria are forced to convert to Judaism

ca 103
Alexander Jannaeus is king
of the Hasmonean Kingdom

ca 101
Galilee is increasingly Hellenized
by Alexander Jannaeus

ca 100
The Sadducees take control
of the Sanhedrin

ca 100
The Pharisees change from
a political to a social movement

THE ROMAN EMPIRE

MAP KEY

- Area ruled by Rome at Julius Caesar's death, 44 B.C.E.
- Acquisitions under Augustus, 27 B.C.E.–14 C.E.
- Area added by the time of Trajan, 117 C.E.
- Territory added by the time of Trajan, but relinquished by Hadrian, 117–138 C.E.

0   400 kilometers

0   400 miles

Present-day drainage, coastlines, and country boundaries are represented. Modern names appear in parentheses.

---

much aided by the fact that Greece and Persia were too busy fighting each other to take any notice. When Alexander the Great defeated Persian King Darius III in 333 B.C.E., it looked as if all of the known world would become a Greek empire. But it was Rome that would reap the spoils in the end.

As Alexander's great realm slowly disintegrated into separate empires and lesser kingdoms, Rome steadily expanded its control of the Italian peninsula. From there, it pushed into the Mediterranean, which inevitably brought it into conflict with the leading power there, the city of Carthage. The result was the series of Punic Wars from which Rome emerged victorious. It was thus perfectly positioned to extend its power eastward, just when the Seleucid king, Antiochus III, made the crucial mistake of

A posthumous bust of a toga-clad Julius Caesar (first half of the first century C.E.) reveals the idealism of the Early Imperial phase in Roman art.

invading Asia Minor and Greece. The Attalid king of Pergamum (today's northwest Turkey) promptly appealed to Rome for help. The Roman Senate was more than happy to oblige, and Antiochus III was sent packing to Syria. Gratefully, King Attalus III bequeathed the entire nation to Rome's care on his death in 133 B.C.E. Thus, by the end of the second century, Rome had suddenly become a major world power, with an appetite for more.

ROME EXPANDS INTO THE NEAR EAST

A major motive for Rome's expansionist policies was control of the eastern basin of the Mediterranean, which was rapidly becoming the nexus of world trade. Rome was anxious to protect its grain shipments; over the past decades, the city of Rome had ballooned to more than 1.5 million people. In addition, Roman senators had discovered that it was far more lucrative to be posted overseas than reap the harvests of their local landholdings. As the case of Gaius

[Pompey] made Jerusalem a tributary to the Romans,
and reduced the whole nation, which had elevated
itself so high before, to its former borders.

JOSEPHUS, *HISTORY OF THE JEWS*

Verres attests, provincial governors could become fabulously wealthy through kickbacks on the sale of mining or trade monopolies and other concessions. This had the unfortunate side effect of widening the gulf between Rome's ruling elites and Italy's vast majority of peasants. One nobleman named Julius Caesar decided to ally himself with this populist cause. It was a smart move, for by 59 B.C.E., Caesar had become the most powerful man in the republic as head of a triumvirate, or "reign of three."

One of these three leaders was Roman General Pompey. He had won universal fame for the efficient way he had cleared the Mediterranean of pirates, who had become a major nuisance for the naval traffic in the region. Pompey next led his legions against King Mithradates VI, long a major irritant to Rome's ambitions in the East. The Roman general was now tantalizingly close to the Seleucid Empire as well as a small nation known as the Hasmonean Kingdom. Rome was at war with neither of them, but in 64 B.C.E., Pompey took the unprecedented step of invading Syria anyway. Historians have posited that Rome wanted a buffer state between its growing empire and the tiresome Parthians, who were making life difficult in the former territory of the Persian Empire. Syrian King Antiochus XIII, the last of the Seleucid Dynasty, was unceremoniously deposed and killed.

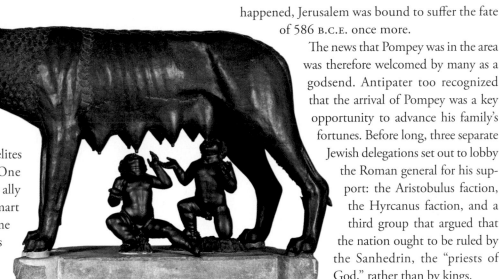

A bronze sculpture of a she-wolf suckling two infants, known as the Capitoline Wolf, illustrates the founding myth of Rome, though its origins are uncertain.

happened, Jerusalem was bound to suffer the fate of 586 B.C.E. once more.

The news that Pompey was in the area was therefore welcomed by many as a godsend. Antipater too recognized that the arrival of Pompey was a key opportunity to advance his family's fortunes. Before long, three separate Jewish delegations set out to lobby the Roman general for his support: the Aristobulus faction, the Hyrcanus faction, and a third group that argued that the nation ought to be ruled by the Sanhedrin, the "priests of God," rather than by kings.

Pompey initially favored Aristobulus's cause, figuring that it would be easier to defeat forces outside the city of Jerusalem than those barricaded inside it. But when Aretas quietly withdrew his forces so as to avoid any quarrel with Rome and Aristobulus started to become impatient, Pompey changed his mind. He advanced on Jerusalem, waited until the Sabbath to launch his attack, and took the city. Aristobulus fled, whereupon Hyrcanus was installed as a puppet prince of Rome with the vague title of *ethnarch* (Greek for "ruler of the people"). Antipater was rewarded with a senior post as well. But the flame of Jewish independence had been extinguished. It would not be rekindled again, save for brief periods of rebellion, until the 20th century.

POMPEY TAKES JERUSALEM

Back in Judea, the throne was still being contested between King Aristobulus II and his older brother, Hyrcanus II. The latter was supported by a man named Antipater, who happened to have a son named Herod. A prominent Idumean nobleman, Antipater had been steadily climbing in the Hasmonean administration when the death of Queen Alexandra forced him to look for new allies. It was Antipater who had persuaded King Aretas III of Nabataea, which was adjacent to Idumea, to come to Hyrcanus's aid. This the king did, by laying siege to Jerusalem, which plunged the nation into despondency. It seemed that unless something drastic

THE REBUILDING OF SCYTHOPOLIS

Soon after the Roman takeover, Pompey instructed his Syrian legate, Gabinius, to identify a location for a new Greco-Roman city. Gabinius chose Beth Shean, the biblical town that once served as the residence of the Egyptian governor, and for a very good reason. Like Megiddo on the west, Beth Shean was perched on the principal trade route across the Jezreel Valley, known as the Via Maris, with easy access to the Jordan River. At that time it was known as Scythopolis, a name that suggests it was settled by Scythian mercenaries who'd retired from Seleucid service. The remains of a Seleucid temple, probably dedicated to the Greek god Zeus, were found on

The city of Scythopolis, the biblical Beth Shean, was a member of the Decapolis and the most Romanized city west of the Jordan River, as witnessed by this second-century theater.

A gold tetradrachm shows the diademed head of King Mithradates VI Eupator of Pontus (r. 120-63 B.C.E.), who was defeated by the Roman General Pompey.

the top of the mound. Scythopolis was the place where Jonathan was killed by assassins on orders of Seleucid King Demetrius II. But since then, the city had burned to the ground.

Gabinius decided to rebuild the city as a Greco-Roman polis, but at the foot of the mound rather than on top. The result is one of the most impressive archaeological sites in Israel. The magnificent theater, the splendid *cardo* (or boulevard) dubbed "Palladius Street," and the *thermae*, or Roman baths, all date from the Early Roman Period, though many of these buildings were extended and embellished during and after the second century C.E. In a nearby cemetery, excavators from the University of Pennsylvania found a sarcophagus with an inscription identifying the deceased as "Antiochus, the son of Phallion," quite possibly the cousin of Herod the Great.

ANTIPATER IN THE ROMAN CIVIL WAR

Twenty years after Pompey's conquest, in 44 B.C.E., Julius Caesar lay dead on the Senate floor, the victim of a conspiracy led by two prominent noblemen, Gaius Cassius and Marcus Junius Brutus. In response, Caesar's 18-year-old grandnephew and heir, Gaius Octavian, formed a triumvirate with Caesar's ablest general, Mark Antony, as well as with General Lepidus, to bring the assassins to justice. The result was the so-called Liberators' Civil War that would last over a decade. Cassius and Brutus, self-styled as the Liberators, fled to the East to raise funds for new legions and convince local leaders that their victory was simply a matter of time.

The matter was of great interest to Antipater, who now ruled Judea as its de facto ruler. Hyrcanus was weak, inept, and more interested

Flavius Josephus

Our understanding of the Roman occupation of Palestine is greatly aided by a Jewish historian named Josephus. Born in Jerusalem around 37 C.E., Josephus was educated in Jerusalem and Rome. During the Jewish Revolt of 66 C.E. Josephus was put in command of a regiment of Jewish militia in Galilee. Following his capture, he was saved from a death sentence after he predicted that Roman General Vespasian would one day become emperor. Indeed, in 69 C.E., Vespasian's own legions pronounced him emperor, and Josephus was released. He eventually went to Rome, where he wrote a book about the Jewish War. He later published another book, *History of the Jews*. Since this book includes a short (though highly controversial) paragraph about Jesus, as well as a less contested section about John the Baptist, Josephus's works were copied by monks throughout the Middle Ages and preserved until modern times.

A 19th-century engraving offers an imaginary likeness of Jewish first-century historian Josephus.

A marble bust depicts Roman general and statesman Gnaeus Pompeius Magnus (106-48 B.C.E.), conqueror of the Hasmonean Kingdom of Judea.

in serving as high priest. Over the past decades, Antipater had steadily cultivated his ties with Julius Caesar, even to the point of fighting by his side while Caesar was battling Egyptian forces. When several years later he was challenged to prove his loyalty to Rome, Antipater ripped off his clothes in a dramatic display of his injuries, saying that he had suffered these in the service of Caesar.

His efforts paid off quite handsomely. Caesar granted Antipater Roman citizenship and even gave him the formal title of *epitropos*, a position comparable to that of prime minister, under Hyrcanus II. Antipater promptly solidified his family's position by appointing his two sons, Phasael and Herod, as provincial governors. Phasael, the elder, received the heartland of Judea and Perea, while Herod was put in charge of the northern province of Galilee. Caesar also granted the Jewish nation a range of exemptions such as the need to provide troops, as other vassal nations were expected to do, and the obligation to sacrifice to the gods of Rome's state religion.

But now Caesar was dead, and Antipater had to quickly recalculate his interests in relation to the Roman Republic. Should he support Caesar's heir Octavian and Mark Antony, or the Liberators? ■

THE RISE OF HEROD THE GREAT

An Idumean Captures the Throne in Jerusalem as a Vassal King

The southern region of Idumea had been conquered by the Hasmonean ruler John Hyrcanus in 125 B.C.E. Large parts of Idumea were pagan, an amalgamation of local deities and Greek gods introduced by the Seleucids. As in the case of Galilee, Hyrcanus then forced every man to convert to Judaism and be circumcised in the process. Josephus claims that this compulsory conversion was done at the behest of the Sadducees, the priestly elite in charge of the sacrificial cult at the Temple.

In time, this would become a serious issue for Antipater and his son Herod in their drive to rule the Jewish nation. Antipater's family, minor Idumean nobility, had also been forcefully converted by Hyrcanus. As a result, Antipater's rise during the reign of Hyrcanus II was broadly resented in Jerusalem circles. Many considered him an Arab upstart with no Jewish pedigree whatsoever. This also applied to his son Herod, since he was the issue of Antipater's marriage to Cypros, an Arab noblewoman from Nabataea, rather than a Jewish woman from Judea. In the minds of the Jews living in Jerusalem, not one drop of Jewish blood coursed through Herod's veins.

Many years later, after Herod had become king of Roman Palestine, he ordered the renowned historian Nicholas of Damascus to invent a bloodline claiming that Herod's family hailed from the priestly elite exiled to Babylon by Nebuchadnezzar, but few in the kingdom were deceived.

HEROD'S RULE IN GALILEE

Nevertheless, Antipater labored tirelessly to advance the cause of his sons. As we saw, both were appointed as provincial governors under Hyrcanus, though in practice it was Antipater who called the shots. This presented Antipater with an acute dilemma when the Liberator Cassius arrived in Syria-Palestine to demand a large tribute for his legions.

This elaborate gold amulet with pendants, possibly crafted in Greece, attests to the wealth of many urban centers of Asia Minor.

Josephus claims that Cassius charged Antipater with raising the exorbitant sum of 700 silver talents. The talent, which in Matthew's Gospel appears in Jesus' parable of the three servants, was roughly worth around $9,000 in modern currency (Matthew 25:14-30). In other words, Antipater was expected to raise around $6.3 million—a near-impossible task in a country as poor as Roman Palestine. Antipater had no choice but to turn to his sons, Phasael and Herod, for help.

Herod eagerly accepted and pursued his fund-raising target with a vengeance. He had inherited his father's ambition and recognized that the road to advancement led through Rome. And few at the time doubted that Cassius and Brutus, who were close to raising some 45 legions—one of the largest armies ever assembled by Rome—would surely deal a blistering defeat to the young and inexperienced Octavian.

Unfortunately, Herod's domain, the province of Galilee, was an agricultural region with no appreciable assets such as mines or timber or any urban centers where concentrations of wealth could be found. What Galilee did have were farmers. These were for the most part subsistence peasants—meaning that they cultivated a small amount of broad-spectrum crops to sustain their families and pay their taxes. By definition, subsistence farmers always operated at the margins of existence. There was little or no room for error, certainly not in times of drought, excessive rainfall, disease, or any other calamity that could swiftly push a farmer into penury.

Of course, this was of no concern to Herod. The purpose of governance in Roman times was not to care for the well-being of one's subjects, but to extract the highest possible tax and tribute. Thus, Herod increased the tax burden to such exorbitant levels that,

Around 37 B.C.E., Herod's troops scoured these caves in the Arbel Heights to flush out resistance fighters loyal to Antigonus, heir to the Hasmonean throne.

> *As soon as Herod captured Jerusalem,*
> *he carried off with all the royal ornaments*
> *and stole from wealthy men whatever he could;*
> *and all this silver and gold he gave*
> *to Antony and his friends.*

JOSEPHUS, *ANTIQUITIES OF THE JEWS*

ca 63
Hyrcanus II is appointed king with Antipater as governor *(epitropos)*

ca 47
Antipater's son Herod is appointed governor *(strategos)* of Galilee

ca 44
Julius Caesar is assassinated on the Senate floor

ca 44
Herod's brutal tax regime in Galilee raises funds for Cassius

Herod's Family Tomb in Jerusalem still retains the round stone used to close the entrance.

as Josephus tells us, he was quickly able to amass his allocation of 350 talents and be "the first to bring in his share from Galilee." Cassius was inordinately pleased.

This unfortunate episode would set the stage for the terrible socioeconomic crisis that swept Galilee in the decades to come and possibly served as an important impetus for the ministry of Jesus. Herod's heavy tax yoke provoked a deep hatred among the population, which Herod was happy to reciprocate. For the remainder of his life, he would use Galilee as a colony to squeeze and exploit, even if this caused hundreds of farmers to be driven from their ancestral lands. It is these victims, these hordes of disposed and impoverished families, who would populate the Gospels as the "multitudes" who cleave to Jesus' words, and inspire the Sermon on the Mount.

THE CROWN OF JUDEA

So catastrophic was Herod's iron-fisted rule in Galilee that around 45 B.C.E., the Galilean peasantry rose in rebellion. This revolt was led by a man named Hezekiah, who quite possibly was a member of the old landed gentry that owed their lands to the Hasmonean Dynasty. Many of these noblemen remained loyal to the Aristobulus faction and opposed the regime of Hyrcanus and Antipater, who openly collaborated with the Roman regime.

In response, Herod mustered his militia and tracked the rebels down to their sanctuary in the cliffs of Arbel. Hezekiah was arrested, brought before a sham tribunal, and summarily put to death. This act lit the fuse of the simmering resentment against Antipater's family, and the nation rose in uproar. Herod was forced to flee to Syria.

This would have been the end of the story of Herod were it not for the fact that in 40 B.C.E., the Parthians invaded Judea. This was done under the nominal pretext of supporting the royal claim of Antigonus, son of the defeated Aristobulus, but in all likelihood, the Parthians simply wanted to expand their sphere of influence at the expense of Roman Syria. If this is true, they certainly succeeded in getting Rome's attention. The Senate was in uproar; Rome's grain lifeline from Egypt was in acute jeopardy. But who could plausibly bring this endless conflict between Hasmonean pretenders to an end?

This is when Herod quite suddenly appeared in Rome. Invited to address the Roman Senate, a rare honor, Herod convinced his audience that he was the man who could rally all of Roman Palestine and send the Parthians packing—with Roman military support, of course. That most of the Jews despised Herod was not a matter that the senators dwelled on at any length. The Romans did not expect their vassal kings to practice democracy. Nor should the small matter of Herod's support for Cassius be held against him. Thus, with Antony's blessing, the Senate not only voted Herod "King of the Jews" but also gave him a Roman legion to drive the Parthians out and seize the throne of Jerusalem.

This sounds easier than it was. It took Herod nearly three years of hard fighting before he could subdue the country. This included

An aerial view of Lower Galilee and the northern shore of the Sea of Galilee illustrates the rich fecundity of this region.

An intimate scene of two women engaged in conversation was executed in Myrina (northern Asia Minor) around 100 B.C.E.

the Galilean gentry, who fielded numerous guerrilla attacks against Herod's forces from their hideaway in the same Arbel Heights where Hezekiah had sheltered earlier. To flush them out, Herod lowered cages filled with soldiers from the top of the mountain. As soon as these came abreast of the cave openings, the soldiers attacked with javelins, grappling hooks, and fire. Anyone found in the cave—man, woman, or child—was killed. Thus, Herod gave notice that he had returned to Roman Palestine, and this time he was determined to stay. ■

MONUMENTS OF THE HERODIAN ERA

King Herod Embarks on a Vast Development Plan in Judea and Samaria

Ever since the restoration of the Temple during the early Persian period, few, if any, major building projects had been undertaken in the former Jewish kingdom. The successive Persian, Greek, Ptolemaic, Seleucid, and Hasmonean rulers engaged more in destroying towns than in building them. The exception was the establishment of various administrative centers at places like Megiddo, Beth Shean, and Dor, and perhaps the restoration of walls and defenses here and there to protect sensitive border areas. For the remainder, these foreign powers restricted their building zest to their poleis, where a Greek lifestyle could be celebrated to the fullest without any concern for local mores or sensibilities. In Roman Syria and Palestine, the most prominent of these Greek cities was the so-called League of the Decapolis ("Ten Cities"), a loose affiliation of independent city-states established from the third century B.C.E. on east of the Jordan River. Only one member city was located west of the river, on the border between Galilee and Samaria: the city of Scytho-polis, rebuilt by Gabinius.

This changed under the rule of Herod the Great. During his 33-year reign, Judea and Samaria saw an unprecedented level of building activity that would change the face of Roman Palestine forever. Much of this was prompted by economic as well as political considerations.

THE HERODIAN FORTRESSES

Fully aware of Judea's tragic history of foreign invasions, Herod first created a defensive bulwark around his kingdom, anchored by a number of fortresses. Several of these fortifications were built at the top of prominent hills or cliffs so as to fulfill a dual function: as both the base for a rapid deployment force in case of internal or external threats and as a palatial refuge for the king and his family. Herod remembered all too vividly how, during the dark days of the Parthian invasion,

This first-century C.E. head of the young Bacchus, god of wine, still has the original silver and colored glass to give the eyes a lifelike appearance.

he had left his family in the modest Hasmonean stronghold on top of a mountain called Masada before he made his way to Rome in an attempt to secure Rome's support. This massive plateau, located close to the Dead Sea, would now become the crown jewel in this string of fortifications.

Excavated by Yigael Yadin in the 1960s, the original Hasmonean fortress was expanded with large cisterns to catch rainwater for elaborate Roman-style bathing facilities built on the site. A palace complex on the west side of the plateau featured an elaborate portico that led to a throne room and a residential section for the king and his family. Ten years after the completion of this palace, in 25 B.C.E., Herod created the most impressive building of all: a "suspended palace" precariously perched on three levels of stepped cliffs. This engineering marvel, located on the northern promontory, offered the king and his guests breathtaking views of the Judean Hills and the Dead Sea as they sipped their cups of Italian wine.

A no less dramatic complex arose on another mound, a volcano-like man-made hill known as the Herodium. Here, Herod's workers filled in the craggy fissures of the hill to create an almost perfectly smooth, cone-shaped fortress, accessible by a steep stairway of hewn stone, and topped by defensive towers. Apparently the place had a special significance for Herod, for it was here that he had defeated a unit of the Parthian army.

Equally dramatic was the fortress of Machaerus, also built on a hilltop and located near the village of Muqawir in today's Jordan, just 18 miles from the Dead Sea. Here too had once stood a modest Hasmonean citadel that Herod expanded into a luxurious fortress. Surrounded by deep ravines, this sheer, impregnable mound rises to a height of 1,100 feet above Dead Sea level. Given its proximity to Nabataea, Herod made this the most heavily fortified stronghold of all, topped by a 100-yard-long wall anchored

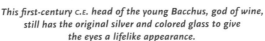

ca 43	ca 43	ca 42	ca 42
Herod suppresses rebellion led by a Galilean named Hezekiah	Octavian, Antony, and Lepidus form a triumvirate in Rome	Caesar's assassins, Brutus and Cassius, are defeated at the Battle of Philippi	The Roman Empire is divided among Octavian, Mark Antony, and Lepidus

KINGDOM OF HEROD THE GREAT

MAP KEY

```
· · · · · · · ·   District or region boundary
▨             Herod's Kingdom
▨             Roman province of Syria
▨             Nabataean Kingdom
• / ○         City of the Decapolis /
              location uncertain
○             Location uncertain
⊙             Herodian fortress
```

Sidon

Damascus

2,814 m
9,232 ft
Mt. Hermon

Leontes

ITUREA

SYRIA

Tyre
Kanah

PHOENICIA

Cadasa
Asor
Raphana

Achzib

Merom
UPPER GALILEE

GAULANITIS

BATANEA

Ptolemais

Capernaum
Bethsaida

Bay of Acco
(Bay of Haifa)

Jotapata
Arbela

Sea of Kinnereth
(Sea of Galilee)

Sycaminium

LOWER GALILEE

Hippos

AURANITIS

Gabae
Nazareth
Philoteria

Mt. Carmel
546 m
1,791 ft

Mt. Tabor
588 m
1,929 ft

Gadara
Abila

Edrei

Dora

Legio

Expanded by Herod the Great and
named in honor of his patron,
Caesar Augustus, this city was
known for its splendid buildings. It
would become a Roman
administrative center.

Caesarea

Scythopolis
Pella
Dion

The Decapolis was a commercial
league whose member cities
enjoyed a measure of autonomy
within the Roman province.

Narbata

Herod the Great built a large
acropolis on the ancient
location of Samaria and
renamed the city Sebaste, the
Greek version of "Augustus."

Sebaste

Mt. Ebal
940 m
3,084 ft

Gerasa

Apollonia

SAMARIA

Neapolis
Amathus

Antipatris

Mt. Gerizim
881 m
2,890 ft

JORDAN

THE GREAT SEA
(MEDITERRANEAN SEA)

PLAIN OF SHARON

Yarqon

Joppa

Lebonah

Alexandrium

Gadara

DECAPOLIS

Phasaelis

Philadelphia

Lydda

Bethel

Archelais

The birthplace of Herod the
Great, an Idumean. He built
magnificent fountains and
baths to beautify the city.

Gazara

JUDEA

Jericho

Cyprus

As a way of garnering favor with
his subjects, Herod instituted a
great building program. Jerusalem
benefited, receiving a market,
amphitheater, theater, a new
building where the Sanhedrin
could convene, and a new royal
palace. In 20 B.C.E. reconstruction
began on the Temple.

Kidron
Emmaus
Mizpah

Esbus

Azotus
Zorah
Jerusalem

Mt. Nebo
802 m
2,631 ft

Medeba

Beth Shemesh
Bethlehem

Ascalon

Hyrcania

PEREA

Anthedon
Marisa
Lachish

Herodium

Salt Sea
(Dead Sea)

Gaza

Hebron

Machaerus

Eshtemoa

Herod the Great constructed an
elaborate monument and temple over
the traditional tomb of the patriarchs.

IDUMEA

Masada
En-gedi

Once a treasure-house
fortress of the Hasmoneans,
it had been torn down by
the Romans. Herod the
Great rebuilt it as a fortress
and prison.

Gaza Strip

Raphia

Beersheba

Malatha

Arnon

Kir-Moab

EGYPT

Besor

NEGEV

NABATEA

```
0        20        40 kilometers
|——|——|——|——|——|
0        20        40 miles
```

*Present-day drainage, coastlines, and country boundaries are represented.
Modern names appear in parentheses.*

PHILISTIA

SHEPHELAH

ca 40
Parthians invade Judea in support
of Antigonus, son of Aristobulus II

ca 40
Herod flees to Rome;
Senate proclaims him
king of Judea

ca 39
Herod lands in Judea
backed by Roman forces
and battles Antigonus

ca 37
Herod besieges Jerusalem
and captures the city

by three corner towers some 90 feet high. Like its sister fortress of Masada (close enough to be signaled in times of danger), Machaerus also featured a palace complex that would serve as the location for a key episode in the Gospels.

SEBASTE

Within his realm proper, Herod focused on the development of Greco-Roman poleis as his Ptolemaic and Seleucid predecessors had done. The purpose of these new cities was twofold: to stimulate the growth of the region's economy and to conform to the wishes of Herod's overlord, the Roman emperor.

Ever since his victory over the Liberators and the subsequent defeat of his rival Mark Antony, Octavian had risen as the unchallenged ruler of the Roman Empire. His foremost ambition was to forge Rome's possessions together in a seamless cultural commonwealth. Only by creating a global economy that would dramatically improve the living standards of the people under his sway, Octavian believed, could the Roman realm be spared the vicious cycle of rebellions that had doomed the empires of old.

To accomplish this vision, Octavian—soon to be granted the honorific "August One," or Augustus, by the Roman Senate—initiated a massive infrastructure project to connect the empire with roads and paved highways. At its peak, the Roman road system covered some 250,000 miles, of which some 50,000 miles were paved. Rome's vassal kings were expected to do their share by launching an urbanization program in each of their domains on the Greco-Roman model. By erasing the native imprint of Near Eastern cities and imposing a uniform stamp of Greek-style temples, theaters, and marketplaces, Augustus believed he could fuse the empire together in a homogeneous world where everyone spoke Greek, everyone bartered using the denarius coin, and everyone could prosper under the benevolent rule of Rome. And in this he was ultimately successful.

Herod too was expected to conform to this model. The king complied by building a new city on one of the most hallowed sites of ancient Israel: the city of Samaria. Repopulated by Alexander the Great's veterans after 331 B.C.E., the city had been destroyed once again by the Hasmonean commander John Hyrcanus during the battles of 108 B.C.E. Work on its restoration began soon after Pompey annexed the city as Roman property, but Julius Caesar decided to formally cede the city to Herod as a gesture of goodwill.

Herod knew what was expected of him. He rebuilt the city as a Greco-Roman polis, complete with a forum, a theater, and a large-scale temple dedicated to Rome. Herod piously named this new city Sebaste, the Greek translation of "Augustus." That building a large pagan temple might give offense to his Jewish subjects did not faze him in the least.

The king then turned to another of Augustus's priorities: the development of swift communications throughout the empire.

This aqueduct, built on orders of Herod the Great between 22 and 10 B.C.E., carried water from a spring some four miles away to his new port city of Caesarea.

This fine oenochoe, or wine vessel, of bronze and silver was probably crafted in Alexandria in the early decades of the first century C.E.

Herod realized that if his kingdom was to benefit from the new Pax Romana, it needed to be plugged in to its network of intrastate commerce. But here was the rub: Palestine had no harbor, at least not the type of port that could accommodate Roman cargo ships. Thus began what was perhaps the most ambitious enterprise of his reign: the development of a large, deep-sea port on the Mediterranean coast near a Jewish fishing township known as Stratonospyrgos, or "Strabo's Tower."

In order to create a deepwater anchorage large enough to accommodate Roman ships, Herod's architects built a vast artificial breakwater by pouring cement made from lime and volcanic ash, imported from Italy. While this massive port, inevitably called "Sebastos," was under construction, Herod also began the development around the harbor of his greatest city yet, known as Caesarea Maritima. It was designed to accommodate the people who would operate the port, from the lowliest dockworker to the wealthiest

The Herodian Fortress

The Herodium was one of the most impressive citadels in Herod's ring of fortifications. While the upper level was primarily defensive in nature, the lower grounds were conceived as "pleasure grounds," in Josephus's words, with "costly royal apartments made for security and for ornament at the same time." As at Masada, all facilities enjoyed ample access to water, which was "brought in from a distance and at great expense." First uncovered in the 1960s by Virgilio Corbo, the site was excavated once more by the Israeli archaeologist Ehud Netzer until his tragic death in 2010. Netzer described how his team uncovered "a palatial resort, a sort of country club in modern terms" complete with a large swimming pool. But nothing prepared them for the discovery of a large mausoleum, similar to the Tomb of Absalom in Jerusalem, and three sarcophagi. One of these, carved from pink Jerusalem limestone, may have contained Herod's body.

The citadel of Herodium, some seven miles south of Jerusalem, was built by Herod the Great as his palace and mausoleum between 24 and 15 B.C.E.

holy city of Jerusalem itself, Herod had begun to build a theater, a hippodrome, and an amphitheater that according to Josephus was designed for "contests of various kinds, including those featuring men fighting wild animals." This, he added, "greatly offended the Jews."

Why did these shocking projects not result in a Maccabee-style rebellion? Perhaps the answer is twofold. On the one hand, Herod's public works program provided employment to thousands of Jews in a land that had very few economic opportunities to offer. As a result, the standard of living in Judea rose perceptibly, as attested by numerous Roman luxury products excavated in the region—though this did not apply to Galilee, as we will see shortly. And second, Herod had begun to build a police state where any hint of insurrection was instantly snuffed out. Jews were encouraged to inform on one another. "Even in the cities and on the open roads, there were men who spied on people meeting," says Josephus. A case in point was a plot, one of several, to kill Herod in his newly built theater. The conspiracy was exposed, and the perpetrators were cut to pieces and thrown to the dogs.

Nevertheless, even Herod realized a gesture was needed to assuage his aggrieved Jewish subjects. In response, he initiated a project that would form a key stage in the story of Jesus: the expansion of the Second Temple into one of the largest sanctuaries of the ancient world. ■

merchant, and eventually it became the largest Greco-Roman city ever built on Israel's soil.

THE JEWISH RESPONSE

To suggest that Herod's subjects were none too pleased with this massive influx of pagan culture would be an understatement. They had suffered willful efforts to impose Greco-Roman idolatry before, particularly under Seleucid rule, but Herod was pushing it to the extreme. In the

THE ART OF THE PERSIAN AND GREEK AGES

Hellenistic Influences Spread Across the Levant

In the wake of Alexander's conquest and the Ptolemaic and Seleucid rule of the region, the Hellenizing influence of Greek culture became widespread. For the next 300 years, many pious Jews in Judea would try to resist this cultural imperialism with varying degrees of success until the arrival of a new and even greater imperialism—the reign of the Roman Caesars. Meanwhile, in the Persian realm, the Achaemenids continued the Persian virtuosity in silver or gold objects—an artisan tradition that would be absorbed in the subsequent Parthian and Sassanid Empires. ■

This portrait of Alexander the Great, executed in Alexandria, conforms to the youthful idealized image of Alexander that became popular after his death.

An octadrachm (worth eight drachmas) shows the twin portraits of King Ptolemy II Philadelphus and Arsinoe II, dated 285-246 B.C.E.

A silver bowl from Hamadan, Iran, is inscribed with the legend "Artaxerxes, king of kings ... son of King Xerxes," and is dated to 465-424 B.C.E.

A fifth-century Greek amphora with two vertical neck handles, used for storing wine or olive oil, was found in Samaria.

A Roman copy of a Greek original, dated around 400 B.C.E., shows the goddess Athena of the so-called Velletri type, wearing a Corinthian helmet.

CHAPTER
5

THE ARCHAEOLOGY OF THE LIFE OF JESUS

The Gospels of Matthew, Mark, Luke, and John

DIVISION OF THE KINGDOM OF HEROD THE GREAT

MAP KEY

— Limit of the kingdom of Herod the Great

⋯⋯ District or region boundary

� Granted to Herod Antipas

▨ Granted to Herod Archelaus

▨ Granted to Salome
(under Archelaus's supervision)

▨ Granted to Salome once
Herod Archelaus was deposed

▨ Granted to Herod Philip

▨ Roman province of Syria

▨ Nabataean Kingdom

● / ○ City of the Decapolis /
location uncertain

○ Location uncertain

⊙ Herodian fortress

Herod Philip built his capital city
at Paneas, referred to as
Caesarea Philippi in the Gospels

Herod Antipas built this
city and named it for his
patron, Emperor Tiberias.

Herod Antipas rebuilt
Sepphoris as Galilee's capital
after its destruction in 4 B.C.E.

The Decapolis was a commercial
league whose member cities enjoyed
a measure of autonomy within the
Roman province.

Herod Antipas held court in a
palace built as part of a fortress; it
was here, according to Josephus,
that Salome danced and John the
Baptist was beheaded.
(Matthew 14:3–12)

THE GREAT SEA
(MEDITERRANEAN SEA)

Sidon
Damascus
Tyre
Kanah
Cadasa
Achzib
Asor
Merom UPPER GALILEE
Paneas
Raphana
GAULANITIS
BATANEA
Ptolemais
Capernaum
Bethsaida
Bay of Acco
(Bay of Haifa)
Jotapata
Arbela
Sea of Kinnereth
Sea of Galilee
Sycaminium
Tiberias
Hippos
AURANITIS
Mt. Carmel
546 m
1,791 ft
Sepphoris
Nazareth
Philoteria
Abila
Gebae
Mt. Tabor
588 m
1,929 ft
Gadara
Edrei
Dora
Legio
Caesarea
Scythopolis
Pella
Gerasa
Narbata
Dion
Mt. Ebal
940 m
3,084 ft
Sebaste
Amathus
Apollonia
Neapolis
Mt. Gerizim
881 m
2,890 ft
Antipatris
Joppa
Lebonah
Alexandrium
Gadara
Phasaelis
Philadelphia
Lydda
Archelais
Bethel
Gazara
Jericho
Mizpah
Cyprus
Emmaus
Esbus
Azotus
Zorah
Jerusalem
Mt. Nebo
802 m
2,631 ft
Medeba
Beth
Shemesh
Bethlehem
Hyrcania
Ascalon
Herodium
Marisa
Lachish
Beth-zur
Anthedon
Hebron
Machaerus
Gaza
Eshtemoa
En-gedi
Gaza
Strip
IDUMEA
EGYPT
Raphia
Masada
Kir-Moab
Beersheba
Malatha
NEGEV

0   20   40 kilometers
0   20   40 miles

Present-day drainage, coastlines, and country boundaries are represented.
Modern names appear in parentheses.

Augustus won over the soldiers with gifts, the populace with cheap corn, and all men with the sweets of repose, and so grew greater by degrees.

TACITUS, THE ANNALS, BOOK I

THE WORLD IN 5 B.C.E.

Galilee and Judea, From 5 B.C.E. to 30 C.E.

IN THE YEAR 5 B.C.E., AUGUSTUS HAD GOVERNED THE ROMAN EMPIRE FOR 22 YEARS. HIS power was now nearly absolute. In 19 B.C.E. the Roman Senate had granted him consular *imperium*, or authority for the rest of his life, and for good reason. Under his command, the Roman Empire had steadily expanded to include northern Africa, the Balkans, Hispania (today's Spain and Portugal), and Galatia in Asia Minor. Augustus had also shrewdly co-opted the ruling elites in these new territories by granting them Roman citizenship and the right to wear a toga. As he had hoped, this soon became the ultimate status symbol in the occupied territories, with many worthies competing with one another for the honor of calling oneself "Roman."

Some communities that rendered exceptional service to the Roman crown could even be rewarded with collective citizenship, as in the case of the city of Tarsus in Cilicia (today's southern Turkey). This city had been so conscientious in remitting its annual tribute to Rome—including the dispatch of mercenary soldiers, as many vassals were expected to do—that the whole community was granted the status of a Roman city. One of the individuals thus favored was a man named Saul (which later became Paul), who many years later would use his citizenship to demand a legal hearing in Rome rather than face a colonial court in Caesarea. The enfranchisement of

Preceding pages: *The rolling fields of the Beit Netofa Valley near Nazareth appear to be as lush as they were in the days of Jesus.*
Right: *This bust of Augustus, founder of the Roman Empire and its first emperor, was probably completed after his death in 14 C.E.*

the provinces became so widespread that two of the empire's most capable emperors, Trajan (crowned in 98 C.E.) and Hadrian (crowned in 117 C.E.), were actually Spanish natives rather than sons of Italy.

Under Augustus's firm but essentially benign rule, living standards steadily rose across the empire, buoyed by the growing demand for timber, metals, oil, wine, and a stunning variety of luxury products. Egypt, a Roman possession since 30 B.C.E., gained renown for its glass, jewelry, alabaster, porphyry, granite, and papyrus. From Africa came large quantities of almonds, walnuts, coconuts, apricots, and peaches, while Syria produced dates, figs, and sugared plums. Most of these delicacies would eventually adorn the banquet tables of Rome's aristocracy, a historically landed class that now saw its fortunes grow hundredfold through overseas service or speculation, or both. Near the end of the first century C.E., Rome's annual receipts totaled 1.5 billion sesterces, roughly the equivalent of $6 billion today.

Wealth seeks an outlet, and found it in the luxuries from the East. The Spice Route through Persia brought Chinese bolts of silk as well as finished silk garments; from India came elephant tusks, amber, pearls, and spices. Meanwhile, caravans on the Arabian Incense Route carried aloes, myrrh, and other perfume agents from Yemen and frankincense from Oman, to burn as incense in Rome's temples. Some scholars have estimated that during the heyday of the Roman Empire, a typical caravan would number 100 camels, each laden with about 500 pounds of cargo and capable of traveling 20 to 30 miles a day. Mercantile centers like Petra in Nabataea and Gerasa and Palmyra in Syria amassed stupendous wealth.

At the same time, Augustus's beautification of Rome itself—by transforming a city of brick into one of marble—launched a similar frenzy across the empire, as every major city tried to outdo its rivals in the splendor of its public buildings. This in turn caused a run on marble quarries throughout Italy, Greece, Asia Minor, and Spain.

This Roman gold pendant from the late first century B.C.E. depicts the head of Medusa, a mythological figure with snakes instead of hair.

THE LATTER YEARS OF HEROD'S RULE

No wonder, then, that King Herod felt a desperate need to tap into this huge trade boom and be recognized among Rome's other vassal kings as an equal. As we saw, he did so by confiscating vast tracts of peasant lands, primarily in Galilee, in order to establish professional estates that churned out surplus yields at greater rates than ever before. The problem was that this new wave of prosperity benefited only an upper class of wealthy merchants, priests, and Hellenized Jewish families. Outside the sparkling cities of Sebaste, Scythopolis, and Caesarea Maritima, the vast majority of Jews, living in rural communities, saw very little of this wealth. Instead, they were taxed to the limit of their endurance.

As a result, popular resentment against the king steadily grew, and soon the country seethed with unrest. Herod was aware of it and urged his personal guard, the 2,000 soldiers of the Doryphoroi ("spear bearers"), to ferret out any hint of sedition. Scores of dissidents were arrested and sent to one of Herod's fortresses, where they were executed. Herod had deliberately weakened the influence of the Sanhedrin by favoring Sadducees over the Pharisaic party and appointing temple officials from priestly families in Babylonia, thus earning their total loyalty. One such priestly family, the house of the high priest Ananas, was particularly favored by the king. Ananas's son-in-law, a man named Caiaphas, would soon sit in judgment of Jesus.

At times, Herod was capable of impressive feats of generosity. When in 24 B.C.E. a severe drought led to an outbreak of famine, he lowered taxes and organized a vast relief effort by importing large quantities of grain from Egypt. The king also offered financial assistance to Jewish expatriate communities in Anatolia and Cyrene (today's Libya). When told that the Olympic Games of 12 B.C.E. faced an acute funding gap, he rushed to fill it so that the games could proceed. And throughout his reign, he made sure that his coins avoided the usual portrait of the Roman emperor or any other representation of humans that could offend the Jewish prohibition on graven images of living beings.

Nevertheless, as he grew older, Herod began to suspect conspiracies around every corner, even in his own family. The king had tried to clad his rule in a cloak of legitimacy by divorcing his first wife, Doris, in order to marry a Hasmonean princess named Mariamne instead. The marriage had the additional benefit of preempting the ambitions of Mariamne's brother, Aristobulus III, who was the legitimate heir in the Hasmonean line. And just to be sure, Herod had Aristobulus drowned just one year after he had appointed the young man as high priest; he was only 17 years old. Herod's sister Salome then convinced the king to execute two of his sons by Mariamne, Alexander and Aristobulus IV, on suspicion of treason. Herod's distrust even turned on Mariamne herself, though she was the mother of five of his children. When one night she refused to share his bed, Herod accused her of adultery and put her on trial, forcing her own mother to appear as a witness for the prosecution. Mariamne was executed, as was her mother shortly after. Long after his wife's death, says Josephus, Herod would "wander around the palace calling for his wife and ordering the servants to bring her to him." Shortly before his death, Herod sealed his calamitous relationship with his family by ordering the execution of his oldest son and heir, Antipater.

And not long after that, a son was born to a rural couple from a hamlet known as Nazareth. ■

This delicate glass kantharos from the first century C.E. illustrates the Roman technique of glassblowing, which was introduced in the Levant around 50 B.C.E.

An image of camel-borne goods harks back to Roman times, when caravans of 50 camels or more were common along the Incense Route across Arabia.

THE LAND OF LOWER GALILEE

A Region of Great Diversity and Fecundity

Matthew's poetic Gospel refers to it as the "Land of Zebulun, land of Naphtali, on the road by the sea, across the Jordan, Galilee of the Gentiles" (Matthew 4:15). But the more laconic narrative of the Gospel of Mark merely states that "Jesus came from Nazareth of Galilee" (Mark 1:9). And in John's Gospel, an incredulous man asks, "Surely the Messiah does not come from Galilee, does he?" (John 7:42).

This rather dismissive attitude to a region that would leave such an indelible print on Jesus' ministry is not surprising. It is likely that none of these evangelists had ever set foot in Galilee when they wrote their stories. Mark, the author of what is generally assumed to be the oldest Gospel, was probably a Roman scribe who around 70 C.E. wrote in Rome for a local Christian congregation. Matthew and Luke, who most likely wrote their Gospels some 10 or 20 years after that of Mark, also lived outside Roman Palestine. Many scholars believe that Matthew produced his text in Antioch on the Orontes in Syria, since Bishop Ignatius of Antioch cited passages from his work as early as 110 C.E. The location of Luke is more difficult to ascertain, but it is possible that this author wrote for a Christian community in Asia Minor, Greece, or Alexandria, given the exquisite elegance of his written Greek.

The similarity of these three Gospels—Mark, Matthew, and Luke—has prompted historians to refer to them as the synoptic Gospels (from the Greek word *synoptikos*, meaning "seen together"). Indeed, close investigation has revealed that both Luke and Matthew used as much as 40 percent of Mark's text, though these two evangelists also used other sources, including a putative text of sayings that scholarly circles refer to as "Q" (for *Quelle*, meaning "source" in German).

The Gospel of John is strikingly different. It is more concerned with Jesus' theological ideas than with the details of his life. Arguably written near the end of the first century C.E., possibly in Ephesus, it dwells at length on sermons and discourses that do not appear in the other Gospels. Nevertheless, this Gospel features some very specific events—such as the wedding in Cana—that do not appear in any of the other canonical texts. John's Gospel may therefore represent a parallel tradition that evolved independent of the synoptic Gospels.

All of this underscores that the evangelists were not the "eyewitnesses" that some Christian traditions hold them to be. Instead, they wrote outside Roman Palestine, using oral and written traditions about Jesus that were circulating in their communities. John, for example, writes that his Gospel is based on "testimony" by a "disciple who is testifying to these things and has written them" (John 21:24).

This explains why the reader who is interested in everyday life in ancient Galilee will not find much information in the Gospel texts. Fortunately, modern excavations in Galilee allow us to fill this gap and complement the New Testament record with many fascinating details.

GALILEE OF THE GENTILES

This bracelet of twisted silver strands from the first century C.E. was excavated in southern Judea.

The most important of these insights is that despite the ongoing Judaization during the Hasmonean era, Galilee remained a highly diverse region. Archaeologist Eric Meyers refers to a "cosmopolitan and multilingual atmosphere" whereby towns with a Greco-Roman imprint lived in uneasy coexistence with rural villages that tended to be more observant of Jewish tenets. Indeed, says Mark Chancey in his Galilean study of 2005, coins and pottery fragments show that these townships were "no less Hellenized and urbanized than anywhere else in the Roman world." One example is the regional capital of Sepphoris, only four miles distant from Nazareth, which excavations show boasted a fairly sophisticated urban population.

ca 37	ca 36	ca 35	ca 32
Reign of King Herod the Great (37-4 B.C.E.) begins	**Herod appoints his 17-year-old brother-in-law Aristobulus III high priest**	**Aristobulus III is drowned on orders of Herod**	**Herod launches war against Nabataea**

Olive groves such as this orchard outside Nazareth evoke the timeless beauty of ancient Galilee.

The whole city was in turmoil, asking, "Who is this?" The crowds were saying, "This is the prophet Jesus from Nazareth in Galilee."

MATTHEW 21:10-11

A fragment of the Gospel of John begins the story of Jesus when he joins followers of John the Baptist in the desert.

ca 32
Roman Senate declares war
on Cleopatra and Mark Antony

ca 31
Strong earthquake
destroys parts of Judea

ca 31
Mark Antony
is defeated by Octavian

ca 31
Mark Antony and Cleopatra
commit suicide

A reconstruction of a first-century C.E. courtyard house in Qasrin, Upper Galilee, suggests what a home in Nazareth may have looked like.

Side by side with these mixed enclaves were some 200 hamlets that clung tenaciously to their Jewish faith and customs. In the words of Jonathan Reed, these villages "did not import foreign wine amphorae, used little or no glass, and befitting Jewish Law, avoided images of humans or animals." Instead they preferred limestone jars and cups, for the Law decreed that liquids such as water or oil remained ritually pure in stone vessels rather than clay pottery—an important concern for many observant Jews, but particularly the Pharisees.

The contrast between mixed urban centers and Jewish-observant hamlets is reflected in the Talmud, a collection of rabbinic writings from around 200 C.E. onward, which makes a clear distinction between a village *(kfr),* a township *('yr),* and a city *(krkh,* similar to the Greek word *polis).* It is also made manifest in the Gospels, where Jesus tells his disciples, "Go nowhere among the Gentiles" (Matthew 10:5). His teaching, at least at this point in the Gospel story, was to be reserved for the Jewish-observant villages of Galilee.

Galilean villages were small, which is probably the reason that Nazareth doesn't deserve even a mention in Josephus's listing of 204 hamlets. Excavations in places like Qasrin in Upper Galilee have shown that a typical village was no larger than eight to ten *dunams* (each *dunam* representing ten families), living over an area of about two acres. Most of these families lived in simple homes of stacked stone, mortared or not, using the basalt stone that was quarried in Lower Eastern Galilee and the Golan Heights.

THE FRUIT BASKET OF THE NEAR EAST

Nazareth and the townships to the west of the Sea of Galilee formed part of the region known as Lower Galilee. According to Josephus, this territory ran from Ptolemais (or Acre) in the west to Mount Tabor and Scythopolis in the south, and the Sea of Galilee in the east. The sea itself is often referred to as Lake Kinneret in Hebrew Scripture, given that its shape was somewhat reminiscent of a harp *(kinor* in Hebrew). Northeast of this region, the landscape became more rugged with craggy highlands of basalt. Basalt does not welcome natural growth, so these hills, roughly between Bethsaida and the foothills of the Golan, sustained little vegetation other than low-level brush and grass. Farther toward the west, around Sepphoris and beyond, the landscape became more lush and fertile. Here terebinth trees, carob brush, and mastic trees hugged the softly undulating hills,

with valleys that burst into a riot of bright colors during spring. Here too were scores of family-tended olive orchards, their silvery leaves glistening in the afternoon sun. While olive oil had a thousand uses in Galilean life, the wood of the tree did not, for it was too gnarly for woodworking.

What set Galilee apart from Judea and Samaria was its abundant fecundity. In the region around the escarpment known as the Nazareth Ridge, natural springs such as the Nahal Sippori provided

The fields surrounding the modern city of Nazareth have changed little since the days of Jesus' boyhood.

A barrel-shaped jar with a ribbed body and loop handle, which was used to store provisions, is dated between 50 B.C.E. and 50 C.E.

a consistent and stable source of water all year, notwithstanding the rather spotty incidence of rain. In 1992, Israeli archaeologist Zvi Gal discovered the secret of these springs: They were (and still are) being fed by large subterranean aquifers, which make Galilee the place par excellence for the growth of fruit and legumes. "Its soil is so universally rich and fruitful, and so full of the plantations of trees of all sorts," Josephus wrote, "that it invites even the most indolent to engage in agriculture, because of its fruitfulness."

This is why, as we saw, the central region of Lower Galilee would consistently attract the greatest density of settlement from the Middle Bronze Age to the Roman era. And it is also the reason that King Herod would seize on Galilee as the territory that could help him fund his vainglorious monuments. ■

BETHLEHEM OF EPHRATHAH

The Place Where the Messiah Would Be Born

Since the earliest of times, the little town of Bethlehem has been closely identified with the birth of Jesus. No Christmas celebration is complete without an image of the stable and the shepherds in the fields. Less known, however, is that the famous Nativity story in the Gospel of Luke is strikingly different from the version in Matthew's Gospel or that the Gospels of Mark and John do not include an infancy narrative at all.

The essential question that confronted Matthew and Luke is how Jesus, who quite clearly spent his childhood in the Galilean village of Nazareth, could plausibly be born in Bethlehem. This was important, because the essential purpose of the synoptic Gospels is to present Jesus as the Jewish Messiah, or "Anointed One"—the term used for Israel's kings—as foretold in Hebrew Scripture. That is why almost every key passage in Jesus' life is framed with biblical references purporting to confirm the fulfillment of biblical prophecy. "All this took place to fulfill what had been spoken by the Lord through the prophet," says Matthew at the beginning of his infancy narrative.

One such prophecy, written by the prophet Micah, stipulated that "one who is to rule in Israel" would be born in "Bethlehem of Ephrathah" (Micah 5:2). Bethlehem, after all, was the place where a widow named Ruth had married a local landowner called Boaz and given birth to Obed, whose grandson would be David, the founder of the Davidic house (Ruth 3:11; I Samuel 16:13). A messiah in the Davidic mold would therefore have to be born in Bethlehem as well.

For Matthew, this prophecy is so important that he quotes it almost in full, combining it with a reference from Samuel: "From you shall come a ruler who is to shepherd my people in Israel" (Matthew 2:6; paraphrasing Micah 5:2 and II Samuel 5:2). But while the association of the Messiah with Bethlehem was important for Matthew and Luke's audience, that may not have been the case for the community that Mark wrote for. In Second Temple Judaism, the concept of the Messiah could mean different things, and not

Shepherds Field near Bethlehem is the place where according to tradition, angels appeared to local shepherds to announce the birth of Jesus.

Inset: *The Domitius Ahenobarbus relief of the late second century B.C.E. depicts a Roman census to determine the property of various classes.*

ca 27
Octavian is named "Augustus"
by the Roman Senate

ca 27
Herod builds an acropolis in
Samaria and names it Sebaste

ca 25
A major drought forces Herod
to import grain from Egypt

ca 25
Galatia, future region
of Paul's ministry, is added
to Roman Empire

all required a Bethlehem birth. For Matthew and Luke, however, a Bethlehem pedigree was of vital importance. But that raised the question of how to reconcile a Bethlehem birth with the fact that Mary was a native of Galilee rather than Judea.

In response, the evangelists arrived at two different scenarios. Matthew claims that Jesus was born in Bethlehem for the simple reason that this is where Mary and Joseph lived. When the three magi from the East follow the star of Bethlehem, they are led to the "place" where Jesus' parents resided as a married Judean couple (Matthew 1:24, 2:9). Matthew uses the Greek word *oikia*, which means "house" or "household," clearly implying a form of permanent residence. What's more, after Joseph and Mary fled to Egypt so as to escape the wrath of Herod, they waited until the king had died and it was safe for them to return. This is when an angel appeared to Joseph telling him not to return to Bethlehem but to move north, "to the district of Galilee," where Joseph then "made his home in a town called Nazareth"—thus restoring the essential thread of the story (Matthew 2:22).

THE QUIRINIUS CENSUS

In the Christian tradition, however, it is Luke's version of the Nativity that dominates the story. In his narrative, Mary and Joseph are an engaged couple, living in Nazareth and expecting the birth of their first child (Luke 2:5). But then an imperial decree from Augustus disrupts their plans. It orders that "all the world should be registered." Luke, a highly educated author who is careful to frame his Gospel with historical references, adds that this census took place "while Quirinius was governor of Syria" (Luke 2:1-2). Since Joseph was a Judean from the house of David, Luke argues, it was incumbent on him to travel to his ancestral home to be registered.

Luke is certainly correct about the first part; we know that during the tenure of the Roman governor Quirinius, a census was undertaken by Coponius, the prefect of Judea and Samaria. The problem is that this census was undertaken at least ten years after the death of Herod, around 6 c.e., when Judea was annexed by Augustus as a Roman crown province. Even so, this census would not have required him to travel to his native home, for the essential purpose of a Roman census was to establish a registry of people and their current property so that an accurate tax rate could be levied. And last, since Joseph and Mary were residents of Nazareth, the Quirinius census would not have affected them at all. Even after the Roman annexation of Judea, Galilee remained an autonomous region ruled by Herod's son Antipas, who operated his own system of tax collection. It is unlikely, however, that anyone among Luke's audience would have been aware of this discrepancy, given that at that time the Quirinius census was already 80 years in the past.

THE CAVE OF THE NATIVITY

In Luke's story, then, Mary and Joseph travel to Bethlehem despite Mary's advanced pregnancy. Unfortunately the guest houses are full, and they are forced to find shelter in the fields, just when Mary's birth pangs begin. Luke doesn't specify the type of shelter in which Mary gives birth, but traditionally it is believed to be a stable, since the newborn Jesus was laid in a "manger," a trough used to feed livestock (Luke 2:6-7).

As Jerome Murphy-O'Connor has argued, however, early Christians had a different place in mind. According to the second-century author Justin Martyr, a native of Samaria, the birth actually took place in a cave. The same suggestion is found in the apocryphal Gospel of James from around 145 c.e. If that is true, and if the idea of a grotto was well established, why did Luke not say so? After all, Jesus' birth in a cave would have matched another reference in Hebrew Scripture, one by Isaiah: "He shall dwell in a lofty cavern of a strong rock" (Isaiah 33:16).

This terra-cotta figure from Asia Minor, dated to the second or third century c.e., depicts a young, affectionate mother with her newborn infant.

In those days a decree went out from Emperor Augustus that all the world should be registered.

GOSPEL OF LUKE 2:1

The Church of the Nativity in Bethlehem, built by Byzantine emperor Justinian in 565 C.E., is one of the oldest continuously operating churches in the world.

The reason, Murphy-O'Connor argues, may be that this could have prompted an uncomfortable parallel to the Persian god Mithra, a Zoroastrian deity whose cult was hugely popular at the time, particularly among Roman troops. The Mithraic Mysteries involved worship in underground caves known as Mithraea, to celebrate his birth from a rock.

Nevertheless, as early as the third century, Christian pilgrims to Bethlehem—including the author Origen—were led to a grotto where Jesus was reportedly born. As in the case of Jesus' burial tomb in Jerusalem, the place was deliberately obliterated in the second century C.E. with a pagan temple—in this case, a temple dedicated to the Greek god Adonis—so as to discourage Christian worship. That changed after Constantine the Great issued the decree of religious tolerance in 313. Queen Helena, the emperor's mother and a devout Christian, tore the pagan shrine down in 327 C.E. and replaced it with a church. This was a five-aisled basilica that culminated in an octagon, a favored Christian motif of Roman architects, to mark the place of the grotto itself. An early visitor to this church was a Roman aristocrat named Paula, who with her daughter embarked on a pilgrimage to Palestine in 382. According to Church Father Jerome, who described her travels in *The Pilgrimage of the Holy Paula,* she found that her visit to the "Grotto of the Savior" in Bethlehem was her most memorable experience. Rebuilt by the Byzantine emperor Justinian in 565 C.E., the Church of the Nativity as it is known today is one of the oldest Roman churches still in use. ∎

THE LOST YEARS AT SEPPHORIS

Antipas Builds a New Capital of His Tetrarchy

The years of Jesus' childhood and early adulthood are a mystery. Neither Mark, Matthew, nor John touches on it, while Luke gives us only the story of Jesus lecturing the teachers in the Temple during Passover, when he was 12 years old (Luke 2:41, 47). For the 21st-century reader, this presents a quandary. Modern psychology has taught us that human beings are shaped by the formative experiences of their childhood and adolescence, but in the case of Jesus, we lack the necessary data. For the Gospel authors, the story begins only when Jesus joins the movement of John the Baptist and is baptized in the Jordan.

What we do know is that these years, roughly from 6 to 28 C.E., were a period of intensive social and political turmoil, not only in Galilee but also in Roman Palestine altogether—which may be part of the reason we hear so little of it in the Gospels.

It is now widely accepted that Jesus must have been born well before 4 B.C.E., because Matthew and Luke are explicit in telling us that Jesus was born in the latter years of Herod's reign (Matthew 2:1). The king died, unmourned, in 4 B.C.E., but he had kept one last surprise. Repelled by the internecine plotting and fighting within his own family, he had decided to withhold the title of *basileus*—"king" of all of Roman Palestine—from any of his sons. Instead, his will decreed that his kingdom would be broken up along familiar tribal lines, with Judea and Samaria split from Galilee once more.

THE KINGDOM IS DIVIDED

Together with Idumea and Samaria, Judea would henceforth be ruled by Archelaus, the king's son by his Samaritan wife, Malthace. Galilee was given to Archelaus's younger brother Antipas, together with the region of Perea on the east bank of the Jordan.

Herod then carved out a third region for his son Philip. It covered the mostly Gentile territory northeast of the Sea of Galilee, including the Gaulanitis (today's Golan region), Batanea, Auranitis, Iturea, and Trachonitis. Finally, the coastal region of Azotus (today's Ashdod), as well as the region around Jabneh and Phaesalis, was given to Herod's sister Salome.

Thus, the great Herodian kingdom ceased to exist. The Gospel of Matthew confirms this division, saying that when Joseph "heard

ca 23
Herod's palace in Jerusalem
and the Herodium fortress are built

ca 23
Archelaus, future ethnarch
of Judea, is born

ca 22
Construction begins
on the harbor of
Caesarea Maritima

ca 21
Work begins on the
expansion of the Second Temple
in Jerusalem

The Roman theater of Sepphoris, originally built by Herod Antipas, was enlarged to a 4,000-seat capacity in the third to fourth centuries C.E.

Water was stored in stone vessels since they were believed to be impervious to ritual impurity, as in the case of this stone measuring cup.

ca 13
Herod designates Antipater II, his son by wife Doris, as his heir

ca 12
Herod's sons Alexander and Aristobulus are added to succession

ca 9
The harbor of Caesarea Maritima is inaugurated

ca 9
Augustus chastises Herod for waging war against Nabataea

that Archelaus was ruling over Judea in place of his father Herod, he was afraid to go [back]" (Matthew 2:19-22).

Joseph may have had good reason not to return to his homestead in Bethlehem, for when the Judeans found out that Archelaus planned to maintain the crushing taxes of the previous regime while refusing to release the king's political prisoners, they staged a massive protest in the Temple forecourt. Archelaus panicked and called out the Herodian guards, who subdued the protesters by force. According to Josephus, some 3,000 men, women, and children were killed. When news of the massacre spread, all of Palestine exploded in revolt. One of the resistance leaders was a Galilean named Judas, who may have been a son of the same Hezekiah who had led a revolt some 40 years earlier. Judas fled to the provincial capital of Sepphoris and helped himself to the arsenal of the Herodian garrison stationed in the city. Soon after, all of Palestine was in flames.

Alarmed, the Roman governor of Syria, Quinctilius Varus, knew he had to act but lacked the legions to do so, lest he leave the eastern frontier undefended. The governor therefore called on all vassal kings in the region to come to his aid. This the local princes did with glee; the prospect of plundering their way through the kingdom of their former adversary, King Herod, must have been an irresistible prospect. And so a horde of brutal mercenaries was let loose on the unarmed peasantry of Galilee with the license to rape, loot, and burn to their heart's content. "All places were full of fire and slaughter," says Josephus, adding that when the Roman legions finally arrived to restore order, they found most villages burned to the ground.

THE REBUILDING OF SEPPHORIS

There is no question that the revolt and subsequent reprisals must have left a deep impact on Nazareth and the couple who lived there with their young son. Nazareth was only four miles from the heart of the rebellion, the city of Sepphoris. When Leroy Waterman began digging at Sepphoris in 1931, followed by James Strange in the 1980s, neither found many traces of the Herodian city, which suggests that the place was truly destroyed.

Of course, Rome did not look kindly on vassal governors who could not keep the peace, and in 6 C.E. Archelaus was removed from his post for gross incompetence. This was the moment that his brother Antipas, ruler of Galilee, had been hoping for. As the next son in line, he had convinced himself that Augustus

A second-century C.E. terra-cotta ink pot, used by scribes to prepare legal documents, is pierced with holes for hanging or carrying.

would turn to him to govern Judea and Samaria. But the Roman emperor demurred. He was heartily sick of these Herodians and their machinations. Instead he annexed the region as a Roman province, to be governed by a Roman official, a prefect. The first prefect was Coponius, and as we saw, he immediately launched a census in Judea, since taxation was now going to be his responsibility.

Deprived of his dream of ruling in Jerusalem and stuck with the rather unimpressive title of "tetrarch" (literally "ruler of a fourth"), Antipas decided to build a magnificent capital of his own—in Sepphoris. Since the place had conveniently been destroyed during the revolt, he could design his new city from scratch and make it the "ornament of all Galilee," as Josephus puts it. For the Galileans, this was something new. No one had ever built a planned city in this region. That also meant that Antipas could not draw from a pool of experienced construction workers. Instead, Antipas did what his Roman masters would do: recruit compulsory labor *ad opus publicum*, "for the sake of public works," in Pliny's words. After all, there were plenty of villages in the vicinity where able-bodied men could be found.

JESUS IN SEPPHORIS

The idea, first suggested by Shirley Case of the University of Chicago, that Jesus and Joseph thus found themselves co-opted in the construction of this new city would explain why we don't hear about Jesus for the next 20 years. Mark's Gospel refers to Joseph as a *tektōn*, which has traditionally been translated as "carpenter" but actually means "artisan" or "skilled worker." Either way, Joseph's skills—and those of his son, who was expected to follow in his footsteps—would have been highly prized for the building project. He may even have volunteered for the work, since much of Galilee's agriculture was still recovering from past depredations, though this is of course pure hypothesis.

The construction of Sepphoris took many years. Throughout Jesus' adolescence, the project must have dominated commercial activity in Galilee and consumed manpower, supplies, and foodstuffs from all over the region. So it is difficult to imagine that such a major undertaking would have left the family of Jesus unaffected. Sepphoris was barely five miles from Nazareth.

Today, the excavations at Sepphoris are still ongoing. Some of the most spectacular discoveries include a theater, carved into the natural

This detail of a third-century mosaic, known as the "Mona Lisa from Galilee," was discovered in a Roman villa of Sepphoris in the 1980s.

A second-century C.E. terra-cotta wine vessel in the shape of a barrel shows that wooden barrels were used to produce or store wine.

slope of a hill and much expanded in the second century; a cardo flanked by comfortable, two-story houses; and two aqueducts fed by the waters of Mount Yona, near Nazareth. There are even indications of a sophisticated sewage system underneath the stone pavement. Remarkably, Antipas did not build any of the Hellenistic facilities his father was so fond of, such as Roman baths, a gymnasium, or temples dedicated to pagan gods. As Mark Chancey and Eric Meyers have shown, the reason is simple: During the time of Jesus, the population of Sepphoris was overwhelmingly Jewish, as attested by the presence of many *mikva'ot,* ritual baths, and vessels made of stone, a material that was considered impervious to ritual impurity. ∎

Herod also built a wall about Sepphoris, which is the security of all Galilee, and made it the metropolis of the country.

JOSEPHUS, *ANTIQUITIES OF THE JEWS*

ca 8
Herod reconciles
with Augustus

ca 7
Alexander and Aristobulus
are tried and executed

ca 6
Herod moves to curb
the influence of the Pharisees

ca 5
Antipater II, Herod's heir,
is charged with treason.

FROM NAZARETH TO THE JORDAN

Jesus Joins the Movement of a Charismatic Dissident

Around 20 C.E., Antipas—who now styled himself as "Herod" Antipas, the name by which he is referred to in the Gospel—decided he had had enough of Sepphoris. He wanted to build a true polis, a Greco-Roman city with all the Hellenistic trappings so admired in places like Scythopolis. A new emperor had been crowned in Rome, which may have encouraged him in his plans. While his relationship with Augustus had always been strained, Antipas had strenuously tried to cultivate contacts with the Tiberius party while Augustus's heir was patiently waiting in the wings. So no one was particularly surprised when Antipas decided to name this new city "Tiberias," in honor of his imperial mentor, and soon made it his new capital.

Tiberias was founded between two ancient fortifications, known as Hammath and Rakkath (Joshua 19:35). What Antipas may not have realized is that this lovely location on the southwestern shores of the Sea of Galilee once served as the cemetery of Hammath. That made the place unclean for observant Jews, and it is very doubtful that many of his Jewish crews working in Sepphoris would have agreed to work on this new site as well. Perhaps Antipas's choice was deliberate, for rumors that the new city was impure virtually guaranteed that it was populated only by Gentiles. That could also be the reason that the Gospels do not refer to the city, even though Jesus traveled extensively in the vicinity.

What happened to Jesus in the subsequent period between 20 and 28 C.E. remains a mystery; perhaps he returned to Nazareth to continue the trade of his father, Joseph, but this is pure hypothesis.

THE VILLAGE OF NAZARETH

Back in Nazareth, Mary's home was now filled with the screams and laughter of many of Jesus' siblings. While this is a controversial issue for Christians who cleave to the doctrine of Mary's perpetual virginity, the Gospel of Mark states that Jesus had four brothers, "James and Joses and Judas and Simon," as well as at least two sisters (Mark 6:3). According to a second-century author named Hegesippus, the sons of Judas—Jesus' nephews—later cultivated

The ruins of ancient Tiberias, founded by Herod Antipas between 14 and 20 C.E., are visible today on the southwestern shore of the Sea of Galilee.

ca 4
Young demonstrators remove
the golden eagle from the Temple

ca 4
Putative date
of birth of Jesus

ca 4
Antipater II
is executed

ca 4
Herod dies; his will divides
his kingdom among his sons

The Jordan River flows near one of the places that tradition has identified with Jesus' baptism by John the Baptist.

a plot of land close to their ancestral home. This home would have been a humble dwelling built of locally quarried rocks and stones, mortared with mud and coated with clay plaster. Built over two levels, with the upper level reserved as sleeping quarters, the house would have been covered with a latticework of wooden beams, palm fronds, and branches, all packed with mud. On the first story was a small enclosed pen where the animals were kept, while a small courtyard held the clay oven where Mary cooked the pita-style bread to feed her family.

A good example of such a first-century home is visible today in the Qasrin archaeological park located close to the Golan Heights in Upper Galilee. In the 1970s, archaeologists uncovered a sixth-century synagogue that today is one of the best preserved synagogues in Galilee. This led to the excavation of several dwellings around the synagogue, which have since been restored.

Conceived as a "Talmudic Village," the open-air museum offers a striking impression of what a village like Nazareth may have looked like.

Various early Christian structures that Bellarmino Bagatti excavated underneath the old Church of the Annunciation during a campaign in the mid-1950s are the only tangible evidence of ancient Nazareth itself, apart from some tombs, cisterns, and storage caves. This site has traditionally been identified with the grotto where Mary received the annunciation from the angel Gabriel. Underneath these layers Bagatti found the remains of granaries and olive presses, which confirm the essential agricultural character of the village. The earliest shrine built on the site dates from the third century; it was replaced by a basilica-type church with a circular apse in the fourth century, only to be destroyed by the Persians in 614. In 1730, the Franciscans built a new church, which was torn down in 1955 to make room for the current edifice. This Church of the Annunciation is the most modern church building in Israel, though its use of bare-faced concrete in the interior, in keeping with the Brutalist aesthetic of the time, is not a very successful space for spiritual reflection.

In March 2015, archaeologist Ken Dark published his excavation of a first-century "courtyard house" underneath the Sisters of Nazareth Convent in Nazareth, very close to the Annunciation Church. Dark believes, partly based on a seventh-century pilgrim account, that this may be the actual childhood home of Jesus.

JESUS LEAVES FOR JUDEA

According to the Gospels, around 28 or 29 C.E. Jesus decided to leave Galilee and join the movement of a prominent dissident, known as John the Baptist, in the Jordan wilderness. That the fame of this preacher was widespread throughout Roman Palestine is attested by Josephus, who wrote that "many joined the crowds about him, for they were deeply stirred at hearing his words." It is possible that John's fame was the factor that drove Jesus to go down to Judea, though there is another possibility that most scholars have overlooked.

In 26, a new Roman prefect had arrived in Judea—the fifth in little more than 20 years. This new official was a member of the Pontii, a minor family of Roman *equites*, or "knights," rather than the aristocratic senatorial class. The primary incentive for a knight to accept a hardship post in a backwater like Judea was to quickly amass—through bribes and commissions—the requisite capital of a million sesterces with which one qualified for senatorial rank. By law, this sum—roughly the equivalent of $4 million—could not be obtained through commerce or financial speculation, which limited one's options and made a diplomatic post overseas much more attractive.

Pontius Pilate soon developed a deep loathing for the population he was expected to rule and could not understand why these

Jews enjoyed exemptions from duties that vassal nations anywhere else in the empire were expected to honor. The prefect thus embarked on a number of deliberate provocations—such as taking Roman standards with silver eagles and other idolatrous symbols into Jerusalem, which predictably caused an uproar—in an effort to show who was in charge. This of course led to a number of protests, which were rapidly and bloodily suppressed.

Above: *A stone from the Roman theater in Caesarea bears the dedication* "[to the gods this] Tiberium [has been dedicated by] Pontius Pilate, Prefect of Judea." Inset: *This marble head of Emperor Tiberius (42 B.C.E.-37 C.E.), the successor of Emperor Augustus, is dated around 10 C.E.*

People from the whole Judean countryside and all the people of Jerusalem were going out to him, and were baptized by him in the river Jordan, confessing their sins.

GOSPEL OF MARK 1:5

Around 28 c.e., tensions rose again when it transpired that Pilate, mindful of the reason that he'd come to Judea initially, was planning to take funds from the Temple treasury in collusion with the high priest Caiaphas. That this theft was ostensibly for the purpose of building a new aqueduct to Jerusalem did not fool the population in the least. Once again, a large crowd of protesters began to gather in the forecourt of the Jerusalem Temple. Pilate ordered his soldiers to infiltrate the throng, and on his signal, they fell on the crowd with their swords. "They slew not only those that had participated in the demonstration," says Josephus, "but even innocent bystanders, who had nothing to do with it." Thousands lay dead or dying in the twisting alleys of Jerusalem.

A wave of revulsion swept the country, and it is plausible to think that this massacre may have prompted many young men and women to join an activist movement like that of John, who preached a radical moral cleansing of Judean society. Luke states that Jesus joined John the Baptist in the Jordan "when Pontius Pilate was governor of Judea, and Herod [Herod Antipas] was ruler of Galilee" (Luke 3:1). Furthermore, in a later passage, his Gospel explicitly cites the Temple massacre by referring to "the Galileans whose blood Pilate had mingled with their sacrifices" (Luke 13:1).

THE JORDAN WILDERNESS

Where, exactly, was John the Baptist's camp of followers based? The Gospels do not give us much information that would allow us to pinpoint the location. The Synoptics speak of the "wilderness" near the Jordan River, possibly near the place where the river flows into the Dead Sea (Mark 1:4). John's Gospel locates Jesus' baptism by John in "Bethany across the Jordan," meaning on the east side of the Jordan in the territory of Perea (John 1:28). Scholars do not agree on the identification of this village. The third-century scholar Origen argued that John actually referred to "Bethabara," which appears on the famous sixth-century Madaba map as a small church on the west side of the Jordan.

After the peace treaty between Israel and Jordan in 1994, a Jordanian excavation team uncovered the remains of two Byzantine churches on the eastern bank, roughly some five miles distant from the Dead Sea near the mouth of the Wadi el-Charrar. Just across, on the Israeli side, is a Greek Orthodox Church from the fifth century, which also claims to be the place of Jesus' baptism. The obvious conclusion may be that during the Byzantine period, the baptism was venerated on both sides of the river.

What both sites have in common, however, is their proximity to the remains of a first-century community at Khirbet Qumran. Excavated by Roland de Vaux from 1951 onward, this site once featured a large complex with a scriptorium, dining hall, and a potter's workshop that produced tall clay jars. As many as six inkwells were found on the site, which suggests some form of organized scribal activity. The prevailing theory is that this community was responsible for storing, and partly copying, the famous Dead Sea Scrolls that were found in 1947 in caves just a stone's throw away. ■

Has Jesus' Childhood Home Been Found?

Under the title "Has Jesus' Nazareth House Been Found?" *Biblical Archaeology Review* announced in 2015 archaeologist Ken Dark's discovery of a partly rock-hewn house in Nazareth, close to the location of the Annunciation Church. The house, probably dating to the first century c.e., ceased to be occupied in the Early Roman period, and after that its site was used for a variety of purposes before a Byzantine church was built there. This Byzantine church has several distinctive features suggesting that it is the Church of the Nutrition, described in a seventh-century pilgrim's account that says that it was built over the house where Jesus was raised as a child. The house itself was a rectilinear structure with some walls cut from the limestone hillside and others built of stone.

This first-century c.e. structure in Nazareth, first published in 2006, is believed by some to be the childhood home of Jesus.

BETHSAIDA, CAPERNAUM, AND CHORAZIN

Three Cities Witness the First Phase of Jesus' Ministry

H aving observed the growing movement of John the Baptist in the region of Perea with considerable alarm, Antipas decided to intervene around 29 C.E. As we saw, this region (today's East Bank of Jordan) was added to Antipas's territory of Galilee under the terms of Herod's will, even though the two regions were not contiguous. Therefore, the Baptist was Antipas's responsibility. As a result, he ordered that John be arrested and—we may assume—his followers scattered.

The Gospels offer a religious rather than a political motive for John's arrest. Mark, whose example is followed by other evangelists, writes that the Baptist's criticism of Antipas's second marriage, to the wife of his half-brother Philip, violated Covenant Law. In fact, this woman, whose name was Herodias, also happened to be the daughter of Antipas's brother Aristobulus and therefore his niece, which made the marriage even more controversial. "It is not lawful for you to have your brother's wife," John told the tetrarch (Mark 6:18).

Josephus sees things differently. He argues that John's movement had simply become too powerful for the tetrarch to ignore. Knowing the history of revolts in the region, and mindful of the fate that had befallen his brother Archelaus, Antipas feared that the Baptist's followers "might empower [John] to raise a rebellion." Whether the historical John the Baptist was indeed contemplating a *levée en masse* is difficult to ascertain; although his language was certainly strident and provocative, he may not have aspired to some form of political activism. Whatever the case may be, John was indeed arrested and later executed on the tetrarch's orders. Josephus adds the interesting detail that John's beheading took place in the fortress of Machaerus, one of the principal citadels that had guarded Herod's former kingdom.

The synagogue of ancient Capernaum, built of white limestone, dates to the early fourth century C.E., although some believe it was built on top of an older synagogue.

Inset: A terra-cotta plate is equipped with a central depression for fish sauce, a highly popular condiment in Antiquity.

ca 1 C.E.
Rome now includes Spain,
Gaul, Britain, and much
of today's Germany

ca 1
Population of the city
of Rome swells to 2.5 million

ca 1
Some of the Dead Sea scrolls
are composed

ca 2
Augustus's grandson
and heir, Lucius, dies

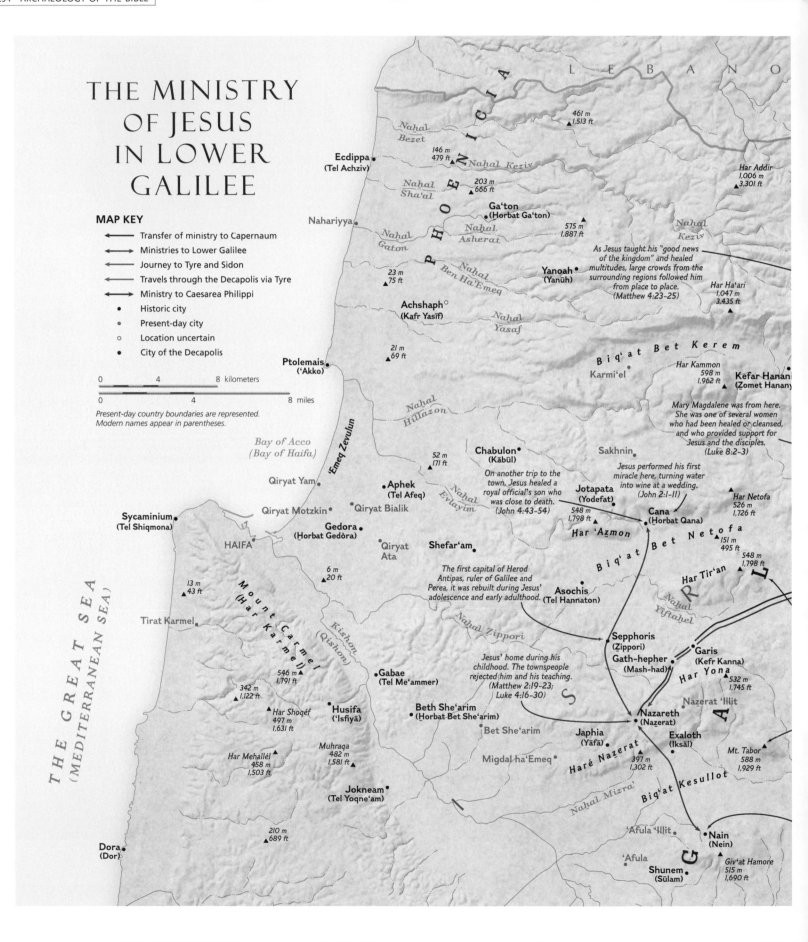

THE MINISTRY OF JESUS IN LOWER GALILEE

MAP KEY

⟵ Transfer of ministry to Capernaum
⟷ Ministries to Lower Galilee
⟵ Journey to Tyre and Sidon
⟵ Travels through the Decapolis via Tyre
⟷ Ministry to Caesarea Philippi
● Historic city
● Present-day city
○ Location uncertain
● City of the Decapolis

0   4   8 kilometers
0   4   8 miles

Present-day country boundaries are represented.
Modern names appear in parentheses.

PHOENICIA

LEBANON

Nahal Bezet

Ecdippa
(Tel Achziv)

146 m
479 ft

Nahal Keziv

Nahariyya

203 m
666 ft

Nahal Sha'al

461 m
▲ 1,513 ft

Har Addir
1,006 m
▲ 3,301 ft

Ga'ton
(Horbat Ga'ton)

Nahal Keziv

Nahal Gaton

Nahal Asherat

575 m ▲
1,887 ft

Yanoah
(Yanūh)

Har Ha'ari
1,047 m
3,435 ft
▲

As Jesus taught his "good news of the kingdom" and healed multitudes, large crowds from the surrounding regions followed him from place to place. (Matthew 4:23-25)

Nahal Ben Ha'Emeq

23 m
▲ 75 ft

Achshaph ○
(Kafr Yasīf)

Nahal Yasaf

Biq'at Bet Kerem

21 m
▲ 69 ft

Karmi'el

Har Kammon
598 m
1,962 ft ▲

Kefar Hanani
(Zomet Hanany)

Ptolemais
('Akko)

Nahal Hillazon

Sakhnin

Mary Magdalene was from here. She was one of several women who had been healed or cleansed, and who provided support for Jesus and the disciples. (Luke 8:2-3)

Bay of Acco
(Bay of Haifa)

52 m
171 ft

Chabulon
(Kābūl)

Qiryat Yam

Emeq Zevulun

Aphek
(Tel Afeq)

Nahal Evlayim

On another trip to the town, Jesus healed a royal official's son who was close to death. (John 4:43-54)

Jotapata
(Yodefat)

548 m
1,798 ft ▲

Cana
(Horbat Qana)

Jesus performed his first miracle here, turning water into wine at a wedding. (John 2:1-11)

Har Netofa
526 m
1,726 ft

Qiryat Motzkin

Qiryat Bialik

Gedora
(Horbat Gedòra)

Qiryat Ata

Shefar'am

Biq'at Bet Netofa

151 m
495 ft

548 m
1,798 ft

Sycaminium
(Tel Shiqmona)

Har 'Azmon

Har Tir'an

HAIFA

6 m
▲ 20 ft

The first capital of Herod Antipas, ruler of Galilee and Perea, it was rebuilt during Jesus' adolescence and early adulthood.

Asochis
(Tel Hannaton)

Nahal Yiftahel

13 m
▲ 43 ft

Mount Carmel
(Har Karmel)

Kishon
(Qishon)

Nahal Zippori

Sepphoris
(Zippori)

Garis

Tirat Karmel

Gath-hepher
(Mash-had)

Garis
(Kefr Kanna)

Har Yona

532 m
1,745 ft

THE GREAT SEA
(MEDITERRANEAN SEA)

546 m
1,791 ft

Jesus' home during his childhood. The townspeople rejected him and his teaching. (Matthew 2:19-23; Luke 4:16-30)

Nazerat 'Illit

342 m
1,122 ft

Har Shoqéf
497 m
1,631 ft

Husifa
('Isfiyā)

Gabae
(Tel Me'ammer)

Beth She'arim
(Horbat Bet She'arim)

Nazareth
(Nazerat)

Japhia
(Yāfā)

Exaloth
(Iksāl)

Muhraqa
482 m
1,581 ft

Har Mehallél
458 m
1,503 ft

Bet She'arim

397 m
1,302 ft

Mt. Tabor
588 m
1,929 ft

Migdal ha'Emeq

Haré Nazerat

Biq'at Kesullot

Jokneam
(Tel Yoqne'am)

Nahal Mizra

210 m
▲ 689 ft

'Afula 'Illit

Nain
(Nein)

Dora
(Dor)

'Afula

Shunem
(Sūlam)

Giv'at Hamore
515 m
1,690 ft

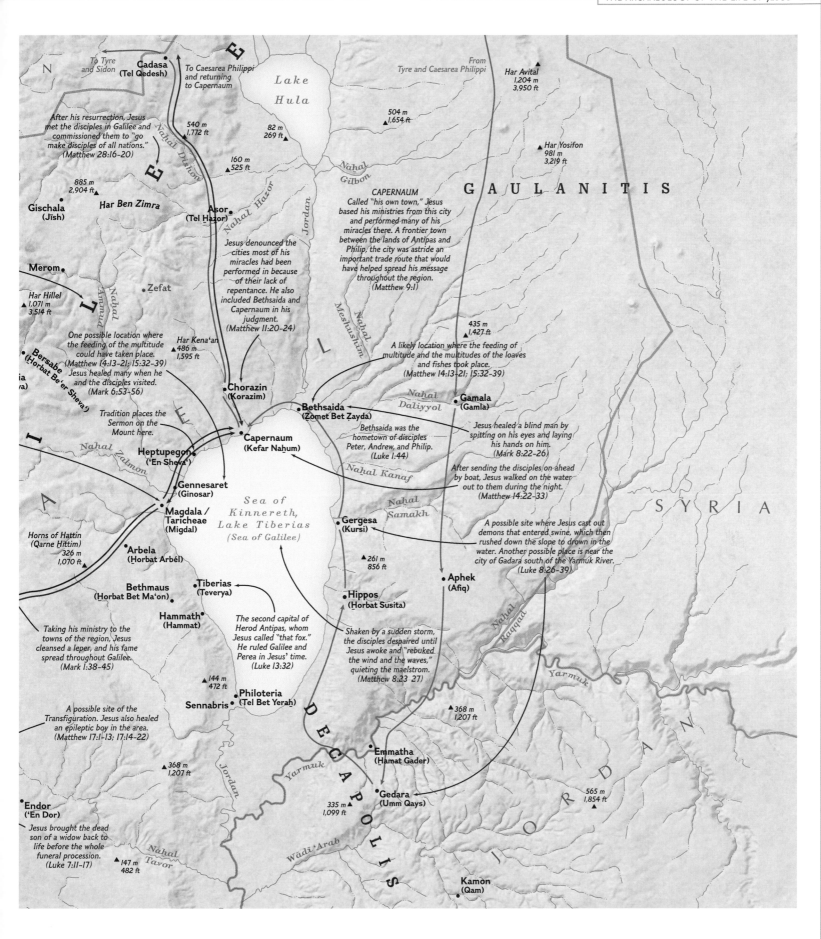

To Tyre
and Sidon

Cadasa
(Tel Qedesh)

To Caesarea Philippi
and returning
to Capernaum

From
Tyre and Caesarea Philippi

Har Avital
1,204 m
3,950 ft

N

E

*Lake
Hula*

504 m
1,654 ft

*After his resurrection, Jesus
met the disciples in Galilee and
commissioned them to "go
make disciples of all nations."*
(Matthew 28:16–20)

540 m
1,772 ft

82 m
269 ft

*Nahal
Gilbon*

Har Yosifon
981 m
3,219 ft

160 m
525 ft

CAPERNAUM
*Called "his own town," Jesus
based his ministries from this city
and performed many of his
miracles there. A frontier town
between the lands of Antipas and
Philip, the city was astride an
important trade route that would
have helped spread his message
throughout the region.*
(Matthew 9:1)

G A U L A N I T I S

885 m
2,904 ft

Gischala
(Jish)

Har Ben Zimra

Asor
(Tel Hazor)

Jordan

*Jesus denounced the
cities most of his
miracles had been
performed in because
of their lack of
repentance. He also
included Bethsaida and
Capernaum in his
judgment.*
(Matthew 11:20–24)

435 m
1,427 ft

Merom

Zefat

Har Hillel
1,071 m
3,514 ft

Nahal Amud

Har Kena'an
486 m
1,595 ft

*One possible location where
the feeding of the multitude
could have taken place.*
(Matthew 14:13–21; 15:32–39)
*Jesus healed many when he
and the disciples visited.*
(Mark 6:53–56)

*A likely location where the feeding of
multitude and the multitudes of the loaves
and fishes took place.*
(Matthew 14:13–21; 15:32–39)

Gamala
(Gamla)

Bersabe
(Horbat Be'er Sheva')

Chorazin
(Korazim)

Bethsaida
(Zomet Bet Zayda)

*Nahal
Daliyyot*

*Jesus healed a blind man by
spitting on his eyes and laying
his hands on him.*
(Mark 8:22–26)

*Tradition places the
Sermon on the
Mount here.*

*Bethsaida was the
hometown of disciples
Peter, Andrew, and Philip.*
(Luke 1:44)

Capernaum
(Kefar Nahum)

*After sending the disciples on ahead
by boat, Jesus walked on the water
out to them during the night.*
(Matthew 14:22–33)

Heptupegon
('En Sheva')

S Y R I A

Gennesaret
(Ginosar)

Nahal Kanaf

*Nahal
Samakh*

**Magdala /
Taricheae**
(Migdal)

*Sea of
Kinnereth,
Lake Tiberias
(Sea of Galilee)*

Gergesa
(Kursi)

*A possible site where Jesus cast out
demons that entered swine, which then
rushed down the slope to drown in the
water. Another possible place is near the
city of Gadara south of the Yarmúk River.*
(Luke 8:26–39)

*Horns of Hattin
(Qarne Hittim)*
326 m
1,070 ft

Arbela
(Horbat Arbél)

261 m
856 ft

Aphek
(Afiq)

Bethmaus
(Horbat Bet Ma'on)

Tiberias
(Teverya)

Hippos
(Horbat Susita)

*Nahal
Raqqad*

Hammath
(Hammat)

*Taking his ministry to the
towns of the region, Jesus
cleansed a leper, and his fame
spread throughout Galilee.*
(Mark 1:38–45)

*The second capital of
Herod Antipas, whom
Jesus called "that fox."
He ruled Galilee and
Perea in Jesus' time.*
(Luke 13:32)

*Shaken by a sudden storm,
the disciples despaired until
Jesus awoke and "rebuked
the wind and the waves,"
quieting the maelstrom.*
(Matthew 8:23–27)

Yarmuk

144 m
472 ft

Philoteria
(Tel Bet Yerah)

368 m
1,207 ft

Sennabris

*A possible site of the
Transfiguration. Jesus also healed
an epileptic boy in the area.*
(Matthew 17:1–13; 17:14–22)

D E C A P O L I S

Jordan

368 m
1,207 ft

Yarmuk

Emmatha
(Hamat Gader)

Endor
('En Dor)

*Jesus brought the dead
son of a widow back to
life before the whole
funeral procession.*
(Luke 7:11–17)

Wādī 'Arab

Gedara
(Umm Qays)

335 m
1,099 ft

565 m
1,854 ft

J O R D A N

*Nahal
Tavor*

147 m
482 ft

Kamon
(Qam)

THE TOWN OF BETHSAIDA

The sudden elimination of their leader left the Baptist's movement in disarray. The Gospel of John suggests that several of his disciples—Philip, Andrew, and Andrew's brother Simon—then gravitated toward Jesus and adopted him as their new rabbi, their "teacher" (John 1:38-41). All three were from Galilee, from a town called Bethsaida.

That distinction is significant, because Bethsaida lay just east of the Jordan River in the Gaulanitis and therefore was part of the tetrarchy of Philip rather than Antipas's territory. One could therefore imagine that when Jesus retraced his steps north, he first sought shelter in the hometown of his new disciples, under the jurisdiction of the tetrarch Philip. For him to walk brazenly into the home territory of the man who had just condemned his teacher would have been rather foolhardy.

Indeed, Bethsaida would later feature prominently in the Gospel stories. Here, Mark places the miracle of restoring a blind man's sight (Mark 8:22), while Luke identifies Bethsaida as the location of the miraculous feeding of the 5,000 (Luke 9:10-17). In all of the New Testament literature, only Jerusalem and Capernaum are cited more frequently. Beth-tsaida, which literally means "house of fishermen," was destroyed during the Roman reprisals of the First Jewish War around 68 or 69 C.E. and was never rebuilt. The ancient ruins lay buried for centuries, while historians speculated where this mysterious city could be. Finally, in 1987, Israeli archaeologist Rami Arav pushed his spade in a tell about a mile or so inland from the Sea of Galilee and struck the remains of a residence made of basalt. A major excavation campaign followed, which ultimately would involve some 15 American universities and colleges. What they found was a sprawling township with many comfortable, two-story residences. These were probably built after Philip elevated the city status to a Greek polis in 30 C.E. At that point, the city was renamed "Julias," to please the widow of Emperor Augustus. One structure, which contained a bronze incense shovel, may have been a temple dedicated to Livia-Julia. The excavations are ongoing and today focus on the likely remains of an Iron Age township located underneath the village that Jesus knew.

CAPERNAUM

Eventually Jesus may have judged that the time was right to cross over into Galilee and set up a base camp in Capernaum, just a few miles distant. There were many reasons that it made sense to do so. Capernaum ("Nahum's Village") was the hometown of Peter's wife, but more important, it served as the nexus of the principal land and sea routes on the Sea of Galilee. This is why the town featured tollbooths (to tax any caravans entering Galilee from Philip's tetrarchy) as well as a sizable port that served shipping traffic across the lake. According to the Gospels, one of these tollbooths was manned by Levi, the son of Alphaeus, who would become a disciple (Mark 2:14).

This suggests that Jesus had already decided what type of ministry he wanted to pursue. Unlike John the Baptist and most other prophets in Hebrew Scripture, who ministered in one place, Jesus wanted to become an itinerant rabbi—one who would actively seek out towns and villages to spread his good news rather than wait for people to come to him. Capernaum served those needs better than any other township in Galilee.

And thus, Jesus formally launched his ministry as a preacher and healer. He did so in the local synagogue, as he would in other towns. In this first phase of his campaign, Jesus was careful to limit his teachings to a Jewish-observant audience. And, says Mark, the people were "astounded at his teaching for he taught them as one having authority, and not as the scribes" (Mark 1:21). Scribes were professional writers who could produce a variety of

A pupil greets his teacher while other students are reading their scrolls in this Roman relief from the second century C.E.

[Jesus] made his home in Capernaum by the sea, in the territory of Zebulun and Naphtali, so that what had been spoken through the prophet Isaiah might be fulfilled.

GOSPEL OF MATTHEW 4:12-14

legal documents for the largely illiterate population of Galilee. Since the prevailing law was that of the Torah, these scribes were considered experts in the application of Mosaic legislation. Mark often lumps them together with the Pharisees as the principal opposition to Jesus' movement.

The remains of the lovely synagogue that today attracts busloads of tourists to Capernaum do not constitute the synagogue where Jesus taught. Discovered in 1905, it was designed as a basilica supported by elegant columns topped with Corinthian capitals, and adorned with expertly carved ornamentation over the lintels. This, and the fact that it was built with limestone rather than the cheaper native basalt, is a clear indication of the great prosperity that Capernaum once enjoyed. But the synagogue dates from the fourth century rather than the first.

A number of scholars have since suggested that this structure may have been built over the remains of an older synagogue. New research indicates that these remains were actually private homes, but that does not deny the possibility that Jesus once taught here; in the first century, larger residences were often used as a *proseuchè,* or "prayer room." Opposite the synagogue are the remains of a Byzantine octagonal chapel, which marks the traditional site of the house of Peter's mother.

CHORAZIN

The third major city of Jesus' initial area of operations, Chorazin, was first settled in the Early Roman Period and experienced rapid growth only from the third century onward, ultimately covering some 25 acres. It was still a young community in Jesus' day and appears in the Gospels only once: when Jesus condemns the three cities of his ministry triangle (Matthew 11:21; Luke 10:13). Discovered in the early 1900s, Chorazin was excavated in the 1960s and the 1980s, with work continuing to this day. Its main structure is a synagogue, built around 300 C.E., that closely resembles the synagogue of Capernaum, albeit crafted from basalt stone. Nearby, several olive oil millstones were found, which suggests that olive oil may have been one of the town's principal products. ∎

Above: *Universities from the United States, Germany, and Poland excavated the ancient city gate of Bethsaida during a campaign starting in 1987.*

Right: *In contrast to Roman glassware, this terracotta flask is typical of the simple earthenware used by most Judeans in the first century C.E.*

AROUND THE SEA OF GALILEE AND BEYOND

Jesus Expands His Journeys Throughout Lower Galilee

During the initial phase of his ministry, Jesus limited his movements to places within a day's walking distance from Capernaum. "Let us go on to the neighboring towns," Jesus says in the Gospel of Mark, "so that I may proclaim the message there also" (Mark 1:38). Here, he typically sought out synagogues as convenient venues to address the local population.

But soon this strategy changed in response to an amazing phenomenon: People began to seek *him* out. "[Jesus] stayed out in the country," Mark says, "and people came to him from every quarter" (Mark 1:45).

The Gospels admit, however, that it was not always clear what attracted these crowds to Jesus: Was it his teachings, or his rumored ability to perform exorcisms, or even miracles?

During this second phase, then, Jesus moved out of the Gennesaret Valley and began to cover distances well beyond a day's march. That may be part of the reason that he chose to recruit a number of disciples from among the local fishermen, for it gave him access to a boat. Most of these boats, which represented a considerable capital investment, were owned by local cooperatives; one such included James and John, the sons of Zebedee, who "were partners *[koinōnoi]* with Simon" (Luke 5:10).

By a stroke of luck, exactly such a boat magically resurfaced from the mud of the Sea of Galilee in 1986 after a severe drought brought water levels to a historic low. It was found near the modern village of Ginosar, some five miles north of the ancient city of Magdala. Magdala was a leading fish processing center; its fish sauce was a highly popular condiment in the ancient world.

Carbon-14 dating revealed that the boat was built sometime between 50 B.C.E. and 50 C.E.—the period straddling Jesus' ministry. With a length of 26 feet and a width of 7.5 feet, the vessel was large enough to comfortably hold as many as ten fishermen as well as their gear and nets.

Amid lush greenery, a waterfall flows into the Banyas River in Israel. The Banyas is one of the main source streams of the River Jordan in Upper Galilee that feed into the Sea of Galilee.

ca 4
Augustus's other grandson, Gaius, is killed; Augustus adopts Tiberius

ca 6
Archelaus is removed from office and banished to Vienne, Roman Gaul

ca 6
Augustus annexes Judea as a Roman province; first procurator is Coponius

ca 6
Quirinius, the new governor of Syria, initiates a census in Judea

ca 6
Annas (Ananus ben Seth)
is appointed high priest
by Quirinius

ca 6
The Roman census provokes
a new revolt; party of the Zealots
is formed

ca 6
Antipas (now known as
Herod Antipas) begins
rebuilding Sepphoris

ca 9
Marcus Ambivulus
succeeds Coponius as
procurator of Judea

THE TOWN OF MAGDALA

While Magdala itself is not mentioned in the Gospels, Jesus most likely did visit the place, for here lived one of his most loyal followers: Mary of Magdala, or Mary "the Magdalene." She was one of several women whom he welcomed as his disciples, which by the standards of ancient Judaism was rather extraordinary (Luke 8:1-5). What's more, Mary must have hailed from an affluent family, for Luke says that she supported the movement with her own funds (Luke 8:2-3). In due course, Mary would become one of Jesus' closest followers and confidants.

Mary Magdalene is often depicted in Western art as "the penitent Magdalene," even though there is no evidence anywhere in the

The main cardo, or boulevard, of the city of Gerasa (today's Jerash, Jordan) led to the main forum, the religious, civic, and commercial center of the city.

Gospels that she lived a sinful or promiscuous life. Centuries later, church fathers conflated her with the "sinful woman" who washed Jesus' feet with her tears. Quite possibly, their motive was to discredit some dissident Gnostic traditions that revered her as a leading Apostle. Not until 1969 did the Vatican explicitly separate the figure of Mary Magdalene from the "sinful woman" character.

Magdala (also known as Magadan or Tarichaea, meaning "fish salters") gained headlines around the world in 2007 when Dina Avshalom-Gorni discovered the remains of a synagogue that may

He came down with them and stood on a level place,
with a great crowd of his disciples and a great multitude of people
from all over Judea, Jerusalem, and the coast of Tyre and Sidon.

GOSPEL OF LUKE 6:17

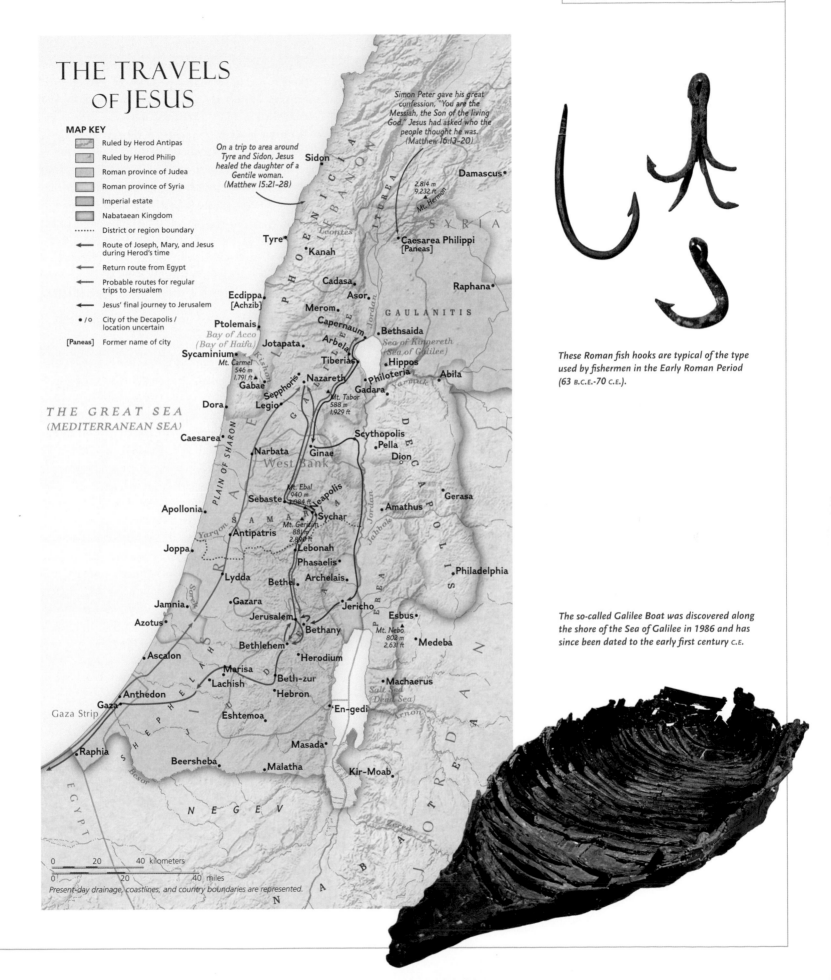

THE TRAVELS OF JESUS

MAP KEY

▢	Ruled by Herod Antipas
▢	Ruled by Herod Philip
▢	Roman province of Judea
▢	Roman province of Syria
▢	Imperial estate
▢	Nabataean Kingdom
········	District or region boundary
←	Route of Joseph, Mary, and Jesus during Herod's time
←	Return route from Egypt
←	Probable routes for regular trips to Jerusalem
←	Jesus' final journey to Jerusalem
• / ○	City of the Decapolis / location uncertain
[Paneas]	Former name of city

On a trip to area around Tyre and Sidon, Jesus healed the daughter of a Gentile woman. (Matthew 15:21–28)

Simon Peter gave his great confession, "You are the Messiah, the Son of the living God." Jesus had asked who the people thought he was. (Matthew 16:13–20)

Sidon
Damascus •
2,814 m
9,232 ft
Mt. Hermon
S Y R I A
• Caesarea Philippi [Paneas]
PHOENICIA
LEBANON
ITUREA
Leontes
Tyre •
Kanah •
Cadasa •
Raphana •
Asor •
Merom •
GAULANITIS
Ecdippa [Achzib] •
Capernaum •
Bethsaida •
Ptolemais •
Jotapata •
Arbela •
Sea of Kinnereth (Sea of Galilee)
Bay of Acco (Bay of Haifa)
GALILEE
Tiberias •
Hippos •
Abila •
Sycaminium •
Mt. Carmel 546 m 1,791 ft
Nazareth •
Sepphoris •
Philoteria •
Gabae •
Gadara •
Yarmuk
Dora •
Legio •
Mt. Tabor 588 m 1,929 ft
Scythopolis •
THE GREAT SEA (MEDITERRANEAN SEA)
Caesarea •
Narbata •
Ginae •
Pella •
Dion •
DECAPOLIS
West Bank
PLAIN OF SHARON
Mt. Ebal 940 m 3,084 ft
Sebaste •
Neapolis •
Gerasa •
Apollonia •
SAMARIA
Sychar •
Amathus •
Mt. Gerizim 881 m 2,890 ft
Jordan
Jabbok
Antipatris •
Lebonah •
Joppa •
Yarqon
Phasaelis •
Philadelphia •
Lydda •
Bethel •
Archelais •
Gazara •
Jericho •
Jamnia •
Jerusalem •
Esbus •
PEREA
Azotus •
Bethany •
Mt. Nebo 802 m 2,631 ft
Medeba •
Bethlehem •
Ascalon •
Herodium •
Machaerus •
Marisa •
Beth-zur •
Lachish •
Hebron •
Anthedon •
Salt Sea (Dead Sea)
Gaza •
Gaza Strip
Eshtemoa •
En-gedi •
Arnon
SHEPHELAH
Masada •
Raphia •
Beersheba •
Malatha •
Kir-Moab •
Zered
N E G E V
EGYPT
NABATEA
Sorek
Besor
Kishon

0   20   40 kilometers
0   20   40 miles

Present-day drainage, coastlines, and country boundaries are represented.

N

These Roman fish hooks are typical of the type used by fishermen in the Early Roman Period (63 B.C.E.–70 C.E.).

The so-called Galilee Boat was discovered along the shore of the Sea of Galilee in 1986 and has since been dated to the early first century C.E.

Mount Tabor

At one point during his journeys, Jesus took his most trusted disciples—Peter, James, and John—on a hill where "he was transfigured before them" (Matthew 17:2). Jesus was joined by two heavenly figures: Moses and Elijah, the leading protagonists of the Law (Torah) and the Prophets (Nevi'im), the two divisions of Hebrew Scripture as it was known in Jesus' time.

The purpose of the Transfiguration is to present Jesus as the fulfillment of Hebrew Scripture prophecy, one of the cardinal ideas of the canonical Gospels. Another motive for this unusual event may be to help early Christians imagine the Resurrection of Jesus, since the actual Resurrection is neither observed nor described in any of the Gospels. Traditionally the Transfiguration is said to have occurred on Mount Tabor in the Jezreel Valley, although some believe that Mount Hermon, today located at the juncture between Israel, Lebanon, and Syria, may have been the place.

A view of the Jezreel Valley and Mount Tabor, which tradition has identified as the site of Jesus' Transfiguration.

date from the first century—one of only seven synagogues from the Late Second Temple Period in Israel that we know of. Like the synagogue of Capernaum, it featured stone benches along its walls, which were decorated with colorful frescoes. Two years later, excavators uncovered a stone block in the center of the synagogue that, astonishingly, appears to be a three-dimensional representation of the Temple itself—the first such image ever. In 2015, Hebrew scholar Rina Talgam speculated that the purpose of the Magdala Stone may have been to "sanctify" the synagogue space even as the actual Temple was still in existence, though others have disputed this claim. Today, the excavations of Magdala continue under the leadership of the Anáhuac México Sur University, resulting in a large cache of oil lamps; amphorae; glass objects; fishnet weights, bells, and bone dice; as well as grinding stones—all roughly dating to the time of Jesus.

GERASA AND GADARA

John Dominic Crossan has documented the ancient levees of no fewer than 15 first-century fishing harbors around the Sea of Galilee, many of which Jesus may have visited. One location that the Gospels cite by name is Gerasa, the "country of the Gerasenes," where Jesus healed a demoniac. Gerasa was one of the Greco-Roman cities of the Decapolis and one of the leading urban centers east of the Sea of Galilee. Indeed, after the demoniac was healed, says Mark, he "began to proclaim in the Decapolis how much Jesus had done for him" (Mark 5:20). Known today as Jerash, located some 30 miles north of the Jordanian capital of Amman, Gerasa was discovered in 1806 and is today one of the best preserved Roman cities in the Near East. The Gospel reference, however, suggests that Jesus merely visited the coastal region, which like many other such satellite regions was considered "the country" of Gerasa in both an economic and political sense. Matthew, however, sets this episode in the "country of Gadarenes," today identified with Umm Qays, also in Jordan (Matthew 8:28). Unlike Gerasa, however, Gadara was completely destroyed by Vespasian after the outbreak of the First Jewish Revolt in 66 C.E., and only a few remains have been found to date.

IN PHOENICIAN LANDS

In the third phase of his ministry, Jesus decided to leave the Galilean heartland altogether in an attempt to reach out to non-Jewish centers in Phoenicia and Decapolis. This represented a break with his original intent to limit his teaching to the "lost sheep of Israel" (Matthew 10:6). Arguably this change of heart, with important consequences for the growth of early Christianity, was in response to the crowds "from beyond the Jordan, and the region around Tyre and Sidon" who traveled down to Galilee to hear the rabbi speak (Mark 3:8).

Jesus first traveled north, probably by taking the trade route from Kinnereth that led past Zefat (today's Safed) and the township of Meiron, a mixed Jewish-Hellenistic city that as "Meroth" would play a key role in Josephus's account of the First Jewish War. A

The shore of the Sea of Galilee, between Capernaum and Chorazin, is the setting for many of the scenes described in the Gospels.

synagogue was built here around the early fourth century that may have influenced the ones in Capernaum and Chorazin.

From Meiron the road led past Gush Halav in the foothills of Mount Meron, renowned for the quality of its olive oil. Given its strategic location on the border with Phoenicia, Gush Halav (or "Gischala") was heavily fortified and one of the last places in Galilee to fall to the Roman legions during the Jewish War. One of the rebel commanders, a wealthy olive oil merchant called John of Gischala, would play a major role in the defense of Jerusalem in 70 C.E.

Beyond Gush Halav, Jesus was in foreign territory. Traveling in the region of Tyre, a major Phoenician port on the Mediterranean coast, he was impressed with a local woman who took offense when Jesus inferred that Gentiles were like "dogs" and healed her daughter (Mark 7:27-30).

THE CITY OF PAN

According to Mark's Gospel, Jesus continued on to Sidon, another Phoenician coastal city some 35 miles north of Tyre, before moving northeast to the hills of the Golan. Here was a town called Paneas, center of the cult of the Greek god Pan. Granted to King Herod as a gift by Augustus in 20 B.C.E., the king had promptly built a large temple "in white marble" dedicated to his Roman master. After Herod's death, his son Philip turned the place into a luxurious spa resort with an expanded sanctuary to Pan—who, perhaps fittingly, was a satyr-like deity in charge of forests and associated pastoral delights. Taking a cue from his father, Philip renamed it "Caesarea"

in 14 C.E., in homage to the Roman emperor, but then added the word "Philippi" to distinguish the city from Caesarea Maritima on the coast. It is under this name, "Caesarea Philippi," that the place appears in the Gospels (Mark 8:27).

In the rather improbable setting of this pagan sanctuary, Jesus decided to reflect on the success of his ministry. He asked his disciples, "Who do people say that I am?" Only one of his followers got it right. Simon Peter stood up and said, "You are the Messiah" (Mark 8:30). In Matthew, Jesus praised Simon Peter with a pun on Peter's nickname (*Petros* in Greek, or "Rocky"): "You are Peter, and on this rock I will build my Church" (Matthew 16:17-18).

Major excavations at Paneas (Banyas as it is known today) did not begin until 1988 and continued well into the 1990s. These campaigns uncovered a large symmetrical complex with two temples, dedicated to Pan and the Greek god Zeus. At its heart was a large palace with subterranean corridors, first published by John Wilson and Vassilios Tzaferis in 1998. The excavators believe that it may have been built by Agrippa II, who in 53 C.E. was installed as ruler of the Gaulanitis by Emperor Claudius. Agrippa would later appear in the Book of Acts of the Apostles as the king who visits Paul during his imprisonment in Caesarea Maritima (Acts 25:12). ■

THE ROAD TO JERUSALEM

Jesus Embarks on the Fateful Journey to Judea

Why did Jesus go to Jerusalem? This is the critical question that forms the linchpin between the story of Jesus' Galilean ministry and the dramatic events that unfolded during Passover around 30 C.E. In principle there is nothing unusual about Jesus leading his followers to the Judean capital. It was Passover, when many Jews throughout the country and from the Diaspora communities throughout the Mediterranean made the long journey to the Temple to offer their paschal sacrifices as the Law required. The problem with this interpretation is that while the Gospels show Jesus visiting the Temple on several occasions, he is never described as making an animal sacrifice, although this was the principal purpose of the Temple sanctuary—certainly during Passover. Jesus considered the Temple "my father's house" (Luke 2:50) but never referred to the sacrificial rites. In this, he may have found inspiration in Hebrew prophets such as Amos, Micah, and Hosea and associated his ministry with their words. "I desire mercy and not sacrifice, and the knowledge of God rather than burnt offerings," Hosea famously said (Hosea 6:6).

Seen in retrospect, for Christians the reason that Jesus went to Jerusalem is clear: to initiate the Passion sequence with which he would redeem mankind. The Gospel of Matthew makes this intent explicit. "See," Jesus said to his disciples as they were on the road, "we are going up to Jerusalem, and the Son of Man will be handed over to the chief priests and scribes, and they will condemn him to death" (Matthew 20:18).

The historian, however, must consider other reasons as well. The revealing episode at Caesarea Philippi depicts a Jesus who, on the threshold of returning to his native land, has begun to question the impact of his teachings. As he passed through the towns and villages of his homeland once more, Jesus was forced to confront the fact that very little had changed. Notwithstanding his sermons and healings, he had failed to attract broad support for refashioning Galilean society as a Kingdom of God. No matter where he looked, there was just as much hunger and poverty as well as egregious wealth as there had been before.

This frustration is what prompts his uncharacteristic outburst in both Matthew and Luke. "Woe to you, Chorazin!" he cried. "Woe to you, Bethsaida! If the powerful deeds performed among you had been done in Tyre and Sidon, they would have changed their ways long ago, sitting in sackcloth and ashes!" (Matthew 11:21; Luke 10:13). This was strong

ca 12
Annius Rufus succeeds
Marcus Ambivulus
as procurator of Judea

ca 14
Augustus dies
and is succeeded
by Tiberius (14-37 C.E.)

ca 15
Valerius Gratus
succeeds Annius Rufus
as procurator of Judea

ca 15
Ishmael ben Fabus
is appointed high priest
in Jerusalem

The theater of Samaria, built by King Herod as part of his new city of Sebaste, overlooks the valley through which ran the ancient road to Jerusalem.

This elegant lusterware pitcher with long neck illustrates the virtuosity of Roman glassblowing techniques in the first century C.E.

ca 16
Tiberius's adopted son, Germanicus, defeats German tribes

ca 16
Eleazar, son of Annas, is appointed high priest in Jerusalem

ca 17
Herod Antipas begins construction of a new city called Tiberias

ca 18
Beginning of a severe drought in eastern China

stuff, for it implied that among the Gentile townships he had just visited, he'd found more faith than in the core cities of his ministry.

Hebrew Scripture has many similar stories of prophets railing at the faithlessness of their following. Jeremiah too had experienced a severe crisis of self-confidence (Jeremiah 20:7). But God had come to his aid. "Stand in the gate of the Lord's house," the Lord had said, "and proclaim there this word … if you truly act justly one with another, if you do not oppress the alien, the orphan, and the widow, or shed innocent blood in this place … then I will dwell with you in this place, in the land that I gave of old to your ancestors forever and ever." A more succinct description of Jesus' Kingdom of God can scarcely be found.

The idea that Jeremiah's dramatic appeal could have inspired Jesus' fateful journey is not entirely hypothetical, for as he stood in the Temple forecourt, Jesus himself would quote from Jeremiah's great Temple Sermon. What's more, the Apostles must have had an inkling of Jesus' plans and realized the risk they were taking by staging a public address during the most volatile time of the year. "They were on the road, going up to Jerusalem," Mark says, "and those who followed were afraid" (Mark 10:32).

JERICHO

Most Galileans traveling to Jerusalem opted for the 80-mile route southward that led from Tiberias through the pleasant Jezreel Valley, past Mount Tabor and the border between Galilee and the Roman province of Samaria and Judea. Long before the city of Sebaste and Mount Gerizim, the holy mountain of the Samaritans, pilgrims would veer sharply left and descend toward the Jordan Valley, where the rolling hills and soothing pastures abruptly changed to the dry, craggy cliffs of the Judean Desert. The purpose of this detour was to avoid any contact with Samaritans, whom as we saw, the Jews of Jesus' time tended to ostracize as schismatics. Early in his ministry, Jesus had instructed his disciples, "Enter no town of the Samaritans" (Matthew 10:5). This route then led to Jericho, where the road once again turned inland, rising steeply to an elevation of over 3,000 feet.

Since its heyday in the Bronze Age, Jericho had regained some of its former glory under King Herod, who surrounded the city with a series of forts, incorporating some of the old fortifications built by the Seleucids during their war with the Maccabees. During the Roman Civil War, Jericho had been bestowed by Mark Antony upon Cleopatra as a gift. She in turn leased the area to Herod, with the understanding that he would tend to her vast palm plantations nearby. But after the fall of the Ptolemaic Dynasty at the death of Cleopatra in 30 C.E., Augustus transferred the city to Herod's

domain. Herod then built a palace, a hippodrome, aqueducts, and a large swimming pool in the area. According to Josephus, this pool was used to drown Aristobulus III.

Because of its strategic location at the nexus of several trade routes, Jericho had a number of toll stations. According to Luke, one of these was occupied by a wealthy tax collector named Zacchaeus, who met Jesus and promptly agreed to give half of his possessions to the poor (Luke 19:1-8).

SYCHAR

The Gospel of John, where the chronology of Jesus' ministry is different from that of the synoptic Gospels, indicates that Jesus and his followers did traverse Samaritan territory. Along the way they stopped to rest in a "Samaritan city called Sychar," which most scholars identify as Shechem, since Jesus sat down near "Jacob's well." When he asked a local Samaritan woman for a drink, she was surprised. "How is it," she said, "that you, a Jew, ask a drink of me, a woman of Samaria?" (John 4:9).

Long eclipsed by the city of Samaria (rebuilt by Herod as the sprawling Greco-Roman city of "Sebaste"), Shechem was now the principal gateway to the Samaritan sanctuary on Mount Gerizim. As a result it had remade itself as a visitors' center of sorts that catered to the needs of the pilgrims. Jesus felt so comfortable in this town that he stayed for two days (John 4:43). His example must have impressed the Apostles, for many months later, they would return to this region "proclaiming the good news to many villages of the Samaritans" (Acts 8:25)." ■

Little remains of the Banyas temple dedicated to Pan, a Greek god in the shape of a satyr, once a major pilgrimage destination as well as a Roman resort.

When Jesus had finished saying these things, he left Galilee and went to the region of Judea beyond the Jordan.

MATTHEW 19:1

THE ROAD TO JERUSALEM

MAP KEY

- Ruled by Herod Antipas
- Ruled by Herod Philip
- Roman province of Judea
- Roman province of Syria
- Imperial estate
- Nabataean Kingdom
- ········ District or region boundary
- ← Route of Jesus to Jerusalem
- • / ○ City of the Decapolis / location uncertain

THE GREAT SEA
(MEDITERRANEAN SEA)

Sidon

Damascus

2,814 m
9,232 ft
Mt. Hermon

ITUREA

SYRIA

Tyre

Kanah

Caesarea Philippi
(Paneas)

Cadasa

Raphana

Ecdippa

Asor

Merom

GAULANITIS

Ptolemais
Bay of Acco
(Bay of Haifa)

Jotapata

Capernaum

Bethsaida

Arbela

Sea of Kinnereth
(Sea of Galilee)

Sycaminium

Mt. Carmel
546 m
1,791 ft

Tiberias

Hippos

Gabae

Nazareth

Philoteria

Sepphoris

Mt. Tabor
588 m
1,929 ft

Gadara

Abila

Dora

Legio

Scythopolis

Caesarea

Narbata

Ginae

Pella

Dion

West Bank

Gerasa

Sebaste

Mt. Ebal
940 m
3,084 ft

Neapolis

Sychar

Amathus

Apollonia

Mt. Gerizim
881 m
2,890 ft

Zacchaeus, a chief
tax collector, was
converted.
(Luke 19:1–10)

Antipatris

Lebonah

Gadara

Philadelphia

Joppa

Phasaelis

Blind Bartimaeus is
given sight by Jesus.
(Mark 10:46–52)

Lydda

Bethel

Archelais

Jericho

Gazara

Esbus

Jamnia

Jerusalem

Bethany
(Al 'Ayzarīyah)

Mt. Nebo
802 m
2,631 ft

Medeba

Azotus

Jesus entered the city to the praising cries of
"Hosanna," meaning "save us" in Hebrew. He would
later be turned over to authorities, crucified, then
buried, and resurrected in the city.
(Matthew 21:9)

Bethlehem

Herodium

Jesus raised Lazarus from the
dead after four days in the tomb.
(John 11:1–44)

Ascalon

Marisa

Beth-zur

Machaerus

Lachish

Hebron

Salt Sea
(Dead Sea)

Anthedon

Gaza

'En-gedi

Gaza Strip

Eshtemoa

Jesus was anointed in the
house of Simon the Leper.
(Matthew 26:6–13; Mark
14:3–9; John 12:1–8)

Masada

NABATEA

Raphia

Beersheba

Malatha

NEGEV

0   20   40 kilometers
0   20   40 miles

EGYPT

Present-day drainage, coastlines, and country boundaries are represented.
Modern names appear in parentheses.

ca 17
Simon ben Camithus is appointed
high priest in Jerusalem

ca 18
Joseph Caiaphas, son-in-law
of Annas, is appointed high priest

ca 19
Tiberius's adopted son,
Germanicus, dies

ca 20
Roman geographer Strabo extols
the wealth of the Arabian Peninsula

THE DISTURBANCE IN THE TEMPLE

Jesus' Action Against the Money Changers Enrages the Priesthood

Most Passover pilgrims from rural areas like Galilee could not afford the high rates of inns in Jerusalem proper. Instead, they camped out on the Mount of Olives, where their families bundled up and slept around improvised campfires. Because Passover fell on the 14th day of the month of Nisan (the equivalent of April 7 in 30 C.E.), nighttime temperatures in Jerusalem could still drop below 40 degrees Fahrenheit.

Jesus and his disciples, however, did not sleep out in the open. Jesus had relatives in the village of Bethany, located on the southeastern slope of the Mount of Olives, just a mile and a half from Jerusalem's city gate. Here lived Martha and Mary, two sisters whom Jesus had visited previously, as well as their brother, Lazarus, whom the Bible says Jesus woke from the dead (Luke 10:39-42; John 11:42-44). Since Jesus' followers were exhausted from the long climb to Jerusalem from Jericho, they decided on a good rest before continuing on to the Temple on the morrow.

Bethany was excavated in the early 1950s by S. J. Saller, who found the remains of four superimposed churches, the first one dating to the end of the fourth century C.E. Several homes from the Early Roman Period, as well as wine presses and cisterns, were excavated as well. Nearby is a cave that since the fourth century has been venerated as the tomb of Lazarus; its name, Lazarium, lives on in the Arab name of the village, which today is El-Eizariya.

THE SECOND TEMPLE

Shortly after dawn, the disciples left the house to witness a magic moment: watching the warm light of the rising sun pass slowly over the Temple sanctuary built by King Herod, setting its golden cornices ablaze. For many followers, this was the first time they had ever laid eyes on this magnificent complex. One disciple later gushed, "Teacher, what large stones and what large buildings!" (Mark 13:1).

The Pool of Bethesda in Jerusalem where John's Gospel places the healing of a paralytic is one of the few locations in the Gospels that have been attested by archaeology. Inset: A Tyrian silver shekel, dated around 68 C.E., was the only type of currency permitted within the Temple.

ca 23
Tiberius's son Drusus dies, leaving Tiberius without an heir

ca 26
Tiberius withdraws from government, passing power to Sejanus

ca 26
Pontius Pilate appointed as procurator of Judea

ca 26
Pilate provokes massive protests in the Temple

John's Gospel claims that at this point, the sanctuary was fully completed, some 50 years after it was begun. Several coins found recently underneath the old Herodian walls, however, suggest that the Temple was not finished until 62 C.E., just eight years before it would be destroyed by Roman legions led by General Titus.

Of course, King Herod did not rebuild the Second Temple from scratch; he merely restored and adorned the structure that had been built during the Persian period. What he did do, however, was to extend this rather modest Temple with two successive courts, which in turn were surrounded by a vast public esplanade, ringed by a double colonnade. The result was an acropolis in the true Hellenistic tradition: a vast sacred precinct of white marble that culminated in the shrine where the presence of the divinity could be felt.

This concept, however, confronted Herod's architects with an acute problem. The Second Temple stood not on level ground but on top of a mound, with little space for anything to surround it. To create the large forecourt that Herod had in mind, the builders had to build a vast, floating platform supported by massive arches and

This mikveh, or ritual bathing pool, excavated just outside the walls of Temple Mount in Jerusalem, was used by pilgrims before entering the Temple.

retaining walls, which would tower high above the Lower City of Jerusalem. Several of these retaining walls are still visible: one of these, the Western Wall, is today the holiest place in Judaism. Only when these massive foundations were in place—which would have taken many years to build—could the architects begin to build the large peristyle, which was supported by a double row of Corinthian columns that embraced the vast forecourt. The purpose of this arcade was to offer welcome shade to worshippers during the heat of midday, but it also sheltered several subsidiary buildings, such as a large basilica known by its Greek name, the Royal Stoa. Here, in a hall known as the Lishkat La-Gazit, or "Chamber of Hewn Stones," sat the 72 members of the Great Sanhedrin, the Jewish Council, which even during the Roman prefecture still exercised considerable autonomy in domestic and religious matters—as we will see shortly.

Upon arriving in Jerusalem from Bethany, Jesus would have taken the Apostles to the monumental staircase leading up to the Double Gate, at the south side of Temple Mount. While the height of each step was roughly the same, the depth alternated between 12 inches and 35 inches, forcing pilgrims to ascend carefully, mindful of the sanctity of the ground. They then entered a tunnel, lit by sputtering torches, which led the worshippers underneath the Royal Stoa into

Then they came to Jerusalem. And he entered the temple and began to drive out those who were selling and those who were buying in the temple.

MARK 11:15

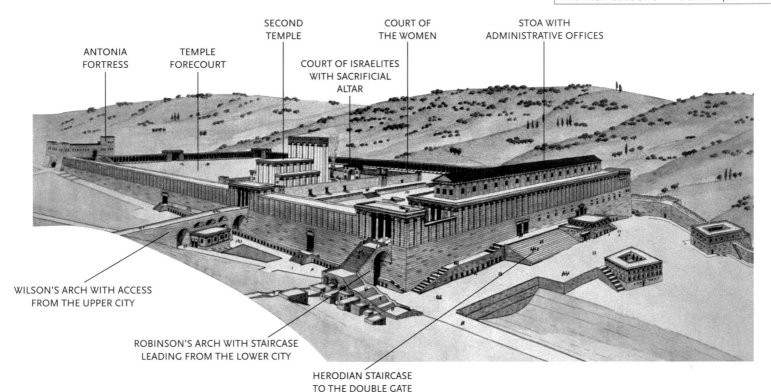

ANTONIA FORTRESS

TEMPLE FORECOURT

SECOND TEMPLE

COURT OF ISRAELITES WITH SACRIFICIAL ALTAR

COURT OF THE WOMEN

STOA WITH ADMINISTRATIVE OFFICES

WILSON'S ARCH WITH ACCESS FROM THE UPPER CITY

ROBINSON'S ARCH WITH STAIRCASE LEADING FROM THE LOWER CITY

HERODIAN STAIRCASE TO THE DOUBLE GATE

the wide forecourt, known as the Court of the Gentiles. While any visitor was welcome here, access to the actual Temple precinct was limited to Jewish worshippers. Foreign visitors were warned that anyone who crossed the *soreg*, the perimeter of this sacred area, would be sentenced to death.

A massive portal then ushered the pilgrims to an inner court, known as the Court of the Women. Here stood 13 horn-shaped depositories, or *shoparoth*, each marked for a particular tithe or offering. From this point, only male pilgrims and their lambs—organized in *kittot* ("sections") of 30 men each—could enter through the Nicanor Gate into the Court of the Priests, which contained a massive altar. Here, priests butchered the animals and tossed their organs on a vast grill so as to offer "a pleasing odor to the Lord" (Leviticus 1:13). As they stood and marveled at the sounds, sights, and smells of sacrificial Judaism, few pilgrims would have noticed a pair of looming towers to the north. Here was the Antonia Fortress, named after Mark Antony, and behind its crenellated walls were Roman auxiliaries, ready to strike at the slightest indication of trouble.

THE MONEY CHANGERS IN THE TEMPLE FORECOURT

But Jesus never got this far. As soon as he set foot in the forecourt, he was dismayed by the hustle and bustle of money changers and animal peddlers, each loudly advertising his

This reconstruction shows Herod's magnificent sanctuary platform, built around the Second Temple Period, between 20 B.C.E. and 62 C.E.

wares and fees. They had a good reason to be there: Priests admitted only sacrificial lambs "without blemish," and only Tyrian shekels were permitted as currency within the Temple. But clearly Jesus was shocked by this commercial frenzy, either because he detested the sacrificial cult or because—as scholar Bruce Chilton has suggested—these vendors used to have their stalls outside the Temple, on the Chanuth, a market on the Mount of Olives. Whatever the case may be, Jesus made "a whip of cords" and "overturned the tables of the money changers and the seats of those who sold doves" (John 2:15; Mark 11:15). Overcome with anger he cried, citing the Book of Isaiah, "Is it not written, 'My house shall be called a house of prayer for all the nations'?" And then followed another quote, far more damning, this time from the Book of Jeremiah: "But you have made it a den of robbers" (Jeremiah 7:11).

This sealed Jesus' fate. It was only two years since the massive protest over the rumor that Pilate—in collusion with the high priest Caiaphas—was stealing from the Temple treasury, as Josephus tells us. Mark writes that as soon as "the chief priests and the scribes heard it, they kept looking for a way to kill him" (Mark 11:18).

Jesus was now a marked man. ■

This censer from the first century C.E. was used to aromatize a room with incense, possibly using frankincense, a resin harvested in southern Arabia.

RECONSTRUCTING THE ROUTE OF THE PASSION

The Path From Gethsemane to Golgotha

T he long journey from the place of Jesus' arrest to the place of his crucifixion and entombment is commemorated by Christians during Holy Week, culminating in the feast of Easter. Most churches feature images of this Passion story, known as the 14 stations of the cross. But the archaeologist who wishes to identify these stations in today's Old City of Jerusalem faces several challenges.

The key problem is that the Jerusalem of Jesus' time no longer exists. That city was thoroughly destroyed following the Jewish Revolt of 66-70 C.E. After the second rebellion of 132-135 C.E., Emperor Hadrian was so fed up with the Jews' refusal to bend their knee that he ordered a new Roman city to be built on the spot, known as Aelia Capitolina, so as to erase any vestige of what remained of the holy city.

Nevertheless, over the past decade, extensive research by archaeologists such as Jodi Magness, Amos Kloner, and Jonathan Reed has uncovered many fascinating details that may help us to imagine the path that Jesus took.

GETHSEMANE

Christian tradition places the scene of Jesus' arrest in a garden, located on the Mount of Olives. The Hebrew *gat-shemanim*, however, refers to an oil press. Such a press was typically set up in a cave to keep the oil cool in summer months and to protect the wooden mechanics from the elements. A cave of this type would have provided Jesus with the privacy and serenity to pray, certainly given that the rest of the mount was teeming with hundreds of pilgrims. Fourth-century traveler Egeria wrote that exactly such a grotto was revered as the location of Gethsemane at the time of her visit. Today, a cave measuring 36 by 60 feet, and supported by four rock-cut pillars, can be seen on the lower slopes of the Mount of Olives. To the right of the altar is a hole in the wall that, according to Jerome Murphy-O'Connor, may have held the weighted wooden beam used to crush the olives.

CAIAPHAS'S PALACE

Following Jesus' arrest on the Mount of Olives, it would have been customary for him to be locked up in the Temple stockade until

ca 28
Rumors circulate of
Pilate's using money
from the Temple treasury

ca 28
A massive demonstration
in Jerusalem is suppressed
by Pilate

ca 28-29
Jesus joins the movement
of John the Baptist
in the Jordan

ca 29
John the Baptist
is arrested by Herod Antipas
and beheaded

These caverns may have formed part of the lower level of the Antonia Fortress, though they were later incorporated in a Roman city gate built in the second century C.E.

Precious perfumed unguents were often kept in delicate glass containers such as this round lusterware flask with twisted neck from the late first century C.E.

ca 29
Jesus leads three
of John's disciples back to Galilee
and begins his ministry

ca 30
Jesus is tried and crucified
on orders of Pilate during
the Passover Festival

ca 34-35
Jewish followers of Jesus,
led by Jesus' brother James,
are marginalized

ca 35
Disciple Stephen
is stoned to death
by a mob

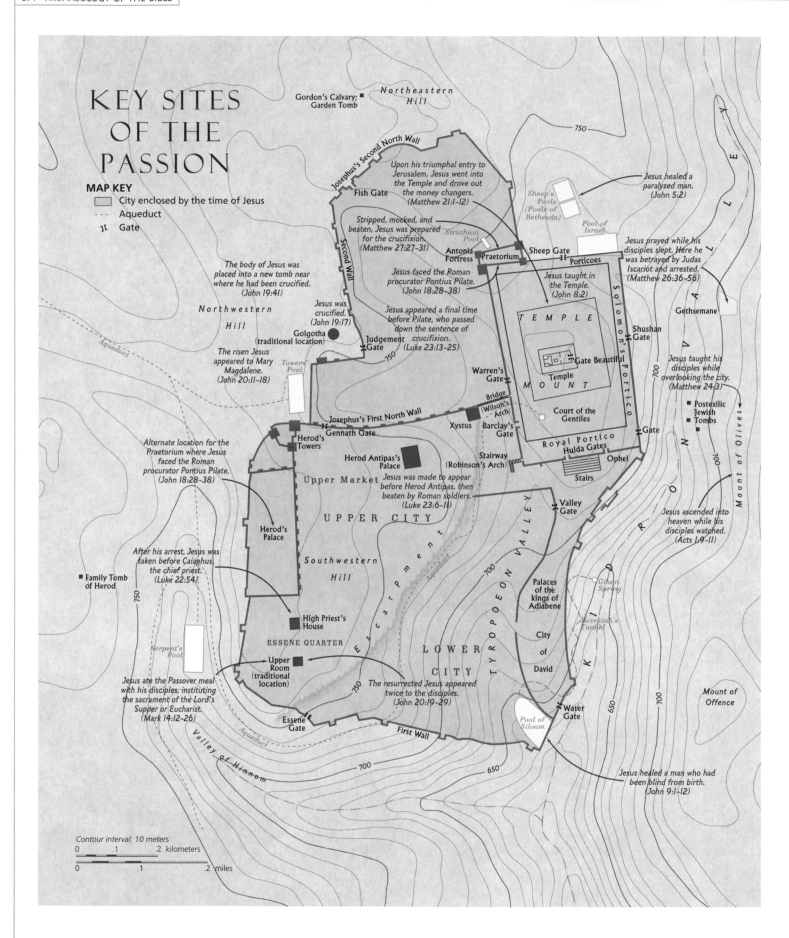

KEY SITES OF THE PASSION

MAP KEY

- City enclosed by the time of Jesus
- Aqueduct
- Gate

Gordon's Calvary; Garden Tomb

Northeastern Hill

Josephus's Second North Wall

Fish Gate

Upon his triumphal entry to Jerusalem, Jesus went into the Temple and drove out the money changers. (Matthew 21:1-12)

Jesus healed a paralyzed man. (John 5:2)

Sheep's Pools (Pools of Bethesda)

Pool of Israel

Stripped, mocked, and beaten, Jesus was prepared for the crucifixion. (Matthew 27:27-31)

Struthion Pool

Second Wall

Antonia Fortress *Praetorium* *Sheep Gate* *Porticoes*

Jesus prayed while his disciples slept. Here he was betrayed by Judas Iscariot and arrested. (Matthew 26:36-56)

The body of Jesus was placed into a new tomb near where he had been crucified. (John 19:41)

Jesus faced the Roman procurator Pontius Pilate. (John 18:28-38)

Jesus taught in the Temple. (John 8:2)

Gethsemane

Northwestern Hill

Jesus was crucified. (John 19:17)

Jesus appeared a final time before Pilate, who passed down the sentence of crucifixion. (Luke 23:13-25)

T E M P L E *Shushan Gate*

Aqueduct

Golgotha (traditional location)

Judgement Gate

Jesus taught his disciples while overlooking the city. (Matthew 24:3)

The risen Jesus appeared to Mary Magdalene. (John 20:11-18)

Towers Pool

Warren's Gate *Gate Beautiful*

M O U N T *Temple*

Postexilic Jewish Tombs

Bridge (Wilson's Arch)

Josephus's First North Wall

Gennath Gate

Xystus

Barclay's Gate

Court of the Gentiles

Solomon's Portico

Gate

Alternate location for the Praetorium where Jesus faced the Roman procurator Pontius Pilate. (John 18:28-38)

Herod's Towers

Herod Antipas's Palace

Stairway (Robinson's Arch)

Royal Portico *Hulda Gates*

Ophel

Stairs

Upper Market

Jesus was made to appear before Herod Antipas, then beaten by Roman soldiers. (Luke 23:6-11)

Valley Gate

Jesus ascended into heaven while his disciples watched. (Acts 1:9-11)

Herod's Palace

U P P E R   C I T Y

Mount of Olives

Family Tomb of Herod

After his arrest, Jesus was taken before Caiaphas the chief priest. (Luke 22:54)

Southwestern Hill

Palaces of the kings of Adiabene

Gihon Spring

Hezekiah's Tunnel

High Priest's House

ESSENE QUARTER

L O W E R   C I T Y

City of David

Serpent's Pool

Upper Room (traditional location)

Jesus ate the Passover meal with his disciples, instituting the sacrament of the Lord's Supper or Eucharist. (Mark 14:12-26)

The resurrected Jesus appeared twice to the disciples. (John 20:19-29)

Mount of Offence

Water Gate

Essene Gate

First Wall

Pool of Siloam

Valley of Hinnom

Jesus healed a man who had been blind from birth. (John 9:1-12)

Aqueduct

Contour interval: 10 meters

0 .... .1 .... .2 kilometers

0 .... .1 .... .2 miles

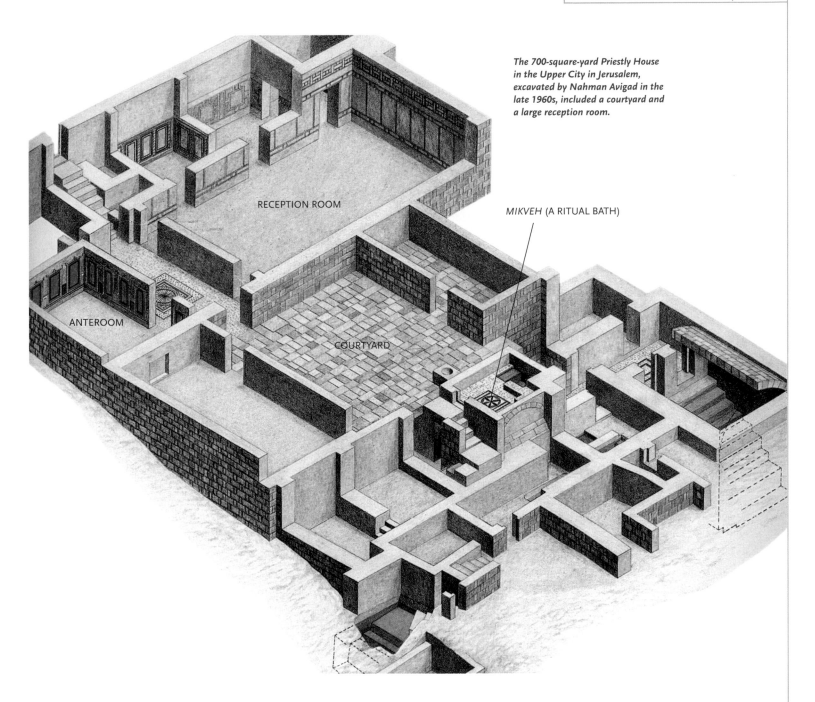

The 700-square-yard Priestly House in the Upper City in Jerusalem, excavated by Nahman Avigad in the late 1960s, included a courtyard and a large reception room.

RECEPTION ROOM

MIKVEH (A RITUAL BATH)

ANTEROOM

COURTYARD

such time that the full Sanhedrin could hear his case. This is exactly what happened to Peter, John, and other Apostles following their arrest. After being held in Temple custody overnight, they were arraigned during a full session presided by "Annas the [former] high priest, [and] Caiaphas" (Acts 4:3; 5:17). The same procedure was followed when Peter was arrested a second time; he was put in a "public prison" and subsequently interrogated by the Sanhedrin (Acts 5:17-18). The reason is that only a full quorum of the Sanhedrin could condemn a man accused of religious crimes to death.

But according to the Gospels, that's not what happened after Jesus was arrested. Instead, Jesus was taken directly to the Jerusalem residence of the high priest, Joseph Caiaphas. This was highly unusual, for his residence, though undoubtedly spacious and comfortable, could never have accommodated all 72 members of the Council in one room. Therefore, the arraignment must have involved only a small group of Caiaphas's handpicked Sadducees rather than the full Council, which usually included a vocal minority of Pharisees. Indeed, during later proceedings against the Apostles, it was Rabbi Gamaliel, a highly respected Pharisee, who came to their defense and ultimately saw them go free. Apparently Caiaphas wanted to avoid such an outcome at all costs.

Although Caiaphas's palace has not been uncovered, we have a very good simile of this setting. In the 1960s, Nahman Avigad found a 2,000-square-foot residence that he called the Priestly House,

In 2015, remnants of Herod's palace in Jerusalem were discovered underneath an old Ottoman building, the Kishle, adjoining the Tower of David Museum.

given the presence of several *mikva'ot,* or ritual baths. The structure, which today is one of six Herodian mansions preserved in the Wohl Archaeological Museum, closely matched the Caiaphas residence as described in the Gospel of Mark. It featured a large reception room, measuring 33 by 21 square feet, that was decorated with stucco ornamentation and frescoed panels in the Herodian manner. The house also featured an inner courtyard with a hearth. It was in one such courtyard that the Bible says Peter stood warming his hands by the fire while Jesus was arraigned inside.

THE PRAETORIUM

According to Mark's Gospel, whose depiction of the Passion was closely followed by the other evangelists, Caiaphas struggled to define a charge that would justify its referral to Roman jurisdiction. Without the backing of the Sanhedrin, Caiaphas could not order a man to death; he had to rely on the Roman authorities to do so. In the end, the high priest trapped Jesus into admitting that he was the Messiah, "the Son of Man seated at the right hand of the Power." That Jesus was actually quoting from the Book of Daniel was

obviously of no consequence to the Romans (Daniel 7:13). If the defendant had aspirations of becoming some sort of Jewish king, then as far as the Roman colonial law, the Ius Gentium, was concerned, he had to be punished, as a political rebel, for sedition.

It is important to recognize that notwithstanding popular perception, Jesus was a colonial subject and therefore did not merit a proper Roman trial, which was reserved for Roman citizens like Paul. All that sufficed for colonial renegades was a brief hearing led by a ranking official to document the defendant's crimes, and that is exactly what Mark's Gospel gives us. Jesus was ushered before the Roman magistrate, in this case Pontius Pilate; the charge was read— the prisoner being accused of claiming to be the Messiah, "the King of the Jews"—and the verdict was rendered.

Mark does not specify the location of this hearing, but John refers to the *praitorion* ("praetorium" in Latin), meaning "the office of the praetor," the highest-ranking official below Pilate. Where this office might have been located is the subject of ongoing debate. One theory places it in Herod's former residence adjoining the Antonia Fortress. Today's Church of the Sisters of Zion, built over the reputed location of the Antonia, has long claimed to be the spot where Jesus was sentenced and scourged. The lower level of the church includes a marble pavement that, some believe, is the Lithostrōtos identified by

John as the place of Pilate's hearing. Recent research, however, suggests that the pavement formed part of a second-century forum, built as part of Hadrian's Roman city of Aelia Capitolina.

Another theory holds that Pilate would have stayed in the most prestigious residence of the city—the former palace of King Herod. This luxurious complex featured gardens and ornamental ponds surrounded by two wings, each offering reception halls, baths, and rooms for upward of a hundred guests. Josephus confirms that this was the residence for Roman prefects visiting the city. In January 2015, archaeologist Amit Re'em announced that he had located remnants of this palace during the excavation of an old Ottoman building, the Kishle, adjoining the Tower of David Museum. Archaeologists had long suspected that this is where the palace was located, especially following excavations by archaeologist Kathleen Kenyon in the 1960s. But the question of where Pilate would have interrogated Jesus remains a subject of dispute.

THE SCOURGING

All of the Gospels state that Jesus was severely scourged before being taken to his place of execution. This was a common procedure for men convicted of violating the Jewish Law or the sanctity of the Temple. The Apostles were flogged after their hearing before the Sanhedrin (Acts 5:40), as was another victim, a man named Jesus son of Ananias, who was arrested during Pentecost of 62 C.E. It is therefore possible that the scourging was applied as punishment for Jesus' disturbance in the Temple, while the Roman sentence of crucifixion was rendered as penalty for his alleged claim to be the Messiah.

The Gospels of Mark and Matthew place the scourging "in the courtyard … of the governor's headquarters," in the presence of "the whole cohort" (Mark 15:16; Matthew 27:27). A Roman cohort—consisting of around 200 soldiers or local auxiliaries—would have been stationed at the Antonia. This makes it likely that Jesus was imprisoned and later scourged in the courtyard of the fortress proper.

THE VIA DOLOROSA

The *Via Dolorosa*, or "Road of Sorrows," in the Old City of Jerusalem is today revered by Christian pilgrims as the path that Jesus followed to his place of execution. It includes 14 stations of the cross, although the last stations, 10 through 14, are contained

The Historical Pilate

The evangelists, and particularly Matthew and John, try to pin the blame for Jesus' death on the Jewish crowd rather than the Roman authorities. This is the purpose of the amnesty, by which Pilate offered the crowd a choice between Jesus and a felon named Barabbas (Mark 15:11). The Jews demanded that Jesus be crucified, thus forcing Pilate's hand.

This scenario reflects the unique pressures the evangelists faced. They lived and wrote under Roman jurisdiction for a largely Greco-Roman audience; it would therefore have been difficult to pin the blame on a high Roman official. What's more, Judea rose in revolt against Rome in 66 C.E., which cast Jews throughout the empire in a negative light. But historically, there is little question that Pilate is the one solely responsible for Jesus' murder. Jewish historian Philo has documented the prefect's "supremely grievous cruelty." That Rome was compelled to remove Pilate from office in 36 C.E. for his violent regime speaks volumes in itself.

within the Church of the Holy Sepulchre. Though the road is a deeply spiritual experience for many Christians, it is of limited value for historians since the streets that Jesus walked no longer exist. The plan of the Old City today is based on the second-century layout of the Roman city of Aelia Capitolina, which further evolved during the subsequent Islamic period. The basic outline of the Roman grid, with two parallel roads—*cardines maximi*—intersecting with a boulevard at right angles, the *decumanus maximus,* is still visible today. As Murphy-O'Connor has shown, the current route of the Via Dolorosa was not established until the 14th century by the Order of the Franciscans, who are custodians of many holy Christian places in Israel. ∎

While affluent families drank wine from silver or glass cups, the poor used a simple earthenware beaker.

They bound him, led him away, and handed him over to Pilate the governor.

MATTHEW 27:2

THE ART OF THE ROMAN AGE
Roman Luxury Items Become Tokens of Wealth

THE ROMAN CONQUEST OF PALESTINE IN 63 B.C.E. INTRODUCED THE UPPER CLASSES OF JUDEA TO THE REFINEMENT of Roman art. Soon, affluent families began to advertise their cultural sophistication by filling their homes with fashionable decorative arts produced throughout the new Roman possessions, including Syria and Egypt. This included glassware, a uniquely Roman specialty following the revolutionary invention of the blowpipe. The artistry of these fine Roman artifacts stands in sharp contrast to the humble earthenware that the less affluent—the vast majority of workers and peasants—continued to use throughout Roman Palestine. ■

A first-century C.E. drinking cup with white barbotine decoration was produced in Roman Egypt.

Oil lamps with scenes from Homer's Odyssey are typical of the kind of terra-cotta lamps that were used throughout the Roman Empire.

A Tyrian silver shekel with an Omer cup from Judea is dated to the fourth year of the Jewish Revolt against the Romans.

A fresco of fishermen, painted in almost impressionist hues, reveals the skill of Roman artists in the first century C.E.

A cameo of Emperor Tiberius carved in carnelian and framed in a gold setting probably dates to the early 30s C.E.

A delicate Roman glass flask with tall neck, found in Palestine and dating from the first century C.E., was probably used for perfumed oils.

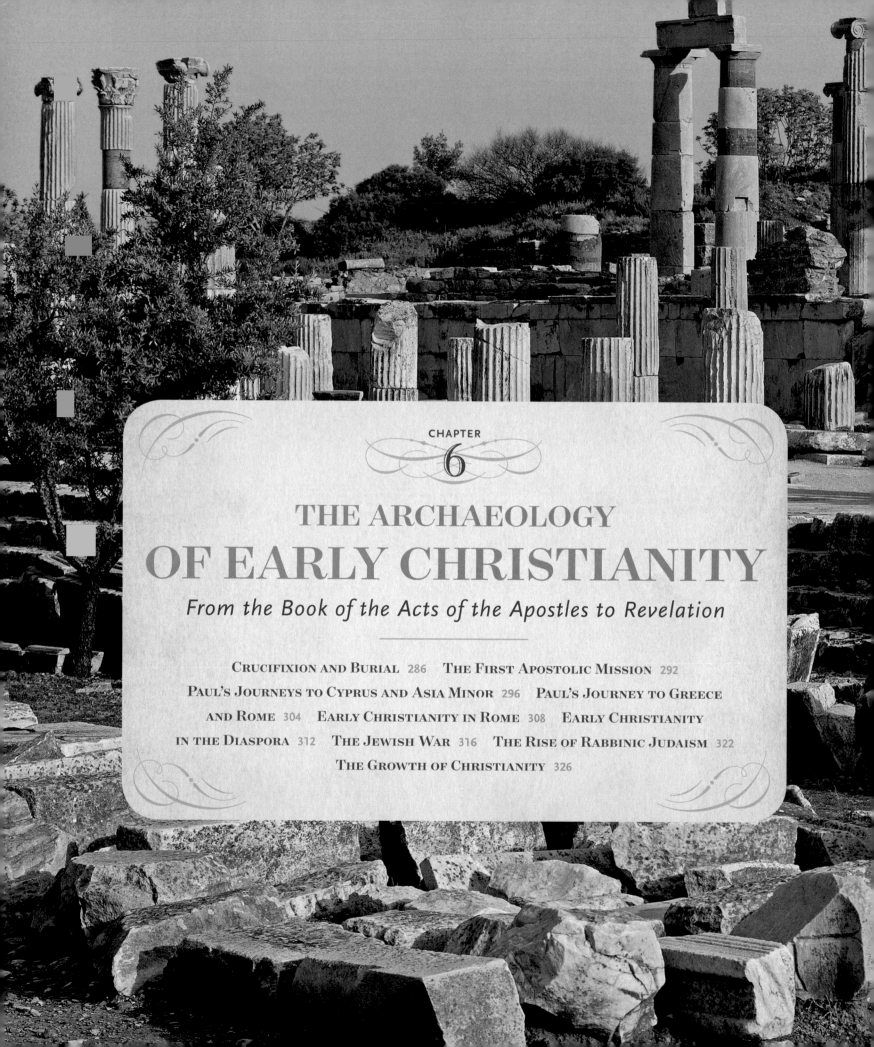

CHAPTER

6

THE ARCHAEOLOGY
OF EARLY CHRISTIANITY

From the Book of the Acts of the Apostles to Revelation

ROMAN PALESTINE

MAP KEY

Roman province of Palestina
Roman province of Syria
Roman province of Arabia
○ Location uncertain
[Jerusalem] Former city name

MARE INTERNUM
(MEDITERRANEAN SEA)

Sidon
Damascus
2,814 m
9,232 ft
Mt. Hermon
S Y R I A
Tyre
Caesarea Philippi
Kanah
Leontes
Cadasa
Raphana
Ecdippa
Asor
Merom
GAULANITIS
Ptolemais
Capernaum
Bethsaida
Bay of Acco
(Bay of Haifa)
Jotapata
Arbela
Lacus Tiberias
(Sea of Galilee)
Sycaminium
Tiberias
Hippos
Mt. Carmel
546 m
1,791 ft
Nazareth
Philoteria
Gabae
Sepphoris
Mt. Tabor
588 m
1,929 ft
Gadara
Abila
Dora
Legio
Yarmuk
Caesarea
Scythopolis
Pella
Narbata
Ginae
Dion
Mt. Ebal
940 m
3,084 ft
Gerasa
Sebaste
Amathus
Apollonia
Neapolis
Mt. Gerizim
881 m
2,890 ft
Antipatris
Joppa
Lebonah
Gadara
Lydda
Phasaelis
Philadelphia
Bethel
Archelais
Gazara
Jamnia
Emmaus
Jericho
Esbus
Azotus
Aelia Capitolina
[Jerusalem]
Bethany
Mt. Nebo
802 m
2,631 ft
Medeba
Bethlehem
Lacus
Asphaltitis
(Dead Sea)
Ascalon
Marisa
Beth-zur
Lachish
Hebron
Anthedon
Eshtemoa
En-gedi
Gaza
Arnon
Gaza Strip
Raphia
Beersheba
Kir-Moab
EGYPT
NEGEV
Zered (Hasa)

Plain of Sharon
Sharon
Shephelah
Kishon
Yarqon
Sorek
Besor
Jordan
Jabbok
PHOENICIA
LEBANON

0   20   40 kilometers
0   20   40 miles

Present-day drainage, coastlines, and country boundaries are represented.

*Then the Roman empire was passed to Tiberius,
the son of Julia, upon the death of Augustus,
who had reigned fifty-seven years.*

JOSEPHUS, *THE JEWISH WAR*

THE WORLD IN 30 C.E.

The Growth of Early Christianity, Circa 30 C.E. to 500 C.E.

IBERIUS WAS WHOLLY UNSUITED FOR THE IMPERIAL THRONE. STRICTLY SPEAKING, he wasn't even Augustus's handpicked heir. That honor went to Augustus's grandchildren, two young boys named Gaius and Lucius Caesar, whom Augustus had adopted as his own sons. That may have prompted Tiberius to withdraw from public life and to flee to Rhodes, where he could sulk in peace.

But this did not last. After young Gaius died in 2 C.E. and Lucius was killed in 4 C.E., Augustus summoned Tiberius back to Rome and made him his heir apparent. Ten years later, Augustus himself lay on his deathbed—after eating figs that had been poisoned by Tiberius's mother, Livia, or so it was whispered. Thus, Tiberius was elevated to the title of Princeps to begin his rule as Rome's second emperor after Caesar.

Eight years later, he changed his mind. Tired of politics, he began to delegate his power to his son Drusus, as well as to his secretary, a knight and officer of the Praetorian Guard named Lucius Aelius Sejanus. In 26 C.E., after the death of his son, Tiberius withdrew from active government altogether, leaving Sejanus in effective control of the empire. For the next four years, this officer instituted an unchecked regime of terror, persecuting his

Preceding pages: *Ephesus, one of the largest Ionian cities on the coast of today's Turkey, was first visited by Paul around 54 C.E. and then became his base for almost two years.* Right: *A flattering portrait of the young Caligula (r. 37-41 C.E.) was probably made in Asia Minor around 40 C.E.*

This gold coin, known as an aureus, was struck during the reign of Emperor Claudius (41-54 C.E.).

A reconstruction of the Forum Romanum shows the heart of the Roman Empire as it would have appeared in the second century C.E.

rivals while favoring men of his own station. One of these was a fellow knight, an otherwise unremarkable officer named Pontius Pilate. As fate would have it, the post of procurator of Judea had become vacant. It is likely that under any other circumstance, Pilate would have never qualified, for he had no known military or diplomatic record. But Sejanus's patronage got him the appointment—with disastrous consequences for Judea, as we know.

But then, soon after Jesus' crucifixion, Sejanus's power came to an abrupt end. He and his followers were arrested on suspicion of plotting a coup d'état, a not unreasonable charge, and duly executed. From that point on, the imperial government muddled along until 37 C.E., when, to everyone's relief, Tiberius died as well. He was succeeded by his great-nephew, an energetic 25-year-old named Gaius, nicknamed Caligula ("little soldier's boot").

HEROD AGRIPPA I

Caligula's reign would eventually descend into abject depravity, but initially his principate showed much promise. In sharp contrast to his predecessor, the young emperor felt it would make more sense to have regions such as Judea governed by local vassals, who knew the territory, rather than Roman governors. One of these was a man named Herod Agrippa, a grandson of King Herod. He also happened to be a close friend of Caligula. Before long, Agrippa was installed as ruler of Philip's former territory of the Gaulanitis. Two years later, Caligula deposed Herod Antipas, the ruler of Galilee and Perea during Jesus' time, and added his territories to Agrippa's domain.

This policy was continued by Emperor Claudius, who in 41 C.E. gave Agrippa control over Judea, Samaria, and Idumea. Thus, for a brief period, Herod Agrippa ruled over a territory that was roughly the size of King Herod's kingdom. Agrippa was also the

one who, according to the Book of Acts, ordered the execution of one of the Jerusalem Apostles, James, the son of Zebedee (Acts 12:1-3).

THE RETURN OF THE PROCURATE

But Judea's autonomy did not last. Agrippa died just three years later, in 44 C.E., and since his son Agrippa II was still underage, Claudius had no choice but to turn the region back into a Roman province. This set Judea on its inevitable spiral into rebellion. Having tasted freedom, the Jewish nation found it very difficult to return to Roman governance and defer to officials who harbored no ambition other than to enrich themselves. Claudius tried to sweeten the pill by reaffirming special rights and privileges that Augustus had accorded to Jews throughout the empire—such as dispensation from the need to sacrifice to the statue of the ruling emperor or serving in the armed forces—but it made no difference.

According to Roman historian Suetonius, this was also a time of rising tensions in certain Roman neighborhoods between observant Jews and those who "were constantly causing disturbances at the instigation of *Chrestus,* arguably a reference to Christ. These conflicts between traditional Jews and Jews who embraced Jesus as the Messiah were a foreshadowing of the deep rifts that would torment Jewish communities in the latter part of the century, as the letters of Paul amply attest. In Rome, the problem escalated to the point that in 49 C.E., Claudius decided to evict all Jews from the city proper—though they drifted back to their homes as soon as the dust had settled. According to the Bible, one of these evicted refugees, a Jewish tentmaker named Aquila and his wife, Priscilla, moved to Corinth, where they would later become close friends with Paul (Acts 18:2).

This portrait of Tiberius (r. 14-37 C.E.) was probably sculpted in 13 C.E., shortly after Augustus designated him as his heir.

THE PATH TO WAR

Just 13 years later, in 62 C.E., the fifth Judean governor in a row named Porcius Festus suddenly died. Before his successor, Lucceius Albinus, could set sail, the high priest Ananus seized the opportunity to arrest and kill "the brother of Jesus, who was called Christ, whose name was James," as Josephus later wrote. This dealt a death blow to the Apostolic movement in Palestine, although as we will see, the momentum of early Christianity had already shifted by that time to Asia Minor and beyond.

Two years later, Rome was ravaged by a massive fire. Emperor Nero, who had come to power in 54 C.E., blamed it on Rome's Christian community, launching a brief but intense period of persecution. "Nero," said the Roman historian Tacitus, "fastened the guilt … on a class hated for their abominations, called Christians [Chrestians] by the populace."

In Palestine, the fuse of all-out rebellion was finally lit when a Greek was seen sacrificing a bird on the doorstep of a synagogue in Caesarea. The ensuing protests were brutally suppressed by the procurator at the time, Gessius Florus. This only fanned the flames, so Florus soon asked for reinforcements from his superior, the governor of Syria. Astonishingly, this Roman legion suffered a humiliating defeat at the hands of the rebels, who promptly declared a new, independent Judea.

Thus, the Jewish nation found itself at war with the most powerful empire on Earth, with far-reaching consequences for both traditional Judaism and a budding new religion called Christianity. ■

CRUCIFIXION AND BURIAL

From Golgotha to the Tomb of Joseph of Arimathea

T he day of Jesus' crucifixion would mark both a beginning and an end. It put an abrupt end to his young ministry, which, to judge by the synoptic Gospels, could not have lasted for much more than 18 months. But by the same token, his crucifixion also became the starting point for a new movement, a *Christian* movement, which would eventually abandon its Jewish roots and embrace the Gentile population of the Roman Empire as a new monotheistic religion.

This was an astonishing development, certainly given the fact that crucifixion was reserved for those whom Rome considered hardened criminals, such as political rebels, pirates, or runaway slaves. That early Christianity was able to capture the imagination of the Greco-Roman world despite its leader's condemnation as an enemy of the state is perhaps unprecedented in the annals of ancient religions.

Although countless stylized depictions of the crucified Christ have inured us to the idea, crucifixion was an intensely shameful and horrific form of execution that could take many hours, if not days. This was the reason that crucifixions were usually performed in public, so that they could serve as a deterrent for anyone else contemplating seditious thoughts.

It was, however, also a time-consuming and labor-intensive business that required a unit of specialists known as *immunes.* That is why victims were not crucified individually but as part of regularly planned group executions. For example, in the case of Jesus, at least two other victims were executed as well that same day (Mark 15:27). It is possible that Pilate had planned such a gruesome display in advance so as to remind the thousands of Passover pilgrims who was in charge.

THE METHOD OF CRUCIFIXION

Contrary to common lore, there was no established procedure by which the Romans crucified their victims. The method varied based on the conditions and resources in the region in question. Wood, certainly a beam strong enough to hold up a human body, was scarce in Judea and therefore expensive. For that reason, it is likely that the Romans set up a permanent killing ground outside the city walls (as was customary for hygienic reasons), with upright stakes, or *stipes,* that could be reused for multiple executions. That meant that Jesus and the condemned men who accompanied him

ca 37	ca 37	ca 37	ca 38
Jewish historian Josephus is born	Tiberius dies, succeeded by Gaius Caligula	Pontius Pilate is recalled to Rome	Jewish pogroms in Alexandria

Some Romans believed that nails such as these could acquire magical powers after being used in a human crucifixion.

The Rotunda of the Church of the Holy Sepulchre in Jerusalem is traditionally identified as the location of the tomb where Jesus was buried.

Inset: A beautiful first-century glass flask with yellow bands and a tall, tapered top would have been used for delicate perfume agents.

ca 40
One of the earliest Christian communities founded in Corinth

ca 41
Agrippa I, grandson of Herod the Great, is appointed king of Judea

ca 41
Claudius confirms the right of Jews to observe their religious practices

ca 42
Caligula is assassinated and succeeded by Claudius

Mary Magdalene at the Empty Tomb

According to the Gospel of Mark, the first people to find that Jesus' tomb was empty were "Mary Magdalene, Mary the mother of James, and Salome." All three had returned to complete the anointing process (Mark 16:1-2). John's Gospel goes further and says that Mary Magdalene was the only person to witness that Jesus had risen (John 20:1). Why is this so surprising? The simple answer is that in ancient Judea, the word of a woman had very little credibility in a Jewish court. Some passages in the Talmud suggest that the testimony of a female witness was inadmissible. Why, then, would the evangelists depict three women as the eyewitnesses of the most important event in Christian theology? Many scholars believe that these authors had no choice, for this is exactly what happened. The incongruity of placing three women at Jesus' empty tomb, even though their word carried little weight, may plead for the historicity of this event.

Opposite: Venetian Renaissance artist Titian (1490-1576) completed "Noli Me Tangere" ("Do Not Touch Me"), showing Mary Magdalene and the resurrected Christ, around 1514. Right: An anklebone fragment pierced by a Roman nail dramatically illustrates the crucifixion procedure Roman forces used in the first century C.E.

would not have carried a full cross, as shown in traditional Christian art, but only a crossbeam known as a *patibulum*. Still, such a beam would have weighed around 70 or 80 pounds, so Mark's claim that a burly bystander named Simon of Cyrene (or "Simon the Libyan") was pressed into carrying the beam for Jesus certainly seems plausible (Mark 15:21).

Most Christian depictions also mistakenly show Jesus affixed to the cross with nails through his hand. The palm of a human hand is far too soft to hold the weight of a male adult. Instead, on the occasions that

nails were used, these were driven just below the wrist, so that the weight was sustained by the radius and ulna bones.

The feet were nailed differently. In 1986, Vassilios Tzaferis, while excavating in Jerusalem, found the skeleton of another first-century crucifixion victim inside an ossuary, or bone box, inscribed with the victim's name: Yehohanan. His calcaneus, or right heel bone, had been pierced by a Roman nail with fragments of wood on either side. This suggests that his feet had been squeezed into a small wooden block, shaped in the form of a U, which was then affixed to the bottom of the upright stake with a single nail. Roman nails were longer than the average modern nail—some six inches in length—with a square shaft some ⅜ inch in width.

Crucifixion does not kill a victim, at least not immediately. Its purpose is to suspend a man by his arms so that breathing becomes very difficult. In order to breathe, the victim must lift himself up, thus adding more strain on his impaled arms and legs that sharply increases the pain. The agony of crucifixion is therefore largely self-inflicted: A victim must choose between intense pain or suffocation. Eventually the condemned will become too exhausted to pull and push himself up to breathe, and dies of asphyxiation. This is why the Romans in the Gospel of John break the legs of the condemned so as to hasten their death before sundown (John 19:32). Without the use of their legs, they could no longer lift themselves to breathe.

GOLGOTHA

The Gospels refer to the execution ground as Golgotha (*Gûlgaltâ* in Aramaic), meaning "place of the skull" (Mark 15:22). This could refer to the Roman practice of tipping the bodies of the condemned in a nearby gully or potter's field. Since the 19th century, at least two possible locations for Golgotha have been suggested. One reason is that the Church of the Holy Sepulchre, which Christian tradition holds to be the place, is located *inside* today's Old City walls rather than *outside*, as an execution ground invariably was (John 19:20; Hebrews 13:12). General Charles George Gordon, the famous "Gordon of Khartoum," believed that Golgotha was located near the so-called Garden Tomb, just north of the Damascus Gate in East Jerusalem. Gordon first published this thesis in an 1884 book, *Reflections in Palestine,* written during a private pilgrimage after his

And when they had crucified him, they divided his clothes among themselves by casting lots.

GOSPEL OF MATTHEW 27:35

These burial niches, known as loculi *or* kokhim, *are from a first-century complex of 63 tombs known as the Tombs of the Sanhedrin in Jerusalem.*

retirement. The Garden Tomb, which still exists, matches the popular image of what Jesus' tomb should look like—certainly for Protestant pilgrims who are taken aback by the crowds and somewhat garish interior of the Holy Sepulchre Church. But modern research has since determined that the Sepulchre Church was indeed located outside Jerusalem's walls during the Early Roman Period.

What's more, second-century documents confirm that Emperor Hadrian ordered a temple of Venus erected on Golgotha, possibly to erase any vestiges of Christian worship. When Queen Helena, the mother of Emperor Constantine, traveled to Jerusalem in 326 C.E. to see the site, a local bishop named Macarius took her straightaway to the Venus shrine. She ordered it torn down and replaced with the first of many successive church structures.

THE TOMB

The Mishnah, a written document of rabbinical discussions dating from the third century C.E., states that condemned men could not be buried in their family plots but in designated graveyards (Mishnah Sanhedrin 6:5). But an exception was made for Jesus. According to Mark, a man named Joseph of Arimathea, who was a member of the Sanhedrin and possibly a member of the Pharisaic faction, intervened with Pilate for the release of Jesus' body. This may suggest not only the extraordinary authority that Sanhedrin members still commanded during the early prefecture, but also the level of support that Jesus may have enjoyed among the Pharisees of the Council; Matthew even calls Joseph "a disciple" (Matthew 27:57).

For most Jews, burial involved being wrapped in a shroud and interred in a trench grave. Only the affluent could afford to carve funerary chambers for themselves in the bedrock of Jerusalem's hills, as in the case of Joseph of Arimathea. Such tombs contained niches, known as *loculi* or *kokhim,* that held the corpse until it was sufficiently decomposed for the bones to be gathered in a separate (and less space-consuming) receptacle, such as an ossuary box. This vacated the niche for another deceased family member. One good example from the time of Jesus is the complex known as the Tombs of the Sanhedrin, a collection of 63 tombs in the Jerusalem suburb of Sanhedria. Revered as a pilgrimage site since medieval times, the tombs were built on the site of an ancient quarry as four distinct burial chambers, organized on two levels. Each contained a number of *loculi* in which the remains would be interred.

In some tombs, such as the Tombs of Kings located in the Sheikh Jarrah neighborhood near Jerusalem's Old City, the chambers also included benches, but these were probably intended for visitors rather than burials. The Tombs of Kings complex also housed several sarcophagi, five of which were recovered by French archaeologist Louis Félicien de Saulcy in 1863. Two of these are now in the Louvre.

THE ROTUNDA

Most scholars accept the Church of the Sepulchre as the place of Jesus' tomb, as well as the location of Golgotha, which must have been in close proximity to one another. One of the earliest visitors to the church, a fourth-century visitor known as the "Bordeaux pilgrim," reported that the Constantinian complex contained two structures: a five-aisled basilica near the reputed location of Golgotha and a separate rotunda (known as the *anastasis*, or "resurrection") over the place of Jesus' tomb. It was, wrote the pilgrim, "a church of wondrous beauty," as no doubt it was, given that it was one of the largest Christian churches built by Roman architects at the time, second only to the large basilica that Constantine was building over the reputed place of Peter's burial on the Ager Vaticanus, or "Vatican Hill."

A similar arrangement, though of more modest dimensions, can still be seen in the 12th-century Crusader church that marks the place of Jesus' crucifixion and burial in Jerusalem today. ■

This Byzantine ivory plaque, dating from the fourth century, is one of the earliest depictions of the crucifixion of Christ.

THE FIRST APOSTOLIC MISSION

From Jerusalem to Antioch, Samaria, and Joppa

The crucifixion left Jesus' movement in disarray. The Gospels imply that at the first sign of trouble, beginning with Jesus' arrest, his disciples had scattered. Only Simon Peter had followed Jesus to the house of Caiaphas, but when confronted by one of the servants, he loudly denied knowing Jesus (Luke 22:55-72). Only the women, including Mary Magdalene, mustered the courage to stay with Jesus through his crucifixion, although John's Gospel places "the beloved disciple" on Golgotha as well (John 19:25).

The Gospels of Matthew, Luke, and John refer to a number of incidents at which the risen Jesus then appeared to his disciples. Most of these took place all over Judea and Galilee, which suggests that many followers had simply returned to their native villages to resume their former life. In one such episode, Jesus even assisted his fishermen-disciples, including Simon Peter, in securing a large haul of fish (John 21:6). But Jesus' resurrection did not imply that he would also resume the leadership of the movement he had started. In Luke's Gospel, Jesus took his followers to Bethany, where the journey of his Passion had begun, and "withdrew from them and was carried up into heaven" (Luke 24:51).

THE ROOM OF PENTECOST

The Book of Acts of the Apostles, which most likely was written by the same author who wrote the Gospel of Luke, picks up the thread of the story from here on. It portrays the followers as somewhat demoralized and rudderless as they huddled together in the "room upstairs where they were staying," immersed in meditation and prayer (Acts 1:13-14). It is possible that this was the same "large room upstairs" *(anagaion mega)* that Luke describes as the place of the Last Supper (Luke 22:12). Some believe this house is the same residence that elsewhere

in Acts is identified as the home of Mary, the mother of the disciple John Mark (Acts 12:12).

Today many Christians visit a large hall on Mount Zion—the so-called Cenacle—that tradition has identified as the place of the Last Supper. At first glance that seems rather unlikely, for the hall is built in a 14th-century Gothic style. After the Islamic conquest of Jerusalem, Suleiman the Magnificent even had it converted it into a mosque in the 16th century, complete with a Qibla ("direction") identifying the orientation toward Mecca that is still visible today. But the claim may not be without merit. According to Christian tradition, the Last Supper hall was built over a synagogue. During the 1948 war, a Jordanian shell exposed the building's foundations, which allowed archaeologist Jacob Pinkerfeld to uncover a section of ashlar stones in the Herodian style, which may—or may not—indicate the remains of a synagogue.

This is where, according to the Book of Acts, the Apostles experienced a divine intervention during the feast of Shavuot ("Weeks" in Hebrew, also known as *Pentecost*, meaning "fiftieth," since the festival occurs seven weeks after Passover, the day after 49 days). "Divided tongues, as of fire appeared among them" and inspired them to go out and proclaim the Gospel to the Shavuot pilgrims outside (Acts 2:3). Thus began the first Apostolic mission, the effort by the Apostles and their followers to continue Jesus' campaign and preach the good news of the heavenly kingdom throughout Judea and beyond.

Their efforts, says Acts, succeeded in bringing many new followers to the movement, which at this point was still fully Jewish observant. The Apostles continued to follow the precepts of the Torah, observe the Sabbath, and preach in the Temple (Acts 2:45, 15:5). But some of these new

An aerial view shows the archaeological excavations of ancient Ashdod-Yam on the coastal plain of Israel.

The Coenaculum, or Hall of the Last Supper,
located on Mount Zion, is believed by some to
have been the place of the Pentecost event.

*Now those who were scattered
went from place to place,
proclaiming the word.*

ACTS 8:4

An earthenware jug with handle and spout, excavated
in Judea, is dated to the late first or second century C.E.

followers, possibly Jews from Diaspora locations whom Acts identified as "Hellenists," did not share the Apostles' reverence toward the Temple. As expatriate Jews, their liturgical life no longer revolved around Temple rites. One outspoken Greek, a man named Stephen, loudly agitated against Temple worship and was condemned to death by the Sanhedrin. One of the men supervising the subsequent stoning was a man named Saul, who "approved of their killing him" (Acts 7:58; 8:1).

SAMARIA AND CAESAREA

Stephen's execution reignited the conflict between Caiaphas and the Jesus movement. The result was an all-out persecution that compelled the Apostles to scatter. Some left for Antioch on the Orontes in Syria, today's Antakya in southern Turkey. This city, founded by Seleucus Nicator, founder of the Seleucid Dynasty, would later emerge as a major center of early Christian activity, centered in the Jewish neighborhood of Kerateion. As we saw, the Gospel of Matthew may have been written here around 80 C.E.

Others sought refuge in towns immediately outside Judea. One of these was Philip, one of seven deacons charged with distributing food among the group of disciples, who decided to go to Samaria, the region of the Samaritans (Acts 6:5). Much to the surprise of his colleagues, Philip found a ready following with "great joy in that city." This suggests that he had been preaching in Herod's city of Sebaste, capital of Samaria (Acts 8:7-8). Encouraged, Philip next traveled to another Greek enclave in Palestine, the coastal cities between Azotus (today's Ashdod) and Herod's magnificent harbor at Caesarea. Despite the fact that he was operating right under the nose of the Roman governor, Philip felt so comfortable that he decided to settle in the city and eventually raised a large Apostolic community, which included his four daughters (Acts 21:9).

LYDDA AND JOPPA

Simon Peter, meanwhile, decided to head west from Jerusalem toward Lydda (today's Lod). Not far from Lod was the village of Joppa, one of the oldest continuously inhabited ports on Israel's coast. Peter was prevailed on to visit this village in order to try to revive a pious woman named Tabitha (or Dorcas in Greek), who had just passed away. Peter agreed, and in a close parallel to Jesus' miraculous resuscitation of the daughter of Jairus, he restored her to life (Acts 9:40).

Joppa, which today is the Tel Aviv suburb of Jaffa, was the subject of an extensive excavation campaign begun by Ze'ev Herzog in 1997. Hebrew Scripture refers to Joppa as the port of entry for cedar wood from Lebanon, used by Solomon to build the First

This ossuary, a box for the second burial of skeletal remains after the body has decomposed, is believed to have contained the bones of the high priest Caiaphas.

Temple and by Ezra for the Second (II Chronicles 2:16; Ezra 3:7). But most buildings discovered by Herzog's campaign were traced back to the Egyptian period of the 18th Dynasty, when the city (known as Yapu or Ya-Pho in the Amarna Letters) served as a major center of the Egyptian administration along the Canaanite littoral. Among others, he excavated a large hall that he ascribed to the period of the Egyptian King Amenhotep III, based on scarabs found among the ruins. Above these Late Bronze and Iron Age remains, Herzog found traces of storerooms and workshops dating to the Ptolemaic and Seleucid periods, but little of the Roman period. This was not unexpected, since the city was utterly destroyed around 67 C.E., during the First Jewish Revolt.

According to Acts, Peter accepted the invitation of a tanner named Simon to stay in Joppa. No doubt its lovely location on the Mediterranean coast had something to do with it. Here, Peter received a vision suggesting that Gentiles should be welcomed as followers as well—provided that they embraced the core tenets of the Jewish Law (Acts 10:28). ∎

The Ossuary of Caiaphas

In 1990, archaeologists made a sensational discovery in a small family tomb that contained several ossuaries from the first century C.E. The most elaborate of these boxes bore an Aramaic inscription: *Yehoseph bar Qypa*, or "Joseph Caiaphas," who may be the high priest Caiaphas who indicted Jesus. During a 2002 press conference, the Discovery Channel and the Biblical Archaeological Society announced another major discovery: an intact ossuary believed to hold the bones of James, based on an Aramaic inscription that read as follows: "James, son of Joseph, brother of Jesus." Reportedly found in the Silwan area in the Kidron Valley, the inscription has since been denounced as a forgery, though the ossuary itself may be genuine. The issue continues to be debated, however.

"The Market of Jaffa" was painted by the German artist
Gustav Bauernfeind (1848-1904) in 1887.

This gold aureus was struck during the
reign of Emperor Tiberius (14-37 C.E.).

A fifth-century Byzantine basilica in Emmaus Nicopolis
marks the location that tradition has identified with
the appearance of the risen Jesus in Emmaus.

PAUL'S JOURNEYS TO CYPRUS AND ASIA MINOR

The Apostolic Mission Moves Beyond Roman Palestine

The man who stood and watched approvingly as Stephen was stoned to death originally hailed from the city of Tarsus, the capital of Cilicia (today's southern Turkey). Highly educated and a mentee of the distinguished Pharisaic rabbi Gamaliel, Sha'ul, or "Saul," was everything that the Apostles were not. Worldly, fluent in Greek, steeped in Scripture as well as Greek philosophy and ethics, Saul saw an opportunity to boost his career in Jerusalem by vigorously persecuting Jesus' disciples. While the Apostles scattered throughout Judea and Samaria, says Acts, Saul initiated a house-by-house search for followers in Jerusalem, "dragging off both men and women" to prison (Acts 8:3). In his letter to the Galatians, written many years later, Saul confessed his ambition to advance "beyond many among my people of the same age, for I was more zealous for the traditions of my ancestors" (Galatians 1:14). His police action was largely successful, for Jerusalem would never again serve as an influential center of early Christianity.

DAMASCUS

Having exhausted his search in the city, Saul turned his attention to the places where the Apostles had reputedly found refuge. He settled on Damascus in Syria. This was a surprising choice, for Damascus fell outside the jurisdiction of the Sanhedrin, and up to this point it had not figured in the Acts narrative as a center of Apostolic activity. Entirely rebuilt by the Romans after its conquest by Pompey in 64 B.C.E., Damascus was a leading Greco-Roman city of the Decapolis. Prior to the devastation wrought by the Syrian civil war begun in 2011, much of Old Damascus still retained the grid of the Roman city, with a cardo and *decumanus maximus* at its core. Governed by Philip as part of his tetrarchy until his death in 33 C.E., the city was briefly ruled by the Roman governor in Antioch before Caligula transferred it to the Nabataean kingdom of King Aretas IV (whose daughter had once been married to

A simple earthenware pitcher with a narrow neck and handle may have been used to serve wine.

Herod Antipas). Acts claims that there were several synagogues in the city, which seems plausible given the city's prominent place in the Diaspora.

But Saul never got that far. Riding on the road to Damascus, "a light from heaven flashed around him." As he fell to the ground, a voice spoke, "Saul, why do you persecute me?" (Acts 9:4; 26:14). Brought to Damascus by his companions, he experienced a conversion and was baptized.

ANTIOCH

To say that news of Saul's conversion was met with surprise would be an understatement. Few people in the Apostolic circles believed him, and they suspected that Saul was merely trying to infiltrate the movement. A similar hostile reception awaited him on his return to Jerusalem; the Greek faction, which seemed to have briefly gained the upper hand in the Apostolic movement, even tried to assassinate him (Acts 9:26-29). In response, Saul withdrew from the Apostolic community altogether and decided to go his own way—with major consequences for the growth of early Christianity.

A new opportunity beckoned. A disciple named Barnabas had asked him to come to Antioch, capital of Roman Syria, where enthusiasm for Jesus' teachings was growing by leaps and bounds. It is here, in Antioch, that the term "Christians" (*Christianos* in Greek) was coined to identify the followers of Jesus, or "Christ" (the Greek translation of Messiah or "Anointed One"; Acts 11:21).

Saul's activity in Antioch was a watershed moment. He was stunned to find that while Jewish communities rebuffed him, many Syrian Gentiles were rather intrigued with the teachings of Jesus. This inspired him to undertake missionary journeys to other urban centers in the eastern Mediterranean, regardless of whether they had large Jewish centers.

ca 52
Antonius Felix replaces Ventidius Cumanus as Roman procurator

ca 57
Paul writes his letter to the Romans

ca 58
Putative date of Paul's arrest in Jerusalem and transfer to Caesarea

ca 60
Porcius Festus replaces Antonius Felix as Roman procurator of Judea

The remains of the massive temple of Apollo in Didyma, where a major oracle was located, illustrates the wealth of the coastal communities of Asia Minor.

As I was on my way and drew near to Damascus, about noon a great light from heaven suddenly shone around me.

ACTS OF THE APOSTLES 22:6

ca 60
Putative date of Paul's
embarkation for Rome

ca 62
Heron of Alexandria designs
a steam engine, water clock,
and water fountain

ca 62
Lucceius Albinus replaces
Porcius Festus as
Roman procurator

ca 62
James, head of the Jerusalem
Church, is killed by
the high priest Ananus

CYPRUS

Together with another disciple called John Mark, Paul and Barnabas then decided to cross over to Cyprus, Barnabas's native region. The plan was for Saul to preach in synagogues throughout the island, from Salamis to Paphos, the Cypriot capital. At this point in the Acts narrative, the name of Saul is suddenly changed to "Paul"—a most telling decision. By switching from the Hebrew "Sha'ul" to its Roman version, "Paulus," at the start of his journey, Paul demonstrated his willingness to adapt his message to a Greco-Roman audience. Indeed, the Cyprus tour was surprisingly successful. Though Acts makes no mention of conversions among the Jewish population, Paul was able to win over a prominent figure—none other than the Roman proconsul, Sergius Paulus. A boundary stone from the reign of Claudius, discovered in Rome in 1887, identifies one of the curators of the Tiber River Authority as Sergius Paulus. Since the stone dates from 47 C.E., this would suggest that Paul's first missionary journey took place in the early to mid 40s, before Sergius Paulus was recalled to Rome.

PERGE AND PISIDIA

From Cyprus, Paul crossed over to Perge on the Pamphylian coast, at which point John Mark decided to return to Jerusalem (Acts 13:13). Though they moved on shortly afterward, Paul would later return to Perge and preach there (Acts 14:25). Poised between the Catarrhactes and Cestrus Rivers, Perge was a highly affluent city. Today it is a major tourist attraction on the coast of southern Turkey, with a well-preserved theater, agora, and stadium—dating from the first and second centuries C.E.

From Perge, Paul and Barnabas traveled to Antioch-in-Pisidia, so known to distinguish it from other cities named after Antiochus. Several decades earlier, Augustus had designated the place as a major settlement area for veterans who had honorably retired from service. As a result, the city had become more Roman and Latinized than the surrounding area. Whether this played a role in the reception to Paul's teachings is not clear. According to Acts, many among the Gentiles "became believers," even though the local Jewish community once again rebuffed him (Acts 13:48).

ICONIUM AND LYSTRA

This type of response was repeated as Paul continued on to Iconium in Roman Lycaonia (today's Konya in Turkey's Central Anatolian District), and the city of Lystra, another 20 miles distant. Here, the animosity of the Jewish community was so strong that Paul was nearly stoned to death (Acts 14:19). By that time, Paul realized that the success of his mission depended less on his ability to convert Jews than on finding a way to welcome the far more numerous and receptive Gentiles. As we saw, Peter had had a similar experience, but he still insisted that Gentile converts should also adopt the Jewish faith and practice, including circumcision. For many

Miletus, a main city of Lydia on Asia Minor during the Roman period, was visited by Paul around 57 C.E.

Gentiles, this was obviously a major deterrent, as Paul well knew. In response, he began to develop a theology that differed substantially from that taught by the original Apostles.

In Paul's view, the saving grace of Christ was meant for all who believed in him, whether Jew or Gentile. Consequently, there was no need to embrace Judaism, for Paul argued that the Jewish Law

had actually been superseded by baptism and faith in Christ. "Real circumcision is a matter of the heart," he wrote in his letter to the Romans; "it is spiritual, not literal" (Romans 2:29). Therefore, Gentiles who agreed to be baptized did not need to be circumcised or follow the kosher laws and rules of ritual purity. "A person is justified not by the works of the Law," Paul wrote, "but through faith in Jesus Christ" (Galatians 2:16).

What this meant, of course, is that Paul's idea of early Christianity would abandon its roots in Second Temple Judaism. And it was this

kerygma, Paul's interpretation of who Jesus was and what his teachings meant, that would emerge triumphant among several other early Christianities, as we will see shortly.

THE JERUSALEM CONFERENCE

Naturally, word of Paul's activity among the Gentiles was met with surprise and concern at the remaining Apostolic mission in Jerusalem. Now led by James, the brother of Jesus, this group had always firmly believed that "unless you are circumcised according to the

This theater in Miletus, a city in Asia Minor that Paul visited during his third journey, was built in the second century C.E.

custom of Moses, you cannot be saved" (Acts 15:1). Inevitably, these two viewpoints were bound to clash.

That confrontation took place during a meeting in Jerusalem around 46 or 47 C.E. Paul's visit to the city was prompted by a terrible famine in Judea, which is described in the books by Josephus. According to Acts, Paul was asked to bring desperately needed supplies from Antioch, though in his letters, he wrote that the purpose of the visit was to defend his work among the Gentiles (Acts 11:27-30; Galatians 2:1-10). The essential question came down to this: If a Gentile's faith in Christ was true, why then should he or she also be required to observe the Law and be

The Son of God

Unlike the synoptic Gospels, Paul emphasized the nature of Jesus as the Son of God rather than the Jewish Messiah. This filial relationship, however, is defined in Jewish terms. In contrast to Luke's Nativity narrative, Paul's letter to the Romans argued that Jesus' biological lineage ran from Joseph back to David "according to the flesh" (Romans 1:3); it was only by virtue of his resurrection from the dead, by the power of the Spirit, that he became the Son of God. The Second Epistle to Timothy, probably written by a disciple of Paul on his behalf, urges its listeners to "remember Jesus Christ, raised from the dead, a descendant of David" (*ek spermatos David*, literally "from the seed of David"; II Timothy 2:8). The idea that a mortal man could still be endowed by the divine spirit as the son of God was fully in line with Hebrew Scripture (II Samuel 7:14).

A 12th-century Byzantine mosaic of Jesus was created for Hagia Sophia in Constantinople, now Istanbul.

circumcised? "Is [God] not the God of Gentiles also?" Paul later wrote (Romans 3:29).

The Jerusalem group did not agree. Even Peter, who had actively worked with Gentile believers in Joppa and Caesarea, now switched sides—"for fear of the circumcision faction," Paul wrote bitterly (Galatians 2:12). Thus, the Jerusalem conference ended in an agreement to disagree. Paul could continue to baptize Gentiles in Syria and Asia Minor if he so desired, while the Jerusalem group would focus their work on circumcised believers only, provided all agreed on one condition: that Gentile followers abstain from defiled things (such as idolatry), illicit sexual activity, and any meat of an animal that had been strangled or contained any blood (Acts 15:20). These so-called Laws of Noah, later cataloged in a compilation known as the *tosefta,* had traditionally been imposed on all foreigners living in Israel (Leviticus 17:10).

Relieved, Paul left Jerusalem, even more determined to propagate his teachings among the Gentiles, not only among the cities in lower Asia Minor but throughout the Mediterranean world. ■

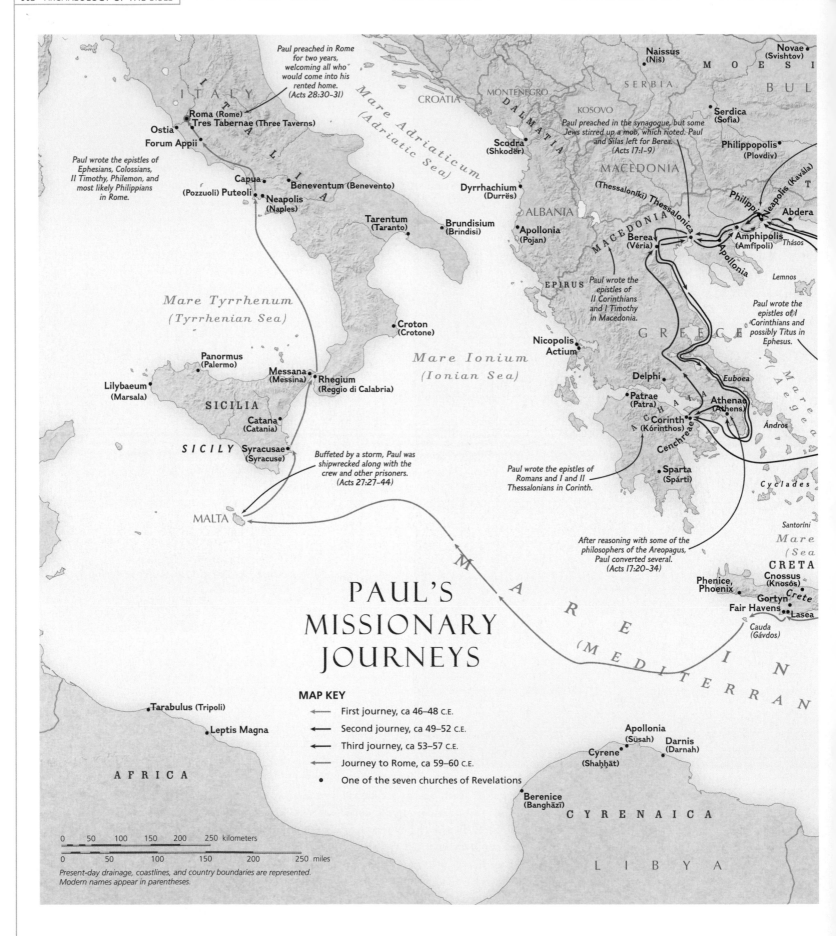

Paul preached in Rome for two years, welcoming all who would come into his rented home. (Acts 28:30–31)

Paul wrote the epistles of Ephesians, Colossians, II Timothy, Philemon, and most likely Philippians in Rome.

Buffeted by a storm, Paul was shipwrecked along with the crew and other prisoners. (Acts 27:27–44)

Paul preached in the synagogue, but some Jews stirred up a mob, which rioted. Paul and Silas left for Berea. (Acts 17:1–9)

Paul wrote the epistles of II Corinthians and I Timothy in Macedonia.

Paul wrote the epistles of I Corinthians and possibly Titus in Ephesus.

Paul wrote the epistles of Romans and I and II Thessalonians in Corinth.

After reasoning with some of the philosophers of the Areopagus, Paul converted several. (Acts 17:20–34)

ITALY
Roma (Rome)
Tres Tabernae (Three Taverns)
Ostia
Forum Appii
Capua
(Pozzuoli) Puteoli
Beneventum (Benevento)
Neapolis (Naples)
Tarentum (Taranto)
Brundisium (Brindisi)

CROATIA
MONTENEGRO
SERBIA
KOSOVO
DALMATIA
Scodra (Shkodër)
Dyrrhachium (Durrës)
ALBANIA
Apollonia (Pojan)
EPIRUS

Naissus (Niš)
Novae (Svishtov)
M O E S I
B U L
Serdica (Sofia)
Philippopolis (Plovdiv)
MACEDONIA
(Thessaloníki) Thessalonica
Berea (Véria)
Apollonia
Philippi
Neapolis (Kavála)
Abdera
Amphipolis (Amfípoli)
Thásos
Lemnos

Mare Adriaticum (Adriatic Sea)

Mare Tyrrhenum (Tyrrhenian Sea)

Croton (Crotone)

Mare Ionium (Ionian Sea)

Panormus (Palermo)
Messana (Messina)
Rhegium (Reggio di Calabria)
Lilybaeum (Marsala)
SICILIA
Catana (Catania)
SICILY
Syracusae (Syracuse)

Nicopolis
Actium
GREECE
Delphi
Patrae (Patra)
Athenae (Athens)
Corinth (Kórinthos)
Cenchreae
Sparta (Spárti)
ACHAIA
Euboea
Mare Aegea
Ándros
Cyclades
Santoríni
Mare (Sea)

MALTA

PAUL'S MISSIONARY JOURNEYS

M A R E   I N

(M E D I T E R R A N

Phenice, Phoenix
Cnossus (Knosós)
CRETA
CRETE
Gortyn
Fair Havens
Lasea
Cauda (Gávdos)

MAP KEY

→ First journey, ca 46–48 C.E.
→ Second journey, ca 49–52 C.E.
→ Third journey, ca 53–57 C.E.
→ Journey to Rome, ca 59–60 C.E.
• One of the seven churches of Revelations

Tarabulus (Tripoli)
Leptis Magna
AFRICA

Apollonia (Sūsah)
Darnis (Darnah)
Cyrene (Shaḥḥāt)
Berenice (Banghāzī)
C Y R E N A I C A
L I B Y A

0   50   100   150   200   250 kilometers
0   50   100   150   200   250 miles

Present-day drainage, coastlines, and country boundaries are represented. Modern names appear in parentheses.

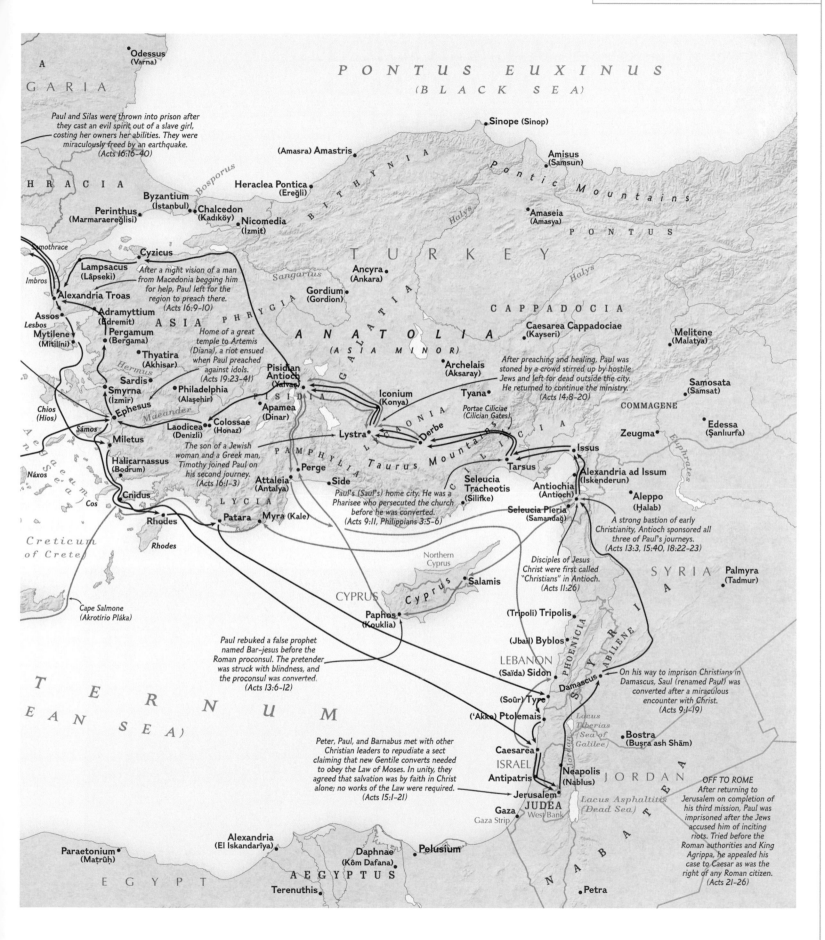

A

GARIA

Odessus
(Varna)

PONTUS EUXINUS
(BLACK SEA)

THRACIA

Paul and Silas were thrown into prison after
they cast an evil spirit out of a slave girl,
costing her owners her abilities. They were
miraculously freed by an earthquake.
(Acts 16:16-40)

Sinope (Sinop)

(Amasra) **Amastris**

Amisus
(Samsun)

Bosporus

Heraclea Pontica
(Ereğli)

B I T H Y N I A

Amaseia
(Amasya)

Pontic Mountains

Byzantium
(İstanbul) **Chalcedon**
(Kadıköy)
Perinthus
(Marmaraereğlisi) **Nicomedia**
(İzmit)

P O N T U S

Samothrace

Cyzicus

Imbros

Lampsacus
(Lâpseki)

After a night vision of a man
from Macedonia begging him
for help, Paul left for the
region to preach there.
(Acts 16:9-10)

Ancyra
(Ankara)

T U R K E Y

Sangarius

Gordium
(Gordion)

Halys

Caesarea Cappadociae
(Kayseri)

C A P P A D O C I A

Melitene
(Malatya)

Alexandria Troas

Assos

Lesbos

Adramyttium
(Edremit)

Pergamum
(Bergama)

A S I A P H R Y G I A

A N A T O L I A

(A S I A   M I N O R)

G A L A T I A

Archelais
(Aksaray)

COMMAGENE

Mytilene
(Mitilíni)

Thyatira
(Akhisar)

Home of a great
temple to Artemis
(Diana), a riot ensued
when Paul preached
against idols.
(Acts 19:23-41)

**Pisidian
Antioch**
(Yalvaç)

Iconium
(Konya)

Tyana

After preaching and healing, Paul was
stoned by a crowd stirred up by hostile
Jews and left for dead outside the city.
He returned to continue the ministry.
(Acts 14:8-20)

Edessa
(Şanlıurfa)

Hermus

Sardis

Smyrna
(İzmir)

Philadelphia
(Alaşehir)

Chios
(Híos)

Maeander

Ephesus

Laodicea
(Denizli)

Colossae
(Honaz)

Apamea
(Dinar)

P I S I D I A

Lystra

L Y C A O N I A

Derbe

Portae Ciliciae
(Cilician Gates)

C I L I C I A

Zeugma

Samosata
(Samsat)

Euphrates

Samos

Miletus

The son of a Jewish
woman and a Greek man,
Timothy joined Paul on
his second journey.
(Acts 16:1-3)

P A M P H Y L I A

Taurus Mountains

Issus

Tarsus

Alexandria ad Issum
(İskenderun)

Aleppo
(Halab)

Halicarnassus
(Bodrum)

Perge

Side

**Seleucia
Tracheotis**
(Silifke)

Antiochia
(Antioch)

S Y R I A

Palmyra
(Tadmur)

Aegean Sea

Cnidus

Attaleia
(Antalya)

Paul's (Saul's) home city. He was
a Pharisee who persecuted the church
before he was converted.
(Acts 9:11, Philippians 3:5-6)

Seleucia Pieria
(Samandağ)

Cos

L Y C I A

Rhodes

*Creticum
of Crete*

Rhodes

Patara

Myra (Kale)

*Northern
Cyprus*

A strong bastion of early
Christianity, Antioch sponsored all
three of Paul's journeys.
(Acts 13:3, 15:40, 18:22-23)

Cape Salmone
(Akrotírio Pláka)

CYPRUS

Cyprus

Salamis

Disciples of Jesus
Christ were first called
"Christians" in Antioch.
(Acts 11:26)

(Tripoli) **Tripolis**
(Tripoli)

Paphos
(Kouklia)

(Jbail) **Byblos**

Paul rebuked a false prophet
named Bar-jesus before the
Roman proconsul. The pretender
was struck with blindness, and
the proconsul was converted.
(Acts 13:6-12)

LEBANON

(Saïda) **Sidon**

P H O E N I C I A

TERNUM

EAN SEA)

Damascus

On his way to imprison Christians in
Damascus, Saul (renamed Paul) was
converted after a miraculous
encounter with Christ.
(Acts 9:1-19)

(Soûr) **Tyre**

ABILENE

*Lacus
Tiberias
(Sea of
Galilee)*

Bostra
(Buşra ash Shām)

('Akko) **Ptolemais**

Jordan

Peter, Paul, and Barnabus met with other
Christian leaders to repudiate a sect
claiming that new Gentile converts needed
to obey the Law of Moses. In unity, they
agreed that salvation was by faith in Christ
alone; no works of the Law were required.
(Acts 15:1-21)

Caesarea

ISRAEL

Antipatris

Neapolis
(Nâblus)

J O R D A N

OFF TO ROME
After returning to
Jerusalem on completion of
his third mission, Paul was
imprisoned after the Jews
accused him of inciting
riots. Tried before the
Roman authorities and King
Agrippa, he appealed his
case to Caesar as was the
right of any Roman citizen.
(Acts 21-26)

Jerusalem

JUDEA

Gaza

Gaza Strip

West Bank

*Lacus Asphaltitis
(Dead Sea)*

N A B A T E A

Alexandria
(El İskandarîya)

Daphnae
(Kôm Dafana)

Pelusium

E G Y P T

A E G Y P T U S

Paraetonium
(Maţrûḥ)

Terenuthis

Petra

PAUL'S JOURNEY TO GREECE AND ROME

Missionary Activity Spreads Across the Mediterranean

The first journey to Asia Minor had yielded mixed results, but the Jerusalem conference had essentially freed Paul to pursue his mission as he saw fit. That he believed he was guided by the Spirit, of that there was no doubt. Although Paul had never met or heard Jesus in the flesh (something of which he was very much aware), he nonetheless claimed to have seen the resurrected Jesus, just as Jesus had appeared to the Apostles. "Am I not an apostle?" he would later write, rather defensively, to the Corinthians; "Have I not seen Jesus our Lord?" (I Corinthians 9:1).

Furthermore, Paul was convinced of the righteousness of his mission to the Gentiles. He had seen firsthand how people throughout the empire, citizen or slave, yearned for an end to the senseless social divisions of the Roman world. He had witnessed the rapture in their eyes as they listened to the promise of a savior who had showed them a path to salvation in heaven and had performed miracles to prove it. The Roman world was ripe for a new form of spirituality, a true spirituality, rather than the Roman state religion that had devolved into a political farce, a cult of imperial propaganda.

In autumn 49, Paul embarked on a second, even more ambitious journey to Asia Minor. Its purpose was to revisit and strengthen the communities he had founded in years past while trying to reach the more affluent and cosmopolitan cities in the West. Barnabas insisted that John Mark should go with them, but Paul refused. In response, Barnabas went with John Mark to Cyprus and was never heard from again. Instead, Paul was accompanied by a disciple called Silas, while in Lystra he found a young man named Timothy who would become one of his most devoted assistants (Timothy 1:1-8).

THE CROSSING TO GREECE
In accordance with their original plan, the group traveled northward into Phrygia, perhaps with the goal of canvassing the Ionian coast, starting with Alexandria Troas (near today's Bozcaada, on

This limestone fragment from Corinth may refer to "Erastus, the city treasurer," who is described in Paul's letter to the Romans.

ca 64
Nero blames the Christians in Rome for a fire that ravaged the city

ca 64
Traditional date for the deaths of Peter and Paul in Rome

ca 64
Gessius Florus replaces Lucceius Albinus as Roman procurator of Judea

ca 65
Seneca is ordered by Nero to commit suicide

In the theater of Ephesus, Paul's companions became embroiled in a dispute with artisans selling statuettes of Artemis in the Temple of Artemis.

We set sail from Troas and took a straight course to Samothrace, the following day to Neapolis, and from there to Philippi.

ACTS OF THE APOSTLES 16:11-12

Most Roman keys were made of bronze by fusing together a mass-produced handle with a shank with custom-made pins.

ca 66	ca 66-70	ca 67	ca 68
Outbreak of the Jewish Rebellion against the Romans in Palestine	Mark writes his Gospel, the oldest of the four canonical Gospels	General Vespasian arrives in Galilee to suppress the Jewish Rebellion	Emperor Nero commits suicide and is succeeded by Galba

These recently excavated terrace houses in Ephesus featured richly decorated rooms that show the high standard of living during the Roman period.

the northern tip of Turkey's western coast). This port city had been built as a strategic bridge between Asia and Europe by Antigonus, another general of Alexander who would establish the lesser-known Antigonid Dynasty. Fittingly, this is where Paul had a vision. He was told to cross the Hellespont and thus bring the good news to the heartland of Greece. At this point, the narrative of Acts suddenly changes from the third to the first person ("we immediately tried to cross over to Macedonia"), which suggests that the author known as Luke had now joined Paul's entourage (Acts 16:10).

Landing at Neapolis in Macedonia, the group made their way to nearby Philippi, where remnants of the famed Via Egnatia are still visible today. Whether this highway was already in place in Paul's day is the subject of debate; although Strabo refers to it in his *Geographica*, published around 23 C.E., it is not clear whether this vast, 550-mile road was fully completed at the time. During the second century, it would reach its fullest extent as the main artery connecting the cities along the Adriatic coast with the Bosporus and the vast hinterland of Asia Minor beyond.

ATHENS

Despite harassment from Jewish protesters in Thessalonica, who denounced him as an apostate, Paul succeeded in establishing a number of early Christian communities in Macedonia. He then continued south, along the Aegean coast to Attica, where the great city of Athens was beckoning him. Now little more than a provincial city in Roman Achaia, Athens nevertheless retained much of its former grandeur, despite the ravages wrought by Sulla in 85 B.C.E. With many of its classical monuments lovingly restored by Augustus, Athens still prided itself on its prominence as the cultural heart of the Roman Empire. Indeed, it still enjoyed the status of a free city precisely so that its schools could flourish unperturbed.

Steeped in Greek philosophy and Stoic ethics himself, Paul must have felt a great yearning to see the fabled city—and to match his wits against its sages in the Agora, where Socrates had once taught. In this he was not disappointed. Taken to Areopagus Hill, from where one could gaze up to the white marble of the Acropolis glistening in the sun, Paul was asked about the meaning of his teachings. What kind of philosophy did he subscribe to? In response, Paul noted that he had seen an altar in the city with the inscription *Agnosto Theo*, "to an unknown God." "What therefore you worship as unknown," he added, "this I proclaim to you" (Acts 17:23).

CORINTH

From Athens it was only a 60-mile journey to the actual capital of Roman Greece, the city of Corinth. Once the largest of all cities in the classical age, Corinth had been utterly destroyed by Roman General Lucius Mummius in 146 B.C.E. It lay abandoned until Julius Caesar, feeling some remorse over the destruction of this lovely city, decided to rebuild it—albeit with the purpose of having it populated by pliable Roman colonists. Although Caesar was assassinated shortly afterward, the experiment succeeded; by the time of Paul's visit, Corinth was once again a prosperous city with a highly diverse population of Roman colonists, native Greeks, and Diaspora Jews. Paul felt so much at home here that he stayed for 18 months, before returning to Asia Minor.

Two years later, around 55 C.E., he felt drawn to the Corinthian community once more. In his letter to the Romans, written in Corinth, Paul refers to "Erastus, the city treasurer," who is quite possibly the aedile—an administrator responsible for public buildings and festivals—listed on a first-century limestone fragment found in Corinth in 1929 (Romans 16:23).

EPHESUS

The only other city to challenge Corinth as a major center of Paul's missionary activity is Ephesus on the coast of Ionia. Though he briefly stayed in the city on the return leg of his second voyage, Ephesus would become Paul's principal base during the third journey, which historians date between 53 and 57 C.E. Here, he came into conflict with local craftsmen who made a living selling statues of the principal deity in Ephesus, the mother goddess Artemis Ephesia, to tourists. Artemis—a different deity from the Greek Artemis, the goddess of the hunt—was venerated in a massive fourth-century temple known as the Artemision. The craftsmen and silversmiths feared that Paul's proselytizing would rob them of their trade to pilgrims. They staged a protest in the city theater, which forced Paul to cut his stay short.

JERUSALEM

After these events, Paul left on his fateful journey to Jerusalem. Here, news of his missionary activities

A Roman copy depicts the Artemis Ephesia, a mother goddess native to Asia Minor who was venerated in the vast Artemision Temple in Ephesus.

Conflict in Corinth

According to Acts, Paul found strong opposition to his teachings among the local Jewish community of Corinth. In fact, they decided to take him to court, accusing him of "persuading people to worship God in ways that are contrary to the law." The presiding judge, the proconsul of Achaia named Gallio, dismissed the charge (Acts 18:12-17). As a polytheistic culture, Rome was tolerant of a wide variety of cults as long as these did not threaten Roman religion. Gallio happened to be the brother of the Roman author Seneca. In the early 20th century, archaeologists found an inscription in the city of Delphi with a reference to a governor named "L. Iunius Gallio" from 52 C.E., which allows us to date Paul's visit.

among Gentiles had caught up with him—not only among the Apostles but also the Jerusalem community altogether. As he tried to enter the Temple, he was arrested by a mob on charges that he "is teaching everyone everywhere against our people, our law, and this place" (Acts 21:28). He was even accused of bringing Gentiles past the *soreg,* the boundary that marked the sacred area reserved only for Jews—an offense punishable by death. The Romans prevaricated, however; unlike Jesus and the Apostles, Paul was a Roman citizen. While the chief priests in Jerusalem demanded that Paul stand trial before the Sanhedrin, Paul successfully appealed to his right of *provocatio,* of being heard by an imperial tribunal in Rome (Acts 25:10). Although the date is uncertain, it is generally believed that Paul embarked on a prisoner ship bound for Rome around 60 C.E. ∎

Now after these things had been accomplished,
Paul resolved in the Spirit to go through Macedonia and Achaia,
and then to go on to Jerusalem.

ACTS OF THE APOSTLES 19:21

EARLY CHRISTIANITY IN ROME

An Early Christian Community Becomes the Nucleus of the Movement

Although Rome has traditionally been the center of Christianity, the origins of its first Christian congregations are rather difficult to determine. Many historians accept the current theory that word about Jesus first circulated among Rome's synagogues in the 30s. Some of these synagogues were probably founded by Alexandrian Jews in the second century B.C.E., when Rome was steadily growing as the dominant economic and political power in the Mediterranean. Scores of inscriptions found in local Jewish catacombs are in Greek rather than Latin.

Jewish life in Rome was interrupted by the praetor Hispanus, who briefly expelled all nonnative Jews (as well as other foreigners) in 139 B.C.E., but a century later, the Jewish contingent in Rome was once again flourishing. It was also sufficiently prominent for Julius Caesar to take notice. As we saw, both Caesar and his heir, Octavian, not only formally recognized Judaism as a religion of the realm but also granted its followers certain privileges—such as exemption from military service, rights of assembly, and the right to observe the Sabbath. Moreover, Augustus authorized the collection of temple tithes throughout the Roman Empire and decreed "that their sacred offerings shall be inviolable," exempt from Roman taxation.

All this suggests a generally positive and constructive relationship between Judaism and the Roman state under the Julio-Claudian dynasty, further illustrated by the fact that many prominent young Judeans (including Herod Agrippa) were sent to Rome to be educated. Jewish philosopher and historian Philo wrote that Augustus respected Jewish congregations and "knew that they had houses of prayer and gatherings within them."

The exception is Claudius's decree in 49 C.E. that expelled the Jews from Rome, although Roman historian Suetonius is careful to identify the reason: that "the Jews constantly made disturbances at the instigation of Chrestus." This suggests that these tensions were internal, between observant Jews and Christian Jews within Rome's

synagogues. Research by Peter Lampe has also shown that Christian communities in Rome were highly diverse, ranging from relatively affluent house chapels, such as the one led by Priscilla and Aquila, to so-called tenement churches, which were located in some of the worst slums in the city. Such socioeconomic factors may have contributed to the tensions between Jewish and Gentile followers of Christ.

THE FIRST CHRISTIANS

In 56 C.E., Paul decided to write a letter to Roman Christians even though he had never set foot in the city and could not claim any role in shaping the Christian presence there. Nevertheless, Paul recognized the importance of the Christian movement in Rome and hoped to secure its support for a new project he had in mind: an evangelizing mission to Spain (Romans 15:24).

Consequently, Paul's letter to the Romans is clearly addressed to a community that was already familiar with much of Jesus' life and teachings. It is perhaps significant that this letter was sent less than two years after the death of Claudius in 54 C.E., when his edict expelling the Jews was rescinded. Several scholars believe that the expulsion order had allowed the Gentile faction among Rome's early Christians to become ascendant and that this inevitably led to conflict when Jewish Christians—including Paul's friends Aquila and Priscilla—were allowed to return. Paul appears to address this conflict when he writes, "Why do you pass judgment on your brother or sister?" (Romans 14:10). But in the next passage, he appears to side with the Gentile faction when he suggests that those who still observe the Jewish Law, including the kosher laws, are "weak in faith."

THE GREAT FIRE

It is in this climate of heightened tensions among Rome's Christian communities that Nero came to power. Although this is often little acknowledged, the new emperor was actually quite popular for the first few years of his reign. He often

This marble bust of Emperor Claudius (r. 41-54 C.E.) from Thasos probably dates from the beginning of his reign.

ca 69	ca 69	ca 70	ca 73
Rome is ruled by three emperors: Galba, Otho, and Vitellius	Vespasian is acclaimed emperor	Titus captures Jerusalem and destroys the Second Temple	Josephus writes *History of the Jewish War*

The Domus Aurea, or "Golden House," was a large villa built by Emperor Nero after the Great Fire of 64 C.E. had destroyed many aristocratic residences on the Palatine Hill.

The outline of the Circus Maximus in Rome is still visible near the ruins of the Domus Augustana, a wing of Domitian's imperial palace on Palatine Hill.

ca 73	ca 75	ca 75-90	ca 79
Jewish rebels on Masada commit mass suicide	Vespasian begins constructing the Colosseum	Putative date of the Gospel of Matthew	Titus succeeds his father, Vespasian, as emperor

promoted social causes, which must have endeared him to many Christians, such as protecting the rights of freedmen or the advancement of a tax cut that greatly benefited the lower classes. But increasingly Nero was distracted by his zeal for the arts. He began to lavish great sums on the construction of theaters, gymnasiums, and gladiatorial circuses, and he often took part in performances himself. Christians generally shunned such amusements, as Nero may have known.

In the sixth year of Nero's rule, around 60 C.E., Paul arrived in Rome to await his trial after being shipwrecked on Malta. Placed under house arrest, he reached out to the "local leaders of the Jews" and strenuously tried to "convince them about Jesus both from the law of Moses and from the prophets." As before, the outcome of his efforts was uneven. "Some were convinced by what he had said," Acts says, "while others refused to believe." Frustrated, Paul warned them that "this salvation of God has been sent to the Gentiles; they will listen" (Acts 28:17-28). It seemed a perfect summary of his long evangelizing campaign among the Gentiles of the realm.

Four years later, on July 18, 64 C.E., a great fire broke out in several shops abutting the Circus Maximus, where many flammable goods were kept. Whipped up by strong winds, the fire gradually consumed or damaged two-thirds of the city and was not brought under control for five days. Soon rumors began to circulate that Nero had deliberately started the fire in order to clear ground for a massive new palace complex, the Domus Aurea ("Golden House"), on the Palatine Hill. Many modern historians are inclined to reject this notion, since the fire did not start close to the Palatine proper; in fact, much of Nero's current palace went up in flames as well. But most accounts do affirm that Nero decided to blame the fire on Rome's Christian community, perhaps to deflect rumors that his zeal for building had inspired the conflagration. As Tacitus wrote, Christians had become "a class hated for their abominations." A great persecution was launched, and many Christians were hideously tortured. According to one source, Nero used Christian men and women, drenched in oil, as human torches in his gardens at night.

Roman state persecution would abate under Vespasian and Titus but then flare up again under Domitian, when many scholars believe the Book of Revelation was written. The reference to the "beast" in Revelation as the number "666" may be a reference to "Neron Kaisar" (Emperor Nero), since the 22 letters of the Hebrew alphabet all have a numerical value. Similarly, the book's references to Babylon probably allude to Rome (Revelation 13:18).

THE MARTYRDOM OF PAUL AND PETER

Bishop Ignatius of Antioch, who was active during this period of Flavian rule, wrote that Paul was swept up in Nero's persecution and executed. Other Church fathers, including Tertullian and Eusebius, later wrote that he was beheaded, which is why Paul's attribute in Christian art is a sword. Another tradition holds that Peter happened to be in the city as well, though there is no indication in the Book

The Burial Place of Peter

According to Church tradition, Peter was buried on a hill called the Ager Vaticanus. In the early 1940s, Pope Pius XII ordered an excavation underneath the current St. Peter's basilica to determine if the tomb of St. Peter could be found. The excavators did discover a white marble *aedicule* (or "shrine") that corresponds to a description of Peter's tomb by a second-century pilgrim named Gaius. Although the grave was empty, the team discovered the remains of a 60-year-old man within one of the nearby stucco walls. In 1950, Pius XII declared that the bones of St. Peter had been found, although the pope admitted that "it is impossible to prove with certainty that they belong to the Apostle."

Underneath St. Peter's basilica, excavators found a pre-Constantinian necropolis including an aedicule, or shrine, that some associate with the remains of the Apostle Peter.

of Acts as to when or why Peter would have made the journey to the Roman capital. The earliest references to Peter's presence in the city appear in the work of Clement of Alexandria and Irenaeus of Lyons, who wrote that both Peter and Paul were responsible for establishing the first Christian community in Rome. While most modern scholars dispute that view, the idea that Peter was martyred and subsequently buried on Vatican Hill has found broad acceptance.

According to Church tradition, other Apostles also died a martyr's death, either in Roman Palestine or Asia Minor, with the exception of John, son of Zebedee. If that is true, then by 66 C.E., just before the outbreak of the First Jewish War, all the principal leaders of the Apostolic mission had been killed. ∎

TIMBER FRAMES TO
REINFORCE WINDOW BAYS

MORTARED RUBBLE
WITH BRICK
OR PLASTER FACING

MAIN STREET
THAT IS PAVED

WEATHERPROOF
TERRA-COTTA TILES

STONE MARKERS TO SHIELD
PEDESTRIAN TRAFFIC

*Various Christian communities were concentrated in the poorer neighborhoods
of Rome, such as this reconstruction of a working-class street in the third century C.E.*

*That night the Lord stood near
him and said, "Keep up your
courage! For just as you have
testified for me in Jerusalem,
so you must bear witness
also in Rome."*

ACTS OF THE APOSTLES 23:11

*A Roman bust depicts Emperor Nero
(r. 54-68 C.E.), who was responsible
for initiating the first state-sanctioned
persecution of Christians.*

EARLY CHRISTIANITY IN THE DIASPORA

Different Christian Movements,
With Their Own Gospels, Begin to Circulate

The Book of Acts depicts the growth of early Christianity as the direct result of the Apostolic mission, and particularly the proselytizing efforts of Peter and Paul. But their campaigns cannot be solely responsible for the rapid spread of early Christianity throughout the eastern Mediterranean and beyond. Modern research by scholars such as Elaine Pagels and Bart Ehrman has shown that, by contrast, a number of other Christian movements were circulating in the region in the decades after the crucifixion. Many of these currents did not conform to Paul's idea of salvation through the Resurrection, and instead emphasized the meaning of Jesus' teachings. Paul was well aware of these alternate movements and fought them whenever he could. For example, after Paul founded the Galatian community, it was approached by Jewish Christians whose message was strikingly different from his own. And although Paul dismissed these proselytizers as "troublemakers," he was sufficiently concerned to urge Timothy to remain in Ephesus to in order to prevent such "heresy" from affecting the church in Ephesus (Galatians 1:7; I Timothy 3-5).

That different ideas about Jesus could circulate in the decades after the Passion events was due to several factors. Most important, there was as yet no authoritative document that described the principal tenets of Jesus' teachings, notably his Kingdom of God doctrine. In an age without mass media other than the rostrum and the spoken word, the memory of Jesus was communicated largely by oral means. Inevitably, these oral traditions began to diverge, depending on the interests and concerns of individual communities. This certainly explains the differences in the four Gospels, but it also suggests the presence of what Ehrman has called multiple "Lost Christianities."

GNOSTICISM

One particular branch of nonconformist Christianity, known as Gnosticism, probably emerged in Alexandria. Gnosticism, based on the Greek word *gnostikos,* or "possessing knowledge," was originally believed to have been the product of many different

ca 79
Pompeii and Herculaneum
are destroyed by the eruption
of Mount Vesuvius

ca 80-90
Putative date
of the Gospel of Luke

ca 81
Emperor Titus dies,
succeeded by his brother Domitian

ca 85-90
Putative date
of the Book of Acts
of the Apostles

A Roman relief from the second century C.E., found in northern Africa, shows a mariner navigating a two-masted coastal vessel known as a corbita.

A stunning pale green glass pitcher from the late first or early second century C.E. with a splayed rim and narrow folded base was found in Asia Minor.

The Monastery of Deir Amba Bishoi near Wadi El Natrun exemplifies the Coptic monastic movement in its search for solitude.

ca 85-100
Putative date
of the Gospel of John

ca 95
Putative date
of the book *Antiquities of the Jews* by Josephus

ca 96
Emperor Domitian
is assassinated and
succeeded by Nerva

ca 98
Emperor Nerva dies
and is succeeded
by Trajan

currents, including neo-Platonism, Zoroastrianism, and various Near Eastern mystery sects. Modern research, however, has shown that Gnosticism formed an authentic and vibrant movement within early Christianity, even though it would share many ideas with other cults, including Persian Manichaeism and pre-Islamic Mandaeism.

The essential thrust of Christian Gnosticism was the rejection of the material world as inherently flawed. Instead, believers should surrender themselves wholeheartedly to the spiritual domain. The way to accomplish this, many Gnostics believed, was through the attainment of gnosis, a secret, intuitive knowledge of the divine, perhaps based on the neo-Platonic premise that each person carried a spark of the divine within.

Gnostic Christians believed that the teachings of Jesus offered a path to this knowledge. In their view, Jesus had revealed a deeply intimate way by which humans could communicate directly with God, without the intervention of a priesthood or complex set of laws. This also explained the reason that Jesus often spoke in parables. True knowledge of God was a precious and potentially dangerous secret, which could be revealed only to those who proved themselves worthy.

The precise character of Jesus himself, however, remained a matter of intense controversy. Some believed he was the embodiment of God in mortal form, as Paul had preached, while others claimed that Jesus was a mortal who, Buddha-like, had steadily achieved a path to perfect enlightenment with the divine. Some, such as the Docetists, argued that Jesus' physical presence had been a mere illusion and that he had always been a divine being. Other sects, including the Ebionites, remained true to their Jewish roots and believed that Jesus had always been a mere mortal. These diverging ideas would plant the seeds for the great conflict about the nature of Christ in the centuries to come.

THE GNOSTIC GOSPELS

Egypt, and particularly the city of Alexandria, was a major center of early Christian and Gnostic activity. From there, Gnostic ideas spread rapidly among both Greek and Coptic-speaking communities; one of these would later bury a collection of Gnostic texts at Nag Hammadi, which on their discovery in 1945 opened the eyes of modern scholarship to this important Christian movement. Among these codices are a number of "Gospel" documents that do not appear in the canon of the New Testament but instead are attributed to authors in Jesus' immediate circle.

The Gospel of Philip, for example, states that "the companion [koinōnos] of the [Savior is] Mary Magdalene." This does not

This text from the Nag Hammadi collection contains the beginning of the Gospel of Thomas.

necessarily imply a romantic relationship; the term "companion" could also suggest that Jesus respected Mary on an equal footing with the 12 male Apostles. When in the same Gospel the disciples confront Jesus about his affection for Mary Magdalene, saying, "Why do you love her more than all of us?" his reply is, "Why do I not love you as [I love] her?"—meaning, he loved all of them equally. Texts such as these indicate that Gnostic congregations welcomed both men and women.

A number of Egyptian Christians, Gnostic or otherwise, decided to move to the desert to further isolate themselves from material concerns. Eventually these hermits formed communities to share their needs for sustenance and worship. The idea of seeking solitude in the desert to be closer to God was not new; many other religions advocated the blessings of meditation in remote places. This was the reason that John the Baptist, as well as the Qumran community, had chosen to live in the Judean wilderness and why Moses received the tablets from God in the heart of the Sinai Desert. What was new, however, was the idea of cenobitic monasticism: the idea of creating settlements where pious men and women could pray and meditate together while pooling their needs for water, food, and security. As Robert Bruce Mullin has noted, the figure of the saintly hermit was the successor to the martyr in some

An Early Gospel?

Among the most intriguing of Gnostic texts is the Gospel of Thomas. It is not a "Gospel" in the traditional sense, for it only provides a listing of specific sayings by Jesus, without any attempt to interpret these in a theological context. References to the crucifixion or Resurrection, for example, are missing. So are any suggestions of Jesus' divinity, which is why this Gospel is perhaps more proto-Gnostic than truly Gnostic. As a sayings document, a common literary genre in Antiquity, the Gospel of Thomas bears a notable resemblance to the hypothetical document referred to by scholars as Q, which, though never found, is believed to have been a source for the parallel materials in the Gospels of Matthew and Luke. In its original form, the Gospel of Thomas may have originated in the first century—as about half of the sayings appear in the canonical Gospels as well.

*Jesus said, "Come unto me, for my yoke is easy
and my lordship is mild, and you will find repose for yourselves."*

GOSPEL OF THOMAS 90

Jean-Léon Gérôme (1824-1904) painted this 1876 reconstruction of a Roman chariot race, one of the most beloved entertainments in the imperial era.

ways. Whereas previously a martyr was glorified by his imitation of Christ's suffering, that role was now passed to the ascetic in his deliberate negation of physical comfort. Several of these hermits, such as Anthony of Egypt, became holy men in their own right and were believed to be capable of performing miracles. Monasticism would eventually spread to Europe and give impetus to the creation of large cloistered orders during the early Middle Ages.

MARTYRDOM

Inevitably, Gnosticism and early Christianity came into conflict with one another. Some scholars, including Pagels, have suggested that Gnosticism threatened the hierarchical model of authority, delegated via bishops and presbyters, that the traditional or "Catholic" (literally "universal") Church was trying to build. Martyrdom, a badge of honor for many traditional Christians (including Ignatius, who looked forward to being "ground by the teeth of the wild beasts"), also became a point of contention. In his *Scorpiace*, or "Antidote to Scorpion's Bite," Tertullian accused those who didn't follow traditional church teachings—including "dissidents" such as Gnostic Christians—of lacking the faith and courage to become martyrs. According to one codex found in the Nag Hammadi collection, the Gnostics countered that it was absurd to think that Jesus would desire such pointless human sacrifice. ∎

ca 110
Oldest known use
of paper for writing
in China

ca 115
Trajan extends
the Roman Empire
into Parthia

ca 115
Outbreak of the Kitos Rebellion
in Libya and Cyprus

ca 117
Putative date
of Tacitus's *Histories*

THE JEWISH WAR

*The Zealots Launch a Desperate Rebellion
Against Roman Rule*

Back in Judea, Claudius's experiment of restoring the restive region as a Roman province was not a success. The procurator Cuspius Fadus remained in office for only two years, and none of his successors lasted much longer. Porcius Festus, the fourth governor since Fadus, died suddenly in 62 C.E. His replacement was Lucceius Albinus, who at the time was still residing in Rome. As he prepared to set sail for Caesarea, the high priest Ananus seized the moment to strike a blow against all members of the Jewish community who opposed the Sadducees in Jerusalem, including Pharisees and followers of Jesus. A reference in one of Josephus's works states that Ananus then won the Sanhedrin's backing to indict "James, the brother of Jesus known as Christ," and had him thrown off the Temple parapet, but this text is the subject of intense debate.

Four years later, rumors swept the city that the new Roman governor, Gessius Florus, had absconded with 17 talents from the Temple treasury. This news, compounded by tensions in Caesarea between Greeks and Jews, led to massive protests. Rather than seeking to calm his province, Florus summoned his auxiliary forces, which turned the demonstration into a bloodbath. But the crowd was not so easily suppressed; soon, Jewish rebels led by the Zealot party took control of the city, prompting many of the elites—including Agrippa II, son of King Agrippa—to flee.

THE ZEALOT PARTY

The Zealot movement originated during protests against the census instigated by the Roman Governor Quirinius in Judea and Samaria. As we saw, Luke used this census to explain why Joseph and Mary traveled to Bethlehem, although historically, it took place some ten years later, in 6 C.E. The resistance against the Roman census was inspired by economic and religious motives. Traditionally, taxes had been paid in kind—as a share of harvest yields, which had been the custom for centuries. Perhaps unaware of this practice, Quirinius

"The Destruction of the Temple of Jerusalem" is the work of classicist artist Francesco Hayez (1791-1881). Inset: Bronze diplomas such as this one, issued to Marcus Papirius in 79 C.E., granted Roman citizenship to a legionnaire after 25 years of faithful service.

ROME AND THE FIRST JEWISH REVOLT

MAP KEY

—— Primary Roman movement, 67 C.E.

----- Secondary Roman movement, 67 C.E.

—— Primary Roman movement, 68 C.E.

----- Secondary Roman movement, 68 C.E.

—— Primary Roman movement, 69 C.E.

----- Secondary Roman movement, 69 C.E.

—— Roman movement, 70 C.E.

—— Roman movement, 71 C.E.

—— Roman movement, 72 C.E.

◉ Jewish fortress

◉ Jewish fort

● Roman garrison

✺ Roman siege

○ Location uncertain

[6] Note location

[19] In June 69 C.E., Emperor Nero committed suicide and the Roman Empire was thrown into turmoil. In the span of a single year, three successors sat on the throne. In the spring of 70 C.E., Vespasian was declared emperor, and Titus took the lead in Judea.

[10] Once Galilee had been subdued, troops were sent to take Joppa, Jamnia, and Azotus. This would secure Roman access to the sea as well as coastal trade routes. Internal strife among the Jews made this task untroublesome for the Romans.

[22] CAPTURE OF JERUSALEM
In May 70 C.E., Titus began the siege of Jerusalem. Legion X set camp on the Mount of Olives, Legion V was placed north of the city, and Legions XII and XV were camped northeast of the city on Mount Scopus. After five months, the city was captured. The residents were taken captive, and most of the buildings razed, including the Temple. Titus turned the destroyed city over to Legion X.

[20] In 70 C.E., Vespasian sent Titus to Caesarea from Alexandria, Egypt, to complete the campaign in Judea.

[18] In spring 69 C.E., General Cerealis was tasked with the capture of Caphethra and Capharabis.

[14] Troops were left to keep control of eastern Idumea while Vespasian turned north, leaving more troops in Adida, as he continued on to Antipatris and Mabartha.

[6] Vespasian ends the revolt in Galilee by capturing Gischala.

[2] With some 60,000 men, Vespasian and his son Titus moved to regain control of eastern Galilee.

[3] With the capture of Jotapata, Rome controlled western Galilee.

[5] After the siege of Taricheae, Titus moved on to besiege Gamala. During the engagement, he sent a detachment to capture Mount Tabor.

[1] Early in 67 C.E., the major city of Sepphoris sided with the Romans and requested a Roman garrison be stationed there.

[9] Legion X wintered in Scythopolis to ensure the control of eastern Galilee.

[4] In the summer of 67 C.E., Titus marched to reclaim eastern Galilee. Vespasian went on to Caesarea Philippi.

[8] In the fall of 67 C.E., Vespasian moved Legion V and XV to Caesarea for winter quarters.

[11] In the spring of 68 C.E., Vespasian set out to capture Perea. Gadara surrendered, and the primary Roman force returned to Caesarea. Legion X went on to capture other cities in the area.

[7] During the 67 C.E. campaigns in Galilee, Vespasian sent one of his generals to disrupt Jewish actions in the area of Mount Gerizim.

[24] In 72 C.E., Roman forces marched on Machaerus. The fortress was besieged, captured, then destroyed.

[13] Vespasian conducted a second campaign in 68 C.E. He marched through Antipatris, Thamna, Lydda, and on to Emmaus where he stationed Legion V. He went on to Betogabris and Caphartobas.

[12] In the summer of 68 C.E., Legion X destroyed the monastery of Qumran.

[15] Vespasian left Mabartha, entered the Jordan Valley, and captured Jericho.

[17] In spring 69 C.E., Vespasian secured Gophna and Acrabeta.

[16] Legion X wintered in Jericho.

[21] Titus set out from Caesarea with Legions XII and XV to capture Jerusalem. Legion V from Emmaus and Legion X from Jericho also marched to the assault.

[23] In 71 C.E., Legion X captured Herodium.

[27] After Masada was taken, Legion X was garrisoned in Jerusalem and tasked with maintaining security in the province of Judea.

[25] In autumn of 72 C.E., Legion X along with auxiliary troops moved against Masada.

[26] In late 72 C.E., Legion X laid siege to Masada. After failed attempts to breach the fortress wall, a massive ramp was built in order to get breaching equipment in place. By the spring of 73 C.E., the ramp was completed, and the fortress walls were breached in May. Once they entered, the Romans discovered that the defenders had burned nearly all the buildings and committed mass suicide rather than face certain defeat and capture.

0 10 20 30 kilometers
0 10 20 30 miles

Present-day country boundaries are represented.

[Titus] Caesar ordered the entire city and the temple smashed to the ground, leaving only the tallest of the towers standing, and part of the western wall to show to posterity.

JOSEPHUS, *THE JEWISH WAR*

This synagogue was built by Zealot rebels fighting the Roman Tenth Legion on the Herodian fortress of Masada between 70 and 73 C.E.. Inset: A marble head of Emperor Titus was carved in 80 C.E., the year after Titus succeeded his father Vespasian.

demanded that the population declare their property in currency value—raising fears that taxes were now to be paid in coin.

The protests eventually coalesced into a resistance movement led by a man known as Judas the Galilean and a Pharisee named Zaddok. Josephus does not tell us whether this man is the same as Judas, the son of Hezekiah, who led a revolt against Archelaus after the death of Herod the Great in 4 B.C.E. Given the frequency of the name "Judas" in first-century Palestine, we should not assume as much.

But what is clear is that this new movement used very different tactics compared to those deployed in previous revolts. It did not take up arms but instead urged the peasantry not to comply with Roman decrees, including the demand to report one's property. It

therefore resembled the modern form of passive resistance, which eschews violence but refuses to abide by what the protesters consider unlawful behavior. And from a Jewish perspective, the census was indeed unlawful. It violated the very principle of the Torah: that the land Quirinius wanted to assess belonged to God, not to Rome. This religious motive is preserved in the name *zelotes*, or "Zealots" itself, a Greek translation of the Hebrew *kana'im*, meaning "zealous followers [of God]."

In the decades to come, the Zealots would steadily grow in prominence, particularly outside the urban centers of Judea. Josephus even accorded them the status of a "Jewish party" on a par with the Sadducees, Pharisees, and Essenes. One Zealot would later

In the Cave of Letters, Yigael Yadin found numerous records of the Bar Kokhba Revolt of 132-135 C.E., including documents of a woman named Babatha.

join the Jesus movement as an Apostle; his name was Simon the Zealot (Luke 6:15; Acts 1:13).

Decades later, in 46 C.E. two sons of Judas the Galilean, Jacob and Simon, moved on the offensive and launched a violent uprising over the crushing tax yoke. They were caught and executed, which hardened the stance of the resisters. The Zealots began to train a potent military wing known as *sicarii* (*sikarioi* in Greek), meaning "dagger men." Thus, when protests broke out in 66 C.E., the Zealots were ready and prepared to exploit the moment.

ROME SENDS REINFORCEMENTS

When it became clear that Florus was no longer in control of the province and the revolt continued to spread, Governor Cestius Gallus of Syria dispatched his only available legion, the 12th Fulminata. Shockingly, these soldiers—for the most part Syrian recruits rather than battle-hardened Romans—were ignominiously defeated at the Battle of the Beth Horon Pass. At that point, the Roman Senate realized that their vassal territory in Palestine was in serious trouble, but Nero was too distracted by his vainglorious pursuits to pay the matter any attention. This respite allowed the rebels to consolidate their control over the country while recruiting and

training thousands of able-bodied men under arms. One of these was Josephus himself, who, due to his priestly class and education, was given command of an infantry unit in Galilee.

Not until early 67 C.E. did Nero finally decide to act. A large expeditionary force was assembled, which consisted of two legendary legions: the 10th Fretensis and 5th Macedonia, both under the command of General Vespasian. The first troop ships landed in Ptolemais, today's Acre, in April 67. Vespasian was soon joined by his son Titus, who brought with him the 15th Legion Apollinaris from Alexandria, as well as various militia forces from nearby vassal kings—including Agrippa II, cherishing the hope of being crowned king in Jerusalem.

The arrival of Rome's armed might—around 60,000 men, by some estimates—led to soul searching among the resisters. Some argued that the time had come for a peace parlay while they still controlled much of the country. Others, led by the Zealots, insisted on continuing the fight to the bitter end. In the end, the Zealots prevailed.

Meanwhile, Vespasian was steadily fighting his way through Galilee. Cities and hamlets that promptly surrendered—such as Tiberias—were treated with mercy, while those that resisted—such as Gamala—were bloodily crushed. In the conflagration, scores of towns and villages that had formed the backdrop of Jesus' ministry were utterly destroyed. Josephus estimates that some 100,000

Galilean Jews were killed or sold into slavery. By 68 C.E., all of the North and the East was under Roman control.

Vespasian, now comfortably settled in the governor's palace in Caesarea, then slowly tightened a noose around the remaining rebel forces, who had retreated into central Judea and Jerusalem. But events in Rome prevented him from delivering the coup de grâce. The death of Nero that same year led to a civil war between the pretenders Galba, Otho, and Vitellius. When news of this messy situation reached Caesarea, Vespasian's troops proclaimed their popular commander as the next imperator of Rome. Vespasian promptly departed for Italy to claim his throne, while leaving his son Titus in command of the battle for Jerusalem.

A pair of sandals, made with three layers of leather, was found in the Cave of Letters in the Judean desert.

THE FINAL ACT

After a brutal and protracted siege, Titus was able to capture the city in 70 C.E. The Second Temple complex, which had been completed only a decade earlier, was burned to the ground. The sacred menorah, the seven-armed lamp stand from the Temple interior, as well as the temple trumpets and the bread of presence, were carried away in triumph—a scene captured in one of the inner panels of the Arch of Titus in Rome that is still visible today. Writing many years later, Matthew's Gospel suggests that Jesus had foretold these events. While his disciples stood and admired the Temple buildings, Jesus had said, "Truly I tell you, not one stone will be left here upon another; all will be thrown down" (Matthew 24:1-2).

The fighting was not over yet. Soon after, the 10th Legion moved into the Judean Desert to mop up the remaining pockets of resistance, which had established themselves in Herod's old border fortresses. The Herodium and Machaerus were quickly overrun, but at Herod's impregnable palace at Masada, the rebels were able to hold out until 73. Along the way, the Romans came across the settlement of Qumran, which had been destroyed by Vespasian's forces in 68, but not before the settlers hid their rolls of Hebrew Scripture and other documents in nearby caves. There they would remain for nearly 2,000 years, until they were brought to light between 1946 and 1947 as the Dead Sea Scrolls.

THE SECOND JEWISH WAR

Once order was restored, the Roman exploitation of the native population continued unabated, following the same pattern that had precipitated the Jewish Revolt. Jewish ancestral lands were appropriated or confiscated as the ruling Roman elite and their collaborators saw fit. Roman taxes placed an intolerable burden on the local peasants. Thus, tensions between Jews and their Roman overlords rose steadily in the first two decades of the second century and erupted again in 131, after Emperor Hadrian announced his intention to build a Roman city on top of the ruins of Jerusalem.

This Second Jewish Revolt was led by Simon bar-Kokhba, who was welcomed by many Jews as the Messiah. Nevertheless, the outcome was never in doubt. After several years of bitter and bloody fighting, the revolt was put down. Near the end, as Roman forces pushed into the desert, a group of Bar-Kokhba's followers fled into a cave system in a wadi named Nahal Hever in the Judean Desert. First discovered in 1953 but only fully explored in 1960 by Yigael Yadin, the so-called Cave of Letters has yielded an unprecedented glimpse into Jewish life in the early second century. A subsequent expedition uncovered another cache that included plates, cups, and a cooking pot; a sickle; a pair of women's sandals; and a bundle of legal documents belonging to a woman named Babatha.

Meanwhile, Palestine became a Roman dependency once more. It would remain under Roman (and later, Byzantine) control until the Persian invasion of 614 and the subsequent Islamic conquest in 637. ∎

The Cave of Letters

Near the end of the Second Jewish Revolt, a group of refugees fled to a number of caves in the Judean Desert where they buried their possessions, including unspun wool and clothing, perfume and cosmetic tools, and a cache of written letters on papyrus. Among them was a bundle of documents belonging to a Jewish woman named Babatha of Maoza, which offers a fascinating glimpse of life in ancient Judea. It included Babatha's marriage contract to her second husband, Yehuda, and deeds related to the disposition of Yehuda's property after his death. Since men were usually older than their brides and mortality rates were high, a woman could be married more than once. Based on this evidence, Ross Kraemer has argued that while first marriages were usually arranged by the woman's parents, a woman would have a greater choice in her second marriage, and even inherit some of his property.

THE RISE OF RABBINIC JUDAISM

The Jewish Religion Survives the Destruction of the Temple

The destruction of the Second Temple on August 29, 70 C.E., was a deeply traumatic event for Jews in Palestine and throughout the Diaspora. In one fell swoop, the very raison d'être of sacrificial Judaism had been wiped from this Earth. Josephus, who wrote as a protégé of the Roman Flavian House, sought to exonerate Titus by claiming that the general had tried to stop the troops from setting fire to the Temple, but this is probably propaganda. The Romans knew very well that the sanctuary served as the focal point of Jewish identity and pride, and it was precisely this pride that they sought to eradicate. Indeed, Titus went on to massacre hundreds of men, women, and children in Jerusalem without compunction, allowing his soldiers to vent their rage on the city that had vexed them for so long. In 1969, Israeli archaeologist Nahman Avigad uncovered vivid testimony of this conflagration when his team excavated the charred remains of the first century "Burnt House." Under blackened pieces of masonry lay the skeleton of a young woman who had died where she fell, still clutching the steps of her home.

Some historians believe that more than 100,000 inhabitants of the city lost their lives, while an equal number may have been sold into slavery. Those who survived were ordered to leave the city, though it is not clear for how long or how often this rule was enforced. The small community of Jewish Christians was also evicted; some of these moved to Pella in the Decapolis, just across the Jordan River.

As a result, most of the factions that had governed the spiritual life of the Jewish nation before the war were scattered or killed. The priesthood of the Sadducees, bereft of their Temple, faded from public life. With them died the rites of animal sacrifice, a key feature of Judaism since the earliest days of Israel.

The synagogue of ancient Tiberias was built while the city served as the center of the Rabbinate after the Second Jewish Revolt.

THE YAVNEH ACADEMY

But several other groups, including the Pharisees, may have survived. One was a man named Yohanan ben Zakkai, who had been a pupil of the renowned Rabbi Hillel and had once led a rabbinical school in Jerusalem. When the war intensified, Yohanan had tried hard to persuade the Zealots to sue for peace. When they refused, he harshly denounced the war party, claiming that they were determined to "destroy this city and burn the house of the sanctuary."

The Romans were aware of the rabbi's efforts. During the early months of Jerusalem's siege, Yohanan was smuggled out of the city in a coffin so that he could plead with Vespasian for a peaceful end to the conflict. In this he was unsuccessful, but Vespasian was sufficiently impressed to allow the rabbi to establish a modest rabbinic school in Yavneh (located some 12 miles south of today's Tel Aviv).

After Jerusalem was destroyed, many of the surviving sages, including members of the Sanhedrin, joined Yohanan in Yavneh to see if they could make sense of what had happened. As several scholars have suggested, this group probably included many Pharisees who for more than a century had debated the practice of the Torah in everyday life. Over time these debates were written down—producing a corpus that would become known as the Oral Law. In doing so, these Pharisees were unwittingly preparing themselves for a time when the Temple and its associated liturgy would no longer exist.

This Oral Instruction (*Torah she-be'al peh*) became the foundation of Jewish spiritual recovery, with Yohanan's academy as its principal center. Engaging wholeheartedly in the study of the Torah, Yohanan said, was in itself a restorative effort. In a sense it created a new Jewish Temple: a *spiritual* Temple, for whenever a group of Jews studied the Law together, the presence of the Lord (*Shekhinah*) was with them. In this

ca 135
Emperor Hadrian builds a new city, Aelia Capitolina, on the ruins of Jerusalem

ca 135
Yohanan ben Zakkai establishes a Jewish religious academy in Yavneh

ca 138
Emperor Hadrian dies and is succeeded by Antoninus Pius

ca 140
The Yavneh Academy in Galilee forms a new Sanhedrin

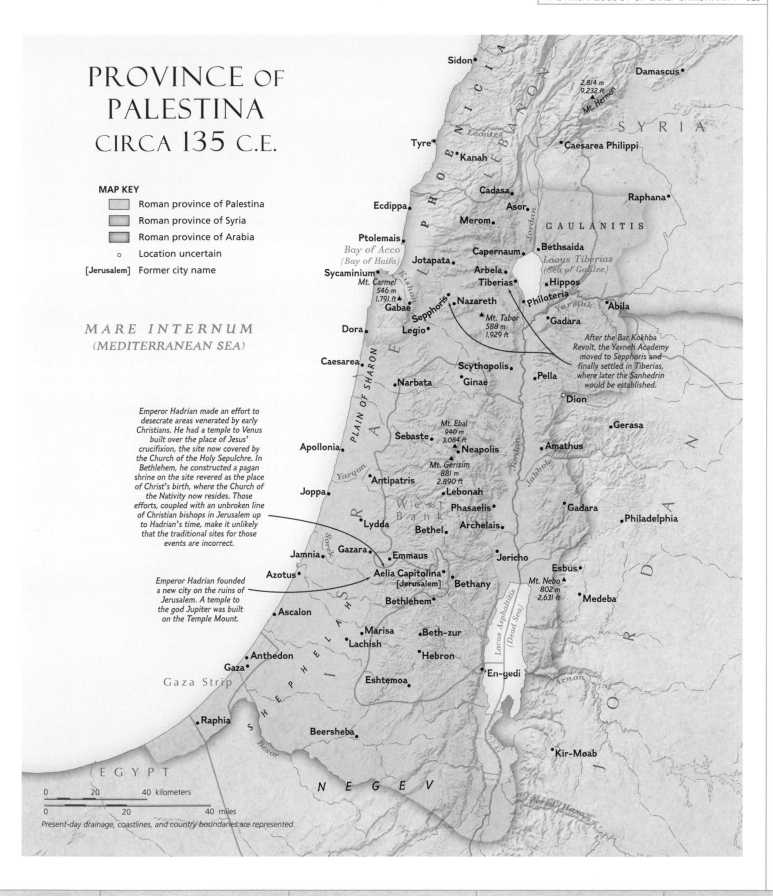

PROVINCE OF PALESTINA
CIRCA 135 C.E.

MAP KEY

Roman province of Palestina

Roman province of Syria

Roman province of Arabia

○   Location uncertain

[Jerusalem]   Former city name

MARE INTERNUM
(MEDITERRANEAN SEA)

Emperor Hadrian made an effort to desecrate areas venerated by early Christians. He had a temple to Venus built over the place of Jesus' crucifixion, the site now covered by the Church of the Holy Sepulchre. In Bethlehem, he constructed a pagan shrine on the site revered as the place of Christ's birth, where the Church of the Nativity now resides. Those efforts, coupled with an unbroken line of Christian bishops in Jerusalem up to Hadrian's time, make it unlikely that the traditional sites for those events are incorrect.

Emperor Hadrian founded a new city on the ruins of Jerusalem. A temple to the god Jupiter was built on the Temple Mount.

After the Bar Kokhba Revolt, the Yavneh Academy moved to Sepphoris and finally settled in Tiberias, where later the Sanhedrin would be established.

Sidon

Damascus

2,814 m
9,232 ft
Mt. Hermon

SYRIA

Tyre

Kanah

Leontes

Caesarea Philippi

Cadasa

Raphana

Ecdippa

Asor

Merom

GAULANITIS

Ptolemais

Bay of Acco
(Bay of Haifa)

Capernaum

Bethsaida

Lacus Tiberias
(Sea of Galilee)

Jotapata

Arbela

Sycaminium

Tiberias

Hippos

Mt. Carmel
546 m
1,791 ft

Gabae

Nazareth

Philoteria

Abila

Sepphoris

Gadara

Dora

Legio

Mt. Tabor
588 m
1,929 ft

Caesarea

Scythopolis

Pella

Narbata

Ginae

Dion

Gerasa

Mt. Ebal
940 m
3,084 ft

Sebaste

Neapolis

Amathus

Apollonia

Mt. Gerizim
881 m
2,890 ft

Yarqon

Antipatris

Lebonah

Joppa

West Bank

Phasaelis

Gadara

Lydda

Bethel

Archelais

Philadelphia

Sorek

Gazara

Emmaus

Jericho

Esbus

Jamnia

Aelia Capitolina
[Jerusalem]

Bethany

Mt. Nebo
802 m
2,631 ft

Medeba

Azotus

Bethlehem

Lacus Asphaltitis
(Dead Sea)

Ascalon

Marisa

Beth-zur

Lachish

Hebron

Anthedon

Eshtemoa

En-gedi

Gaza

Gaza Strip

Beersheba

Arnon

Raphia

Besor

Kir-Moab

EGYPT

NEGEV

Jered (Hasa)

0   20   40 kilometers

0   20   40 miles

Present-day drainage, coastlines, and country boundaries are represented.

ca 161
Antoninus Pius is succeeded by Lucius Verus and Marcus Aurelius

ca 169
Lucius Verus dies; Marcus Aurelius reigns as sole emperor

ca 177
Commodus, son of Marcus Aurelius, becomes co-emperor

ca 180
Marcus Aurelius dies; Commodus reigns as sole emperor

Let your house be a gathering place for sages.
And wallow in the dust of their feet, and drink in
their words with gusto. Let your house be open wide.

YOSE BEN YOEZER AND YOSE BEN YOHANAN IN MISHNAH, TRACTATE AVOT I

they could also point to Diaspora Jews, who had long since built a community life around the synagogue and the interpretation of the Torah, rather than the sacrificial rites at the Temple in Jerusalem. Diaspora communities continued to flourish throughout Asia Minor, Greece, and the Italian peninsula, as well as in Egypt, Carthage, and Spain. Their use of the synagogue as a center of prayer and scriptural study had shown that the Jewish religion could continue to prosper on the strength of its laws, prayer, and ongoing rabbinic study.

The necropolis of Beth She'arim ("house of strangers") was one of the most prominent Jewish burial grounds in Late Antiquity.

Thus, Judaism found a way to survive. The period of Second Temple Judaism, with its focus on pilgrimage and sacrificial rites, had come to an end. But a new period, the era of Rabbinic Judaism, was about to begin. This form of Judaism is still with us today.

THE JEWISH PATRIARCHATE

The Roman authorities always realized that Judaism as a religion posed no threat to the state. There were flourishing Jewish communities throughout the Empire—in Spain, Egypt, Greece, Asia Minor, and Rome itself—whose economic life was closely intertwined with the local and international commerce of the empire.

The mosaic floor of the fourth-century synagogue in Tiberias features a Torah ark flanked by two large candelabra.

The Mishnah

The Oral Law—a corpus of commentary by rabbinic sages about the daily application of the Torah as illustrated by actual cases—was first codified in the early third century B.C.E. in a book known as the Mishnah (meaning "teaching"). Probably edited by Rabbi Yehuda ha Nasi ("the Prince"), its purpose was to provide a systematic reference for legal arguments and precepts based on the Torah. It is organized around six basic subject areas, (subdivided into 63 tractates and 531 chapters): Seeds (Agricultural Laws), Appointed Times (Jewish festivals), Women (Marriage Laws), Damages (Civil Law), Holy Things (sacrifice), and Purities (issues of cultic purity).

establishment of a new Sanhedrin, with considerable autonomy in local jurisdiction. The Romans realized that the Jewish rabbinate could act as a stabilizing and moderating force over the restive Jewish nation. At the head of the Sanhedrin stood the patriarch, a position that eventually became a hereditary office for those of Davidic pedigree. In many ways, the position would acquire a religious authority not dissimilar from that of the high priest during the Second Temple Period. Thus began the heyday of the Jewish patriarchate in Judea. ∎

That is the reason why, even at the peak of the First Revolt, Emperor Vespasian never revoked Judaism's status as a lawfully recognized religion. Jews formed too critical a part of the empire's social fabric to be ignored or ostracized—although the same could not be said for Christian communities, both Jewish and Gentile.

In the aftermath of the devastation of the Bar Kokhba Revolt, the Yavneh Academy decided to move to Galilee. It was first established in Beth She'arim before moving to the former capital of Galilee, Sepphoris, and finally settling in Tiberias, on the shores of the Sea of Galilee. This, as we saw, had originally been a largely Gentile city founded by Antipas, but in the second century, it rapidly became the center of a Jewish renaissance. In 140, Simeon ben Gamaliel succeeded in securing Roman approval for the

A large glass jug with wide splayed mouth and handle from Syria reveals the artistry of Roman glass-blowing techniques in the third century C.E.

THE GROWTH OF CHRISTIANITY

*The Christian Movement Grows
Despite Tensions From Within and Without*

While Roman Palestine was convulsed by the First Revolt, the Christian movement continued to grow apace in the Mediterranean. The Book of Revelation, written by the author known as John of Patmos, is dedicated to seven churches located in Asia Minor, none of which (except for Ephesus) were known as Christian communities in Paul's time. These include Smyrna (today's Izmir), Pergamum (near today's Bergama), Thyatira (modern Akhisar), Philadelphia (today's Alaşehir), and Laodicea on the Lycus (near modern Eskihisar), all located in western Turkey.

Many of these communities confronted the need for some form of organization. In Paul's day, the notion of a formal hierarchy was never seriously contemplated; after all, followers firmly believed that Jesus would return in their lifetime, whereupon Christ would establish his new kingdom. But the rise of Roman persecution and the continuing challenge from dissident factions gave urgency to the development of some organizational structure. Paul had written to the Corinthians that "God has given the first place to apostles, second to prophets, and third to teachers" (I Corinthians 12:28). Consequently, those communities that followed the "Catholic" model of Christianity began to appoint priestly leaders, or presbyters, on the strength of their ability and faith. Eventually these prelates claimed that their authority derived from the apostolate itself, and so the title of bishop emerged.

In the meantime, the rising pitch of the First Revolt accelerated the polarization between Jewish and Gentile followers of Jesus. Gentiles, quite naturally, were at pains to distance themselves from the rebellion taking place in Judea, and they went out of their way to assure their local communities that they were loyal and patriotic citizens. This may have

This citadel underneath the Damascus Gate in Jerusalem formed part of the triumphal gate built by the Romans in the city of Aelia Capitolina in the second century B.C.E. Inset: A bronze coin displays the chi rho symbol—the first two initials of Christos, the Greek translation of "Messiah"—as well as the alpha and the omega, another reference to Christ.

ca 185	ca 193	ca 200	ca 215
Bishop Irenaeus proposes a New Testament canon of Matthew, Mark, Luke, and John	Emperor Septimius Severus permits a persecution of Christians	The Huns invade Afghanistan	The Baths of Caracalla are built in Rome

ca 249
Emperor Decius persecutes
all who refuse to worship
Roman gods

ca 261
Emperor Gallienus ends
the persecution of Christians

ca 300
Bishop Eusebius codifies
the first canon of the
New Testament

ca 313
Constantine the Great issues
the Edict of Milan,
tolerating all religions

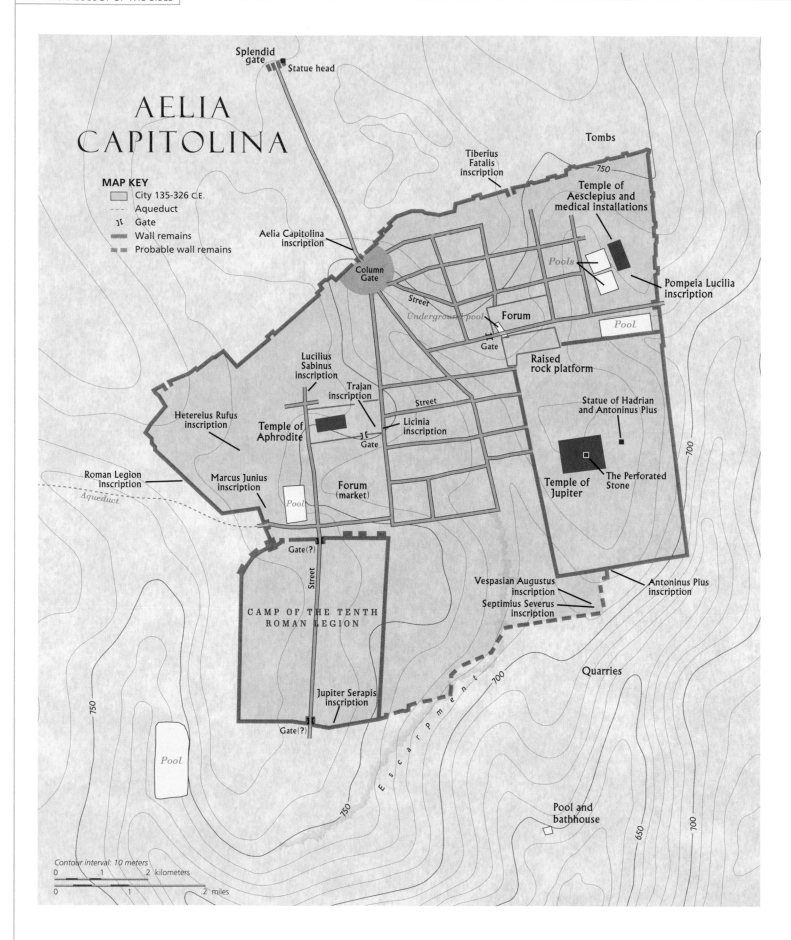

AELIA CAPITOLINA

MAP KEY

- City 135-326 C.E.
- Aqueduct
- Gate
- Wall remains
- Probable wall remains

Splendid gate

Statue head

Aelia Capitolina inscription

Column Gate

Tiberius Fatalis inscription

Tombs

Temple of Aesclepius and medical installations

Pools

Pompeia Lucilia inscription

Street

Underground pool

Forum

Pool

Gate

Raised rock platform

Lucilius Sabinus inscription

Trajan inscription

Street

Statue of Hadrian and Antoninus Pius

Hetereius Rufus inscription

Temple of Aphrodite

Licinia inscription

Gate

Temple of Jupiter

The Perforated Stone

Roman Legion inscription

Marcus Junius inscription

Aqueduct

Pool

Forum (market)

Pool

Vespasian Augustus inscription

Septimius Severus inscription

Antoninus Pius inscription

Gate (?)

Street

CAMP OF THE TENTH ROMAN LEGION

Quarries

Jupiter Serapis inscription

Escarpment

Gate (?)

Pool

Pool and bathhouse

Contour interval: 10 meters

0 .1 .2 kilometers

0 .1 .2 miles

750

750

700

700

650

700

750

*The oftener we are mown down by you, the more in number we grow;
the blood of Christians is seed.*

TERTULLIAN OF CARTHAGE, *APOLOGETICUS*

A reconstruction of the pagan temple of Venus, built by Emperor Hadrian in Aelia Capitolina, was painted by the French artist James Tissot (1836-1902).

been the incentive for the author known as Mark to write the first Gospel—in Rome, for a Roman audience. As we saw, Mark's Gospel emphatically deflects the blame for Jesus' execution from the Roman procurator to the Jewish crowd attending his trial. At the same time, Gentile Christians may have felt a strong need for a form of scripture that was uniquely Christian rather than Jewish—an authoritative source that explained Jesus' teachings and deeds that was based on the teachings of Paul rather than the Torah.

CHRISTIANITY IN THE SECOND AND THIRD CENTURIES

As the movement entered its second century, Christian communities were flourishing throughout the Roman Empire; by one estimate, some 300,000 Christians could be found in Asia Minor alone. Christian communities sprang up in unexpected corners of the Empire, founded by unknown missionaries well beyond the orbit of the Apostles James, Peter, Paul, Thomas, or John. Many of these Christians came together for

communal worship in so-called house churches, so as not to arouse the suspicions of their neighbors. Paul himself was familiar with several such house churches, including the one led by Aquila and Priscilla and a follower named Nymphas in Laodicea (I Corinthians 16:19; Colossians 4:15). One such house was found in Dura Europos in Syria, dating from the 230s. It even featured several frescoes in a style that is not dissimilar to the paintings of the more famous Dura Europos synagogue nearby, built around the same time frame. These frescoes are preserved in the Yale University Art Gallery; the fate of the house church itself, now in ISIS-held territory, is uncertain.

Hostility toward Christians was not universal. Many Romans were secretly impressed by the way Christians practiced acts of compassion, such as clothing the destitute, feeding the poor, and burying the indigent. Partly for this reason, it is not clear to what extent the Roman prohibition of Christianity was truly enforced during the second century C.E. There were doubtless

A marble bust depicts Emperor Hadrian (r. 117-138 C.E.), who ordered the construction of a Roman city on the ruins of Jerusalem.

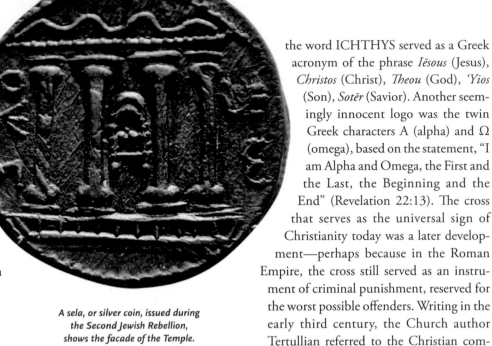

A sela, or silver coin, issued during the Second Jewish Rebellion, shows the facade of the Temple.

episodes of conflict, but these may have been instigated by citizens who harbored suspicions about Christian worship and its practice of eating "Christ's body" and drinking "Christ's blood." Negative attitudes toward Christians also stemmed from the fact that Christians cherished rather unconventional social ideas that were deemed disruptive to Roman society. For example, the Christian emphasis on love (*agapè* in Greek, meaning charitable love) as a force that transcended class boundaries was often ridiculed in a culture where classes were rigorously separated, and love in a religious sense was usually associated with sensuous Dionysian rites.

The most disturbing aspect of Christianity in the eyes of many Romans, however, was the rather unpatriotic refusal by Christians to offer sacrifices to the Roman gods or the reigning emperor. In the early second century, Pliny the Younger complained that there were so many Christians in Bithynia and Pontus (the Black Sea coastal region of today's Turkey) that pagan demand for sacrificial animals had dropped precipitously. Augustus had always emphasized the role of the Roman state religion as the sole element that could fuse the disparate peoples and cultures within the empire together. It was this "faith of our fathers" that gave Roman civilization its moral foundation.

Little wonder, then, that the Roman historian Tacitus referred to Christianity as a "deadly superstition," and Pliny the Younger called it "a superstition taken to extravagant lengths." It reinforced the impression that Christianity was a foreign cult, profoundly at odds with Roman interests, which by the third century would lead to a sharp increase in discrimination against Christians. Just as Domitian had rejected any cult that refused to recognize him as *dominus et deus* (Lord and God), so too would Emperor Decius in 250 order that all citizens obtain a *libellus,* certified proof of faithful sacrifice to Roman gods, on pain of death. Scores of Christians submitted. Those who refused to comply, including Pope Fabian, the 20th pope since Peter, were promptly executed.

A NASCENT ICONOGRAPHY

In response to this oppression, Christians developed secret emblems and symbols to identify oneself as a member of the flock. One such emblem was the *ichthys* symbol—the Greek word for fish—rendered as a word or in the stylized form of a fish. While innocuous on the surface, the symbol carried a double meaning. The fish signified the apostolic task of serving as "fishermen of men," and the word ICHTHYS served as a Greek acronym of the phrase *Iēsous* (Jesus), *Christos* (Christ), *Theou* (God), *'Yios* (Son), *Sotēr* (Savior). Another seemingly innocent logo was the twin Greek characters A (alpha) and Ω (omega), based on the statement, "I am Alpha and Omega, the First and the Last, the Beginning and the End" (Revelation 22:13). The cross that serves as the universal sign of Christianity today was a later development—perhaps because in the Roman Empire, the cross still served as an instrument of criminal punishment, reserved for the worst possible offenders. Writing in the early third century, the Church author Tertullian referred to the Christian community as *crucis religiosi,* or "devotees of the Cross." The crucifix, the depiction of a figure attached to a cross, would not gain currency until the fifth century.

At the same time, Christians began to imagine what Jesus could have looked like. In the Jewish world, where the representation of humans and animals was proscribed, this was of course anathema—which is why no contemporary image of Jesus has survived. As we saw, Jesus lived and ministered in a devoutly observant environment where the precepts of the Torah were scrupulously adhered to.

But Gentile Christians harbored no such compunction. They had been raised in a culture where Greek and Roman gods were glorified in human form, in paintings and sculpture, precisely

Catacomb Art

In Rome proper, many Christians were buried in underground burial networks known as catacombs, which were dug in the soft volcanic rock. As the practice became widespread, large subterranean networks were developed along the main roads to Rome, such as the Via Appia, the Via Ostiensis, and the Via Tiburtina. In Rome alone, excavators have identified more than 60 catacomb networks, some equipped with multiple galleries at a depth of 60 feet. Many of these catacombs were adorned with scenes from Hebrew Scripture and the Gospels in which Jesus, for lack of a precedent, was sometimes depicted as a young Apollo.

because the sheer perfection of their physical beauty identified them as divine. As Europeans, these Gentiles did not share the ephemeral mysteries of the East. Whereas Palestinian Jews were content to contemplate the divine in transcendent and intangible terms, Gentiles yearned for a physical manifestation of the God they wished to worship.

Thus, the very first representations of Jesus and the Apostles appear, in fresco, on the damp walls of catacombs in which Christians were often interred. Most Christians did not follow the Roman practice of cremation, in part because they believed that

the body of the faithful would rise again on the Day of Judgment. The problem was where to bury the dead, given that Christianity was not officially tolerated and any form of human burial within the city limits was forbidden. In response, many Christians turned to the subterranean burial chambers known as *catacumbae,* or "catacombs," which were already in use as a burial place for the poor. In the Via Latina catacomb, for example, discovered only in 1955, archaeologists found a number of colorful frescoes that depict Jesus delivering his Sermon on the Mount to a large group of toga-clad followers. The vivid brushwork of these paintings is entirely in line with the style of Roman first-century portraiture. From these humble beginnings, a formal iconography of Christ would emerge in the centuries to come. ∎

A room in the catacombs of Domitilla with oculi for burial of the deceased also features a fresco of Christian martyrs Veneranda and Petronilla.

THE ART OF IMPERIAL ROME

The Arts of Antiquity Reach Their Apogee

DURING THE FIRST AND SECOND CENTURIES C.E., ROMAN ARTISTS REACHED A LEVEL OF CREATIVE VIRTUOSITY THAT would not be matched until the High Renaissance of the 16th century. This artistic excellence found expression in virtually every genre, including the casting of bronze sculptures, fresco painting, glassblowing, and the crafting of delicate luxury items in silver and gold. Only in the third century did Roman art begin its long decline that would ultimately produce the more stylized art of the Byzantine era, which focused on the ephemeral quality of mosaics to depict sacred Christian themes rather than the physical realism of the pagan world. ■

Roman gold flasks with a splayed top, such as this sample from the first century C.E. found near Knidos (today's Turkey), are rare.

A delicate blue-tinted glass flask is a fine example of Roman glassblowing techniques developed in the mid-first century C.E.

This head of Constantine I (306-337 C.E.), now at the Capitoline Museum in Rome, once belonged to a bronze statue of the emperor.

An equestrian statue depicting Emperor Marcus Aurelius (r. 161-180 C.E.) was installed on the Campidoglio in Rome.

A first-century C.E. Roman fresco depicts Bacchus, the Roman equivalent of Dionysus, with his companion, the satyr Silenus.

The aureus, the most valuable currency unit in the Roman Empire, was worth 100 sesterces and carried the image of the emperor—in this case, Vespasian (r. 69-79 C.E.).

No one whatsoever should be denied the opportunity to give his heart to the observance of the Christian religion, of that religion which he should think best of himself.

CONSTANTINE THE GREAT, EDICT OF MILAN

EPILOGUE

After Coming Close to Being Eradicated, Christianity Triumphs in the Empire

NEAR THE END OF THE THIRD CENTURY, THE PRESSURE ON CHRISTIANS TO CONFORM to the Roman state reached a fever pitch. As the empire was threatened by barbaric invasions on all fronts, patriotism surged; citizens were expected to show their loyalty to the state. These same invasions also prompted a complete overhaul of the imperial system originally created by Augustus. Instead of one ruler, four rulers —two emperors and two vice-emperors, or "caesars"—were needed to lead Roman forces at critical fronts throughout the realm. This tetrarchy became known as the Dominate, led by Diocletian as the senior ruler. Each emperor established a forward headquarters near sensitive frontiers: one in Milan, facing Transalpine Gaul, and one in Nicomedia in the East, to confront the incursions from eastern Europe. As it happened, Nicomedia was just a few miles distant from a city called Byzantium.

One night, Diocletian's palace was consumed by fire. In an eerie replay of what had occurred more than two centuries earlier during the reign of Nero, the blame fell on the local Christian community. Churches—such as they were—were either confiscated or razed, and all Christian worship was outlawed. Many church leaders were arrested, tortured, and put to death. This was perhaps the most critical moment in the history of the nascent movement. Had Diocletian's rule been longer, Christianity may well have been fatefully crippled or even extinguished.

Opposite: The central crossing of the Church of the Holy Sepulchre in Jerusalem, known as the Catholikon Dome, was originally built during the 12th-century Crusader period. Right: A bronze coin depicts Emperor Diocletian (r. 284-305 C.E.), the emperor who nearly succeeded in crushing Christianity within the Roman realm.

An aureus, or gold coin, depicts Emperor Diocletian (r. 284-305 C.E.), who established a tetrarchy of four Roman rulers, known as the Dominate.

A reconstruction of Diocletian's palace in Spoleto, built around 305 C.E., suggests the immense size of the complex, which at its peak housed 9,000 people.

But mercifully that didn't happen, for Diocletian—in many ways one of the most capable leaders in Roman history—was in poor health. In 305 C.E. the emperor abdicated, thus forcing his co-emperor, Maximian, to do the same. As a result, their subordinates, Caesar Galerius in the East and Constantius I Chlorus in the West, were allowed to succeed them. These new emperors jockeyed to nominate their own "caesars," but this process soon devolved into a 20-year civil war between various pretenders to the throne. By 312, only two imperial claimants were still standing: Constantine, the son of Constantius, and Maxentius, the son of Maximian. After a prolonged battle of attrition, the two foes met for a last and decisive clash not far from the city of Rome, near a crossing over the Tiber River known as the Milvian Bridge.

On the eve of this battle, something strange happened. Christian author Lactantius, a scholar who would later become the tutor of Constantine's son, wrote that Constantine had a dream in which he was told to decorate the shields of his soldiers with "the heavenly sign of God": the monogram of Christ (the Greek letters chi and rho, the first two letters of the Greek word *Christos*). Constantine's biographer, Eusebius, however, claims that Constantine had a daylight vision of a luminescent cross in the sky, blazing with the Greek words *en toutoi nika* ("by this [sign] conquer"). Whatever the case may be, Constantine went on to defeat his rival and became the undisputed leader of the West—crediting the Christian God for his victory.

The following year, in 313, the emperor issued the famous Edict of Milan, which granted all religions—including, most emphatically, Christianity—unlimited freedom to worship. In 324, Constantine also defeated his rival in the East, Emperor Licinius, thus extending his policy of religious tolerance throughout the Roman Empire. Less than 80 years later, Emperor Theodosius II outlawed all pagan cults, including the Roman state religion. In all, it had taken 350 years for the ideas of a Galilean rabbi to conquer the world and become the sole religion of the Roman Empire.

Scholars have pointed out that similar decrees of tolerance had been issued before, notably by Emperor Gallienus as well as Diocletian's caesar, Galerius. But Constantine's policy had by far the greatest impact. While the events on the eve of the battle near Milvian Bridge are shrouded in church hagiography, there is no question that Constantine had long been a devoted monotheist, certainly given the popularity of the sun god in his legions. His mother, Helena, was a devoted Christian; perhaps the Edict of Milan was her suggestion.

THE DESIGN OF A CHRISTIAN "TEMPLE"

In 326, Helena sailed for Roman Palestine herself, determined to turn this Jewish province into the "Christian Holy Land." For the next decade, Helena—backed by the full financial resources of the Roman realm, soon based in Byzantium—devoted herself to marking the key locations of Jesus' birth, death, and resurrection with prominent churches, using state-of-the-art Roman architectural engineering. And although

Constantine himself was not baptized until he lay on his deathbed, the emperor fully supported her endeavors and actively abetted the growth of the Church. He promised full restitution of all confiscated Christian property throughout the realm. Christians who had been exiled were invited back and offered key positions in the imperial administration. Most important, Christian communities were invited to build churches, sometimes with the support of the state.

The question was, however: What should an official temple to the Christ look like? Since Christian worship was a communal activity, unlike the individual nature of pagan worship, the archetype of a Roman temple was not appropriate for church liturgy. Most Christians would probably have been offended to worship in a building so redolent of polytheism. Instead, Constantine's architects adopted a building type that had been used for centuries: the basilica. Based on the Greek stoa, it had always served as the center of civic administration in cities throughout the realm. Usually these basilicas ended in an apse, so as to accommodate a statue of the reigning emperor. This space would now serve as a different focal point: for the placement of the altar.

Thus, a basilica rose in Bethlehem, over the reputed site of Jesus' birth, as well as on the Mount of Olives, the traditional site of Jesus' ascension into heaven. In addition, as we saw, Helena commissioned a large basilica and *anastasis* over the place of his crucifixion and entombment in Jerusalem. In Rome, meanwhile,

This impressive colonnaded atrium from Diocletian's palace in Spoleto (today's Split, Croatia) is a fine example of Roman architecture in Late Antiquity.

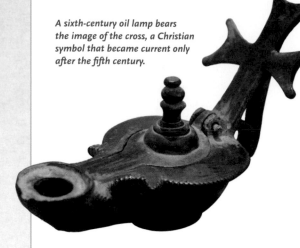

A sixth-century oil lamp bears the image of the cross, a Christian symbol that became current only after the fifth century.

The presbytery of the Basilica of San Vitale in Ravenna, Italy, begun in 527 and completed 20 years later, is covered with mosaics using themes from the Bible.

Constantine ordered a vast, five-aisled basilica to be built on the Ager Vaticanus, Vatican Hill, the traditional location of Peter's grave. St. Peter's Basilica took 25 years to build and stood for more than a thousand years—vivid testimony to the excellence of Roman engineering in Late Antiquity. Here, in 800, Charlemagne was crowned emperor of the Holy Roman Empire. The church was torn down in 1506 and replaced with the current St. Peter's Basilica, based on designs by Bramante and Michelangelo.

THE CHRISTIANIZATION OF PALESTINE

For the Jewish Patriarchate in Palestine, which had continued to govern the region in semiautonomous fashion, the sudden "Christianization" of Judea came as a shock. The rabbinate observed with alarm how Jerusalem was refashioned in a Christian mold. Temple Mount, a location that featured so prominently in the Gospels, was ignored as the principal focus now shifted to the reputed place of Golgotha, where Helena's Church of the Holy Sepulchre rose high above the city. Thousands of pilgrims, monks, and prelates followed, changing the face of Jerusalem forever.

Even greater changes were to come when Theodosius II made Christianity the official and sole religion of the Roman state. While the emperor stopped short of proscribing Judaism, Jewish citizens were marginalized and evicted from all administrative positions. A new law forbade the construction of synagogues, although the remains of synagogues from the fourth through the sixth centuries, including those in Capernaum and Chorazin, may show that this law was routinely ignored. The power of the rabbinic court, the Sanhedrin in Tiberias, was drastically curtailed. In its stead, the Christian bishop in Jerusalem was elevated to the status of patriarch. A heavy tax was levied on Jewish communities, including the Samaritans, which plunged many households into poverty. In response, both Jews and Samaritans rose in revolt in 352. In a sad replay of the tax revolts during Jesus' lifetime, these were bloodily suppressed.

Eventually, however, Judaism reached an accommodation with the Christian presence and was allowed to prosper to some degree, as is evident from the beautiful mosaics found in the sixth-century synagogue of Beit Alpha, in the shadow of Mount Gilboa, east of the Jezreel Valley.

A marble head of Constantine I (306-337 C.E.) formed part of a colossal statue in Rome.

THE TRIUMPH OF CHRISTIAN ART

Now freed from all proscription, the full artistry of Roman artists and sculptors was unleashed on the creation of Christian artifacts and monuments. What had previously been hidden in catacombs and home chapels could now come out into the open. An immediate outlet was the development of elaborate sarcophagi for well-to-do Christians. For these, sculptors deftly switched from the traditional motifs of Amazon battles or Dionysian rites to scenes from the Gospels. Since the iconography of Christ was still fluid, many sarcophagi relied on pagan models, just as the catacomb artist had done a century or two earlier. In one such tableau from the late fourth century, Jesus appears as a toga-clad philosopher with curly hair and beard, surrounded by the attentive disciples of his apostolic school.

But Roman art itself was in decline, as its artists could no longer match the virtuosity and naturalism of painters and sculptors from centuries past. As the Roman realm passed in the Byzantine epoch, its artists found an entirely different form of expression in the medium of the mosaic. Quite in contrast to the anthropomorphic cults of ancient Rome, Byzantine art embraced the ephemeral quality of mosaics to evoke the heavenly sphere of the sacred, rather than the earthly pleasures of the pagan world that soon would be lost forever. ∎

A fifth-century Christian sarcophagus of Jesus and the Apostles depicts Jesus as a toga-clad philosopher with curly hair and without a beard.

APPENDIX: THE SCRIPTURES

This appendix lists the books of Hebrew Scripture and their arrangement in the Christian Old Testament, as well as the works of the New Testament, from which this book has cited extensively.

Hebrew Scripture is traditionally organized into three divisions: the Torah or Law, also known as the Laws of Moses; the Nevi'im or Prophets; and the Ketuvim or Writings. In Jesus' lifetime, only the first two divisions were collectively recognized as Scripture. That is why Jesus often refers to the Bible as "the Law and the Prophets" (Luke 16:16). Nevertheless, although the third division was still being formed in the first century c.e., Jesus was most likely familiar with some of these books, specifically the Psalms.

The New Testament literature includes the Book of Acts of the Apostles, which covers the early development of the Christian Church; the Letters or Epistles attributed to Paul; additional apostolic letters; and the apocalyptic book of Revelation.

THE HEBREW SCRIPTURES (TANAKH)

	THE PROPHETS (NEVI'IM)	THE WRITINGS (KETUVIM)
	Former Prophets:	
Genesis	Joshua	Psalms
Exodus	Judges	Proverbs
Leviticus	Samuel (I and II)	Job
Numbers	Kings (I and II)	Song of Solomon
Deuteronomy	*Latter Prophets:*	Ruth
	Isaiah	Lamentations
	Jeremiah	Ecclesiastes
	Ezekiel	Esther
	Twelve Minor Prophets:	Daniel
	Hosea	Ezra-Nehemiah
	Joel	Chronicles (I and II)
	Amos	
	Obadiah	
	Jonah	
	Micah	
	Nahum	
	Habakkuk	
	Zephaniah	
	Haggai	
	Zechariah	
	Malachi	

THE BOOKS OF THE OLD TESTAMENT

THE LAW (TORAH)	THE PROPHETS (NEVI'IM)	THE WRITINGS (KETUVIM)
		Deuterocanonical/ Apocryphal:
Genesis	Isaiah	Tobit
Exodus	Jeremiah	Judith
Leviticus	Lamentations	Esther
Numbers	Ezekiel	The Wisdom of Solomon
Deuteronomy	Daniel	Ecclesiasticus
Joshua	Hosea	Baruch
Judges	Joel	Letter of Jeremiah
Ruth	Amos	*Additions to Daniel, including:*
I Samuel	Obadiah	Prayer of Azariah
II Samuel	Jonah	Song of Three Jews
I Kings	Micah	Susanna
II Kings	Nahum	Bel and the Dragon
I Chronicles	Habakkuk	I Maccabees
II Chronicles	Zephaniah	II Maccabees
Ezra	Haggai	I Esdras
Nehemiah	Zechariah	Prayer of Manasseh
Esther	Malachi	Psalm 151
Job		III Maccabees
Psalms		II Esdras
Proverbs		IV Maccabees
Ecclesiastes		
Song of Solomon		

THE BOOKS OF THE NEW TESTAMENT

THE GOSPELS	TRADITIONAL ATTRIBUTION	POSSIBLE DATE
Matthew	Matthew (Levi)	75-90 c.e.
Mark	Mark, Peter's interpreter	66-70 c.e.
Luke	Luke, Paul's attendant	75-90 c.e.
John	John (disciple)	85-100 c.e.
ACTS	**TRADITIONAL ATTRIBUTION**	**POSSIBLE DATE**
Acts of the Apostles	Luke, Paul's attendant	75-90 c.e.
	Isaiah	Lamentations
PAULINE EPISTLES	**TRADITIONAL ATTRIBUTION**	**POSSIBLE DATE**
Letter to the Romans	Paul	56-57 c.e.
First Letter to the Corinthians	Paul	54-55 c.e.

	TRADITIONAL ATTRIBUTION	POSSIBLE DATE
Second Letter to the Corinthians	Paul	55-56 C.E.
Letter to the Galatians	Paul	50-56 C.E.
Letter to the Ephesians	Paul (pseudonymous)	80-95 C.E.
Letter to the Philippians	Paul	54-55 C.E.
Letter to the Colossians	Paul	57-61 C.E.
First Letter to the Thessalonians	Paul	50-51 C.E.
Second Letter to the Thessalonians	Paul	50-51 C.E.
First Letter to Timothy	Paul (pseudonymous)	90-110 C.E.
Second Letter to Timothy	Paul (pseudonymous)	90-110 C.E.
Letter to Titus	Paul (pseudonymous)	90-110 C.E.
Letter to Philemon	Paul	54-55 C.E.
Letter to the Hebrews	Paul (pseudonymous)	60-95 C.E.
GENERAL EPISTLES	**TRADITIONAL ATTRIBUTION**	**POSSIBLE DATE**
Letter to James	James, brother of Jesus	50-70 C.E.
First Letter of Peter	Peter (pseudonymous)	70-90 C.E.
Second Letter of Peter	Peter (pseudonymous)	80-90 C.E.
First Letter of John	John (disciple)	ca 100 C.E.
Second Letter of John	John (disciple)	ca 100 C.E.
Third Letter of John	John (disciple)	ca 100 C.E.
Letter of Jude	Jude, brother of Jesus	45-65 C.E.
PROPHECY	**TRADITIONAL ATTRIBUTION**	**POSSIBLE DATE**
Revelation	John (disciple)	70-100 C.E.

FURTHER READING

ANCIENT MESOPOTAMIA AND EGYPT

John Baines and Jaromír Málek, *Cultural Atlas of Ancient Egypt*. Andromeda Oxford, 2000.

Stephen Bertman, *Life in Ancient Mesopotamia*. Oxford University Press, 2005.

Manfred Bietak, *Avaris, the Capital of the Hyksos: Recent Excavations at Tell el-Daba*. British Museum Press, 1996.

Jeremy Black and Anthony Green, *Gods, Demons and Symbols of Ancient Mesopotamia*. British Museum Press, 2004.

Robert Cargill, *The Cities That Built the Bible*. HarperOne, 2016.

Eric H. Cline, *From Eden to Exile: Unraveling Mysteries of the Bible*. National Geographic, 2006.

Dominique Collon, *Ancient Near Eastern Art*. Trustees of the British Museum, 1995.

W. D. Davies and Louis Finkelstein (eds.), *The Cambridge History of Judaism*, Vols. 1-3. Cambridge University Press, 1999.

Jean-Pierre Isbouts, *The Biblical World: An Illustrated Atlas*. National Geographic, 2007.

E. O. James, *The Ancient Gods: The History and Diffusion of Religion in the Ancient Near East and the Eastern Mediterranean*. Castle Books, 2004.

Michael Roafs, *Cultural Atlas of Mesopotamia and the Ancient Near East*. Andromeda Oxford, 2004.

David M. Rohl, *Pharaohs and Kings: A Biblical Quest*. Crown Publishers, 1995.

T. L. Thompson, *The Historicity of the Patriarchal Narratives: The Quest for the Historical Abraham*. De Gruyter, 1974.

J. Gardner Wilkinson. *The Ancient Egyptians: Their Life and Customs*, Vols. 1-2. Studio Editions, 1994.

ANCIENT ISRAEL

Eric H. Cline, *1177 B.C.: The Year Civilization Collapsed*. Princeton University Press, 2014.

William G. Dever, *The Lives of Ordinary People in Ancient Israel: Where Archaeology and the Bible Intersect*. Eerdmans, 2012.

Trude Dothan and Moshe Dothan, *People of the Sea: The Search for the Philistines*. Scribner, 1992.

Israel Finkelstein and Amihai Mazar, *The Quest for the Historical Israel*. Society of Biblical Literature, 2007.

Israel Finkelstein and Neil Asher Silberman, *The Bible Unearthed: Archeology's New Vision of Ancient Israel and the Origin of Its Sacred Texts*. Free Press, 2001.

Ann E. Killebrew, *Biblical Peoples and Ethnicity: An Archaeological Study of Egyptians, Canaanites, Philistines, and Early Israel, 1300-1100 B.C.E.* Society of Biblical Literature, 2005.

Philip J. King and Lawrence E. Stager, *Life in Biblical Israel*. Westminster John Knox Press, 2002.

T. C. Mitchell, *The Bible in the British Museum: Interpreting the Evidence*. British Museum Press, 1988.

George F. Moore, *A Critical and Exegetical Commentary on Judges*. Scribner's, 1895.

Neil Asher Silberman and David B. Small, *The Archeology of Israel: Constructing the Past, Interpreting the Present*. Sheffield Academic Press, 1997.

Ephraim Stern, *Archaeology of the Land of the Bible, Vol. 2: The Assyrian, Babylonian, and Persian Periods*. Doubleday, 2001.

Bart Wagemakers (ed.), *Archaeology in the "Land of Tells and Ruins."* Oxbow Books, 2014.

THE SECOND TEMPLE PERIOD

A. B. Bosworth, *Conquest and Empire: The Reign of Alexander the Great*. Cambridge University Press, 1988.

Robert Cargill, *Qumran Through (Real) Time: A Virtual Reconstruction of Qumran*. Gorgias Press, 2009.

C. E. Carter, *The Emergence of Yehud in the Persian Period*. Sheffield Academic Press, 1999.

Daniel Harrington, *The Maccabean Revolt: Anatomy of a Biblical Revolution.* Michael Glazier, 1991.

Richard Horsley, *Galilee: History, Politics, People.* Trinity Press, 1995.

Jodi Magness, *The Archaeology of the Holy Land, From the Destruction of Solomon's Temple to the Muslim Conquest.* Cambridge University Press, 2012.

Lawrence H. Schiffman, *Reclaiming the Dead Sea Scrolls: The History of Judaism, the Background of Christianity, the Lost Library of Qumran.* Doubleday, 1995.

THE ERA OF JESUS

Marcus J. Borg, *Jesus: Uncovering the Life, Teachings, and Relevance of a Religious Revolutionary.* HarperSanFrancisco, 2006.

Mark A. Chancey, *The Myth of a Gentile Galilee.* Cambridge University Press, 2002.

Bruce Chilton, *Rabbi Jesus.* Doubleday, 2000.

John Dominic Crossan, *Jesus: A Revolutionary Biography.* HarperCollins, 1994.

John Dominic Crossan and Jonathan L. Reed, *Excavating Jesus: Beneath the Stones, Behind the Texts.* HarperCollins, 2001.

Craig Evans, *Jesus and His World: The Archaeological Evidence.* Westminster John Knox Press, 2012.

Richard Horsley, *Jesus and Empire: The Kingdom of God and the New World Disorder.* Fortress Press, 2003.

Jean-Pierre Isbouts, *In the Footsteps of Jesus: A Chronicle of His Life and the Origins of Christianity.* National Geographic, 2012.

Amy-Jill Levine (ed.), *Historical Jesus in Context.* Princeton University Press, 2006.

Jodi Magness, *Stone and Dung, Oil and Spit: Jewish Life in the Time of Jesus.* Eerdmans, 2011.

Byron R. McCane, *Roll Back the Stone: Death and Burial in the World of Jesus.* Trinity Press International, 2003.

John P. Meier, *A Marginal Jew: Rethinking the Historical Jesus,* Vols. 1-3. Doubleday, 1994.

Jacob Neusner, *Judaism When Christianity Began: A Survey of Belief and Practice.* John Knox Press, 2002.

Jonathan L. Reed, *The HarperCollins Visual Guide to the New Testament.* HarperCollins, 2007.

Donald Senior, *Jesus: A Gospel Portrait.* Paulist Press, 1992.

Fabian E. Udoh, *To Caesar What Is Caesar's: Tribute, Taxes, and Imperial Administration in Early Roman Palestine (63 B.C.E.-70 C.E.).* Brown Judaic Studies, 2005.

EARLY CHRISTIANITY

Bruce Chilton, *Rabbi Paul: An Intellectual Biography.* Image/Doubleday, 2005.

James D. G. Dunn (ed.), *The Cambridge Companion to St. Paul.* Cambridge University Press, 2003.

Bart Ehrman, *Lost Christianities: The Battles for Scripture and the Faiths We Never Knew.* Oxford University Press, 2003.

Jas Elsner, *Imperial Rome and Christian Triumph.* Oxford University Press, 1998.

Craig A. Evans (ed.), *The World of Jesus and the Early Church.* Hendrickson Publishers, 2011.

Elaine Pagels, *Beyond Belief: The Secret Gospel of Thomas.* Random House, 2003.

Elaine Pagels, *The Gnostic Gospels.* Random House, 1979.

J. M. Robinson (ed.), *The Nag Hammadi Library.* E. J. Brill, 1977.

Note: The Biblical Archaeology Review *referred to in this book is published by the Biblical Archaeological Society, 4710 41st Street N.W., Washington, DC 20016. On the Web: www.biblicalarchaeology.org.*

ABOUT THE AUTHOR

Dr. Jean-Pierre Isbouts is a historian and doctoral professor at Fielding Graduate University in Santa Barbara, California. He has published widely on the origins of Judaism, Christianity, and Islam, including two bestsellers: *The Biblical World* (National Geographic, 2007) and *In the Footsteps of Jesus* (National Geographic, 2012). His other books include *Young Jesus: Restoring the Lost Years of a Social Activist and Religious Dissident* (Sterling, 2008); *From Moses to Muhammad: The Shared Origins of Judaism, Christianity and Islam* (Pantheon, 2010); *Who's Who in the Bible* (National Geographic, 2013); *The Story of Christianity* (National Geographic, 2014); and *Jesus: An Illustrated Life* (National Geographic, 2015). An award-winning filmmaker, Dr. Isbouts has also produced a number of programs, including *Charlton Heston's Voyage Through the Bible* (GoodTimes, 1998), *The Quest for Peace* (Hallmark, 2003), and *Young Jesus* (PBS, 2008). He lives in Santa Monica, California, where he and his wife, Cathie, serve as Eucharistic ministers at St. Monica's Church. His website is www.jpisbouts.org.

BOARD OF ADVISERS

Dr. Robert R. Cargill is assistant professor of classics and religious studies at the University of Iowa, where he teaches biblical studies, Second Temple Jewish literature, archaeology, and early Christianity. He is the author of *Cities That Built the Bible* and can be seen regularly on TV, where he has hosted shows like Nat Geo's "Writing the Dead Sea Scrolls."

Steven Feldman works with early-career scholars in a variety of academic disciplines to help them transform their dissertations into first academic books. Previously he served as Web editor and director of educational programs for the Biblical Archaeology Society and managing editor of *Biblical Archaeology Review* and *Bible Review*, published by the Society. He holds degrees from the University of Chicago Divinity School and the College at the University of Chicago.

Jodi Magness (www.JodiMagness.org) is the Kenan Distinguished Professor for Teaching Excellence in the Department of Religious Studies at the University of North Carolina at Chapel Hill. She specializes in the archaeology of Palestine (modern Israel, Jordan, and the Palestinian territories) in the Roman, Byzantine, and early Islamic periods. Since 2011, she has directed excavations at Huqoq in Israel's Galilee (www.huqoq.org).

ACKNOWLEDGMENTS

Archaeology of the Bible is the culmination of many years of research into a nexus that has fascinated me as a historian for much of my career: the crucial intersection of Bible and science, of biblical narrative and archaeological data.

Once again, I thank Lisa Thomas, head of National Geographic's Book Division, for collaborating on the concept for this book and for her strong and unerring support throughout. In the same breadth I express my deep gratitude to my wonderful editor, Barbara Payne, on this, our sixth book, together. Many thanks also to the superb team at National Geographic, including Sanaa Akkach for her beautiful, stirring layout designs, Matt Propert for his excellent photo research, Jon Bowen for his wonderful maps, and Beverly Miller for her incisive copyedit.

Special thanks are due to the panel of distinguished scholars who reviewed the manuscript, specifically Jodi Magness, Kenan Distinguished Professor for Teaching Excellence in Early Judaism at the University of North Carolina at Chapel Hill; Robert Cargill, Assistant Professor of Classics and Religious Studies at the University of Iowa; and my dear friend Steven Feldman, previously the director of educational programs for the Biblical Archaeology Society and managing editor of *Biblical Archaeology Review* and *Bible Review.*

In addition, I have profited from the research of many other scholars too numerous to mention, though I have tried to identify them as much as possible in the text, as well as in the Further Reading section. Needless to say, any errors in the narrative are mine alone.

Thanks are due to my agent, Peter Miller, and his staff at Global Lion Intellectual Property Management. And finally, I express my deepest gratitude to my wonderful wife, Cathie, who continues to be my muse and my indefatigable companion during our many journeys through the Middle East.

ILLUSTRATIONS CREDITS

All photographs by Pantheon Studios, Inc., unless otherwise noted.

Front cover, © Mark Millan/500px Prime; back cover (LE), Tim Gerard Barker/Getty Images; back flap, Fielding Graduate University; 2-3, Michael Melford/National Geographic Creative; 6, Maynard Owen Williams/National Geographic Creative; 10 (LO), Pascal Partouche/SkyView Photography; 11, Richard T. Nowitz/Corbis; 14-15, NASA/JPL-Caltech/STScI; 19, Dean Conger/National Geographic Creative; 20-21, Kent Kobersteen/National Geographic Creative; 22, telesniuk/Shutterstock; 23, David Doubilet/National Geographic Creative; 24-5, "The Garden of Eden With the Fall of Man," ca 1615 (oil on panel), Brueghel, Jan (1568-1625) & Rubens, P.P. (1577-1640)/Mauritshuis, the Hague, the Netherlands/Bridgeman Images; 27 (UP), photostockam/Shutterstock; 29 (UP), Balage Balogh/ArchaeologyIllustrated.com; 31 (LO), De Agostini Picture Library/Getty Images; 34-5, Network Photographer/Alamy Stock Photo; 36 (UP), Balage Balogh/Archaeology Illustrated.com; 38-9, Gordon Gahan/National Geographic Creative; 44-5, Frans Lanting/lanting.com; 48-9, Kunsthistorisches Museum,

Aegyptisch-Orientalische Sammlung, Vienna, Austria/Erich Lessing Culture and Fine Arts Archives; 50-51, Michael Melford/National Geographic Creative; 53, Dr. Steven Collins; 54, "Abraham Turning Away Hagar," 1837 (oil on canvas), Vernet, Emile Jean Horace (1789-1863)/Musee des Beaux-Arts, Nantes, France/Bridgeman Images; 55, six foundation stones, reign of King Lipit-Ishtar, ca 1934-1924 B.C.E. (clay), Babylonian/Private Collection/Photo © Christie's Images/Bridgeman Images; 61 (UP), Thomas J. Abercrombie/National Geographic Creative; 66, Scala/Art Resource, NY; 70-71, Kenneth Garrett/National Geographic Creative; 74 (UP), courtesy Israel Antiquities Authority; 74 (LO), Urmas Ääro/Alamy Stock Photo; 75, William Cook/National Geographic Creative; 76, "Joseph Explaining Pharaoh's Dreams," by Jean Adrien Guignet (1816-1854), oil on canvas/De Agostini Picture Library/G. Dagli Orti/Bridgeman Images; 78 (RT), François Guenet/Art Resource, NY; 80-81, "Joseph, Overseer of Pharaoh's Granaries," 1874 (oil on panel), Alma-Tadema, Lawrence (1836-1912)/Dahesh Museum of Art, New York, USA/Bridgeman Images; 82, Kenneth Garrett/National Geographic Creative; 83, collar in the form of the vulture goddess Nekhbet, from

the tomb of Tutankhamun (ca 1370-1352 B.C.E.) New Kingdom (gold inlaid with semiprecious stones), Egyptian 18th Dynasty (ca 1567-1320 B.C.E.)/Egyptian National Museum, Cairo, Egypt/Photo © Boltin Picture Library/Bridgeman Images; 87 (LE), Egypt, detail of statue representing the Pharaoh Ahmose I (ca 1560-1546 B.C.E.), founder of the 18th Dynasty/Louvre, Paris, France/De Agostini Picture Library/G. Dagli Orti/Bridgeman Images; 87 (RT), Kenneth Garrett/National Geographic Creative; 90 (UP), Kenneth Garrett/National Geographic Creative; 91, Greg Girard; 93, Patrick Frilet/Hemis/Corbis; 94 (LO), Andrea Jemolo/akg-images; 94 (UP), Mark Millmore; 96, Relief showing Akhenaten and his family/Egyptian National Museum, Cairo, Egypt/Bridgeman Images; 97, bpk, Berlin/Aegyptisches Museum und Papyrussammlung, Staatliche Museen, Berlin, Germany/Margarete Büsing/Art Resource, NY; 101, Travel Ink/Getty Images; 103 (LE), mummy of Seti I, face detail/De Agostini Picture Library/Bridgeman Images; 104-105, Universal History Archive/Getty Images; 107, Mitsuhiko Imamori/Minden Pictures/National Geographic Creative; 112-13, HIP/Art Resource, NY; 114-15, Kenneth Garrett/National Geographic

INDEX

Boldface indicates illustrations.

ARCHAEOLOGY OF THE BIBLE

Since 1888, the National Geographic Society has funded more than 12,000 research, exploration, and preservation projects around the world. National Geographic Partners distributes a portion of the funds it receives from your purchase to National Geographic Society to support programs including the conservation of animals and their habitats.

National Geographic Partners
1145 17th Street NW
Washington, DC 20036-4688 USA

Become a member of National Geographic and activate your benefits today at natgeo.com/jointoday.

For information about special discounts for bulk purchases, please contact National Geographic Books Special Sales: specialsales@natgeo.com

For rights or permissions inquiries, please contact National Geographic Books Subsidiary Rights: bookrights@natgeo.com

Library of Congress Cataloging-in-Publication Data

Names: Isbouts, Jean-Pierre, author.
Title: Archaeology of the Bible : the greatest discoveries from Genesis to
 the Roman era / best-selling author of In the footsteps of Jesus, Jean-Pierre Isbouts.
Description: Washington, DC : National Geographic Partners, 2016. | Includes
 bibliographical references and index.
Identifiers: LCCN 2016028720| ISBN 9781426217043 (hardcover : alk. paper) |
 ISBN 9781426218200 (hardcover deluxe : alk. paper)
Subjects: LCSH: Bible--Antiquities.
Classification: LCC BS621 .I83 2016 | DDC 220.9/3--dc23
LC record available at https://urldefense.proofpoint.com/v2/url?u=https-3A__lccn.loc.gov_2016028720&d=DQIFAg&c=uw6TLu4hwhHdiGJOgwcWD4AjKQx6zvFcGEsbfiY9-EI&r=Ar3XRLWsOd9X4qagesooQpv_FSetDc1lkl9pxdILrhw&m=kBUL_JCFRdAwtu1R_10q8XByoiVtMTV8EnvH0UyMmgs&s=ooXk93wnnphXOCtAS-smcJO_NbSfd86om8OUCWq2NkA&e=

Printed in the United States of America

16/QGT-RRDML/1

A New Look at a Life
Destined to Change the World

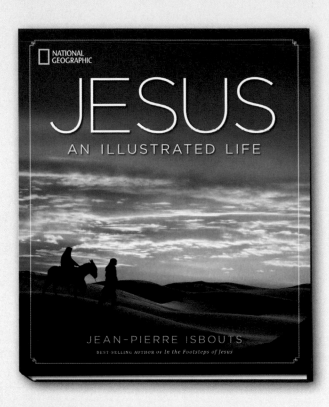

Using the latest scientific and archaeological finds, acclaimed author Jean-Pierre Isbouts provides an in-depth look into Jesus' everyday life. Through exquisite photographs, rare period artifacts, and detailed maps, the times and places Jesus walked the earth are vividly portrayed.

Also by Jean-Pierre Isbouts

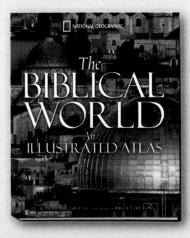

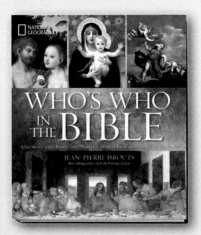

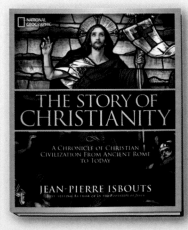

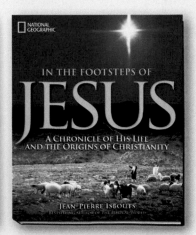